TRUTH IN AMERICAN FICTION

TRUTH
IN
AMERICAN
FICTION

THE LEGACY OF
RHETORICAL IDEALISM

Janet Gabler-Hover

THE UNIVERSITY OF GEORGIA PRESS
Athens and London

© 1990 by the University of Georgia Press
Athens, Georgia 30602
All rights reserved

Designed by Debby Jay
Set in Janson
The paper in this book meets the guidelines
for permanence and durability of the Committee on
Production Guidelines for Book Longevity
of the Council on Library Resources.

Printed in the United States of America

94   93   92   91   90   5   4   3   2   1

Library of Congress Cataloging in Publication Data

Gabler-Hover, Janet.
Truth in American fiction: the legacy of rhetorical
idealism / Janet Gabler-Hover.
p.   cm.
Includes bibliographical references.
ISBN 0-8203-1247-9 (alk. paper)
1. American fiction — 19th century — History and criticism.
2. Truthfulness and falsehood in literature. 3. Ethics in
literature. 4. Truth in literature. I. Title.
PS374.T78G3   1990
813'.309353 — dc20
90-31609 CIP

British Library Cataloging in Publication Data available

To my husband,
for his gift of the will to believe

Contents

Acknowledgments

Many spirits contribute to the conception of a book. I would like to thank Thomas Cooley for first suggesting to me that the subject of rhetoric in *The Bostonians* remained surprisingly unexplored. I would also like to thank Edward P. J. Corbett for introducing me to rhetoric at roughly the same time. A good friend, James D. Wilson, suggested that I expand my study of the historical link between rhetoric and literature beyond the works of Henry James. My teachers Lyman Leathers and Thomas Joswick inspired my love for nineteenth-century American literature.

Colleagues have also proven generous in their response to the manuscript. Virginia Spencer-Carr read an intermediate draft of this work and offered both encouragement and suggestions on style. Matthew Roudané read the original version of Chapter 1 and offered consistent support for the ongoing composition of the manuscript. Terence Martin and Leland Person reviewed the manuscript wisely and sympathetically. Their constructive criticism and requests for substantive revision contributed to the quality of the book.

I have also received assistance in research and editing. My colleagues in the Department of English at Georgia State University under the direction of Virginia Spencer-Carr granted me a quarter of released time to pursue my scholarship. Debbie Fraker-Lanius provided invaluable research assistance on the Hawthorne and Melville chapters. Kristan Sarvé-Gorham and Michele Simms-Burton assisted in the editing of the manuscript. I would also like to thank Karen Orchard, Gertrude Calvert, and the editorial staff at the University of Georgia Press for their efforts to improve and support the book.

Sections from several of the chapters have appeared in printed form elsewhere. I acknowledge with thanks permission from the University of Texas Press and from *Texas Studies in Literature and Language* to reprint material from Chapters 5 and 6 that first appeared in *Texas Studies*, and permission from the *South Central Review* and the *Journal of Narrative Technique* to reprint published material that appears in altered form in Chapters 4 and 5.

In conclusion, I wish to thank the two individuals whose unfailing faith in my work carried me through what often seemed insurmountable frustrations. William J. Scheick has supported and encouraged my professional efforts. Professor Scheick's choice to be a mentor and a nurturer in our profession as well as a catalyst for academic excellence exemplifies for me the ideal in our profession. Professor Scheick has made a significant difference in both my faith in and demands upon myself. Finally, I thank my wonderful husband, Bill, who respects the critical scholarship in a field quite alien to his own career simply because it is my field. Bill's patience with my struggles to understand is exceeded only by his patience as the bemused but always intelligent audience for my rough drafts. In spirit, Bill is my reader with the one heart and mind of perfect sympathy.

TRUTH IN AMERICAN FICTION

Introduction

For the essential thing is heat, and heat comes of sincerity. Speak what
you do know and believe; and are personally in it; and are answerable
for every word. Eloquence is *the power to translate a truth into language
perfectly intelligible to the person to whom you speak.*
　　　　　　　　　　　　　　　　　—RALPH WALDO EMERSON,
　　　　　　　　　　　　　　　　　1867 Lecture on Eloquence

Wayne Booth has suggested that stories (or other objects) allow
three questions to be asked: "those that the object seems to *invite* . . .
those that it will *tolerate* or respond to, even though perhaps reluctantly; and those that *violate* its own interests or effort to be a given
kind of thing in the world."[1] Most readers would probably agree that
major novels not only invite such generic questions as What is my plot?
and Who are my characters? but also the more profound ones such as
What values are implicit within my fictional world? and What am I
saying about what is or should be important in life? (even if those questions are asked only to be problematized). Most readers might even
imagine the same ethical questions posed in very specific terms in specific novels. The focus of this study is the ethical status of language
in late eighteenth- and nineteenth-century American novels so I will
turn to this issue as an example of one ethical question commonly perceived. Most critics of nineteenth-century American fiction today, for
example, discover the subject of language itself as a value-laden part of
the fictional ethos in nineteenth-century American novels.[2]

Although disagreements do, from time to time, arise about the
nature of the questions novels invite us to ask, it is much more likely
that we will disagree about the answers we imagine we receive. Readers

1

are divergent, "what we retain from reading is highly selective and dependent upon our own consciousness, which in turn is dependent upon our own experience and previous knowledge,"[3] also, one should add, upon our critical predisposition.

Thus it may seem surprising that, because of a certain uniformity in the critical disposition of recent scholars of nineteenth-century American literature, the answer deduced about the critical status of language in nineteenth-century American fiction has a certain sameness about it. The present-day critical community is on the whole predisposed to view the literary text as indeterminant and to view language in the literary text as obdurately, defiantly (and morally) nonreferential. Indeed, if a critic does not find this quality of open-endedness in a work of nineteenth-century fiction, he or she is apt to dismiss it. Fred G. See, for example, elevates the fiction of Harriet Beecher Stowe over that of Nathaniel Hawthorne because of See's Saussurean/Derridean literary/ethical scheme. This is because Stowe at least sets out "to dissolve the paternal authority of theological language," whereas Hawthorne returns in *The Scarlet Letter* "not only to the familiar institutions but to those dogmatic literary signs which are the cold trace of presence." And Herman Melville thereby "eclipses" Hawthorne, because "Hawthorne evaded what Melville faced: . . . the collapse of systematic meaning." Actually, however, this devaluation of Hawthorne in deconstructionist terms is rare. It is much more likely that Hawthorne's works are praised as deconstructionist, as part of the move "sometime in the nineteenth century" when "the sign begins to reorient itself toward signifiers — toward an order which conceived itself as fragments rather than essential unity."[4] Hawthorne's romance form is seen, for example, as the perfect medium for the "play of significance." Hawthorne overdetermines his symbolism in *The Scarlet Letter* as a way of expressing a "loss of confidence in the sacred grounding of signs."[5]

Underlying these deconstructionist readings are some potent inferences about the author or critic who does *not* engage in the deconstructive project: first, that he or she is naive, not fully in command of the complexities of life or of the literary text. In Murray Krieger's words, recent criticism "would have us avoid the thematizing act in its search for a purity that would celebrate method while suppressing substance, that would celebrate structural functions while suppressing ideology. Such an emphasis, with its fear of the ontological and its consequent suppression of the worldly *references of words*, has led to an imbalance and, in some quarters, a smugness that regards with disdain the critical concern with the moral and ideological consequences of literary works."[6]

Second, deconstructionists imply that the author who affirms closure and referential language or the critic who does not deconstruct it is engaged in something immoral. As Booth eloquently remarks,

> we encounter a curious contrast between two claims made by the theorists of open-endedness. On the one hand, they all celebrate freedom and variety in readers' responses (thus illustrating my previous point that just about everybody on our scene is an "ethical" critic); on the other, they assume that certain privileged literary techniques and forms are invariably better for readers than certain others, and that readers *who read for closure* are at fault. [and authors who write for it?] Open-ended techniques provide, for all readers on all conceivable reading occasions, and in contrast to the old intrusive omniscient authoritarian methods, just what we all most need.[7]

The reading that I offer here of late eighteenth- and nineteenth-century American literary texts challenges the assumption that the metaphysics of deconstruction is an invariably better (more complex and more moral) literary technique to adopt in interpreting fiction than the metaphysics of referentiality. It is my belief that major works of nineteenth-century American fiction engage in the metaphysics of referentiality and thus invite rather than merely tolerate readings that offer closure and a distinctive moral/ethical program. For better or for worse, the fictional metaphysics of these novels, including Charles Brockden Brown's *Wieland or the Transformation*, Nathaniel Hawthorne's *The Scarlet Letter*, Mark Twain's *Adventures of Huckleberry Finn*, and Henry James's *The Bostonians, The Wings of the Dove*, and *The Golden Bowl*, affirms the truth-telling power of language. These authors' novels do so, of course, complexly, achieving "their harmony without denying ironic undercuttings."[8] In addition, these texts offer a transcendental referent for language that is not bound up in the ideological conventionalities that are condemned by deconstructionists as immoral. For after Jacques Derrida stresses that it is philosophically impeccable to acknowledge that referential language merely points to an absence,[9] his next move is to condemn referential language as authoritative, to link referential language with those tyrannizing institutions and power structures that through language wield authority:

"The Socratic word does not wander, stays at home, is closely watched: within autochthony, within the city, within the law, under the surveillance of its mother tongue" (124).

For Fred See, following Jacques Lacan, the freedom being tyrannized over by referential language is sexual desire, which "tries to work free of an engulfing law by entering the play of signs." [10] More usually, the authority wielded by language in nineteenth-century American texts is seen to be political. For Nina Baym, the Puritan society in *The Scarlet Letter* is complicit with the tyrannizing power of language; Hester "is the pre-civilized nature goddess opposing Western civilization, the impulsive heart defying the repressive letter of the law." [11]

Among the polyvalences of the novels that I examine in this study, "conventional" language is indeed ironically undercut, but conventional language — that language bound up with social law and authority — is not undercut for the purpose of celebrating in general the inevitable indeterminacy of language. Instead, conventional language is portrayed in league with the project of suggesting that meaning is indeterminant, and *this* suggestion — that meaning *is* indeterminant — is persuasively shown to be immoral.

We still have not established, of course, that critics are right in assuming that their present-day preoccupation with the ethical status of language was equally shared by nineteenth-century American authors. How concerned were these authors with the truth-telling properties of language and, a more difficult question to address, how would they have understood the word *truth*? Besides much textual evidence (Hawthorne wrote *The Scarlet Letter*, Twain showed Huck's absorption with truth and lies in the very first paragraph of *Adventures of Huckleberry Finn*) there *is* a strong cultural influence that seems to have worked its way into the very texture of the novels that nineteenth-century American authors wrote.

No movement influencing early American thought so engaged the heart of the American public as the study of rhetoric. This rhetoric, a hybrid form exported from the religious centers of great universities in Scotland, flourished in the newly emerging educational and cultural centers of America and was taught well into the 1850s to American college students, largely those studying for the ministry or law. Books like Hugh Blair's *Rhetoric and Belles Lettres* (1783) and George Campbell's *Philosophy of Rhetoric* (1776), as well as the study of Greek and Roman rhetoric, found a cultural life that lasted well into the final decades of nineteenth-century America. This movement in rhetoric — a

movement manifesting itself in a variety of forms throughout the nineteenth century but in its ethical principles remaining essentially the
same — directly touched many of the century's great American authors.
A few of the influences include Charles Brockden Brown's admiration
for Hugh Blair's work and Nathaniel Hawthorne's instruction at Bowdoin by Samuel Newman, one of America's prominent rhetoricians.
Hawthorne's short stories were often published alongside periodical
treatises on rhetoric that may have influenced his work, as my chapter on *The Scarlet Letter* suggests. Mark Twain befriended and read the
work of Henry Ward Beecher, an influential exponent of American
rhetoric in the 1860s. Among other influences, Henry James boarded
during his college year at Harvard with the fourth Harvard Boylston
Professor of Rhetoric and Oratory, Francis J. Child.

The language ethos of this rhetorical movement provided American
authors with a common ground of moral reference with their audiences. One of the products of the movement, for example, was a community basis for authors' and readers' understanding of *truth*. Barnet
Baskerville summarizes nineteenth-century periodical essays on oratory by noting that "the insistence upon truth (frequently italicized or
spelled out in capital letters) occurs again and again in the literature."
And in periodicalists' assumptions about truth,

> one is struck by the fact that . . . truth is readily ascertainable and has
> the same appearance to all men. One marvels at the calm assurance of
> these men that the orator has only to lay hold of truth in order to be elo-
> quent and successful. The orator, apparently, has a clear choice, truth or
> falsehood. The upright man will choose truth every time. A possible ex-
> planation of this certainty about the nature of truth is that these writers
> are using the term in a metaphysical sense. They are talking not about
> probability or demonstrable fact, but about eternal verities, intuitively
> perceived.[12]

When nineteenth-century Americans considered "the great duty of
veracity to the unchanging principle in which it is founded," as one
periodicalist in the 1830s phrased it,[13] a transcendent referent for language was implied. As Chapter 1 of this study suggests, the metaphysical referent for truth in the rhetorical ethos was a Christian
one. The eighteenth- and nineteenth-century rhetorical renaissance
was impelled by ministers such as Hugh Blair, George Campbell, and
Henry Ward Beecher. But contrary to the Derridian conjunction of
letter/religion/law/tyranny, the Christian message urged by the rhe-

torical movement was benevolent, not doctrinal. When rhetoricians urged the importance of truth, they were implicitly advocating a behavior of selflessness and generosity; these were the Christian virtues. A domesticated version of Christian truth also applied on the level of concrete experience. One should not lie to another (or to oneself), the ethos implied, about felt emotion or concrete experience.

Trust was an important part of this. For friendship and community, truth was essential:

> Why are we required, in all our communications with another, to speak the truth? Why is this so positively enjoined in the Scriptures? and why is it urged with so much zeal by those, who do not avail themselves of the authority of Divine inspiration? To questions like these, we answer — Because the vital interests, because the very being of society depends upon it. Society could no more live and prosper without mutual truth, than material bodies could exist without the principle of cohesive attraction. Though liars may associate for temporary purposes, there must be some truth between them; some ground amid the general ruins of falsehood for them to stand upon, or they can maintain no friendly intercourse whatever.[14]

In *Wieland*, by Charles Brockden Brown, or in the novels of Henry James, the destabilization of the communicative grounds between two individuals results in nothing less than an epistemological disequilibrium, often expressed as psychic violence — rape or abuse. When Carwin insinuates himself into Clara Wieland's life, he does so by using an eloquence culturally codified to be synonymous with trustful relations and with truth. His ultimate progress through this linguistic deceit into the closet of Clara's private chamber is akin to sexual violence. A characteristic example of such violence in a James novel, although the novel is not examined in this study, occurs in *What Maisie Knew*. When little Maisie Farange realizes that because of her parents' parsimoniousness she will get no education, there will be "no sequel to the classes in French literature with all the smart little girls," James relates that "she was to feel henceforth as if she were flattening her nose upon the hard window-pane of the sweet-shop of knowledge." Within the cultural code of truth as selfless behavior, little Maisie's trusting attempt to keep up her part of the ethical bargain is pure pathos: " 'Look here, she's *true*!' " exclaims the romantic Captain to Maisie about her mother, and, even though earlier in this same scene Maisie feels an intimate embrace with her mother "as if she had suddenly been thrust, with a smash of glass, into a jeweller's shop-front," Maisie has "so little desire to assert the contrary that she found herself, in the intensity of her response, throbbing with a joy." [15]

In both instances, fictional characters are victims of their unreflexive faith in one of the systematized features of the nineteenth-century rhetorical ethos, although, as my chapters on James's fiction will argue, this unswerving faith, one might say reverence, for this feature of the ethos gives James's characters who have it the ability to redeem the corrupt world. This feature throughout the history of rhetoric has been commonly called the Quintilian principle, after Roman orator Marcus Fabius Quintilian, who is usually credited with originating the concept although echoes of it are certainly present in Cicero and arguably even in Aristotle.[16] What this good-man-speaking principle implied, simply enough, was that "truth was the very heart of genuine eloquence," as Baskerville puts it. "Nor did many of them [the commentators on oratory] flinch from defending the necessary concomitant of this position—that it is impossible to be eloquent in defense of the wrong or untrue," he continues to say.[17] The Quintilian principle in its nineteenth-century form urged belief in the intrinsic morality of rhetorical eloquence, suggesting that only a virtuous speaker could be sufficiently eloquent to be believed.

Such an easy faith in the inevitable virtue of eloquence can well be imagined as a vulnerable spot in the rhetorical ethos for ironists and those intent on satirizing the social scene. Rhetoricians who perpetuated the principle had a personal stake in doing so, for they had to combat the age-old fear that "a clever tongue [is] suspect." [18] They were, in this aspect, some shrewd author might perceive, confidence men. In addition, though, as Chapter 1 discusses, the ethical rhetoricians of the time thought that by investing rhetoric with a necessary moral dimension they could compel aspiring orators to be virtuous. This ambition may seem absurd, but it lies at the heart of the ethical rhetoric compelled by James's virtuous characters in *The Wings of the Dove* and *The Golden Bowl*. One "truth" I would like to suggest is that late eighteenth- and nineteenth-century American authors responded to the rhetorical tradition in very different ways. Charles Brockden Brown comments directly on the easy confidences and self-deceit directly nurtured if not fostered by enthusiasm for rhetoric during his own time. Mark Twain and Nathaniel Hawthorne allude to the tradition as they portray a society in which the letter is indeed tyrannized by the law as opposed to conjoined, ideally, with selflessness and benevolence. Henry James, finally, looks to the Quintilian principle (and to the importance of telling the truth) as a principle of "good faith," which may redeem his fictional world, at least, by the power of its "associational magic." [19]

Unquestionably, I bring to bear many of my own ethical beliefs in the analysis of these works of American fiction. My own usual predilection toward closure is an uneasy mate with the practice of deconstructive criticism that insists on language's indeterminacy and on the problematics of interpersonal communication. In this study, I am drawn to the interpretation of novels that seem to speak to my own system of values. This does not mean, though, that I am imposing my values upon the empty ciphers of the literary texts.[20] Instead, I would like "to hold out," to quote Murray Krieger, "for the possibility that a single verbal structure can convert its elements so that we read them under the aegis of metaphorical identity with its claim to presence." [21] I derive the sense that the literary work *is* present to make specific claims upon the reader's understanding through its particularized codes and language. "When I read as I ought," Georges Poulet once said, "my comprehension becomes intuitive and any feeling proposed to me is immediately assumed by me." [22]

Recent research into the reading process has suggested, of course, that one's intuitive comprehension of the literary text will be based on one's selective attention to details different than those attended to by another reader's intuitive comprehension.[23] A case in point is a comparison between John Auchard's analysis of language in *The Wings of the Dove* [24] and my counteranalysis of it as published in *Texas Studies in Literature and Language* and expanded in this study. I reviewed Auchard's book after writing my own essay on the novel. My thesis was that the importance of truth-telling in *The Wings of the Dove* was central to an understanding of the novel. Auchard's view was diametrically opposite: he believes that James retreats, in *The Wings of the Dove*, from the false presence of words into the mystic recesses of a profound nothingness. To my dismay/amusement, a side-by-side analysis of the two readings suggested, at least initially, that interpretation might be based upon a selective attention directed on the part of two critics to discrete passages in the literary text.

Alert to this disparity, I presented both Auchard's and my view of language in the novel when I was teaching it in a graduate course. In our quest for a synthesis (or a "right" or "wrong" reading), my students and I focused on a central passage that Auchard had read for his thesis,

one not "present" to my analysis. It was the famous "Bronzino" passage, where Milly stands in front of a portrait Lord Mark has pointed
out as bearing resemblance to herself. Auchard analyzes the final lines
where Milly notes the portrait as "a very great personage — only unaccompanied by a joy. And she was dead, dead, dead. Milly recognized her
exactly in words that had nothing to do with her. 'I shall never be better than this.' " Auchard discovers in these final lines, "as final effect, an
antithesis to words," since the referential ambiguities of "she," "her,"
and "this" in the passage are obscure, as he explains at some length.[25]
Oddly enough, to me the passage always seemed comprehensible. Its
comprehensibility requires the text immediately preceding it and following. Milly, turning away from the portrait because it is dead, dead,
dead, and unaccompanied by a joy, opposes it because she at present
has joy: she has just experienced her own "pink dawn of an apotheosis"
in the life of the London social scene. The haunting resemblance between a dead person and herself is an unwelcome reminder of her own
hubristic attempt to "live." (She has already projected onto others her
own repressed fear of death through her noting of their "kind, kind
eyes.") Lord Mark here performs his later more dangerous role of de-
flating Milly's project to "live." But in this instance, Milly's response is
to "recognize," that is, to give due honor, to royalty, but paradoxically,
by denying the woman in the portrait, turning away from her deadness
with the utterance of words that had nothing to do with "her" — that
is, nothing to do with the woman in the portrait. Instead, Milly turns
to her own living image in the social scene where Milly feels elevated
among the living to divine status. She says, "I shall never be better
than *this*" — "this" in sweeping reference to the life she presently embraces on that social afternoon. She thus subordinates the dead portrait,
bravely, to her living image of herself.

Ultimately, with any close readings, it finally becomes a matter of
which reading seems most persuasive, whether it is open-ended and
suggestive of language's indeterminacy, or suggestive of the closures
that seem tacitly invited by many nineteenth-century American novels.
Finally, in this introduction, I want to illustrate an openness to the
tacit invitations of the literary text through discussion of the indeterminacy of one nineteenth-century American novel, Herman Melville's
The Confidence-Man. The same values are brought to bear in this reading as are brought to bear in reading in the other literary works in this
study. Similarly also, Melville's awareness of contemporary and classical rhetoric becomes clear in the interpretation of the novel. But in

Melville's case, it is much less obvious how the allusions to rhetoric are being thematically used. One point that might be inferred from this reading of *The Confidence-Man* is that any commitment to values of "closure," "trust," or "truth" on the part of the critic may not prohibit him or her from perceiving that particular novels, in this case Melville's *Confidence-Man*, may not easily "tolerate" such a reading.

    "But even if experience did not sanction the proverb, that a good laugher cannot be a bad man, I should yet feel bound in confidence to believe it, since it is a saying current among the people, and I doubt not originated among them, and hence *must* be true, for the voice of the people is the voice of truth. Don't you think so?"

    "Look, sir, all this to the right is certain truth, and all this to the left is certain truth, but all I hold in my hand here is apocrypha."
               —HERMAN MELVILLE, *The Confidence-Man*

Herman Melville's *The Confidence-Man: His Masquerade* (1857) depicts a mysterious stranger afoot on the Mississippi steamer *Fidèle* selling his commodity of confidence to various and sundry American "pilgrims"[26] on a sunny April first presumably during Melville's own time. That the fools-day joke redounds on Melville's reading audience seems likely, since the message about the virtues of confidence and charity is unclear to many readers. The editors of the Newberry Edition of the novel comment that

    in all his appearances, both day and night, he [the Confidence Man] pleads for confidence or its equivalent and argues winningly, however dubious his motives, against distrusting anything in human nature, physical nature, or the cosmos. Most of his listeners, it seems, prove too trusting, but a few too skeptical. Just which characters—those with warm soft hearts and heads or those with cold ones, "philanthropists" or "misanthropists"—have the author's approval is uncertain; perhaps none unqualifiedly. It seems to be left ambiguous whether, underneath everything, he calls for a difficult, even impossible, balance of heart and head or despairs of any trustworthy basis for moral judgments.[27]

One point generally agreed on is that the Confidence Man is a con artist, at least as he is depicted in the first half of the novel in his shape-shifting disguises and in the novel's two final scenes. The Confidence Man's apparent scams seem to suggest it, and the historical genesis of the term *confidence man* is cited as the predominant source for Melville's novel. Scholars have proven that Melville knew from the newspapers of the twice-famous swindler "William Thompson." Melville appropriated incidents from Thompson's career for his novel, and also the name *con-fidence man*, which newspapers coined to memorialize this consummate con artist. Soon, as Tom Quirk reveals, the term was extended by the media to connote swindlers in all walks of life.[28] But intrepid Melville scholars have even challenged this certain assumption, starting with Philip Drew in 1963, who states that "we may search in vain for the episode which establishes that any of the confidence-men is a swindler. Every incident narrated is innocent in itself and innocent to a trusting eye, but filled with dubious circumstance to the reader who is himself without confidence." Lawrence Buell agrees, noting that "we may suspect . . . the cosmopolitan . . . but we can't prove it," and he concludes that "as a result, the reader is enticed into a continuous guessing game." Buell alleges that the book is "carefully rigged to invite and then to frustrate a hard-and-fast interpretation." [29]

These doubts are a long way from Elizabeth Foster's ambitious and courageous statement in her 1954 introduction that *The Confidence-Man* "needs to be decoded. Furthermore, it can be." [30] This determination coupled with the symbolic allusiveness of Melville's novel predicts the formal closure of allegory, and, as Buell points out, the novel seems to invite it. Since biblical references in the novel abound as they do in all Melville,[31] many allegorical readings of the novel uncover a religious message. What that message *is*, however, is up for grabs. Whereas Nathalia Wright sees this novel as Melville's closest approach to heresy, John W. Schroeder convincingly argues that Melville urges in this novel the necessity for a strict adherence to conservative Christian faith. Inevitably, the allegorical meaning of the central figure the Confidence Man differs from one reading to another. Sometimes he is interpreted as the Devil, but occasionally as Christ, or God, or perhaps as a pagan trickster god.[32]

Ivor Winters wrote in 1938 that "in *Pierre* and *The Confidence-Man* alike it is assumed that valid judgment is impossible, for every event, every fact, every person, is too fluid, too unbounded to be known." [33] It is just this literary slipperiness and boundless indeterminacy that those committed to fictional meaning attempt to decode, seldom willfully, usually with a strong invitation from the literary text. John Shroeder's canny reading of the novel comes close, in my view, to cracking the case.

Shroeder points to literary sources for Melville's novel that provide a context and a set of literary cross-references for our understanding of the religious allegory in *The Confidence-Man*. Akin to John Bunyan's *Pilgrim's Progress* and Nathaniel Hawthorne's "Celestial Railroad," Melville's tale presents "a great Vanity Fair," which is, in this case, "situated on an allegorical steamboat . . . presumably sailing . . . on the symbolic level, for the New Jerusalem of nineteenth-century optimism and liberal theology" but, which is, in reality, "inclining its course dangerously toward the pits of the Black Rapids Coal Company. Aboard the vessel we have pilgrimmaging mankind. And among these pilgrims, the confidence-man is inordinately active." The Confidence Man according to this reading is the Devil, or, in his lesser guises, one of his agents. The Devil asks his victims for "confidence that the world has no dark side" and the "penalty for its payment is . . . damnation."[34]

Schroeder's analysis compels through its discovery of literary allusion and repetitive pattern in the novel. He likens the various names of the Confidence Man, Truman, Francis Goodman, and the Happy Man, an epithet for the Herb Doctor, to Spenser's Sansfoy, Sansjoy, and Sansloy. He also ties in the various manifestations of the Confidence Man to the Devil through the associational imagery of snakes and Indians (Melville's synonyms for the Devil) that always accompanies them. In Schroeder's analysis, the "true" Christian, Melville says, avoids damnation by acknowledging always "the natural evil of the Universe," which "represents to man a perpetual emblem of his fall and consequent perilous spiritual state."[35] There is much to reassure one in this reading. Although redemption does not occur to the foolishly optimistic characters in the pages of the novel, the reading satisfies because salvation is now possible outside the novel's pages: the reader has been redressed; he or she has Melville's prescription for life; he or she either endorses it or patronizes it and thus averts the potential chaos of recognizing a problematical ethics in the novel.

No doubt in these modern times many scholars reject such a pat allegorical reading of *The Confidence-Man* on principle, but that is not a valid reason for doing so. Shroeder's allegorical scheme is Promethean in its attempt to absorb a number of the subtle nuances as well as larger themes of *The Confidence-Man*. Since the work of John Shroeder and Elizabeth Foster, no one has questioned that the easy optimism of Melville's age is the novel's central satirical target, yet, ironically, consideration of this point makes Shroeder's allegory break down for many readers. Many readers sense, as did Elizabeth Foster, that *The Confidence-Man* is virtually split in half on the issue of confidence: "The first half satirizes credulity and the second half points out the evil consequences of too much distrust."[36] Trust in the good nature of one's fellow men would constitute a virtual heresy in Shroeder's reading. What Shroeder does not see that many others do is an apparent shift in narrative point of view on the issue of man's nature and best mission in life after the Confidence Man takes on the role of the Cosmopolitan. Shroeder reads the Devil imagery connected with the Cosmopolitan as unambiguous and sees no change in the attitude of this Confidence Man's request for trust. Yet he tacitly admits that his allegory is potentially complicated by the Cosmopolitan: "I have not offered any explanation as to why Noble [a lesser agent of the Devil] and Goodman [the Cosmopolitan], if both are from the pit, should unknown to one another carry on their long conversation." Further, Shroeder feels compelled to reveal, out of what must be a sense of critical integrity, that he has "not attempted to unriddle the tales of Goneril, Charlemont, and China Aster."[37] No critic has attempted to "unriddle" all the tales, encounters, and criticism of fiction in *The Confidence-Man* to satisfy the requirements of his or her thesis. Nevertheless, Shroeder intimates a rent in the fabric of his allegory. The text certainly invites Shroeder's reading but does not seem to tolerate it.

Yet Melville's rhetorical layering of allusion seduces us with what Derrida calls in one instance "the *pharmakon*." The "word," Melville's literary word, seduces us, in its implicit but suggestive reference to an authoritative absence, to recover the hidden "*logos*" — "father," "sun," "capital" (82), or, in this instance, literary meaning. Laurence Buell concludes triumphantly that "it is a misdirection of energy . . . to work oneself into a state of romantic agony, or ennui, speculating about the obscurities of *The Confidence-Man*."[38] But Herman Melville, who confided to Nathaniel Hawthorne that he could "neither believe, nor be comfortable in his unbelief,"[39] simulates in *The Confidence-Man* a perversely allusive but evasive universe which condones neither certain knowledge nor skepticism. It condones instead the emotional risk of misdirected energy, energy that misfires, misses its mark. Our infection by Melville's allusion is both poison and remedy ("poison and remedy" is what Derrida interprets to be the dual meaning of the *pharmakon*, which he suggests is falsely opposed by Socrates to the *logos*); to understand it as either a poison or a remedy exclusively is to understand too well. Confidence in *The Confidence-Man* is an ethical sin because it shuts us off from the emotional energy that binds us all together: our mutual awareness of the absurd misdirectedness of our quest to believe opens up in us the floodgates of fellow feeling, emotional empathy, pity. Rhetoric, equally serving in the novel as the manifestation of misdirected energy and repressive, immoral confidence, functions in *The Confidence-Man* as a strand of allusion equal in magnitude to biblical allusion. The Confidence Man is consummately an orator — and Melville uses his knowledge and fascination with rhetoric, contemporary and classical, to play that for all it is worth.

In the 1830s, when Herman Melville was a boy, he dreamed of going to college and becoming a great orator.[40] This seems to have been a common dream for young American men growing up in the first part of the nineteenth century. Ralph Waldo Emerson, born in 1803, shared a similar love of oratory. Emerson's son Edward writes that "eloquence, in boyhood and youth, had been his idol,"[41] probably in part because Emerson studied at Harvard with Edward T. Channing, one of the most inspiring and idealistic professors to become a Boylston Professor of Rhetoric. Melville, because of his family's financial hardships, had no such good fortune as to pursue in any formal way his dream of becoming an orator, but published information on the volumes known to be in Melville's possession shows clearly that rhetoric was a continuing interest.

Because some of Melville's library was dispersed after his lifetime, some knowledge of Melville's reading must be conjectured from the literary allusions in his fictional texts. Undoubtedly Melville had read at least parts of Hugh Blair's popular *Rhetoric and Belles Lettres* (1783). Melville lists "Blair's Lectures, University Edition," among the Man-of-War library in *White-Jacket:* "a fine treatise on rhetoric, but having nothing to say about nautical phrases such as *'splicing the main-brace,' 'passing a gammoning,' 'puddinging the dolphin,'* and *'making a Carrick-bend.' "*[42] Scholars have also tentatively attributed to Melville an anonymous essay appearing in an 1847 *Yankee Doodle* entitled "A Short Patent Sermon, According to Blair, the Rhetorician."[43]

Melville's interest in rhetoric is documented most heavily in the classics. He owned a copy of Plato's *Phaedrus*, one of the two dialogues commonly thought to be Plato's discourse on rhetoric. He also owned a copy of Demosthenes' *Orations, The Three Dialogues of Cicero on the Orator* (the *de Oratore*, the *Brutus*, and the *Orator*,) and a copy of Aristotle's *Rhetoric*.[44] From the allusions to rhetoric in *The Confidence-Man*, it also seems clear that Melville read the *Confessions of St. Augustine*, which addresses the topic of Augustine's training in and convictions about rhetoric. Melville may also have read Plato's *Gorgias*, Plato's other dialogue on rhetoric. As Merton Sealts suggests, Melville read a wide range of Plato and alluded to Plato often in his literary works.[45]

Probably the reason that scholars have not researched this suggestive connection between Melville's knowledge of rhetoric and the depiction of that consummate orator the Confidence Man is that persuasive tactics employed by the Confidence Man seem already accessible to Melville through his knowledge of contemporary confidence men.[46] Also, many of these persuasive tactics make good common sense. Melville and the audience of his time period did, however, have a contemporary context for understanding such rhetorical actions. It was not just in American universities that rhetoric and public speaking had an impact; a preoccuption with oratory and eloquence also "infected" the pages of contemporary periodicals, and there were vivid descriptions and praise for adroit rhetorical skills. From 1853 through 1855, *Putnam's New Monthly Magazine* as just one example could be found running a series of essays featuring prominent orators, rhapsodizing on their abilities and instructing would-be orators and audience alike about what good oratory should be. *Putnam's* on rhetoric is a good source to link with Herman Melville since Melville was actively contributing to *Putnam's* from 1853 through 1855 because of his dire financial straits.[47] In all probability, Melville also subscribed to the magazine;[48] it seems very likely that he would have at least owned copies of those issues in which he published. And in those issues, he could have read about contemporary oratory. Given his own interest in oratory, it seems likely, again, that he did.

Some of the descriptions of the oratory in these periodical essays evoke Melville's Confidence Man. Each orator in *Putnam's* series was singled out for a particular kind of oratory. Rufus Choate, for example, was singled out as "the first and foremost of *made* orators."[49] Melville's 1855 January through July issues of *Putnam's* are in the Melville Collection of the Harvard College Library.[50] *Putnam's* discussion of Rufus Choate's 1855 April essay is an interesting one to consider in connection with Melville's Confidence Man.

Putnam's describes Rufus Choate as "a great actor, an artist, but an actor after all" (348). (One recalls that in *The Confidence-Man* the Cosmopolitan quotes Shakespeare's famous lines from *As You Like It* about the world as a stage and all men and women merely players.) The similarity between Melville's Confidence Man and *Putnam's* Rufus Choate is a shared theatricality, eclecticism of materials, and proclivity for metaphor or analogy to bridge over potential logical flaws in the argument. Choate uses language, *Putnam's* says, "drawn from all the sources of literature, and men's talk, common and uncommon; from the Bible and the newspapers, from some Homeric stanza and from the chat of our streets; from books the people love, and books they never heard of; simple words, long-legged words, all mixed up and stuck together like some bizarre mosaic, showing forth some splendid story, in all its infinite variety of hues" (352). This last description may bring to mind the Cosmopolitan's "vesture barred with various hues" (131). Though the Cosmopolitan's is an outward dress, various costumes are a part of the Confidence Man's, much as his language, so it seems evocative that *Putnam's* repeatedly describes Choate's persuasive language in the metaphor of clothes, his "rainbow hues or sulphureous fires" (350) and the way he can "dress his thought as he pleases, plain, or in gay, rhetorical attire, in kitchen garments, or in coronation robes" (351).

Interesting also is that Choate most excels in his persuasive and evasive use of similes and arguments. His "imaginative conception" and "distorting description . . . carry him right over weak spots in the argument of the case, as the skater swift as light skims in safety the cracking and bending ice" (350). In Choate's crafting of similes and arguments "he reveals his real essential power, for the force of his will and his intellectual passion is such, that he compels us in spite of ourselves to admire and sympathize with what in another man's mouth we might entirely condemn" (353). The implicit fear of such a word-wizard yet the subsequent and inevitable conviction of the audience are familiar dynamics in *The Confidence-Man*. One notable instance occurs when the Missouri bachelor suspiciously follows the analogies drawn from nature by the Confidence Man in his guise as a Philosophical Intelligence Officer to prove that a bad boy can be redeemed. The Missouri bachelor grudgingly admits, "That sounds a kind of reasonable, as it were—a little so, really. In fact, though you have said a great many foolish and absurd things, yet, upon the whole, your conversation has been such as might almost lead one less distrustful than I to repose a certain conditional confidence in you, I had almost added in your office also" (127). Other resonances seem present. The Confidence Man as portrayed by the narrator in both company and solitude can be found characterized in the remark that "a serio-comic cast is perceptible" in Rufus Choate's work, and the comment that Choate orates as if "the sepulchral Hamlet" would "give one rib-shaking laugh" might be applied to the unsolved mystery of Melville's reference to Hamlet in the novel's second half.[51] Hamlet, as Choate, and as the Confidence Man, sometimes seems to utter "such a funny little vein of thought, dashed into some solemn and high-keyed conception, like a woof of woolen shot with silver tissues" (353).

Most of Choate's metaphysical traits are more reminiscent of the Confidence Man in the second half of the novel. To turn to the Confidence Man in his more plebian disguises, one can look at an essay entitled "Of Fitness in Oratory" that was published in the April 1854 issue of *Putnam's*, pages 417 through 423, after the second installment of Melville's "The Encantadas," which appeared in that issue, pages 344 through 355. This essay provides several important links between rhetoric and our understanding of *The Confidence-Man*. It illustrates that the term *confidence man* may not refer exclusively to the realm of entrepreneurial swindling associated with William Thompson; it territorially establishes the term *confidence* within the province of rhetorical theory so that Melville's Confidence Man can be understood equally as an allusion to the tradition of rhetoric. Melville's Confidence Man does not seem to be out for money, after all; he is selling convictions, ideas — he is selling words.

How to trust an orator — and how to inspire trust if you were one — was one of the central concerns of oratory during Melville's time. According to the *Putnam's* article "Of Fitness in Oratory," only one solution was available, one way to "inspire *confidence* at the first look" (italics added): orators could conquer mistrust if they made it seem as though they had their audience's interests at heart. In other words, "everyone who observes their [the orators'] proceedings" must be "convinced that his own interests will be advanced thereby."[52] This would mean that the orator, to make his mark on a variety of audiences, or, in other words, to inspire confidence, must be adaptable. Many Melville scholars in establishing the religious context for *The Confidence-Man* have noted the resemblance between the Confidence Man's adaptive guises and a statement about rhetorical adaptability made by St. Paul. That statement might be phrased: "The Apostle Paul, to attain his great objects the easier, practised this considerateness towards the prejudices of his contemporaries, and became all things to all men *that by all means he might save some*." Curiously and perhaps not coincidentally, this statement comes from "Of Fitness in Oratory" (420). Could it be that this 1854 essay caught Melville's eye?

One additional feature of "Fitness in Oratory" is that adaptability is presented as a moral necessity which inclines toward a moral end. The orator must first and foremost study "his hearer under the influence of a true zeal for his welfare," and there are echoes of moral Platonism in the description of the adaptive process: "If the orator therefore would penetrate into our inner life and renew there the traces of forgotten thoughts and feelings, if he would indeed *address* us, let him make use of the customary words in which we are wont to hold converse with ourselves" (421). The orator is to awaken, in the "hearer," what lies within that hearer's inmost soul. This reference is surely derivative of Plato's *Phaedrus*, where Plato states that true knowledge is a remembering of what our souls once saw as they made their journeys with the gods.[53] This remembering is something which the lover (or rhetorician) can lead us toward.

Possibly Melville parodies this notion of a "really virtuous transaction" (423) in *The Confidence-Man* in several ways, both to comic effect. In chapter 17, "A gentleman with gold sleeve-buttons," the Confidence Man in the guise of the man in gray soliciting for the Seminole Widow and Orphan Asylum approaches a wealthy man, "who, like the Hebrew governor, knew how to keep his hands clean" (36). The Confidence Man's pitch to this philanthropist has the markings of his being in rapport with this "good" man, but it is not the wealthy gentleman but the man in gray who supposedly stirs himself with his own words about a universal benevolent society: "The master chord of the man in gray had been touched, and it seemed as if it would never cease vibrating. A not unsilvery tongue, too, was his, with gestures that were a Pentecost of added ones, and persuasiveness before which granite hearts might crumble into gravel" (42). This overdone description of the virtuous rhetorical transaction becomes almost whimsically funny when we realize that the ever-resourceful Confidence Man is putting on a one-man show as both orator and audience in default of finding an involved auditor. And even after reproducing the whole drama of the virtuous transaction for the benefit of the gentleman, the gentleman with the gold sleeve buttons refuses to be moved by this process: he "remained proof to such eloquence" and listened "with pleasant incredulity" (42).

In another instance, the Confidence Man's pliable adaptability suffers a comic misfire. As the man with the weed—a grieving widower of sorts—the Confidence Man senses he will be successful in approaching a university student within his present guise, inveighing against the cynicism of Tacitus, but with sentimentalized "diffidence" that changes "from soliloquy to colloquy, in a manner strangely mixed of familiarity and pathos." He proceeds in this gambit by assuming an air of melancholy "with a sort of sociable sorrowfulness" (25). But this time the Confidence Man has misjudged. He discovers that the student's possession of Tacitus is no touchstone to the student's character and that he has too glibly assumed from a stereotype of the sophomore that this particular student will admire melancholy. Undaunted, however, the resilient Confidence Man simply adapts to his audience's more insensitive and optimistic interior. He reencounters the student, and the Confidence Man is reincarnated as a "brisk, ruddy-cheeked man"—the man with the ledger of the Black Rapids Coal Company, something a pragmatic and self-interested sophomore might go for—and he converges with the student, correcting his initial error by identifying the man with the weed—his prior self, of course—as "a little cracked" (46).

Although I have read these fictional instances as Melville's parody of a "really virtuous transaction," Melville's target for satire could hypothetically be his Confidence Man instead of virtuous rhetoric itself. Melville could be supporting the view in "Fitness in Oratory" that the rhetorician without moral virtue will inevitably make some mistakes in the adaptive process because he lacks virtue. "Fitness in Oratory" points out that sagacity and shrewdness alone do not secure the best results; those

> are best secured by morality. It is not at all impossible that a crafty spirit may succeed in discovering one or another weak side of a character, with the design of bringing it into leading-strings; yet, to gain an enlarged appreciation of the views, feelings, and condition of a man, so as to be able to operate with beneficent and ennobling results upon his character, something more than cunning is necessary; prudence, indeed, is necessary, but such a prudence as follows the guidance of conscientious feeling, and of a disinterested spirit which looks with a genial sympathy upon the various circumstances of men. (419)

This very moral outlook, which begins by rejecting Cicero for his exclusive concentration on shrewdness and sagacity, rests uneasily side by side with the essay on the flamboyant antics of Rufus Choate, yet the nineteenth-century periodical essays on rhetoric maintained an uneasy truce between rhetorical rhapsodizing and rhetorical moralizing. A reading of the Confidence Man as the Devil could easily determine that mistakes made by the Confidence Man are the hints by which Mel-

ville encourages readers to make those fine-line distinctions between
sophistry and a "really virtuous transaction." The question thus invites
itself: Did Melville endorse and, through negative example, illustrate a
distinction between good and bad rhetoric in *The Confidence-Man* (despite the fact that the air of genial disinterest used to characterize the
"virtuous" rhetorician in the last passage is used in Melville's novel to
describe the Confidence Man)?

My answer would be emphatically no, but not because Melville
lacked awareness of sources that expressed the moral view. According
to Richard Weaver, Plato's *Phaedrus*, which picks up ostensibly on the
difference between the lover and the nonlover, is actually a discourse
on language: there are two types of rhetoric (two types of lovers) and a
"semantically purified" or "neuter language" (the nonlover). According
to Weaver, neuter language is not really the subject of Plato's dialogue,
since Plato rejects semantically purified language as an impossibility.
This is because the guise of neutral language is undoubtedly a cover
for some hidden suasiveness, just as Phaedrus's teacher Lysias pretends
to be a nonlover to advance his sexual interests in Phaedrus. Plato's
real concern, in Weaver's view, is the two potentials of rhetoric: "It can
move us toward what is good; it can move us toward what is evil." [54]
The immoral rhetorician, Plato says, "let[s] truth go to hell and stay
there" (65). On the other hand, the virtuous rhetorician will analyze
the unique soul of his audience so as to communicate "convictions and
virtues" (61) convincingly, stirring the response of the audience so that
it is compelled to pursue its own spiritual good.

Melville plays around with the *Phaedrus* in the opening scene of
The Confidence-Man although, of course, it is still not established that
he endorses exploitation of Plato's dialogue. From this opening scene
comes one of the issues most debated about the novel: the identity
and symbolic meaning of the deaf and mute man in cream-colors, who
writes verses on a slate from 1 Corinthians about the value of charity in
the novel's opening. The questioning goes something like this: Is this
"lamb-like" man an avatar of the Confidence Man, or, as Elizabeth Foster suggests, is he the ineffable symbol of a God who "is unknowable. If
He hears us, He gives no sign" [55]? The critic may not be able to vouch
for the mute man's identity, but one can turn to the *Phaedrus* for at
least one possibility of what he symbolically means.

One of the most remarkable reevaluations of the *Phaedrus* in recent
times is Jacques Derrida's in his 1981 *Dissemination*, and, curiously,
Derrida's chosen emphasis on the text of the *Phaedrus* illuminates how

Melville might have used it in *The Confidence-Man*. Although Derrida spends much time analyzing Plato's concluding myth about King Thamus of Egypt (a symbol for the *logos*) and the divinity Theuth (a symbol for the written word), Derrida suggests that Plato's discussion of language stemming from this myth motivates the entire dialogue in the *Phaedrus*. Plato's purpose is to discriminate between the written word, or the *pharmakon*, and living speech, the "undeffered *logos*" (71). Derrida notes that Plato disparages the written word as mere "mime of memory, of knowledge, of truth" (105). This is because the written word is not sustained by a living soul. Instead, the written word is only good "for *hypomnēsis* (re-memoration, recollection, consignation) and not for the *mnēmē* (living knowing memory)" (91): living memory can only be pursued through a dialectical quest, through living language. In support of Derrida's reading, one might consider how Plato in the opening of the dialogue mocks Phaedrus's dependency upon a written speech for relating Lysias's views. Not only does Phaedrus have to depend on the written speech, but he also has to read it rather than recite it by heart since his memorizing power has weakened thanks to his dependence on the written word. The written word, then, for Plato, represents death, for it "substitutes the breathless sign for the living voice, claims to do without the father (who is both living and life-giving) of *logos*, and can no more answer for itself than a sculpture or inanimate painting, etc" (92).

It seems possible that Melville is dramatizing Plato's preference for living speech over the written word at the beginning of *The Confidence-Man*. The lamblike man trying to urge the virtue of charity faces an audience that is hostile to virtue, the initially antagonistic audience that Plato says one should expect. Melville's conception of the lamblike man quoting Corinthians as both deaf and dumb dramatizes Plato's view that the written word lacks access to the rhetorical process: the deafness and dumbness of the messenger underscore that the written word cannot "speak" and that the audience, conversely, cannot "listen." How unresponsive the written word is—how much it constitutes an inflexibility—is illustrated by Melville's comment that "the word charity [on the slate], as originally traced, remained throughout uneffaced, not unlike the left-hand numeral of a printed date, otherwise left for convenience in blank" (5). *Charity* as a written word is only an inflexible transcription whose meaning does not change through time or interaction. Hence the written word, despite and because of its implacable stolidity, itself represents a trace, an absence; it cannot speak for itself in response to the hostility of the audience and it subsequently cannot bring the audience to virtue: "Illy pleased with his pertinacity, as they thought it, the crowd a second time thrust him aside, and not without epithets and some buffets" (4).[56]

The written word on the Confidence-Man's slate can only convert the already converted, "A Charitable lady," in chapter 8, who has been reading 1 Corinthians, "to which chapter possibly her attention might have recently been turned, by witnessing the scene of the monitory mute and his slate" (43). But the author of the written text is not present to the word, and, further, the long-term fate of the written word is that it will be forgotten: "The sacred page no longer meets her eye; but, as at evening, when *for a time* the western hills shine on though the sun be set, her thoughtful face retains its tenderness *though the teacher is forgotten*" (italics added) (44).

So the written word at the beginning of *The Confidence-Man* is at best productive of subtle suggestions about the virtue of confidence. It has effects in the scene with the widow and in at least one other instance. Those critics wishing to connect the man in cream colors with the Confidence Man's other avatars, even though he is not on Black Guinea's list, also need to consider the other character who disseminates words as a possible avatar of the Confidence Man, the "somewhat elderly person, in the quaker dress" (52–53), mentioned in chapter 10. Watson Branch notes several requirements for candidacy for the role of Confidence Man: each avatar must replace his predecessor, no two can appear together, and avatars will often allude to each other in the language of double entendres.[57] Although the man in the traveling cap carrying the ledger-book is the avatar in chapters 9 through 15,[58] the Quaker who has distributed the "Ode on the Intimations of Distrust in Man, Unwittingly Inferred from Repeated Repulses, in Disinterested Endeavors to Procure His Confidence" is described as having left the scene of distribution by chapter 10, so he does not appear simultaneously with chapter 10's man with the traveling cap. Further, there is evidence of implicit endorsement of one avatar by the other, in that the Quaker's reference to "repeated repulses" certainly could qualify as an oblique comment on his other experiences as avatar, and the "ge'mman wid a big book" endorses the other's poetry by calling attention to it. Finally, the Quaker's method of operation parallels that of the lamblike man: he "quietly" distributes his message and elicits some muted response from a "little dried-up man" who comments that the ode "works on my numbness not unlike a sermon" (53).

Apart from these few less than hearty responses to the written word, living speech in *The Confidence-Man* is portrayed as the mode of conviction. But does that equally mean that Melville endorses Plato's assertion (as Derrida sees it) that living speech is morally superior? Not necessarily. In *The Confidence-Man*, Melville plays several games with the central metaphor Plato uses to describe a "really virtuous transaction."

In the *Phaedrus*, to describe the flight of the soul to virtue for the less metaphysically inclined in his audience, Plato likens the soul to a "composite union of powers in a team of winged horses and their charioteer. Now all the gods' horses and charioteers are good and of good descent, but those of other beings are mixed. In the case of the human soul, first of all, it is a pair of horses that the charioteer dominates; one of them is noble and handsome and of good breeding, while the other is the very opposite, so that our charioteer necessarily has a difficult and troublesome task" (28). Plato goes on to say that the mortal soul once had wings and was immortal; it had a "blessed vision" of divine truth and gazed at spectacles of heaven "in the pure light of final revelation" (34). The charioteer in the mortal's soul can be responsible for the regrowth of the soul's immortal wings if the soul can regain its memory of divine beauty. This will help the charioteer to subdue the corrupt horse in his soul, which, through its wanton lust and procreation, prevents the "stump" of the soul's wing from blossoming (35). Thus, says Plato, "let this tribute, then, be paid to memory, which has caused us to enlarge upon it now, yearning for what we once possessed" (34). The virtuous orator will thus induce in his audience, by virtue of his living word, this memory of divinity and yearning for spiritual good, a good which to Plato implies self-control, honesty, kindness toward others.[59]

Plato's charioteer of the soul in *The Confidence-Man* becomes a jockey, and Melville's allusion to Plato's metaphor materializes in the words of "a limping, gimlet-eyed, sour-faced person" (12) — the man with the wooden leg who doubts Black Guinea's authenticity in chapter 3. This man responds to the Methodist minister's request for a charitable judgment of Black Guinea by retorting, "here on earth, true charity dotes, and false charity plots." At this juncture, the minister requests that the wooden-legged man suppose how he, with his vile words, would be judged without charity. To this, the wooden-legged man answers, as " 'some such pitiless man as has lost his piety in much the same way that the jockey loses his honesty' " (14).

Anyone recalling Plato's metaphor of the charioteer and horses in the *Phaedrus* may suspect that Melville is making a sexual joke of Plato's metaphor. The jockey who has lost his honesty has a "stump" instead of a wing; he obviously is riding, in a virtuous sense at least, the wrong horse. When the minister (who obviously cannot recall or has not read his *Phaedrus*) does not understand, the sarcasm continues as the wooden-legged man extends his allusion: " 'Never you mind how it is'—with a sneer; 'but all horses aint virtuous, no more than all men kind; and come close to, and much dealt with, some things are catching [an allusion to sexual disease?]. When you find me a virtuous jockey, I will find you a benevolent wise man' " (15). The minister mumbles, " 'Some insinuation there,' " and the cynical man responds, " 'More fool you that are puzzled by it.' " Of course, the wooden-legged man's declaration is tautological: a virtuous jockey is a benevolent wise man in Plato's pages, but the wooden-legged man implies that there are no benevolent wise men in the world, since the loss of male piety—virginity—seems certain (except with shrewd characters such as the Missouri bachelor).

The horse metaphor resurfaces in chapter 4 in the scene between the merchant, Mr. Roberts, and the Confidence Man as John Ringman. The Confidence Man's vigilant eye for the mark has enabled him to pick up Roberts's dropped business card in his guise as Black Guinea—ironically, it is Black Guinea's "advanced leather stump" (17) that covers the card—which indicates what horse Black Guinea is riding. Ringman's entry into Roberts's intimacy depends on his being able to convince Roberts, through his knowledge of Roberts's name, that they were formerly business acquaintances. His whole scam depends on debunking Roberts's memory, which bears no recollection, of course, of Ringman. Ringman plays on the difference between faithless and faithful memories and asks Roberts to ask himself whether "in some things this memory of yours is a little faithless." In contrast, Ringman says, Roberts should "trust in the faithfulness of mine" (19). If Roberts had read the *Phaedrus*, he would have known he was being approached by a soul with a dubious rider, because Ringman's subsequent analogy used to illustrate why human beings must sometimes rely on the memory of others proceeds in the following way: " 'In my boyhood I was kicked by a horse, and lay insensible for a long time. Upon recovering, what a blank! No faintest trace in regard to how I had come near the horse, or what horse it was, or where it was, or that it was a horse at all that had brought me to this pass' " (20). Being kicked by a horse implies that

Ringman, as his soul's charioteer, lacks self-control since he is obviously being kicked, or dominated, by the more corrupt of his horses. But Ringman's discourse on memory also tarnishes Plato's credibility. He has only his friends' judgment to rely on, Ringman concludes, to trust that the horse that kicked him even existed. By extension, readers of Plato have only friend Plato's word to rely on to jar their memory that the soul has a charioteer and divine horses.

Melville's view in *The Confidence-Man* would seem to be that there are no virtuous men in the participatory world of rhetoric, in other words, that there is no such thing as virtuous rhetoric, in other words, no valid division between the written and spoken word in terms of ethical worth, and, further, that there is no division within the spoken word between virtuous rhetoric and sophistry. For Herman Melville in this novel as for Jacques Derrida in *Dissemination*, exploding Plato's myth of a possible separation between one type of language and another seems to be a moral necessity. For Derrida, "Socrates' bite is worse than a snake's since its traces invade the soul" (118). Derrida plays Socrates' rhetorical figuration of the written word as a *pharmakon*—both poison and remedy—against Socrates himself, suggesting that fragments and forms of this figuration for death attach themselves to Socrates throughout the dialogue. Socrates, through "the dialectical inversion of the *pharmakon* or of the dangerous supplement" (123), creates a false myth of supplementarity, an invasive exterior (the written word/death) and a pure interior (the spoken word/life). In Plato's myth, "the restoration of internal purity must thus reconstitute, *recite* . . . that to which the *pharmakon* should not have had to be added and attached like a *literal parasite:* a *Letter* installing itself inside a living organism to rob it of its *nourishment* and to *distort* . . . the pure audibility of a voice" (128). The Socratic word, according to Derrida, is an exclusionary principle—and the living word is synonymous with truth, law, dialectics, philosophy—that enacts a dialectical inversion of "the dangerous supplement" so that death seems "both acceptable and null" (123). But the ethical danger that Derrida implies in this process, which motivates him to say that the *pharmakon* or poison that we all await was well deserved by Socrates (119), is that the desire to mythologize a dangerous exterior and then to control it results in political fanaticism, as in the instance of the scapegoat during Greek times who was often burned alive after being taken outside the city: "The city's body *proper* thus reconstitutes its unity, closes around the security of its

inner courts, gives back to itself the word that links it with itself within
the confines of the agora, by violently excluding from its territory the
representative of an external threat or aggression" (133).

Melville unofficially dedicated *The Confidence-Man* "to victims of
Auto da Fe,"[60] to victims, one might say, of the tyrannical exclusionary
process at work. In *The Confidence-Man*, once the spoken word becomes
the novel's center of attention, the living language of sophistry takes
the role of the *pharmakon*, as opposed to the living *logos* of virtuous
rhetoric. And in the first half of the novel, as Melville dramatizes this
process, the Confidence Man/Devil/Stranger serves as both victim
and parodic advocate of this exclusionary process. He is a foreigner, a
stranger, estranged from the body politic; his position is actually akin
to the position of the *pharmakon* or written word in Plato's myth, as
the *teknē* Theuth: "As a substitute capable of doubling for the king, the
father, the sun, and the word, distinguished from those only by dint
of representing, repeating, and masquerading, Theuth was naturally
also capable of totally supplanting them and appropriating all their attributes" (90). In the first half of the novel, the Confidence Man is
Theuth appropriating the attributes of the *logos*. Most critics believe
that the first half of the novel warns against credulity, but it may be
that the problem with the people in the first half of the novel is their
demand for unqualified certitude, a need which the Confidence Man
satisfies by masquerading as the *logos*. This expungement is demanded
because a state of confidence more problematic would require indeterminacy, emotional risk. But emotional risk seems the "truth" of moral
life for Melville.

Melville's view is intimated in the Confidence Man's second encounter with the merchant. The Confidence Man, the man with the
ledger for the Black Rapids Coal Company, discusses with the merchant the story of Goneril, which the Confidence Man narrated to the
merchant in his role as the man with the weed to solicit his sympathy
and funds. The merchant has been moved, by the account of the perfidy of Goneril, to a consideration of the hardness of life. Ironically,
the Confidence Man as the man with the ledger now has to remove
the doubt he had inculcated in the merchant when he was the man
with the weed soliciting confidence. He does so by warning that "to
admit the existence of unmerited misery . . . was . . . not prudent"
(65). Admitting the existence of misery (the *pharmakon*/death) might
shake one's "conviction of a Providence," the *logos*, and unflinching
faith in Providence is "of the essence of a right conviction of the divine

nature." The Confidence Man's position is that of the *logos*; the unfortunate experience of the man with the weed with his wife Goneril is a *pharmakon*. It is, indeed, absent from its author; it is the narrator's story of the good merchant's story of the man with the weed's story of a story that is apocryphal, that only purports to exist. The denial of the *pharmakon* breeds confidence; it prohibits "too much latitude of philosophizing, or, indeed, of compassionating, since this might beget an indiscreet habit of thinking and feeling which might unexpectedly betray him upon unsuitable occasions" (66). Thus the *pharmakon* must be expelled, or it must be repressed, so that the body politic of the *logos*, or, in this instance, of Divine Providence, remains pure. A whole range of human emotions, including compassion, get denied in the process, then, of affirming an unqualified confidence. The merchant, for example, cannot pity the man with the weed in the story, for that would be acknowledging that the *logos* has been invaded by the *pharmakon*; the merchant must consider him a "lucky dog . . . after all" for losing a shrewish wife, whose possible shrewishness must also be qualified. Expelled from the story also is acknowledgment of the man's loss of his beloved child.

In *The Confidence-Man*, then, Melville seems to present the Platonic quest for truth as a selfish demand for a certified *logos* and as a tyrannizing process that excludes the problematics of human emotion. It is difficult, though, in terms of this thesis, to interpret the significance of Melville's Platonic Indian-hater, Colonel John Moredock. In some ways the Indian-hater seems ethically impeccable, especially if the novel is read as Shroeder's type of religious allegory. As Hershel Parker points out, Melville adds biblical allusion to Judge Hall's account of the story, and there seems to be a "similarity of the dedication of the Indian-hater to the way Jesus would have begun a life as His follower." Both Parker and Shroeder find Indians to be connected with the Devil in this novel, so that the Indian-hater is that altruistic man, a dedicated Christian who would pursue Evil "at the cost of forsaking human ties."[61]

This analysis seems convincing, especially since Melville's tone in narration of Moredock's story seems at its most unambiguous and at its least ironic. One's impression from the folk-heroic tone of this story about a hero never even seen who battles evil is that Melville finds this hero admirable. Thus it may be that in his account of the Indian-hater Melville diverges from Derrida's complete rejection of Plato's mythological pursuit of the *logos* to the extent that the Indian-hater is

exempt from the participatory rhetorical world. The Indian-hater does
not involve himself with the community intentions of language. He is
a hater, not a lover (although he loves his family, he never sees them),
and his forsaking of human ties does not bind him up in the hypocrisies
of pursuing Platonic purity while indulging in the messiness of human
emotions. The Indians, perhaps, in Melville's symbolic sense, are not
human but the embodiment of an idea, which the Indian-hater pursues
relentlessly as a higher truth, but solitarily and without implicating
those he loves by forcing them to do the same.

But the messy emotional life of the Missouri bachelor makes the
bachelor seem a more endearing and plausible character. The emotions
of the Missouri bachelor keep him uncertain, never able to have full
confidence or full doubt in man's virtue or lack of it. As the Cosmopolitan says of him, " 'I seized that lucky chance, I say to inspect his
heart, and found it an inviting oyster in a forbidding shell. His outside is but put on. Ashamed of his own goodness, he treats mankind
as those strange old uncles in romances do their nephews—snapping
at them all the time and yet loving them as the apple of their eye' "
(156). The Confidence Man makes his mark upon the Missouri bachelor only once, and the bachelor's final credulity, despite his admirable
resistance of the herb doctor's casuistry, is what damns him, according
to Shroeder. The Missouri bachelor believes in St. Augustine's doctrine of original sin—so he admits to the Confidence Man as Pitch,
the Philosophical Intelligence Officer. This belief is the one he should
not have relinquished, in Shroeder's view, for it would have saved him
from the sin of nominal Christianity.

Pitch tries to persuade the Missouri bachelor to hire one more boy
for labor since, contrary to the bachelor's experience, not all boys are
bad and even bad boys can be redeemed. After a series of dubious
analogies drawn from nature to prove his point, Pitch finally succeeds
by producing his trump card, the one he has held in reserve since the
Missouri bachelor told him that one of his former laborers, a very
polite boy, "very politely stole my pears" (118). Chapters 4 through 10
of Book 2, "The Sixteenth Year," of St. Augustine's Confessions are
entitled "Robbing a Pear-tree." Augustine blames this sin on the influence of companionship: "But since the pleasure I got was not in the
pears, it must have been in the crime itself, and put there by the companionship of others sinning with me." [62] In some occult passageway of
the Confidence Man's devious mind, he has deduced from the bachelor's reference to the pears that the Missouri bachelor who is examin-

ing the risks of companionship has in mind, at least unconsciously, St. Augustine. Several interchanges later, Pitch inquires, " 'But you have a little looked into St. Augustine I suppose,' " and the Missouri bachelor answers that " 'St. Augustine on Original Sin is my textbook.' " After the Missouri bachelor rejects Pitch's examples of other saintly people who from bad starts had reformed, Pitch points out that St. Augustine was first " 'the saint's irresponsible little forerunner—the boy.' " " 'All boys are rascals, and so are all men' " (125), the Missouri bachelor exclaims, but he begins to fidget—and he is hooked.

Not only does Augustine reject companionship of all but a very select few as conducive to sin, but he also rejects his own profession of rhetoric. Rhetoric, to St. Augustine, is sophistry, and sophistry and companionship are bound up in the world of sin as opposed to divine authority. The Confidence Man's use of St. Augustine himself as the argument to defeat original sin (or easy redemption) is a cruel trick to play on St. Augustine. But what the Confidence Man brings up in pointing out the rascal in the saint is that communion with the divine is hard won by fallible humans, and then only at the cost of isolation. And although rhetoric and companionship are equally dubious propositions in *The Confidence-Man*, they are still the necessary sustenance for all but a rare few.

I have so far suggested that the Confidence Man in the first half of the novel has played a role much like Theuth in Derrida's version of Plato's myth, with his theatrical whimsicality and his masquerade as the certitude of *logos* to give the people what they want. This disguise is played with a vengeance against the intentional fallacy of the *logos*—against the concept of a hidden authority that does not exist. But in the Confidence Man's scene as the Cosmopolitan with the Missouri bachelor, he is identified as a genial misanthropist by the bachelor: " 'You are Diogenes, Diogenes in disguise. I say—Diogenes masquerading as a cosmopolitan' " (138). Despite the Cosmopolitan's cry of protest that he has been "taken to belong to a side to which he but labors, however ineffectually, to convert," it appears that the bachelor's recognition of mutual identity and offer of friendship in a problematical world convert the Confidence Man; he drops his masquerade of certitude, or turns certitude against itself with irony, and acknowledges language as the *pharmakon*—as the ambiguous verbal interchange of problematized human relationships. He also represents the view that the concept of the *logos* is an alienating dimension of human relations.

From chapter 25 of *The Confidence-Man* until the novel's closing frame in which the Cosmopolitan converses with the barber, several changes occur in the narrative presentation of the Confidence Man that seem significant. The Confidence Man is now approached by others whereas in the past he was the one to approach, and, although the Confidence Man has been persistently called "stranger" in the novel's first half and as the Cosmopolitan is called "stranger" in his scene in chapter 24 with the Missouri bachelor, from chapter 25 until the closing frame he is consistently referred to as the Cosmopolitan and his companions in discourse are referred to as "stranger." Perhaps this suggests that the Cosmopolitan's more balanced and cautious yet companionable approach to human relations familiarizes him to the world, while the falsely genial approaches of Mark Winsome, Egbert, and Charlie Noble, now all called "stranger," estrange them from the world as they operate under the hidden sign of the *logos*.

Tom Quirk expresses the view of most critics of *The Confidence-Man* when he suggests that "the second half of this double-edged satire ridicules those who refuse to have confidence,"[63] but Melville's satire is actually more complex than this description would indicate, for Mark Winsome, his disciple Egbert, and Charlie Noble are all confidence men. They are not like the barber who hangs out the sign "No Trust." Instead, Winsome and Egbert operate under the *logos* of universal benevolence, and Charlie Noble operates under the *logos* of the universal goodness of man. The Cosmopolitan as Frank Goodman links Winsome's and Charlie Noble's views by calling Egbert "Charlie" in his hypothetical example about friendship. The similarity between them is that they transmit the myth of the *logos* as a means of exercising power over men and of avoiding the risk involved in genuine human experience.

The Cosmopolitan's exposure of their real lack of confidence is only a first step toward dispelling the myth of the *logos*, the myth of confidence itself, and a demonstration that "those red men who are the greatest sticklers for the theory of Indian virtue, and Indian loving-kindness, are sometimes the arrantest horse-thieves and tomahawkers among them" (147). The irresponsibility in selling confidence — that men are good, that there is a divine benevolence, that rhetoric is virtuous and tells the "truth" — is that it discourages people's acceptance of risk as the true means to human relations. When Charlie Noble refuses to loan money to Frank Goodman, not only does he expose Noble's understandable but, in this case, morally hypocritical lack of confidence, but Goodman betrays Charlie's serious ethical lack — his unwillingness, out of any warmth or companionship for his fellow human being, to take a risk.

To choose to operate under the power of a bogus certainty rather than to be willing to participate in the risk of indeterminate human relations is considered immoral by Melville, as the Cosmopolitan's dealings with Mark Winsome and Egbert reveal. Goodman tries twice, with Winsome and with his disciple, to demonstrate how their philosophies estrange them from humanity. Winsome's certitude about the universal benevolence of nature in its relation with men does not stand up, of course, to Goodman's example of the rattlesnake that bites men, but, when Goodman introduces this *pharmakon*/poison into the purity of the *logos*/nature and human relations, Winsome expels it, pointing out that the snake is *labeled* as a *pharmakon* because of its rattles, so that the fault does not devolve onto the *logos*, but on the human agent who has not expelled the poisonous *pharmakon*/snake from the system of nature by killing it. Since expulsion of the *pharmakon* is possible, since "a proper view of the universe" is that it "is suited to breed a proper confidence" (191), then living agents are accountable for the impurity of nature, which they are obligated to expel from the system. Hence human pain requires no compassion because there was really no risk of being bitten, if the person had only had confidence in reading the label, just as any evil can be expelled from the *logos* if people would only "read" the labels of evil.

Confidence in reading the labels means confidence that they *can* be read, and it is tempting to tie in this proposed confidence in a label with the confidence in Melville's culture during his time that the truth or falsity of eloquence — another label — could be read. It is also tempting to speculate that Melville knew something of Emerson's reverence for eloquence, since Melville's character Mark Winsome was based on Emerson. Emerson was a popular lecturer throughout his career, and his most popular lecture was entitled "Poetry and Eloquence."[64] This lecture was first delivered in 1847 in Boston, and it continued to be a mainstay of his lecture series. Emerson's "Eloquence," however, did not appear in published form until 1870.[65] In addition, Merton Sealts has provided some convincing evidence that the lecture Melville heard Emerson give in New York on February 5, 1849, was "Natural Aristocracy,"[66] although it is imprecise from Sealts's footnotes how Emerson's lecture "Eloquence" has been ruled out; "Eloquence" was Emerson's second-to-last lecture in "The Mind and Manners" series in London in 1848 and Sealts identifies the lecture Melville heard as Emerson's

second-to-last in the "Mind and Manners" series delivered in 1849 in
New York. According to information that Sealts alludes to but does
not fully disclose since it is from the manuscript notes of another
scholar, apparently Emerson's "Mind and Manners" series was altered
for New York, although it is surprising that he would delete such a
popular essay as "Eloquence." "Eloquence" was published in the *Boston
Journal* in 1847, according to Sealts, but it is still improbable that Melville, although in Boston in 1847, read it. Nevertheless, Emerson's first
essay titled "Eloquence," for there were two, exhibits the enthusiasm
for Platonic virtuous rhetoric that Melville's *Confidence-Man* seriously
questions. Virtuous eloquence, stated Emerson, is "when the orator
sees through all masks to the eternal scale of truth, in such sort that he
can hold up before the eyes of men the fact of to-day steadily to that
standard, thereby making the great great, and the small, small, which
is the true way to astonish and to reform mankind." [67] Emerson's second "Eloquence," which was first delivered in 1867, was considerably
more polemical, stating that "no act indicates more universal health
than eloquence" and declaring his own adamant faith in the inherent
virtue of eloquence: "Will you establish a lie? You are a very elegant
writer, but you can't write what gravitates down." [68]

As we shall see in Chapter 1, Emerson's statement is a recasting
of the famous Quintilian principle asserting that liars cannot be eloquent. As expressed by Hugh Blair, whom Emerson mentions in his
second essay, "without possessing the virtuous affections in a strong degree, no man can attain eminence in the sublime parts of eloquence." [69]
Although Melville may not have heard Emerson on eloquence, he had
read Blair, and it is possible that by contributing the following statement to the Cosmopolitan's debunking irony, Melville is parodying the
Quintilian principle: "Even if experience did not sanction the proverb,
that a good laugher cannot be a bad man, I should yet feel bound in
confidence to believe it" (163).

After reading *The Confidence-Man*, no one feels bound in confidence
to believe that eloquence is always "true," but Melville's point seems
further extended to suggest that eloquence can never be true, at least,
that one cannot know it to be so. The labels of language are not trans-
parent, and they require the risk of interpretation out of the love of
companionship rather than the tyranny of the allegorical *logos* that
expresses its need for power and control. Melville's shrewdest demonstration of this point occurs in the scene between Frank Goodman

and Charlie Noble, when they sit down in "convivial expectancy" to drink their wine. "The stranger," Charlie Noble, claims that they have a "friendship at first sight," and the Cosmopolitan responds that this sort of friendship "is the only true one, the only noble one. It bespeaks confidence" (160). Truth, nobility, confidence, all are synonyms for the *logos*. This blind imposition of the *logos* upon the radical indeterminacy of friendship denies the possibility of experience, the suggestion that in friendship there might be any risk. (Friendship is an immediately readable label.) Of course, Noble has no confidence whatsoever, and his goal is to get Goodman inebriated through a sense of false security so that Noble can take advantage of him. But Goodman, of course, is urging Charlie to drink also, and a battle for power ensues. There is really no battle for the Cosmopolitan, or Goodman, however. He is merely exposing Noble's hypocritical stance on confidence, but, further, Noble's essential immorality, for the Cosmopolitan deliberately problematizes the situation for Charlie and exposes that Charlie, for the sake of human companionship, is unwilling to take a risk.

The risk devolves upon the wine bottle that the Cosmopolitan orders, and that Charlie refuses to drink, which arrives in

> a little bark basket, braided with porcupine quills, gayly tinted in the Indian fashion . . . bearing the capital letters, "P.W."
>
> "P.W.," said he [Noble] at last, perplexedly eying the pleasing poser, "now what does P.W. mean?"
>
> "Shouldn't wonder," said the cosmopolitan gravely, "if it stood for port wine. You called for port wine, didn't you?"
>
> "Why so it is, so it is!"
>
> "I find some little mysteries not very hard to clear up," said the other, quietly crossing his legs. (161)

Of course, Charlie's fear (that the Cosmopolitan deliberately initiates and aggravates by his subsequent discussion of poisoned wine) is that "P.W." stands for "poisoned wine," but it could also stand for "port wine," or "pure wine," or "perplexing wine," or "pleasing wine," *pure* being the only one of these *p* words not present in the text surrounding this description, and, thus, the Cosmopolitan, through his pleasing poser, problematizes the *logos*, shows that the *pharmakon*, or poison, can never be exterior to but is always implicit in rhetoric. The Cosmopolitan likewise problematizes the purity of the human heart, which is much like "each bottle of port" (161) so that when the Cosmopolitan pledges (another *p* word) that the wine is pure with his "whole heart," even truth, as represented by the word *pledge*, has been robbed of a potentially transcendental referent based on emotion.

In *The Confidence-Man*, Melville denied a transcendental status to truth because he believed in the ethics of risk, in "a kind of man who, while convinced that on this continent most wines are shams, yet still drinks away at them; accounting wine so fine a thing, that even the sham article is better than none at all," and in a "man of a disposition ungovernably good-natured who might still familiarly associate with men, though, at the same time, he believed the greater part of men false-hearted — accounting society so sweet a thing that even the spurious sort was better than none at all" (162). For Melville, the divine authority of the *logos* could only be a confidence game perpetuated by knaves or fools either to tyrannize over and to deny or repress the realities of human experience. In fact, in Melville's view, the confidence game itself — the need to impose an authoritative order on the world — creates some of the more brutal human realities such as the auto da fe, which means, in one interpretation, the religious theater of faith.

But for the other authors in this study, Charles Brockden Brown, Nathaniel Hawthorne, Mark Twain, and Henry James, the accessibility of and necessity for some form of truth is central to their ethical vision, and it is only through trust, which is established by truthful human relations, that human beings with fragile emotions can feel safe to share those emotions with each other. The concept in nineteenth-century American literature that truth was knowable and that truth was morally necessary was a cultural legacy of the historical rhetoric that will be discussed at greater length in the first chapter of this book. The thesis of this book is that Brown, Hawthorne, Twain, and James confirmed in one way or another the legitimacy of this rhetorical conception of truth, responding out of a strong moral conviction just as Melville did when he rejected it.

1

A Full Heart and a Well-Equipped Mind: The Legacy of Rhetorical Idealism in Nineteenth-Century America

🌿

> The central element of Henry Ward Beecher's character was his sensitiveness to truth.
>
> —JOHN R. HOWARD, 1887

The love of rhetorical study from the end of the eighteenth century into the final decades of the nineteenth century engrossed Americans of all sorts, those people intellectually and philosophically inclined but also those literate and perhaps not so literate within the popular culture. Training in rhetoric began in America with the establishment of universities and private preparatory schools at the end of the eighteenth century and was soon a part of the curriculum in public schools. Essays on rhetoric, or on oratory, practically interchangeable terms during this time, also appeared frequently within the pages of American periodicals, and the terms of rhetorical idealism derived from the rhetorical study of the time could be heard in the speeches and in the written praise of the orators who for many Americans practically became folk heroes. As one scholar of nineteenth-century oratory explains, "Nineteenth-century Americans displayed an enthusiasm for 'eloquence' and 'oratory' which is difficult for the modern reader fully to appreciate. Young men who aspired to leadership in any field were counseled that the cultivation of eloquence was the surest, speediest avenue to success."[1]

My interest in this chapter is to track one of the most profound assumptions about language to come out of this rhetorical movement

35

and to reveal that this assumption about language, despite the changing fate and direction of rhetorical study throughout the nineteenth
century, remained constant. The rhetorical study that began in American universities and filtered down into the popular culture was notable
for its unswerving faith in the truth-telling power of language and for
its insistence on the moral necessity of telling the truth. This faith
in and reverence for the truth was an omnipresent theme throughout
the nineteenth century, and, strangely enough, despite the increasing
scientific skepticism as the century wore on about the epistemological status of such concepts as truth, the rhetorical conception of truth
was sufficiently entrenched within the culture to ensure that truthful
language retained its integrity for many Americans.

In writing about oratory as it was perceived throughout the nineteenth century, Barnet Baskerville observes that

> one is struck by the fact that truth is readily ascertainable and has the
> same appearance to all men. One marvels at the calm assurance of these
> men that the orator has only to lay hold of truth in order to be elo-
> quent and successful. The orator, apparently, has a clear choice, truth or
> falsehood. The upright man will choose truth every time. A possible ex-
> planation of this certainty about the nature of truth is that these writers
> are using the term in a metaphysical sense. They are talking not about
> probability or demonstrable fact, but about eternal verities, intuitively
> perceived.[2]

Indeed, contrary to what Baskerville suggests, rhetoricians *were* concerned with the demonstrable facts of experience, but the truth that
orators referred to when they used *truth* in a metaphysical sense can be
identified in the nineteenth century very firmly. Since Hugh Blair and
many of the rhetorical theorists who succeeded him in influence over
the American conception of rhetoric were ministers, the eternal verities founded on the intuitive private inquiry to which Blair leaves the
process of truth-seeking in his *Rhetoric and Belles Lettres*[3] were invariably implied to be Christian virtues, and truth-telling was inevitably
connected with the concept of ethical responsibility. In this respect, the
rhetoric of Blair and his successors in the American rhetorical tradition
was thoroughly conversant in the classics, not just with the more pragmatic rhetoric of Aristotle but, actually, more responsive in its ethical
cast to the more idealistic discourses in rhetoric found in Plato. In the
Gorgias, for example, Socrates articulates that spiritual truth implies
self-control, honesty, and compassion in our behavior toward others.[4]

These are the Christian virtues as Blair and later rhetoricians would have known them.

Truth to the late eighteenth- and nineteenth-century American implied humanitarian virtues, but it also implied an equal reliance on the reality of experience. To lie implied that someone was consciously telling a falsehood that one knew to be contrary to experience, and thus to lie deliberately was to violate the larger truth of man's shared humanity. As one periodical essayist expressed it in the 1830s, not only is lying "the offspring of a selfish spirit," but "he, who utters a single lie, sins not only against society, but against himself, — against soul and body, — against his temporal no less than his eternal interests."[5] Conscious deception implied a desire to do ill to another and the abuse of the trust established between individuals. Trust in a relationship formed the truth of the relationship upon which the individual could act. Further, lies could damage an individual not only by inducing him or her to commit acts destructive to self but also by making the individual doubt his or her experience. *Truth* and *truthfulness* were companion terms in late eighteenth- and nineteenth-century morality.

Among the thinking Americans upon whom the rhetorical conception of truth had a compelling influence were the authors considered in this study, Charles Brockden Brown, Nathaniel Hawthorne, Herman Melville (as we have seen), Mark Twain, and Henry James. Each of these authors shared common sources for their knowledge of the rhetorical tradition, but the later authors in the period actually had an awareness of an accumulatively wider range of sources. Of course, the authors also allude to the cultural context of rhetorical theory in response to the other social issues and intellectual discoveries of their time, but the fundamental basis of their various responses to the rhetorical tradition of truth-telling language is their private and separate ethical visions, and it seems likely that Herman Melville would have responded to the rhetorical conception of truth similarly were he writing in 1850 or 1900. Nevertheless, it will be useful to give a basic overview of the rhetorical movement in America from its beginnings until the end of the nineteenth century as it relates to this conception of truth so that each author in this study can be seen in the context of his more immediate influences.

When Charles Brockden Brown wrote *Wieland* in 1798, the American rhetorical movement that so fervently espoused truthful language was an enthusiasm sweeping the country, as Brown himself was aware as a member of the Belles Lettres Club in Philadelphia in 1792 and

as an admirer of Hugh Blair's *Rhetoric and Belles Lettres*.[6] The emphasis on truthful language was a feature of the moral rhetoric textbooks
that were used in rhetoric instruction in America in the late eighteenth
century, the most prominent rhetoric during Brown's time being that
of the Scottish rhetorician Hugh Blair. Blair's rhetoric was first published in England and in America in 1783,[7] and William Charvat mentions that Blair's and other derivative rhetorics "were almost household
books in America." Blair's rhetoric was the standard text for the course
of rhetoric that was required in all college curriculums, and on into
the nineteenth century it was also widely used in local schools in small
American towns. Fifty-three editions of Blair's rhetoric were published
in America in the eighteenth and nineteenth centuries, fourteen of
them after 1835.[8]

Blair's rhetoric was not the only source for America's early enthusiasm for rhetoric, and it is interesting that other rhetorical influences
in America during Brown's time were combining the ideal of truth not
only with the Christian virtues of brotherly love and virtuous honesty
but also with the early political ideals of American democracy. Thomas
Jefferson was one of many important thinkers of his time influenced
by a young Scottish rhetorician, James Ogilvie, who came to America
after the Revolution in 1795 before the age of twenty.[9] Jefferson even
sent Ogilvie a set of Cicero's volumes to thank him for one of Ogilvie's
speeches. Ogilvie was also a particular friend of Washington Irving,
whose nephew mentioned in Irving's biography the widespread and
lasting influence of Ogilvie on American oratory. Ogilvie's plan was
to educate the masses through the concept of eloquence, a term emphasized throughout rhetorical treatises, particularly in Blair's. Ogilvie
lectured throughout the Southeast to promote his campaign. His subject matter was declared to be devoid of politics and religion, but he
clearly embraced democratic and Christian ideals.

Ogilvie's rhetoric was received with an idealized adoration. Francis
Walker Gilmer, a former student of Ogilvie's whom Jefferson sent to
Europe to negotiate the first faculty for the University of Virginia, testified that " 'Ogilvie inspired me with new desires. He touched some
sympathetic chord which instantly responded, and from that moment
I felt that there was a divine spark in the human mind, at least in
mine, which might be fanned into flame and which was infinitely of
more value and of more enjoyment, than the mere pleasures of sense.' "
This rhetorical combination of feeling and imagination that embraced
some higher truth was complementary to American democracy. As one

scholar notes, "Ogilvie was as much a product of his age as he was a maker of it. Raw America, with little time for the more subtle literary arts, and supremely interested in politics, saw 'eloquence' as the means to a limited aestheticism and to practical politics at the same time." [10]

A typical theme for a thesis on oratory at Yale in 1776 was "Eloquence always flowers and rules among a free people." The *State Gazette* of South Carolina in 1790 announced college oratorical exhibitions that would "display the proficiency of the youth in the useful, ornamental, and sublime art of eloquence, so essentially important in a Republic." [11] Predictably, the Boylston Chair of Rhetoric and Oratory at Harvard, endowed by Nicholas Boylston in 1771 and activated in 1806, was first occupied by a politician no less important than John Quincy Adams. [12] Indeed, at least one modern scholar has suggested that rhetoric and democracy were symbiotic companions in the emergence of the new nation, [13] and the notion that truthful rhetoric flourishes best in a democracy is advocated by one of the more famous Boylston professors of rhetoric to be discussed in this chapter, Edward Tyrell Channing.

Hence it was within this atmosphere of great enthusiasm and faith in rhetorical eloquence as the inevitably virtuous voice of a new American democracy that Charles Brockden Brown wrote his novel *Wieland, or the Transformation,* and it is certainly in allusion to this enthusiasm that Brown depicts his central character Theodore Wieland, a representative of enlightened America, placing in Wieland's temple of worship a bust of Cicero and dramatizing Wieland's reading of rhetorical treatises with his friend Pleyel. But *Wieland* is a response also to the darker side of the rhetorical tradition that late eighteenth- and nineteenth-century rhetorical theorists sought to repress. Since *truth* and *truthfulness* were coveted companion terms in late eighteenth- and nineteenth-century rhetorical morality, it is all the more curious to consider rhetoric's traditional problematic relationship with *sophistry* and with *the truth.*

The potential for sophistry has always been a problem for rhetoricians trying to justify the study of rhetoric. In the late eighteenth and nineteenth centuries, it was the rhetoricians like Hugh Blair, and then, later, George Campbell, Edward Tyrell Channing, Ralph Waldo Emerson, and Henry Ward Beecher who perpetuated the notion that truthfulness was tantamount to virtue, and imperative. This urging of truth, however, was not only an ethical priority for these advocates of rhetoric but also a necessary strategy for counteracting the suspicion that rhetoric was the study of how best to deceive people. Most rhetorics of the time, including the early generative ones of the Scottish rhetoricians Hugh Blair, George Campbell, and Richard Whately, mention that rhetoric is "apt to suggest to many minds an associated idea of empty declamation, or of dishonest artifice; or at best, of a mere dissertation on Tropes and Figures of Speech. The subject indeed stands perhaps but a few degrees above Logic in popular estimation; the one being generally regarded by the vulgar as the Art of bewildering the learned by frivolous subtleties; the other, that of deluding the multitude by specious falsehood." [14]

Suspicion of rhetoric as sophistry can be traced back to Plato, somewhat ironically, since American nineteenth-century theorists are essentially Platonists in their call for a virtuous rhetoric, but this suspicion reemerges throughout the history of rhetoric, in part as a result of the way rhetorical study is conceptualized from one time period to the next. For quite some time before the rhetorics of Blair, Campbell, and Whately, the province of rhetorical study had been drastically reduced by the plan of late sixteenth-century logician Peter Ramus, who challenged the classical Aristotelian divisions of rhetoric by reassigning the two ancient rhetorical divisions of invention and arrangement to logic, thus leaving only style and delivery to the rhetorical scholar. Rhetoricians like Blair and Campbell were aware that when rhetoric is equated solely with style, it becomes vulnerable to charges of sophistry. Eighteenth- and nineteenth-century rhetoricians responded to this charge against their discipline by insisting on the implicit moral value of rhetorical studies and by distinguishing between an inferior form of rhetoric they called sophistry and a superior form that they often referred to as rhetorical eloquence. Despite Blair's avowed adherence to Ramus's narrower definition of rhetoric—Campbell was the only one to insist openly that rhetoric should be equated with moral philosophy—Blair and his American rhetorical successors (who had Plato and the other classical rhetoricians as known sources as well as the rhetoric of Blair) tried to build back into their rhetorical system the notion that rhetoric involved a depth and honesty central to scholarly humanism. And thus rhetoricians focused squarely on the absolute moral necessity of telling the truth as a way of imparting ethos to their discipline.

But the rhetoricians went to further lengths to assure their audiences that rhetorical study was morally beneficial. Hugh Blair's *Rhetoric and Belles Lettres* contained the first of the time period's influential rhetorical counterstatements to the accusation that rhetorical eloquence could be deceptively persuasive, and Blair dealt with this problem as did his successors: he expressed an optimism that downplayed the potential moral danger in rhetoric by deeming it practically nonexistent, by suggesting that persuasive language, if it were persuasive, could not be untrue. Blair was thus the first to respond to the suspicion of detractors that rhetoric actually promoted sophistry by placing his defense within the context of the Roman orator Quintilian's good-man-speaking principle. According to Quintilian, "the perfect orator . . . cannot exist unless he is above all a good man."[15] Blair, in his rhetoric, echoes Quintilian, proclaiming one thing certain, "that without possessing the virtuous affections in a strong degree, no man can attain eminence in the sublime parts of eloquence. He must feel what a good man feels, if he expects greatly to move or to interest mankind."[16] Several decades later, George Campbell's *Philosophy of Rhetoric*, which was actually written earlier than Blair's but first published in America in 1818,[17] had also expressed this belief. Eloquence, felt Campbell, was "more friendly to truth than to falsehood, and more easily retained in the cause of virtue than in that of vice." Campbell fully agreed that "in order to be a successful orator, one must be a good man; for to be good is the only sure way of being long esteemed good, and to be esteemed good is previously necessary to one's being heard with due attention and regard. Consequently, the topic hath a foundation in human nature."[18]

Here begins the history of an interesting debate about rhetoric in America in the nineteenth century, for, contrary to what one might suppose, the debate about language that emanated from rhetoric was not about whether truth was ascertainable or about whether there was essentially any difference between truth and falsehood. Rather, the debate concentrated upon the Quintilian principle itself, upon whether persuasive language, artfully invented, could be so potent as to sway a vulnerable audience to believe falsehood rather than the truth. During the early reign of enthusiasm for Blair's optimistic rhetoric in America, Professor John Quincy Adams rarely mentioned Blair in his rhetoric classrooms at Harvard because he judged the Quintilian principle advocated by Blair's rhetoric to be unrealistic, and he sensed the potential harm in a student's precipitous equation between eloquence and honesty.[19] As Chapter 2 will suggest, within this atmosphere of optimistic and unqualified belief in the inherent truth-telling nature of rhetorical eloquence, Charles Brockden Brown writes satirically about rhetorical eloquence and enthusiasm in *Wieland*, sounding a warning call to those carried away by a facile notion that all persuasive language imparts the truth.

The trend of American enthusiasm for rhetoric did not abate during the first two quarters of the nineteenth century, which are the historical backdrop for Nathaniel Hawthorne's thematizing about rhetoric in *The Scarlet Letter*. Indeed, it intensified and matured beyond what seems to have been the rather giddy reception of rhetoricians such as James Ogilvie. The rhapsodizing about the histrionics of various eloquent rhetoricians continued. Chapter 3 on Hawthorne's *Scarlet Letter* characterizes the catchphrases used by popular periodicals beginning in the first quarter of the nineteenth century that describe the rhetorical process in an idealized fashion. Eloquence is described, for example, as "immortal" and as a "heaven-drawn song" in one periodical essay in the *United States Magazine and Democratic Review* in which one of Hawthorne's sketches also appeared.[20] Other oratory is described as "a cataract of jewels," and words are "like repeated bolts of irresistible power."[21] Rhetorical eloquence is enchantment, in one instance operating "as by an invisible wand"[22] and in another with a "touch and demolition, as if magic were employed."[23]

But the rhapsodizing about rhetoric as enchantment in the periodicals is accompanied by moralizing about the virtue inherent in and produced by the rhetorical process. One study of the proliferation of periodical essays written on rhetorical eloquence from 1815 to 1858 in the *North American Review*, the *Southern Review*, the *Knickerbocker*, the *Southern Literary Messenger*, and the *American Review* states that these essays generated "a conception of the way the world ought to be, and the writers in the periodicals left a record attesting to the vigor of rhetoric in that conception." The rhetoric in these journals, this study finds, was eclectic and idealistic, combining classical and Scottish rhetorical sources to suggest the humanizing influence of effective rhetorical argument: "'The soul vents its fullness in spontaneous gushings. Link by link the chain of irresistible argument is forged. With cumulative power, the lightnings of truth flash conviction on the doubtful, and dismay on the corrupt.'"[24] The melodrama and idealism in this passage go hand in hand. It was directed to the taste of the American public, and the message was not about rhetoric's intricacies (tropes, grammar, and the like). It was about the way rhetoric was considered to be pure inspiration and to impart inevitable truth.

One of the primary influential sources for this view of moral rhetoric during Hawthorne's time was Edward Tyrell Channing, the third Boylston Professor of Rhetoric and Oratory at Harvard, who taught rhetoric to many of the great writers and thinkers of his day, including Ralph Waldo Emerson, Oliver Wendell Holmes, Charles Francis

Adams, Richard Henry Dana, Jr., Henry David Thoreau, Edward Everett Hale, Francis J. Child, and Charles Eliot Norton.[25] Channing taught at Harvard from 1819 to 1851, and his lectures to Harvard seniors, composed over the period 1819–46, came out in published form. Channing's lectures reveal that he is representative of and perhaps at least partially responsible for the view of rhetoric during his time, for, aside from his less than mainstream discouragement of flamboyant rhetoric, Channing asserted two fundamental precepts of rhetoric to his students: first, that the rhetorician has a moral obligation to tell the truth, and, second, that one can have faith that the audience will compel truth from the rhetorician. Both points are established for Channing by the distinction he makes between the state of oratory during the time of "the ancient republics" and during his own democratic times in which, Channing states, "there has never been a serious doubt amongst us that there were ample opportunities and inducements, in the free states of these times, to call forth and perfect the highest qualities of oratory."[26] Channing's account of ancient times and his conception of the virtuous rhetorician seem to owe much to Plato's *Gorgias*, since both Channing and Socrates stress that in ancient times the orator appealed to the selfish interests of the audience and flattered the audience to win conviction rather than telling the truth.[27] But Channing stresses that in his day,

> I would mention the importance of character to all successful eloquence. It is his virtues, his consistency, his unquestioned sincerity that must get the orator attention and confidence now. He must not rely too much upon the zeal or even the soundness with which he treats a question under immediate discussion. His hearers must believe that his life is steadily influenced by the sentiments he is trying to impress on them, — that he is willing to abide by principle at any hazard, and give his opinions and professions the full authority of his actions. . . . No festival eloquence will do then, no vain mockery of art, no treacherous allurements from a close and sober inspection of the truths upon which we are to act. We want then the orator who feels and acts with us; in whom we can confide even better than in ourselves; who is filled with our cause, and looks at it with solemnity and wisdom.[28]

Channing's expressed faith in the ability of the audience to discern the difference between truth and falsehood is also the means by which Channing the teacher compels his own audience of would-be orators to be honest. Since, with the discerning audience of his own day, "the subject is more thought of than the orator, and what he says must come from the subject rather than from his art," Channing warns his class of students that "the excitement" that the orator "would produce must follow and mingle with conviction, not take the place of it;—the splendor that surrounds him must be the natural light of truth, not the false brilliancy that startles and blinds." [29]

The faith that Channing expresses in the ability of the audience both to discern and to compel honesty is the inheritance Scottish rhetoric derived from Scottish faculty psychology, according to the modern-day editors of Channing's lectures. The philosophy of faculty psychologist Thomas Reid "provided a kind of built-in moral integrity, an optimism about the nature of man," and a belief that "man's active and rational powers, if he allowed them to operate together, produced happy men and strong societies." [30] Nevertheless, Channing derives his faith in the audience's ability to compel virtue just as much if not more strongly from his own knowledge of rhetoric—from the earlier rhetorical statement of this faith in the Quintilian principle.

This same expressed faith in the audience's ability to compel virtue is illustrated in a story that circulated in New England during the 1830s and 1840s, although it was not put into published form until 1864. The story was about Bronson Alcott's encounter with a confidence man, who asked Alcott for a loan of five dollars. Alcott's friends chided him for being so trusting, but the eventual outcome of the story proved Alcott the victor. The confidence man paid back the money to Alcott because his conscience would not let him swindle anyone so trusting. [31] Interestingly, however, this anecdote about Alcott differs from Channing's description of the audience, for while Channing's faith in the audience is contingent on its intelligent discernment, the story about Alcott reveals an audience without discernment, necessarily, but with faith in the honesty of the orator. Thus the Quintilian principle in the nineteenth century could as easily be interpreted to imply that an orator would be compelled by his or her audience's intellectual discernment or by his or her audience's virtue.

Ralph Waldo Emerson's first lecture, "Eloquence," a very popular lecture first delivered in Boston in 1847, reiterates the belief of his rhetoric professor that the audience has an innate desire to be compelled by virtue: "If the speaker utter a noble sentiment, the attention deepens, a new and highest audience now listens, and the audiences of the fun and of facts and of the understanding are all silenced and awed. There is also something excellent in every audience,—the capacity of virtue. They are ready to be beatified. They know so much more than the orator,—and are so just! There is a tablet there for every line he can inscribe, though he should mount to the highest levels." [32]

Channing urges his other rhetorical precept—the moral obligation of the rhetorician to tell the truth—not on the basis of ethical principle alone, but he pragmatically reinforces it by warning his students of rhetoric that only the honest speaker will be believed. Nevertheless, faith in the audience to discern truth and exhorting the orator to be honest were two discrete precepts that could be subscribed to separately. Although rhetorical theorists continued to use the Quintilian principle throughout the century both to compel honesty from would-be orators and to reassure audiences not to be suspicious of rhetoric, as in Brockden Brown's time, when John Quincy Adams refused to teach the Quintilian principle in his classroom because of its potential harm, there were also those in Hawthorne's time who questioned the ability of the audience to separate truth from sophistry and to compel honesty while still exhorting the orator to tell the truth.

The most well-known skeptic and the one who became the model for all other invectives against nineteenth-century American oratory [33] was Thomas Carlyle, who wrote the "Stump-Orator," which appeared as Number 5 in his *Latter-Day Pamphlets*, published in 1850. Emerson was greatly displeased with one of Carlyle's essays in this volume because of its criticisms of American culture.[34] Given Emerson's unqualified love of eloquence, he was probably also displeased with Carlyle's "Stump-Orator." The purpose of Carlyle's essay is to take issue with the habit of mankind "for several centuries back, to consider human talent as best of all evincing itself by the faculty of eloquent speech." And he does so by emphasizing the audience's vulnerability to being deceived:

> False speech,—capable of becoming, as some one has said, the falsest and basest of all human things:—put the case, one were listening to *that* as to the truest and noblest! Which, little as we are conscious of it, I take to be the sad lot of many excellent souls among us just now. So many as admire parliamentary eloquence, divine popular literature, and suchlike, are dreadfully liable to it just now: and whole nations and generations seem as if getting themselves *asphyxiaed*, constitutionally, into their last sleep, by means of it just now.[35]

Carlyle in "Stump-Orator" shows a lack of faith in the audience's ability to distinguish between virtuous eloquence and "sham-excellent" or sophistic speech, but he does so with a moral purpose of impressing upon audience and orator alike how vital it is that the truth be spoken. Thus Carlyle rejects the current version of the Quintilian principle, but he shares Channing's conviction about the moral necessity of truth. These were the two most typical responses to the ethics of rhetoric from the beginning until the end of the nineteenth century: either, as Emerson and Channing, one held an optimistic view that a discerning and innately virtuous audience would compel honest rhetoric, or one feared, as did Plato, that sophistry could be misperceived by an audience as eloquence (especially when the audience's self-interest was concerned) and thus concentrated solely on urging the sense of moral responsibility in the orator.

One periodicalist of Hawthorne's time begins his essay "Importance and Obligation of Truth" by praising those literary works which "awaken an abhorrence of all falsehood and duplicity, — by depicting, on the one hand, beautiful images of truth and honor, and presenting, on the other, the disastrous consequences of sacrificing veracity to the interests or the caprice of a moment." [36] This essay appears only pages away in the same 1834 issue of the *New England Magazine* in which Hawthorne published one of his literary sketches.[37] Hawthorne's *Scarlet Letter* can be considered as a work of literature about the disastrous consequences, both to oneself and to one's intimates, of sacrificing veracity.

Nathaniel Hawthorne was taught rhetoric at Bowdoin by one of America's prominent rhetoric professors, Samuel Newman, who wrote the first American rhetoric textbook widely used in schools.[38] While at Bowdoin Hawthorne read Hugh Blair,[39] and it seems almost inevitable that during the first half of the nineteenth century, when the study of rhetoric at universities included the classics, Hawthorne would also have read the *Gorgias* and *Phaedrus*, Plato's two dialogues on rhetoric.

Hawthorne may also have been familiar with Channing's lectures, either directly or through his acquaintance with Ralph Waldo Emerson or one of Channing's other students, and, as Chapter 3 of this study reveals, he was probably also familiar with much of the current commentary on rhetoric that appeared in the pages of the periodicals in which he published. So he would have been familiar with the concept of the Quintilian principle, which suggested trust in the innate discernment of the public audience, and he also would have been aware of the strong moral strain in rhetorical theorizing of his time.

Channing's high estimation of his audience is constituted from his faith in the openness and receptivity present in American democracy, in this "advanced society," where "amidst the ceaseless flashing of ideas and theories, the minds of even the unlearned are made inquisitive by all that surrounds them."[40] But Hawthorne's opinion of American democracy as depicted in the "Custom-House" section of *The Scarlet Letter* is that the American political system (which arbitrarily ousted him from power because he was not a Whig) exercises the tyranny and despotism of authority. In *The Scarlet Letter*, Hawthorne rejects the larger implications of the Quintilian principle that an audience can compel an orator's virtue. In fact, he satirizes this expectation when he describes the Reverend Dimmesdale's eloquence in laudatory contemporary terms and simultaneously portrays the audience's inability to perceive Dimmesdale's eloquence as sophistry.

Not only does the audience fail to perceive that Dimmesdale is an adulterer, but Dimmesdale projects his own responsibility for admitting the truth upon his audience, assuming that its infallible ability to see the truth will thus force the truth out of him. Instead, the audience fails to see that Dimmesdale's religious rhetoric in *The Scarlet Letter* is bound up with the rhetoric of the law and that both serve the spurious truths of authority rather than the genuine truth of felt, human experience. Hawthorne emphasizes in *The Scarlet Letter* the necessity for self-motivated ethical virtue, for a language expressive of emotional truth that opposes the language of desire/adultery/law/religion. Hester Prynne and Dimmesdale's adultery in *The Scarlet Letter* is portrayed in complicity with the law, as the force which by opposing the law is actually inscribed within it. But emotion—love, compassion for the suffering of others, caritas, selflessness—is for Hawthorne a transcendental referent for truth that can free language from the bonds of external authority. When Hester Prynne and Arthur Dimmesdale "take shame upon themselves" and admit their adultery, they free themselves from it, and, by releasing their daughter, Pearl, from the bonds of sophistic secrecy, they give back to themselves (if only briefly for Dimmesdale) and they bequeath to Pearl the gift of an emotional life.

One might say that Hawthorne confirms the Quintilian principle if Pearl can be seen to compel her mother's honesty, and, to the extent that Pearl succeeds, one would be accurate in saying so. Nevertheless, the nineteenth-century American authors considered in this study demonstrate a cautious faith in the Quintilian principle. Neither Hawthorne, Twain, nor James portrays the public world to be open, virtuous, or as intelligent as Channing does. Instead, these authors all profess a faith in the possibility of a virtuous rhetorical transaction—

even one, possibly, compelled by the virtue of the audience—but all such virtuous transactions take place only when the audience has been narrowed down to one, and a relationship of truth shared by two characters is like a port in the storm of public corruption that makes truthful language such a difficult proposition.

In Mark Twain's *Adventures of Huckleberry Finn*, public language in pre–Civil War America seems irredeemably corrupt. "Lying," writes the author of the 1834 essay on the importance of truth, "is generally, if not always, the offspring of a selfish spirit,"[41] and human selfishness is the reason for the hypocrisy in *Huckleberry Finn*, where the "truthful" language of social convention and authority in forms such as slavery, Tom Sawyer's game playing, the King and Duke's scams, or Pap's persuasive rhetoric of reform is actually deceptive in terms of its relationship to the transcendental referent of felt human emotion and experience. For Mark Twain, an openness to suffering is the key to the transcendent truth of felt human emotion, and in espousing this view in *Adventures of Huckleberry Finn*, Twain had a source in a well-known rhetorician of his time, the minister Henry Ward Beecher.

Mark Twain admired some of the rhetoricians of his time who retained strong ties to eighteenth-century Scottish rhetoric and the succeeding tradition of rhetoric in nineteenth-century America. He had read John Henry Newman's much talked-about *Apologia Pro Vita Sua*. Newman was a former student of the eminent eighteenth-century rhetorician Richard Whately. Twain also admired the prominent American rhetorician Henry Ward Beecher. He owned the entire collection of Beecher's Plymouth Pulpit sermons dating from 1868 through 1884. Twain and Beecher knew each other socially and professionally, dining together from time to time and encouraging each other's professional work. Twain even considered publishing Beecher's work as a means of infusing life into his own publishing firm.[42]

The principal element contemporaries like Beecher and John Henry Newman extracted from eighteenth-century rhetoric was a passion for telling the truth. Mark Twain shared his admiration for Beecher with the rest of his culture, and what was most admired was Beecher's apparent reverence for the truth. Beecher was a Presbyterian minister born into a well-known religious family in New England in 1813. His rhetorical training was extensive, both in his studies at Amherst College and at Lane Seminary. At Amherst, Beecher was required to study Campbell, Blair, Whately, and American rhetorician Samuel Newman. After his education, Beecher lived for a time in relative poverty while he preached in the midwestern frontiers and edited the *Western Farmer and Gardener*. He then moved to Brooklyn Heights to preach at the Congregationalist Plymouth Church, where he wrote his famous Plymouth Pulpit Sermons.

One of the prominent features of Beecher's ministry was his lifelong dedication to and faith in the virtue of rhetorical eloquence and the necessity for telling the truth. In an 1876 speech delivered in Philadelphia at the opening of that city's School of Oratory, Beecher attests to a school of oratory as "one of the noblest institutions that could be established in your midst; one of the most needed," since "there is nothing that draws men more quickly to any centre than the hope of hearing important subjects wisely discussed with full fervour of manhood; and that is oratory—truth bearing upon conduct, and character set home by the living force of the full man." [43]

Beecher shared a similar concept of truth with all the other rhetorical theorists of his age. Truth implies the Christian (or Platonic) virtues of love and charity for one's fellow man:

> First, in the orator is the man. Let no man who is a sneak try to be an orator. The method is not the substance of oratory. A man who is to be an orator must have something to say. He must have something that in his very soul he feels to be worth saying. He must have in his nature that kindly sympathy which connects him with his fellow men, and which so makes him a part of the audience which he moves that his smile is their smile, that his tear is their tear, and that the throb of his heart becomes the throb of the hearts of the whole assembly. A man that is humane, a lover of his kind, full of all earnest and sweet sympathy for their welfare, has in him the original element, the substance of oratory, which is truth. [44]

For Beecher, however, the truth becomes even more specifically defined within the New Testament Christian scheme. Truthful oratory is the spiritualizing influence on man in Beecher's Christianized version of Charles Darwin's theory of natural evolution. In the world, Beecher says,

> the underflow of life is animal, and the channels of human society have been taken possession of by lower influences beforehand. The devil squatted on human territory before the angel came to dispossess him. Pride and intolerance, arrogance and its cruelty, selfishness and its greed, all the lower appetites and passions, do swarm, and do hold in thrall the

under-man that each one of us yet carries—the man of flesh, on which the spirit-man seeks to ride, and by which too often he is thrown and trampled under foot. The truth in its attempt to wean the better from the worse needs every auxiliary and every adjuvant.[45]

One of the primary ways of seeking out the spiritual truth of redemption, according to Beecher, was to undergo the experience of suffering. One's awareness of suffering in the world was actually the central dynamic in Beecher's version of the Quintilian principle, because the person who acknowledged suffering as the inevitable human condition had a firm hold on the truth of human emotion. Beecher cast doubt on any person who was "able to ward off all suffering; that never does suffer; that never will suffer; that can live in the midst of human life and all its unfoldings and environments and contrive to maintain itself inviolate from suffering. It is inconsistent with our fundamental notions of true manhood, that a being should go through this life in the conditions in which men live, and be able to shield himself entirely from suffering."[46]

To Beecher's mind, those who attempt to avoid suffering are avoiding the truth of human experience and the surest wellspring of empathy—empathy, that great ability to feel for others by virtue of one's own misery, that great moral reservoir of compassion that would restrain man's crueler survivalist instincts. Awareness or lack of awareness of one's own suffering or the suffering of others is a similar index of the truth-telling capacity of characters in *Adventures of Huckleberry Finn*. In this novel, Mark Twain reinforces the message of Henry Ward Beecher that truth implies an openness to the experience of suffering, and Twain suggests also that institutionalized conventions or lies that serve to repress the reality of suffering for whatever selfish reason actually promote suffering by seeking to deny its existence. The largest metaphor for suffering in the novel is the institution of slavery, which hides behind a lie of purported benevolence and the myth that blacks are lesser beings who do not suffer, but there are many other lies as well, such as Tom Sawyer's fantasies of violence that serve to deny the reality of death through dramatic catharsis.

While one considers that Twain's depiction of institutionalized lies in *Adventures of Huckleberry Finn* actually satirizes the condition of his own contemporary society, one should not ignore the further irony Twain directed toward his audience by having Huck assume that everyone tells lies, for, as we have seen, people in the nineteenth century perceived themselves as valuing the truth. Indeed, national praise of a public figure such as Beecher typically centered on his ability to tell the truth. Beecher, for example, can "clothe the bare bones of fact with such living power that the pictures were recognized as truthful and vivid to the last degree."[47] An 1872 essay in *Scribner's Monthly* calls Beecher "a social force" because he is "comprehensive enough in his survey of the truth to afford a support for all."[48] *Atlantic Monthly*, January 1867, praises Beecher's "complete extirpation of the desire of producing an illegitimate effect; it is his sincerity and genuineness as a human being" which gives him "this easy mastery over every situation in which he finds himself."[49] *The New York Tribune*'s obituary of Beecher praises "what power could be exercised" from a "full heart and a well-equipped mind."[50] Despite the possibility that Twain's satiric inversion of truth and lies might further redound on Henry Ward Beecher, who went on trial for adultery in the 1870s, the plain fact seems to be that it did not. Not only did Twain staunchly defend Beecher when he went on trial but he also seemed clearly to value Beecher's apprehension about the relationship between truth and painful experience and to dramatize a similar relationship in *Adventures of Huckleberry Finn*. Twain's irony devolves instead on the contemporary reading audience, who would squirm uncomfortably when they inferred from Twain's text that their own purported reverence for truthful language was actually a facade for moral hypocrisy.

Nevertheless, Twain does uphold one instance of a virtuous rhetorical transaction in the novel, and, in this instance, the Quintilian principle holds true because the orator and the audience each numbers one. This scene does not occur between Huck and Jim, whose verbal interchanges are too fraught with the damaging misinformation of the conventional culture to be completely compelling, but occurs when Huck reveals to Mary Jane Wilks the truth about the Duke and the King. In this one instance, Mary Jane's trust and empathy have compelled Huck's honesty, and, again, as in the anecdote about Bronson Alcott, honesty is compelled not by Mary Jane's keen discernment but by her obvious possession of innate virtue and trust.

The debate about the Quintilian principle did not diminish in rhetorical circles throughout the third quarter of the nineteenth century. In 1867, Emerson delivered his second "Eloquence" lecture in Chicago, and this time, perhaps in response to Carlyle's invective against rhetoric in "Stump-Orator," of which Emerson's son writes that Emerson was well aware,[51] Emerson resoundingly invokes the Quintilian

principle, twice even in the opening epithets.[52] In this version of "Eloquence," Emerson emphasizes that the successful orator must primarily
be truthful, "for the essential thing is heat, and heat comes of sincerity.
. . . Will you establish a lie? You are a very elegant writer, but you can't
write up what gravitates down."[53]

An angry debate about the virtues of rhetorical study occurred in
the March 4 and 11, 1875, pages of the *Nation*. *Nation* editor E. L.
Godkin had condemned the effects of rhetorical study as "almost as
baneful as those of excessive alcohol; as destructive of manliness, of
simplicity; and of power, as productive of fatuous conceit and self-
worship. It is almost certain to produce, too, love of notoriety; and
when once this takes possession of a rhetorician, it consumes him
utterly." Godkin's argument about the sophistic nature of any studied
orator is an old argument now leveled against abolishing rhetoric as a
discipline in schools. The March 11 response to this editorial reiterates the earlier century's defense: "It is an ill-considered position, if
not a vulgar prejudice, to suppose that training in rhetoric and elocution, whether in writing or speaking, means the increase of fluent, easy
writing or fluent, declamatory speaking—in short, that rhetoric means
what is called 'mere rhetoric,' which means either vicious rhetoric, or
writing or speaking by men who have too little to say. Rhetoric is the
art of enabling men who have something to say to say it to the best advantage." The editorial concludes that rhetoric "is, in fine, to restore,
as far as can be, the broken relations between thought and expression,
emotion and utterance."[54]

The preceding argument about whether or not to study the art of
persuasive speaking has some basis in the century-old debate concerning whether rhetoric is an acquired talent or a natural skill. Nevertheless, the underlying assumption of Godkin's editorial is that *consciously
contrived language* is dangerous. Of course, any persuasive language is
in a sense consciously contrived, and, thus, Godkin's resistance to the
study of rhetoric implies his suspicion about the basic rhetoricity of
language itself.

Rhetorical enthusiasts continued throughout the third quarter of the
nineteenth century to utter reassurances that rhetorical eloquence was
truthful. An 1863 essay in the *Universalist Quarterly Review* diffidently
noted that rhetoric is considered by some "a kind of system of leger-
demain which enables its masters and proficients to 'make the worse
appear the better reason;' a scheme without honor or virtue." This is
"most unjust," similar to the persecution of Christ. Rhetoric is like

"those beautiful and truthful words of our Saviour." It is "beneficent, and kind; bestowing its favors on every hand, opening its bounty and satisfying many an esthetic and intellectual want."[55] An 1874 essay in the *Presbyterian Quarterly* angrily responded to the charge that rhetoric serves "the lowest purposes of sophistry and deceit";[56] and there is a great deal of humor to be found in the repeated assurance of one 1863 essay in the *National Quarterly Review* that "earnestness is the indispensable condition of eloquence. To be eloquent a man must be in earnest. True, he may not be eloquent, though he be in earnest; but he cannot be an orator in any true sense of the term unless he is in earnest. All eloquence, therefore, is the fruit of earnestness."[57]

This apologistic conviction that persuasive rhetoric necessarily "postulates a full mind and a full heart"[58] could be perceived by rhetoricians to be a dangerous assumption, and one to hold this view was Francis J. Child, the fourth Boylston Professor of Rhetoric and Oratory at Harvard from 1851 to 1876. Child was at best a reluctant professor of rhetoric, and when Charles W. Eliot came to Harvard as president in 1869, he created a separate chair of English for Child. One reason for Child's halfheartedness about rhetoric may well have been his reservations about public oratory. In his senior year at Harvard, Child had written a condemnatory essay on rhetoric entitled "The Moral Views of Plato as Unfolded in the *Gorgias*," and Child apparently shared Plato's view that orators are most likely to be sophistic and audiences are most probably ignorant and easily seduced. Child was professor of rhetoric while Henry James was at Harvard in law school from 1862 to 1863, and James and Child were fellow boarders at Miss Upham's during that year. It is likely that in their many conversations this view would have been discussed.

More than any other author in this study, Henry James explores in most depth and with most subtlety the validity of the Quintilian principle. His potential sources for this concern are multifold. There are any number of rhetorical studies of which he could have been aware, including *The Philosophy of Rhetoric* by George Campbell, which his brother William quotes in his work, and Hugh Blair's *Rhetoric and Belles Lettres*, which was ubiquitous in the first half of the nineteenth century in the education of American youth. It seems possible also that James knew of one or both of Emerson's famous "Eloquence" lectures, which came out in published form in the 1870s. And it seems unlikely that Henry James would have required the impetus of Francis J. Child to read Plato's dialogues on rhetoric.

James's knowledge of the current rhetorical scene in his own time is illustrated in *The Bostonians,* which depicts quite accurately the fervor for oratory in Boston in the 1870s and the catchphrases used to describe this oratorical eloquence. In this novel, James expresses doubt about the transformative power of the rhetorically eloquent to convert an audience to virtue. Although Verena Tarrant's rhetoric is employed in the service of feminism in this novel, her message that brotherly love and unity between the sexes should result from their mutual apprehension of suffering bears the Christian ethos of contemporary rhetorical idealism, and Verena does seem able to persuade her public audiences to engage with this message on some level; indeed, several scenes in *The Bostonians* suggest the benevolent heart of the multitude.

But in James's psychological novels, personal conversion, whether it takes the form of spiritual or epistemological growth, can occur only on the personal level. And in *The Bostonians,* through his portrayal of the exploitative rhetorical tactics of Basil Ransom and Olive Chancellor, James suggests with what facility rhetorical sophistry can pass itself off as rhetorical virtue, and he suggests with what facility rhetorical virtue can be subdued by rhetorical sophistry. Both Olive Chancellor and Basil Ransom operate according to political agendas of power based on hatred or on a desire to subdue and tyrannize over the opposite sex. Thus in their rhetoric, the power of the *logos,* or of the living word, becomes enslaved to authority, and rhetoric that passes itself off as eloquence is really sophistry, while virtuous rhetoric—Verena's— becomes enslaved to tyranny. Olive Chancellor, for example, follows the precepts of rhetorical idealism, basing her use of Verena's rhetoric on the concept of women's suffering and founding her own rhetorical strategies with Verena on Plato's definition of the virtuous rhetorical lover in the *Phaedrus.* James's dramatization of Olive's self-deceit as she fancies herself employing virtuous rhetoric to serve the sophistic ends of hatred and selfishness sheds powerful doubt on the transformative capability of rhetorical idealism in the real world of dogma and political conflict.

Nevertheless, the concept of the Quintilian principle powerfully appealed to Henry James. The notion that rhetorical persuasion *could* be linked to the rhetorical ethos of truth had for James the moral resonance, the ring of moral necessity, that it had for the other rhetorical idealists of his age, but James had to find a way to create fictional conditions in which the Quintilian principle could plausibly prevail. In the fictional worlds that James creates in *The Wings of the Dove* and *The*

Golden Bowl, he wills the Quintilian principle into functional operation by enabling the rhetorically virtuous heroines in these novels, Milly Theale and Maggie Verver, to woo the male protagonists away from sophistic lovers far more fascinating and far more seductive through the more potent persuasion of their truthful rhetorical ethos.

This statement about the truthful ethos of Maggie Verver and Milly Theale would be challenged by many James critics who believe that Milly Theale in *The Wings of the Dove* and Maggie Verver in *The Golden Bowl* compromise their own truthful status in these novels by resorting to lies.[59] But there is a subtle yet significant difference between the conditionally temporary way that Milly Theale and Maggie Verver suspend the literal truth of the factual world to enact changes upon it and the way that Kate Croy and Charlotte Stant deliberately and consistently contort the truths of experience as their functional way of life. The difference lies in the way Milly Theale and Maggie Verver employ the power of imagination in league with their hold on experience as a means of temporarily suspending the corrupt factual world so that it can be transformed at first experimentally and then actually into a world that can entertain truth.

The relationship between the imagination and experience in the rhetorical truth-seeking process was eventually confirmed in nineteenth-century rhetorical theory. Even at the beginning of the century, most rhetoricians believed that truth was derived from a mixture of knowledge gained from experience and pure spiritual intuition, and this spiritual intuition that entailed a grasp of the eternal verities could be considered a forerunner of the aesthetic imagination conceived by Beecher later in the century to be a spiritualizing influence. But first and foremost, rhetorical theorists such as George Campbell adhered to the truth of experience, and, in doing so, Campbell and all who followed in his wake were true faculty psychologists. Both Campbell and Richard Whately, for example, examined how knowledge is derived from experience, although Whately left this problem for his logic text and not for his *Elements of Rhetoric.*

Unlike Whately, who applied rigid scholastic methods for determining experiential truth, George Campbell rejected syllogistic reasoning as inadequate to the description of the way one really lives and makes decisions. Campbell relied on the power of the memory as a decision-making tool, asserting that "the clear representations of . . . memory, in regard to past events, are indubitably true."[60] He also believed that "such principles cannot be confirmed through reason; neither can they

be confirmed through the senses. But they must be true, for 'it is impossible, without a full conviction of them, to advance a single step
in the acquisition of knowledge especially in all that regards mankind,
life, and conduct.' " [61] Thus in counting the memory absolutely essential to the learning process, Campbell established a pragmatic basis
for epistemological understanding that anticipated William James. Important nineteenth-century public rhetorical figures built upon this
principle of the retention of experience in their efforts to describe the
truth-seeking process.

Despite this dependence on experience, the typical nineteenth-century rhetorician also confirmed the role of the imagination in seeking
the truth. Hugh Blair did indeed perpetuate the faculty psychologist's
distrust of imagination; he even went so far as to suggest that the
imagination was strongest in primitive peoples. And Richard Whately
also disregarded appeals to passions and to the imagination in his system of rhetorical argument. Nevertheless, as early as 1827, Bowdoin
Professor of Rhetoric Samuel Newman extolled the imagination. He
adopted a Coleridgean division between the fancy and the imagination
and observed that "the most admired works in the art of painting are
not exact imitations. They are the creations of the painter, and have
no archetype in nature." [62] Campbell also observes that "if the orator
would prove successful, it is necessary that he engage in his service all
these different powers of the mind, the imagination, the memory, and
the passions." [63] John Henry Newman writes that "the heart is commonly reached, not through the reason, but through the imagination,
by means of direct impressions, by the testimony of facts and events,
by history, by description." [64]

The flourishing of English departments in the late nineteenth century was one reason for the marriage between rhetoric and the imagination. Ironically, Blair's *Rhetoric and Belles Lettres*, despite its slant on
imagination, paved the way in its concentration on literary taste for
literature departments in major late nineteenth-century universities,
and these English departments studied works of the literary imagination. American universities after the 1870s introduced the German
concept of elective courses into their curriculum, and rhetoric as a
studied discipline began to fall by the wayside. On one hand, it was
perceived as an outmoded and even dangerous discipline when time
could be spent on the sciences, and on the other it was seen as useful
only for teaching composition. [65] Thus many courses in rhetoric, and
rhetoric professors themselves, were assimilated into English depart-

ments, and they brought their rhetorical ideals right along with them. The rhetorical ethos of truth, for example, can be seen in the 1899 statement of Harvard English professor Lewis Gates, who had a strong influence on Frank Norris and perhaps also, then, on the strains of Platonism in Norris's writing. Even though Gates taught rhetoric at Harvard during philosophically skeptical times, he asserted that "subtle and elusive as [truth] may be, it is nevertheless something tangible and describable and defensible." [66]

The marriage between rhetoric and art which thus began to occur toward the end of the nineteenth century allowed imagination an equal status with experience in truth-seeking apprehension. Such a marriage is predicted in the third quarter of the century in the rhetorical philosophy of Henry Ward Beecher, who saw truth as a union between the philosophies of Aristotle and Plato. The perfect man in his search for truth uses his experience, his heart, and his imagination, "his feet standing on solid facts, his head goes philosophizing, and his heart is the balance between them." [67] For Beecher, spiritual evolution occurred through the imagination. Beecher's religion shared this conviction with the aesthetics of the time. One can see in Beecher's philosophy how Hugh Blair's belletristic conception of taste as a product of culture and tradition fed into modern aesthetic notions that contact with culture refined the imaginative sensibilities, rendering the individual liable to higher truths. "It was through a quiet familiarity with these things" (paintings), comments Beecher, "that I came to have an insight into them. As soon as *I* changed, by culture, *pictures* seemed to change, too. And now when I look at a picture, I am not such a fool as to see merely what stares out from the canvas; I see its finer and less obvious features." [68] .

But the imaginative vision was infused with experience and with feelings from the heart, the old rhetorical formula revivified. Indeed, taste and culture as refinements of the imagination already intimated that imagination was blended with experience. Those necessary moral components that once constituted rhetoric were now the requisites of artistic appreciation:

> Into the composition of taste, therefore, two differing elements are introduced; these make up its warp and woof; and the entire cloth in its magnificence and beauty of pattern, figure, and texture, is impossible without them. They are imagination and reason; whose procuring powers are susceptibility and naturalness, and a sound and true judg-

ment. But there is a still highest element to be taken into account. A good head and a good heart are essential to the full enjoyment of the moral beauties and glories of composition.[69]

The idealistic conception of truth was as fraught toward the end of the nineteenth century with value-laden virtues of Christian benevolence and humanity as it was at the beginning. This truth was also linked with telling the truth, as truth was equally known through experience and apprehended by imagination.

Henry James seems to incorporate a similar blend between imagination and experience in the apprehension of truth in his later novels. In *The Wings of the Dove* and *The Golden Bowl*, Milly Theale and Maggie Verver both use the powers of imagination spiritually to intuit a better world, and they present the imagination of that truth as their persuasive arguments to the male protagonists in the novels. In both novels, the reality of experience is temporarily suspended — not denied — until the experiment of a spiritualized conception of truth (with its own basis in a conceived reality: Maggie *is* married to Amerigo, despite his adultery; Milly *is* alive and Densher *does* have a connection and a past with her despite his relationship with Kate) has the opportunity to redeem the corrupt world and make it "true." James, in the realistic tapestry of *The Bostonians*, cannot see beyond the helplessness of a spiritually conceived notion of truth to transform the corrupt world, so in these later two novels, he confers an authorial dispensation to suspend temporarily this world so that the truth can be brought about in it, brought about, in *The Wings of the Dove* and *The Golden Bowl*, by the faith of women with good heads — James, by the way, gives to both his heroines a discerning intelligence — and sound hearts. In these two novels, then, James makes the most commanding nineteenth-century statement of faith in the Quintilian principle, and he does so because he wishes to urge, as did his predecessor Nathaniel Hawthorne, the presence of spiritual truth in the world as a moral necessity.

2

Eloquence a Virtue?
The Evils of Credulity and Imposture
in *Wieland*

Philosophy owes its precision to history, and history is enlightened by the beams of rational philosophy. The presence of the muses softens the severer genius of the law, and without their kindly influence even the study of nature becomes harsh and unpleasing. The pleasures of taste on the contrary, are often carried to a vicious extreme, unless corrected by a seasonable mixture of philosophical severity.

— CHARLES BROCKDEN BROWN,
Lecture to Belles Lettres Club

The gothic invites a conception of epistemological chaos, of a universe in which the normal, everyday bases for judgment of the world have been eroded, often by the supernatural. Moral axioms do not fare well in such a world. They do not fare well in the criticism of gothic novels either. Donald Ringe's landmark essay on Charles Brockden Brown's darkly gothic *Wieland* not only mentions the novel's lack of systematic ethics but objects to it. Because *Wieland* "fails to provide any system of value in terms of which the characters could have corrected their errors and acted more wisely than they did," Ringe calls *Wieland* "an intellectually truncated book." [1]

Even today, when the modern scholar is trained to avoid certain questions, there is still the desire to find purpose in *Wieland*. *Wieland* is a troubling story of inspired madness and senseless violence, set in the apparently placid environment of eighteenth-century enlightened America. An innocent and virtuous young heroine, Clara, tells

59

the disturbing story of how her brother Theodore slaughters his cherished family when instructed to do so by celestial voices. Theodore believes in these voices because of earlier strange experiences. Unfortunately, the improbable inventions of a crafty ventriloquist have set Wieland on his erroneous way toward believing that his senses are responding to mystical experience. Theodore's Enlightenment training causes him to believe in the account of his senses. The earlier deception leads to Theodore's madness and to personal catastrophe for the Wielands. Witness to the devastation, one is drawn behind the veil of the authorial presence in the novel to ask why.

The question of values in *Wieland* seems an impenetrable challenge. Ringe suggests that the novel functions mainly as a "systematic questioning" of Enlightenment tenets, and critics have largely endorsed this view ever since.[2] Alan Axelrod's brilliant tour de force on *Wieland* suggests Brown as the ultimate iconoclast. Axelrod finds that "some imp of the perverse seems always to knock down whatever figure Brown's imagination suggests—no matter how exemplary. Abraham, Cicero, Socrates—in *Wieland* all wobble on their pedestals."[3]

Despite the way *Wieland* has tended to confound, the narrative of the novel is nevertheless subtly interwoven with a steady discourse on ethics. Starting in the preface, continuing in the epigraph, concluding with the epistolary moralizing in the final pages of the unraveling subplot, ethics in the novel evolve in response to the fearsome power of voices, the fearsome power of language, language specifically in the sense of its rhetoricity—in its power to seduce or to persuade. *Wieland* initiates a voice of its own raised in warning to a contemporary audience carried away by the trend in popular rhetoric.

Brown himself was familiar with and qualifiedly admired contemporary rhetoric. He admired Hugh Blair.[4] Brown was aware that Blair's introduction of belle lettres to the discipline of rhetoric was his notable contribution to eighteenth-century rhetoric. Belle lettres referred to principles of good taste and sound criticism and to the use of literary models to gain a sense of good style. In the mainstream of this trend, Brown was a member of the Belles Lettres Club in Philadelphia in 1792.

Brown shows his familiarity with Blair's principles of good taste as applied to fiction in his preface to *Wieland*. Brown asserts his moral purpose as a writer of fiction, one "neither selfish nor temporary," but one that "aims at the illustration of some important branches of the moral constitution of man."[5] He considers it "the business of moral painters to exhibit their subject in its most instructive and memorable forms. If history furnishes one parallel fact, it is a sufficient vindication of the writer; but most readers will probably recollect an authentic case, remarkably similar to that of Wieland" (3).

Brown defers to Blair's advice about the novel in Blair's rhetoric. Blair had insisted on the novel's moral purpose and on its basis in reality, on what "may actually occur in life; by means of which what is laudable or defective in character and in conduct, may be pointed out, and placed in an useful light."[6] One might question whether Brown had Blair in mind when he wrote his preface, since such moral reassurances in prefaces were commonplace in the early American novel. Terence Martin has observed that eighteenth-century American novelists characteristically tried "to pass" their work "off as true" because of the American distrust of the imagination. This distrust was inherited from Puritan beliefs and strengthened by the metaphysics of Scottish commonsense philosophers such as Dugald Stewart and Thomas Reid.[7] The popular Scottish rhetoric of the time, according to William Charvat, also implicitly contained the influence of commonsense philosophy, including the disparagement of the imagination, and rhetoric at this time meant first and foremost Blair's.[8] Along with Brown's intimate knowledge of Blair's work, this possible link between Blair's rhetoric and the defensive preface makes it even more probable that Brown's preface responded to Blair.

Whether Brown agreed in principle with the letter and the law of his own preface is an arguable point. Several scholars have suggested that Brown's defense of his fiction in the preface implies his own distrust of fiction and of the imagination and exhibits his ambivalence about being an author. Mark Seltzer notes that Brown is uncertain about the perceived usefulness of his work. Michael D. Bell argues even more specifically that Brown sincerely shared Blair's reservation about fiction, witnessed in Brown's fear of artful literary expression leading "to artificiality and deception."[9]

But there does seem to be an overpunctiliousness in the preface reminiscent of Twain's inflated deference to his audience in the preface to *Adventures of Huckleberry Finn*. Brown's response to the cautionary measures placed on fiction by the discipline of rhetoric may well be the ensuing novel—which cautions primarily against rhetoric, not fiction. "From Virtue's blissful paths away / The double-tongued are sure to stray," Brown moralizes in the epigraph. Clara concludes that "if Wieland had framed juster notions of moral duty, and of the divine attributes; or if I had been gifted with ordinary equanimity or foresight, the double-tongued deceiver would have been baffled and repelled" (244). And Clara begins her manuscript hoping that it "will inculcate the duty of avoiding deceit" (5).

Whether or not Brown subscribes to Blair's moral restrictions on fiction, he could hardly have missed the irony in Blair's setting of rigid restrictions not on rhetoric but only on fiction. Blair and the rhetorical sentimentalizers of his day blocked the notion that rhetoric could be dangerous or that convincing rhetoric could possibly be deceitful or sophistic. As a noted scholar on Blair has commented, "Blair spent a lifetime teaching his subject, practicing it, and indeed, trying to save souls by it." [10] Eighteenth-century rhetoricians saw rhetoric as an ame-liorative force. They reasoned that sophistry posed no danger, and they did so on the basis of Quintilian's good-man-speaking principle. Blair borrowed the belief from Quintilian that "in order to be a truly eloquent or persuasive Speaker, nothing is more necessary than to be a virtuous man" (2:228). The reassuring implication of this was that no scoundrel could ever be persuasive. Brown must have thought this simplicity odd coming from a man who put such rigid restrictions on literature.

Equally unsettling for Brown must have been Blair's facile assump-tions about the unique discerning abilities of the rhetorical audience. Why did Blair put so much faith in rhetoric and so little in fiction? The audience for both forms of discourse was the same. He clearly intended the good-man principle to serve as a deterrent for all would-be sophists. But in his zeal for virtuous rhetoric, he seemed to forget that the audience for rhetoric was the same one that presumably could be seduced by fiction. Blair thought rhetoric "the fountain of real and genuine virtue" from which "are drawn those sentiments which will ever be most powerful in affecting the hearts of others." Therefore, "bad as the world is, nothing has so great and universal a command over the minds of man as virtue" (2:230–31). Blair implied that an audience will by nature be moved only by the eloquence of virtue. Therefore, the audience could assume that if it were being moved, it was not in the hand of a sophist. "One thing is certain," Blair emphasized, "that without possessing the virtuous affections in a strong degree, no man can attain imminence in the sublime parts of eloquence. He must feel what a good man feels, if he expects greatly to move or to interest mankind" (1:13).

This implied trust in the ethical virtue of the eloquent speaker may

well have generated a form of American rhetorical innocence, one sufficiently alarming that an American author might feel compelled to
write a work of fiction to disarm it. Some alarm about false confidence
in rhetoric seemed to be in the air. Harvard's first Boylston Professor of
Rhetoric, John Quincy Adams, responded negatively to the American
naïveté about rhetoric when he took his chair in 1806. He thought the
Quintilian principle was implausible and possibly dangerous because
students would assume that an effective speaker was virtuous.[11] But
Adams's view was outnumbered by the thirty-nine editions of Blair's
Lectures which were published in America before 1835.[12]

Adams's reservation can be set against the illustrative case of James
Ogilvie, who was a cause célèbre after he arrived in America from Scotland in 1795 to proselytize in the name of rhetoric. Thomas Jefferson
gave Ogilvie a job teaching rhetoric in small academies in Virginia.
Ogilvie soon moved to the capital of Virginia, bringing with him a
plan to travel around the country teaching the virtues of "eloquence."
Ogilvie toured major American cities, ending up in 1815 as a lecturer
at Columbia College. He strongly influenced such important Americans as George Ticknor, Thomas Jefferson, and Washington Irving
and other noted politicians and scholars. But there were always dissi-
dent voices raised in protest against this optimistic rhetoric. A New
York literary critic ruthlessly followed Ogilvie's lectures, satirizing his
sentimental view of rhetoric.[13]

Brown may not have known of Ogilvie when he wrote *Wieland*, but
he certainly knew about America's enthusiastic reception of rhetoric.
Brown's knowledge of America's romance with rhetoric seems apparent in his portrait of Clara Wieland. The initially ingenuous Clara —
that the more experienced narrator Clara writes about in epistolary
form in retrospect in this novel — projects a gardenlike innocence into
her cloistered world, and it seems largely based on her conception
of rhetoric, which does not account for the presence of the serpent.
Wieland presents a bildungsroman, the chronicle of the loss of Clara's
rhetorical innocence, and the testament to Clara's loss of faith in Quintilian's good-man-speaking principle.

In view of Clara's recounted naïveté in this novel, one might wonder
about her reliability as a narrator. In *Wieland*, it is a partially wiser Clara
who narrates in retrospect, so as to "inculcate the duty of avoiding
deceit," her earlier errors in judgment when she was a more trusting
self. At times Brown does seem to undercut even the wiser Clara's
retrospective judgment of her own psychological *reasons* for misjudg-

ing Carwin's, or Wieland's, rhetoric, but he never casts doubt upon Clara's reliability as an initial perceiver or eventual retrospective narrator of the actual events that transpired. Clara is reliable; she is just not fully cognizant, it seems, of the psychological implications of what she is saying. There is no textual evidence, however, that Clara contrives the narration of events in any way flattering or prejudicial to the audience's opinion of herself. If Brown intended the reader to suspect Clara's veracity, then he would have suggestively hinted to his reader the possibility of that doubt by embedding within Clara's narrative instances of self-contradiction. Instead, Brown employs a narrator who recounts events reliably. Clara tells the truth, she is reliable, but it seems that she is still self-deceived about her own role in the past disaster that she is describing. Nevertheless, through the device of Clara's narrative, Brown shows the disastrous effects of a false confidence in rhetorical eloquence and, through their acquaintance with Clara's initial misjudgments of rhetorical eloquence and eventual insight into the possibility of deception, the audience is warned against making Clara's initial mistake of naively assessing and relying upon rhetorical eloquence as a basis for judgment of truthfulness.

Brown implies in *Wieland* that rhetorical eloquence can lead to flawed standards of judgment. In the introduction to his rhetoric, Blair comments that rhetoric "serves to add the polish" to knowledge and science, which "must furnish the material that form the body and substance of any valuable composition." He hastens to assure, however, "that none but firm and solid bodies can be polished well" (1:4), and thus by reassuring that rhetorical style cannot be eloquent (polished well) unless its logical content is firm and solid (another version of the Quintilian principle that reassures that only the true can be eloquent), Blair can be read to imply that the judgment of style can be used as a standard for the judgment of content, since only truthful content will result in successful style. Not only does Brown parody this statement in *Wieland*, but he suggests further that confidence in style can encourage neglect of content, warning against the facile judgments that may result. Brown borrows Blair's body/polish metaphor so that he can parody it, not coincidentally in a passage where Clara describes the emblem of the Wielands' worship of rhetoric—a bust of Cicero that they had placed in their temple. Her brother had purchased the bust from an "Italian adventurer," who "copied this piece from an antique dug up with his own hands in the environs of Modena. Of the truth of his assertions we were not qualified to judge; but the marble was pure and polished, and we were contented to admire the performance, without waiting for the sanction of connoisseurs" (23–24). Clara's description of the Wielands' contentment with the polish of the performance suggests an American audience content to be entertained by eloquence and to be reassured that they need not bother with the difficult task of judgment. At the least, the Wielands did not care to address a more rigorous principle of judgment than rhetorical eloquence. Brown's allusion may imply the way that rhetoric was oversimplified by its American enthusiasts. As *Wieland* will suggest, "waiting for the sanction of connoisseurs," which was certainly another one of Blair's and rhetoric's principles, implies an alternate viable form of judgment, but a young American culture might pick and choose those precepts from rhetoric that suited it best.

Narrating in retrospect, Clara Wieland reveals that she has learned two disillusioning things through the course of events in the novel: the potential potency of sophistry and the potential weakness of a rhetoric endowed with virtue. One scholar has convincingly pointed out the resemblance between Carwin and Milton's Lucifer.[14] To pursue that analogy further, one might say that Clara's initial encounter with Carwin's eloquence initiates her fall from rhetorical faith.

As *Wieland*'s tale unfolds, Clara reveals that in her past she lived in idyllic isolation with her brother, his wife, his wife's brother Pleyel, and their ward, Louisa Conway. Strange incidents had already occurred in this community, instigated by Carwin, by the time Clara first spied Carwin, but none of them had disturbed her greatly until this time. It is only after Clara meets Carwin that she spends a gloomy day, obsessed with ominous forebodings:

> Why was my mind absorbed in thoughts ominous and dreary? Why did my bosom heave with sighs and my eyes overflow with tears? Was the tempest that had just passed a signal of the ruin which impended over me? My soul fondly dwelt upon the images of my brother and his children, yet they only increased the mournfulness of my contemplations. The smiles of the charming babes were as bland as formerly. The same dignity sat on the brow of their father, and yet I thought of them with anguish. Something whispered that the happiness we at present enjoyed was set on mutable foundations. Death must happen to all. (54–55)

Only after meeting Carwin does Clara think of death, of mutability. The retrospective Clara here reminisces accurately about her past feelings, but her own ability to interpret her suggestive imagery, even in retrospection, does not extend to an understanding of the psychological implications of her past actions, which Brown leaves up to the reader to deduce. Modern psychoanalytical critics tend to equate seeking a meaningful presence in language with the desire to avoid the gap that is death,[15] and Brown as artist may be extending the symbolic implications of Clara's discoveries about language beyond her own ability to interpret them. This does not mean that Clara is an unreliable narrator; rather, the author is exploring with his reading a level beyond Clara's psychological naïveté that her own retrospective narrative is the means of suggesting, but that Clara does not intuit. From the imagery that Clara calls forth at this point to describe her forebodings from her first meeting with Carwin, the reader can conclude that this meeting undermines Clara's confidence in language, which results in this odd prescience of death. Another issue emerges from the passage. Clara intuitively transferred onto her brother her concerns provoked by Carwin; this transference implies that Clara based her confidence in her brother's stability on his love of rhetoric, a confidence now unbalanced, on a subconscious level, by Clara's new uncertainty about language.

As Clara suggests, Carwin's rhetoric disconcerted her because of the discrepancy between his verbal eloquence and his slovenly appearance. Following principles of virtuous rhetoric, Clara implies that she assumed that his outward "style" should be a window on the inner character of his eloquence. The rhetorical split between style and content in this instance is represented by the split between the person's language and his outward appearance. "Style" appears still as the outward manifestation of something inward, but "rhetoric" becomes now the content itself, since the American innocent judging eloquence as inherently truthful considers rhetorical style itself as a source of evidence. Clara first judges Carwin as a country rustic. She immediately connects his outward rusticity with a corresponding inward lack of eloquence. She wonders idly about whether such a rustic could dissolve the bonds between ignorance and agriculture: "I asked why the plough and the hoe might not become the trade of every human being, and how this trade might be made conducive to, or, at least, consistent with the acquisition of wisdom and eloquence" (51). It is important to remember that *eloquence* was the rhetorical catchword of the day, implying not only stylistic grace but rhetorical truth; an interesting elitist connection between *wealth* and *truth* at times creeps in. The ingenuous Clara assumed that a country rustic, lacking in polished appearance, could not be *eloquent*. When she hears an eloquent voice in her kitchen and then is forced to connect it with Carwin, she becomes tremendously disconcerted.

Ironically, Clara tells us that Carwin's voice represented to her the very ideal of eloquence. She heard him imploring her maid for a cup of water, and she tells us that she "cannot pretend to communicate the impression that was made upon me by these accents." She cannot begin

> to depict the degree in which force and sweetness were blended in them. They were articulated with a distinctness that was unexampled in my experience. But this was not all. The voice was not only mellifluent and clear, but the emphasis was so just, and the modulation so impassioned, that it seemed as if an heart of stone could not fail of being moved by it. It imparted to me an emotion altogether involuntary and incontroulable. When he uttered the words "for charity's sweet sake," I dropped the cloth that I held in my hand, my heart overflowed with sympathy, and my eyes with unbidden tears. (52)

There is a notable similarity between Clara's response to Carwin's elocution and a former pupil's reminiscence about James Ogilvie's rhetorical skills in the *Southern Literary Messenger* (1848): " 'Ogilvie inspired me with new desires. He touched some sympathetic chord which instantly responded, and from that moment I felt that there was a divine spark in the human mind, at least in mine, which might be fanned with flame.' "[16] Both responses show the American's idealization of eloquence and reliance upon it as something noble and inevitably truthful.

Clara relates in retrospect that Carwin's unseemly appearance unbalanced her faith in rhetoric. Clara had related "the idea of superior virtue" with "that of superior power" (46), and she recalls her dismay at discovering that Carwin's superior power of rhetoric could not be associated in her mind with the idea of superior virtue. Her disenchantment began when she discovered that the ideal of eloquence she had so strongly admired belonged to the rustic she had so patronizingly dismissed. She expects her audience to imagine her reaction, to imagine "my surprize, when I beheld the self-same figure that had appeared an halfhour before upon the bank," and it is as if in her instructional mode of inculcating the duty of avoiding deceit, she anticipates that her audience will sympathize with her original expectation that truth and eloquence were connected. Because of her faith in eloquence, Clara relates, she had "conjured up a very different image" to go with the eloquent voice in her kitchen. True to Clara's faith in rhetoric, "a form, and attitude, and garb, were instantly created worthy to accompany such elocution; but this person was, in all visible respects, the reverse of this phantom." And Clara believes that her audience will not perceive it as strange that she "could not speedily reconcile myself to this disappointment" (52).

This passage, which dwells so much on Carwin's rhetoric and on how it disconcerted Clara, leads directly into the scene in which Clara discusses death and mutability. And not surprisingly, the dawning of Clara's suspicions about rhetoric immediately cause her to turn intuitively, although subconsciously, to suspicions of her brother, whose reverence for rhetoric and rhetorical skills had always provided Wieland, Clara assumed, with a check against his irrationality. The brother's mind, Clara relates, "was enriched by science, and embellished with literature" (23). But more specifically, Clara tells us that she took note that "the chief object of his veneration was Cicero" (24). Clara's unswerving faith in her brother was matched by her unswerving faith in rhetoric; both were problematized at the same time.

The subsequent events that Clara narrates illustrate that the greatest source of her distress was the unpredictability of rhetoric. Carwin's ventriloquism alternately warned and assailed her in her bedroom closet and in her riverbank retreat, but did not distress her as did the ambiguity of his rhetoric. Clara became obsessed with Carwin, an obsession she did not herself understand, but the reader is left with perhaps less uncertainty about the psychological nature of Clara's obsession. The reader has a fuller psychological insight than Clara as he or she reads about how Clara became determined to discover the source of Carwin's eloquence and to reconcile it with his chameleon-like appearance. It is as if by finding the key to that mystery Clara feels on a subconscious level that she will regain the epistemological equilibrium once given her by her faith in rhetorical eloquence. Since Pleyel once knew Carwin, Clara narrates, she asked him to seek out Carwin's mystery, only to discover that "he had assiduously diverted the attention of the latter to indifferent topics, but was still, on every theme, as eloquent and judicious as formerly" (68). Predictably, Carwin's suspect evasiveness disconcertingly coupled with his rhetorical eloquence causes the rhetorically optimistic Clara existential distress: "From the death of my parents, till the commencement of this year, my life had been serene and blissful, beyond the ordinary portion of humanity; but, now, my bosom was corroded by anxiety. I was visited by dread of unknown dangers, and the future was a scene over which clouds rolled, and thunders muttered" (69).

Clara's recounted anxiety quite possibly derived from her loss of stable grounding in an extremely safe epistemological structure. At the base of that structure lay the Quintilian principle. Carwin's rhetoric unsettled it; Clara reveals that she could not reconcile his eloquence with his virtue. Bemused, Clara dwelt on Carwin's rhetoric:

> He was sparing in discourse; but whatever he said was pregnant with meaning, and uttered with rectitude of articulation, and force of emphasis, of which I had entertained no conception previously to my knowledge of him. Notwithstanding the uncouthness of his garb, his manners were not unpolished. All topics were handled by him with skill, and without pedantry or affectation. He uttered no sentiment calculated to produce a disadvantageous impression: on the contrary, his observations denoted a mind alive to every generous and heroic feeling. They were introduced without parade, and accompanied with that degree of earnestness which indicates sincerity. (71)

Nevertheless, Clara narrates that she realized, much to her consternation, "I could not deny my homage to the intelligence expressed in it, but was wholly uncertain, whether he were an object to be dreaded or adored, and whether his powers had been exerted to evil or to good" (71).

Clara could not square Carwin's eloquence with his character. She admitted to herself that Carwin's secrecy about his past life "was prompted by the shame, or by the prudence of guilt" (73). Yet she dwelt on the skill with which Carwin could "seem" to tell the truth. When Carwin suggested a human cause for the disembodied voices the Wielands had been hearing, Clara narrates that she admitted that "those that were most coherent and most minute, and, of consequence, least entitled to credit, were yet rendered probable by the exquisite art of this rhetorician" (74).

It is clear that what most disturbed Clara was Carwin's ability to seem but not to be truthful. Because of the deductions that she made from Carwin's "exquisite art," she was unnerved shortly after to find Carwin emerging from her bedroom closet, apparently intent on violating her honor. In retrospect, Clara recollects how she paused in midflight from the bedroom to go over her own grounding in the Quintilian principle, how even in midflight her own expectation that the rhetorical ideal would predict experience could cause her to pause and wonder "why should such a one be dreaded" since his "society was endeared to us by his intellectual elevations and accomplishments" and he "had a thousand times expatiated on the usefulness and beauty of virtue" (91).

Clara discloses that she was finally forced by the reality of the situation to conclude that a successful rhetorician, one who seemed the soul of virtue itself, was not necessarily virtuous. She reveals that she was finally in what the reader may perceive as an existential position, as she was forced to ask herself, "And who was he that threatened to destroy me?" (93) only to find that "nothing could be discerned through the impenetrable veil of his duplicity" (94).

The Quintilian principle is again challenged in the subplot that Clara narrates. A Mrs. Stuart turns out to be the mother of the Wielands' ward, Louisa Conway, and it turns out that Mrs. Stuart has also been misled by rhetorical eloquence, this time by a dashing scoundrel named Maxwell. "Maxwell," Clara recounts, "though deceitful and sensual, possessed great force of mind and specious accomplishments. He contrived to mislead the generous mind of Stuart, and to regain the esteem which his misconduct, for a time, had forfeited. He was recommended by her husband to the confidence of Mrs. Stuart" (240). The eloquent but deceitful Maxwell proceeded almost to the point of compromising Mrs. Stuart. Again, the point is made that a sure reliance on the virtue of an eloquent man is a dangerous thing indeed.

The Quintilian principle is implied to be doubly confounded in *Wieland* when Clara's disclosure of Pleyel's suspicions of her suggests that a rhetorician's virtue does not necessarily produce conviction. Clara relates discovering that virtue is not a fail-safe weapon against evil or skepticism. Confronted with the villainous Carwin emerging from her closet, Clara reveals that she regarded her state as "a hopeless one" and that she "was wholly at the mercy of this being" despite the resources of her "personal strength, [her] ingenuity, and [her] eloquence," which she now "estimated at nothing." Clara discloses that she was suddenly forced to realize that virtuous rhetoric, that "the dignity of virtue, and the force of truth, I had been accustomed to celebrate; and had frequently vaunted of the conquests which I should make with their assistance" (90), would be of no practical use in the presence of a villain.

Clara narrates that she was sufficiently disillusioned about the power of rhetorical eloquence that, when Pleyel was deceived by Carwin's mimicry into thinking her a fallen woman, she doubted that her rhetoric could convince him otherwise. Nevertheless, she reveals that this realization dismayed her and made her "[burn] with disdain," as she questioned, "Would not truth, and the consciousness of innocence, render me triumphant?" (113).

The answer to Clara's question, she discovers, was a dismaying "no." In devising a plan to meet once more with the threatening Carwin, she finally realized that truth would not gain her the interview she desired. She went to find out what he had to tell her, only to discover that she would have to compromise her virtue to do so. Clara also reveals that after first gathering resolve for the interview, she also realized that she would have to lie to her sister-in-law Catherine in order to steal away for the interview. Faced with her dilemma, Clara narrates, she absorbed the subtle possibility that there was occasionally more benefit in lying than in truth: "The views with which I should return to my own house, it would therefore be necessary to conceal. Yet some pretext might be invented. I had never been initiated into the trade of lying. Yet what but falsehood was a deliberate suppression of the truth?" (142). "To deceive by silence or by words is the same," Clara relates that she concluded. And with this realization, Clara's initiation into the ambiguities of rhetoric was complete.

Nevertheless, the initiated Clara—the narrator of *Wieland*—never fully relinquishes a disturbing blindness about the credibility of her brother's rhetoric. Indeed, the reader is unsure if the narrator is cognizant that a less credulous faith in Theodore's rhetorical innocence might indeed have caused her more initial wariness about the wisdom of Wieland's religious enthusiasm. To the end of Clara's narrative, and, thus, one must assume, in her wiser stance as the retrospective narrator who has penetrated Carwin's sophistry, Clara continues to believe in Theodore's rhetoric despite his heinous crimes, and here is where the reader may consider Clara's narration of the experiences recounted as truthful, but then pursue beyond Clara's factual recounting of her words the possible psychological significance of her own continued deception about her brother. Clara reveals that even after reading the transcription of Theodore's forensic oratory, she found him "supreme in misery; thus towering in virtue!" (223) and was appalled at herself for considering that she should "inflict death upon [this] menacer" when her own life was threatened by him. It is interesting that Clara's first narrated reaction to the manuscript was denial: she retreated into the dream world from which previously all her warnings about her brother had come. But when she returned to the manuscript, she was lured by the rhetoric, by her brother's unflagging insistence on his own virtue. Clara describes herself as having been moved by the manuscript; her "faculties were chained up in wonder and awe" (177).

For Clara, then, filial love and rhetorical faith are inseparable, and this is one unreflective and emotional response from which she never disengages herself. The narrator Clara, in retrospect, is like the ingenue Clara in her continued belief that to love Wieland is to believe in his rhetoric. Continuously, Wieland's insistence on his own virtue forms a substitute for her for actual evidence of that virtue. During Wieland's trial, she concludes that "not for a moment did he lay aside the majesty of virtue" and that, therefore, "surely there was truth in this appeal: none but a command from heaven could have swayed his will; and nothing but unerring proof of divine approbation could sustain his mind in its present elevation" (181). Clara's love for Theodore approaches the irrational in this instance, since, in the name of virtue, she undercuts the very epistemological grounds for virtue by suggesting that the question of virtue itself is morally relative. "How does one know what *is* virtue," she seems to ask, "and how can one judge it?" Perhaps it is only an appearance of virtue, and one consistently presented, since one can never know for sure. But Clara's inability to discern sophistry in her brother is suggested in the literary text to have a psychological base, and even her original inability to perceive Carwin's sophistry seems suggested by Brockden Brown to have psychological motives. Through planting psychological undercurrents in his narrator's recounting of events of which his narrator is unaware, Brown implies that Clara's self-deceptions have an unacknowledged psychological motivation. And Brown thus offers revelatory suggestions in *Wieland* about the psychological desires that might motivate a willed belief in the Quintilian principle. Indeed, he intimates that the Quintilian principle and the respect for style that it produced could easily be corrupted, solipsistically appropriated by the rhetorician or by the judging audience as a means of eclipsing all other forms of judgment and of rationalizing or legitimizing one's own egotism.

The key to Brown's caution against the dangers of rhetorical style may be found in Blair's own rhetoric, which, with its scientifically analytical emphasis on style as it related to audience effects, could be misconstrued to confer legitimacy on a rhetorician whose sole concern was rhetorical style and on an effete audience whose only concern was analyzing the pleasures of style and these effects of pleasure on themselves. The deemphasis on content in Blair's rhetoric is probably explained by the exclusion in his *Lectures on Rhetoric and Belles Lettres* of the classical topic of invention from its rhetorical scheme, following the initiative of sixteenth-century French logician Peter Ramus, who redistributed the classical topic of invention to the science of logic. Even though Blair emphasized that careful, disciplined thought must accompany rhetorical expression, as one rhetorical scholar has observed, "Blair's exclusion of invention was characteristic of his belletristic bias, which caused him to pay more attention to style than to any other aspect of rhetoric." [17]

Actually, there seems to be some ambivalence in Blair's remarks about style. Blair links style organically with content, suggesting that style always has "some reference to an author's manner of thinking. It is a picture of the ideas which rise in his mind, and of the manner in which they rise there" (1:183). Nevertheless, Blair cautions "that the love of minute elegance, and attention to inferior ornaments of composition, may at present have engrossed too great a degree of the public regard. It is indeed my opinion, that we lean to this extreme; often more careful of polishing style, than of storing it with thought" (1:7). Thus on one hand, Blair writes that concerns with taste and belles lettres "necessarily lead us to reflect on the operations of the imagination, and the movements of the heart" (1:9–10), but, on the other, he warns, "I will not go so far as to say that the improvement of taste and of virtue is the same; or that they may always be expected to coexist in an equal degree. More powerful correctives than taste can apply are necessary for reforming the corrupt propensities which too frequently prevail among mankind" (1:13–14).

Terence Martin discusses faculty psychologist Dugald Stewart's fears of imaginative fiction "rendering the mind callous to actual distress." Apparently Stewart also feared that such fiction might "cultivate a false refinement of taste, inconsistent with our condition as members of society." [18] Through his depiction of the emotional undercurrents of Clara's judgment of rhetoric, which emerge in Clara's naive account and of which she seems apparently unaware, Brockden Brown seems to reflect in *Wieland* his own concern with the similar distancing effects of rhetorical study. In Clara's account both of her brother's enthusiasm for rhetoric and of her own moral judgments of the world around her, Brown seems to intimate that the study of taste that Blair's rhetorical text pursues may encourage a certain distanced callousness as it scrutinizes emotions and situations for their potential effect upon the sensibility.

The reader can see the nature of Theodore's rhetorical interests, for example, from the honest rendition of them offered up by Clara without judgment. It seems clear that Theodore's love of rhetoric focused on elocution, perhaps the least invention-oriented aspect of rhetoric. In addition, Theodore most admired Cicero. Cicero's "name alone," according to Blair, "suggests everything that is splendid in oratory" (2:26). Nevertheless, Blair finds what appears almost to be an ethical problem with Cicero's "harmonious style." "His love of it," claims Blair, "is too visible; and the pomp of his numbers sometimes detracts from his strength" (1:262). Clara reveals that Theodore used Cicero scrupulously to select "a true scheme of pronunciation for the Latin tongue, and in adapting it to the words of his darling writer. His favorite occupation consisted in embellishing his rhetoric with all the proprieties of gesticulation and utterance" (24). Thus, although Clara does not explicitly make this observation or appear to draw inferences from it, the reader may conclude that Theodore's rhetorical interests suggest him to be more interested in the flair of rhetoric than in the sense. His own religious enthusiasm seems inflamed by an indulgence in the flashier aspects of rhetoric. And, by Clara's account, he finally becomes an oratorical exhibitionist at his own trial. In his discussion of style, Blair warns that "attention to style must not engross us so much as to detract from a higher degree of attention to the thoughts." Significant, I believe, to Brown's own estimation of present-day rhetorical enthusiasm, Blair adds that he fears "that the present taste of the age in writing, seems to lean more to style than to thoughts" (1:407). An interesting echo of that thought is expressed satirically by American author Hugh Henry Brackenridge in his preface to *Modern Chivalry* (1792–1815) at a roughly contemporaneous time. It is possible that in this preface Brackenridge may also be satirizing an audience whose assurance of moral principles is actually undermined by a preoccupation with style. In his own ironic tone of modest proposal, Brackenridge discloses that since "it is not in the power of human ingenuity to attain two things perfectly at once," his work is being experimentally "undertaken with a view to style, regarding thought as of secondary importance," since "to expect good language, and good sense at the same time, is absurd." Brackenridge concludes that this "will be all the better for those who like light reading, and do not wish to be troubled with the labour of thinking," making a final thrust at the facile thinking processes of his audience.[19] The case of Theodore Wieland may suggest to the reader an exaggerated example of the moral danger implicit in being an egocentric enthusiast who neglects the pursuit of thought for the hedonistic pleasure of rhetorical style.

Although in retrospect Clara only discloses this point without an apparent understanding of its significance, the style of her father's autobiographical manuscript is what engrossed Clara when she read it, not its thought. One can only speculate on the frightening possibilities of what this relatively uneducated fanatical member of the Camissard sect, in his extreme guilt-ridden agitation, might actually have written in this manuscript. Yet Clara read the manuscript with the emotional detachment of an analytical audience that deemphasizes content and prides itself on being a connoisseur of rhetorical style: "The narrative was by no means recommended by its eloquence; but neither did all its value flow from my relationship to the author. Its style had an unaffected and picturesque simplicity. The great variety and circumstantial display of the incidents, together with their intrinsic importance, as descriptive of human manners and passions, made it the most useful book in my collection" (83).

In this passage Clara recounts herself as having judged her father's manuscript by one of the rhetorical standards of taste which Blair cites as "simplicity," which is "essential to all true ornament" (1:3). And the muted and distant tone of Clara's evaluation seems reminiscent of the scholarly rhetorical dissection of emotions. Such dissections suggestively promote the displacement of emotions as a function of audience. They do so by encouraging one to develop a self-consciousness about himself or herself as the judging audience upon whom the emotions of others gain significance only in the context of how those emotions produce, for the audience, a gratifying stylistic effect. The often impersonal nature of the rhetorical analysis of audience response potentially encourages the audience to focus on itself solipsistically as the judging center of the universe, upon whom all other people exist simply as stylistic effect.

Although she seems unaware of it, Clara Wieland unwittingly reveals herself to have been one such judging audience, who, in her evaluation of others in terms of their ability to gratify her, exhibits the characteristic of a self-indulgent, hedonistic audience who is not herself fulfilling a necessary moral role in the rhetorical process. She demonstrates this, for example, by recounting the premium she put on those events that could arouse her curiosity. The emotion of curiosity is one such audience effect scrutinized in Blair's rhetoric in a dispassionate and ego-centered way. In Blair's rhetoric, curiosity is both intellectually dissected and anesthetized as a gratifying emotion, and there is no ethical consideration of the potential emotional dynamics involved in arousing such an emotion. Blair mentions that curiosity is a form of novelty "which has no merit to recommend it, except its being uncommon or new, by means of this quality alone, produces in the mind a vivid and an agreeable emotion." And he goes on to explain that curiosity occurs when "new and strange objects rouse the mind from its dormant state by giving it a quick and pleasing impulse" (1:91).

Although Clara seems unaware that she has played the role of egocentric audience, she betrays this fact as she relates how she egocentrically interpreted the significance of the actions of others in terms of their significance for herself. One effect that the actions of others could produce upon her was curiosity, and the description Clara provides of her own responses of curiosity betrays an unintentional cruelty, since her self-absorption caused her to be disturbingly callous about the fact that the actions of others have emotional consequences for themselves as well as for Clara. Clara's retrospective narration reveals that she was and may still be capable of unreflectively seeing the pain of others as an emotion of benefit to her, especially as that emotion was related to her boredom and curiosity. "The sound of war had been heard," she relates, "but it was at such a distance as to enhance our enjoyment by affording objects of comparison." With frightening nonchalance, Clara concluded that "revolutions and battles, however calamitous to those who occupied the scene, contributed in some sort to our happiness, by agitating our minds with curiosity, and furnishing causes of patriotic exultation" (26). Now, in a dispassionate and objective sense, this effect of war may well be an accurate one to perceive, but Clara depicts herself as having totally ignored the harm of war to those involved in it. Through Clara's own unwitting depiction of her absorption with the judgments of rhetorical scholasticism, Brockden Brown implies that on a psychological level Clara emotionally isolated herself—just as the Wieland community was isolated in all respects—from the pain of her fellow men, concentrating instead on how the novelty of their pain eased her boredom. She unwittingly perceived herself in terms of her existence with others as an audience that needed to be entertained and mollified. And in this self-indulgent frame of mind, she did not consider her potentially active role as audience in compelling the rhetorician's sense of ethos. Like the small-town river folk who are entertained by the Duke and the King in *Adventures of Huckleberry Finn*, Clara, at least to an extent, sought only to be gratified. Clara betrays her own emotional self-absorption in a way that may seem comical to the reader when she recounts unjudgmentally her reaction to Pleyel's first misinformed knowledge "of the death of his Theresa." Theresa, as Clara recounts, was Clara's foreign rival for Pleyel's affections. Clara relates her feelings upon hearing that "this woman was then dead. A confirmation of the tidings, if true, would speedily arrive." One might assume that this discovery would elicit Clara's concern for Pleyel. Instead, Clara tells us without apparent compunction that she immediately reflected on the significance of this news for herself: "Propitious was the spirit that imparted these tidings. Propitious he would perhaps have been, if he had been instrumental in producing, as well as in communicating the tidings of her death" (46).

Clara also does not seem aware that her focus on herself as indulged audience rather than as possible corrective audience perhaps encouraged her fatal neglect of the full implications of her brother's "thrilling melancholy." She reveals that she thought about her brother's emotional state only in terms of its consequence for herself: "It hindered the element in which we moved from stagnating. Some agitation and concussion is requisite to the due exercise of human understanding" (23). Clara's narration reveals that she thereby distanced herself from her brother's individual emotions, diffusing their potentially threatening immediacy at least partially for her own gratification. The suppressed fear of Wieland that Clara may not know that she felt seems symbolically present to the reader in Clara's recounting of her dreams.

Clara expresses a similar emotional solipsism about the supernatural events that occurred to her father and about the supposedly disembodied voice of Catherine heard by Wieland and Pleyel: "My wonder was excited by the inscrutableness of the cause, but my wonder was unmixed with sorrow or fear. It begat in me a thrilling, and not unpleasant solemnity. Similar to these were the sensations produced by the recent adventure" (34–35). One cannot lay all this emotional solipsism at rhetoric's door. But Clara depicts herself, although unwittingly, as unreasonably buoyed into a self-confidence about her own judgments, judgments which often sound like aphorisms culled from a rhetoric text. She also shows herself as having practiced a subtle elitism based on her assumption that style is class-based, as illustrated by her recounted assumption that the rustic Carwin would not be eloquent. In sum, Clara reveals herself as having indulged in emotional self-absorption; she in essence saw herself as the audience for rhetoric, just as Blair examines the audience in his *Lectures*, and she inquired of herself how emotions would affect *her* in the same way that the rhetorician scrutinizes the methods of persuasion upon an audience. Her recounted innocence seems, in the reader's retrospect, willful. She did not take upon herself the moral responsibility an audience has to judge and to distinguish between virtuous rhetoric and sophistry. Instead, she concentrated upon which rhetoric would best seduce her emotions. Her excessive credulity about the implied virtue in eloquence allowed her to avoid the responsibility of judging the rhetoric of others. And because of this credulity, she remained smugly enveloped within her own emotional self-absorption. It is difficult for at least this reader not to conclude that Clara, despite her more experienced awareness of the potential for rhetoric to be sophistic as the retrospective narrator of *Wieland*, is unable to judge her own deficiencies as audience, and that *this* continued undercutting of the narrator's judgment, although not of her veracity, is the richest unresolved irony in the text.

Nevertheless, the irony at Clara's expense does not fault the potential for stable and sound rhetorical judgment. The reverse side of excessive faith in rhetoric would be total skepticism, to which Brown seems equally opposed, and Pleyel represents this skeptical perspective in the novel. Pleyel himself is described by Clara as an artist, but he is not portrayed as really respecting the purpose of art or as taking it seriously. Clara relates that Pleyel "was prone to view every object merely as supplying materials for mirth. His conceptions were ardent but ludicrous, and his memory, aided, as he honestly acknowledged, by his invention, was an inexhaustible fund of entertainment." Although Clara describes Pleyel as "the champion of intellectual liberty," who "rejected all guidance but that of his reason," Pleyel's reason was defective because it was restricted solely to what his senses told him; he rejected completely evidence based on an educated faith or on analogy. In discussions of religion, Pleyel "could find nothing but reasons for doubt" (25). He also doubted the Ciceronian oration for Cluentius because "to rely on the exaggerations of an advocate, or to make the picture of a single family a model from which to sketch the condition of a nation, was absurd" (30). It is difficult to imagine that Brown would endorse Pleyel's view as he has Clara dutifully recount it, since Brown in *Wieland* in effect attempts to sketch the conditions of his nation from a single family sketch. Brown explains in his preface that there is a moral purpose for painting a moral sketch from "one parallel fact" (3). Pleyel's "reason" did not help him in the realm of moral judgment. Brown assumes a moral purpose for literature arising out of an alternate sphere of evidence that Pleyel's skepticism would not make possible.

One sees the weaknesses of Pleyel's skepticism twice in his affairs with women. When Clara recounts that Pleyel received no letter from his fiancée Theresa, she describes Pleyel as being "seized with the torments of jealousy, and suspect[ing] nothing less than the infidelity of her to whom he had devoted his heart" (40). This hasty and irrational conclusion suggests an individual who should rely more on his recollection of the historical past, since Theresa has apparently given him no cause for suspicion before.

Donald Ringe mentions that all that Pleyel "hears and sees is perfectly accurate. His senses correctly report the sights and sounds that have been generated. But in every case his mind makes an unjustified inference, and his imagination augments his error." [20] Actually, Blair's rhetorical philosophy emphasizes a basis for judgment that Pleyel discounted: the experience of the past. Blair's rhetoric emphasizes tradition and majority consensus as a strong basis for evaluative judgment. Pleyel's imagination was disjunctive; the reader can infer from Clara's descriptions that Pleyel could not make connections between the present and the past. Clara relates that "Pleyel's temper made him susceptible of no durable impressions" (61). Appropriately, Clara informs her audience that while the bank bounding her brother's land was crowned "by the horticultural skill of my brother," the shore that bounded Pleyel's lands "is deformed with mud, and incumbered with a forest of reeds," and "the ditches by which they are bounded" are "mantled with stagnating green" (47). Nothing durable seems to flourish on Pleyel's lands; in the symbolism of metaphysical landscaping common to nineteenth-century fiction, this reference may have significance.

Even Theodore, according to Clara, was able to tell his sister that he was "ready to question his own senses when they plead against you" (109). But Clara finally realized that only the weight of her rhetoric could be set against Pleyel's senses. Pleyel accepted only the judgment of his senses and determined Clara a fallen woman rather than trusting in the evidence of her past. Clara relates that she realized Pleyel's lack of trust, which caused her great perplexity. She knew that she had only her "own assertion" to "throw in the balance against" Pleyel's suspicion (111). Clara had asked herself, one recalls, whether the force of truth would not be able to convince Pleyel of her innocence. She had then calculated the credibility of her rhetoric by the eloquence of her innocence and on the weight of her past experiences: "Could the long series of my actions and sentiments grant me no exemption from suspicion so foul?" (105). Nevertheless, despite her faith in her own integrity, Clara rightly predicted Pleyel's disbelief, ruefully acknowledging that "Pleyel is sceptical in a transcendant degree" (111).

To add injury to insult, Pleyel then went on at length about Clara's past virtuousness and her rhetoric:

> Here is exemplified, that union between intellect and form, which has hitherto existed only in the conceptions of the poet. I have watched your eyes; my attention has hung upon your lips. I have questioned whether the enchantments of your voice were more conspicuous in the intricacies of melody, or the emphasis of rhetoric. I have marked the transitions of your discourse, the felicities of your expression, your refined argumentation, and glowing imagery; and been forced to acknowledge, that all delights were meagre and contemptible, compared with those connected with the audience and sight of you. I have contemplated your principles, and been astonished at the solidity of their foundation, and the perfection of their structure. (121–22)

And through Clara's heart-wringing account of this discourse between herself and Pleyel, which Brown does not undercut, a startling reversal of Brown's theme is suggested: Pleyel *should* have based his judgment of Clara's present rhetoric on the Quintilian principle. Despite apparent sensory evidence to the contrary, Clara's eloquence should have reminded Pleyel of her virtue.

If both arguments against and for the Quintilian principle are implicitly presented in *Wieland* as true, then one of the important issues raised by this novel is the question of when one should trust rhetorical eloquence and when not, the same question that Herman Melville addresses in *The Confidence-Man:* should we trust rhetoric or not? The question might be rephrased, how does one, or can one indeed, detect the difference between virtuous or moral rhetoric and sophistry? And the question as raised in *Wieland* is an epistemological one: how does one arrive at certainty in an uncertain universe? Brown goes to pains to emphasize that uncertainty. His gothic world of inscrutable events that his created narrator Clara is careful to say may or may not have been supernatural creates an epistemological instability that makes it difficult to condemn Theodore Wieland's failure to doubt the validity of celestial voices urging him on to murder. Indeed, Alan Axelrod concludes that the novel's crucial truth is its "unremitting and unresolved ambiguity, a paradoxical revelation of the absolute limit of revelation."[21]

But the point seems to be suggested in *Wieland* that if human beings cannot trust the universe, they better be able to trust each other. Perhaps Brown goes to such great pains to establish the unreliability of natural and religious phenomena to point out the importance for judgmental purposes of reciprocated human trust. Since man is set against the instability of the universe, it is very important that man's truths and understandings can be verified through verbal communication. Knowledge, based on trust, must not be undermined by dishonesty. Clara recounts that in hindsight, Carwin acknowledged his mistake in deceiving Clara when he emerged from her bedroom closet: "Seldom have I felt deeper mortification, and more painful perplexity. I did not consider that the truth would be less injurious than any lie which I could hastily frame" (208).

Axelrod claims that "Carwin's double tongue proclaims the relativity of man's knowledge," yet he also astutely observes that despite Carwin's rhetorical skill, "Carwin lacks the moral principle by which he might regulate his powers."[22] The existence of Carwin's double tongue—or of sophistry in the universe—does not prove the nonexistence or impossibility of moral rhetoric. Indeed, Brown seems to create Carwin to advocate the necessity for virtuous rhetoric. After witnessing the catastrophes wreaked by his double tongue, Carwin himself, Clara relates, decided to write a narrative "as a lesson to mankind on the evils of credulity on the one hand, and of imposture on the other," as he relates his purpose to Clara (212). This seems also to be the message in *Wieland*, which is aimed both at the potential rhetorician and at the potential rhetorical audience. Through the example of Carwin that Clara faithfully reports, Brown gravely warns the would-be sophist of the far-ranging consequences of his imposture. Discussing the epistemological uncertainty depicted in *Wieland*, Ringe suggests that "Clara's mind breaks under the strain almost as if it were shattered at perceiving the truth of what has happened, a truth that could not be finally established without the self-revelatory speeches of the other characters,"[23] and, indeed, Clara's account is dependent on the truthful self-revelatory speeches of others, as all accounts of even one's own life are always intertextually dependent on the self-revelatory speeches of others. Verbal deception undermines one basis for man's knowledge, the verifiability of his conceptions that he receives from others.

But through his narrator Clara, who depicts her own gullibility, and through his own subtle implications about Clara's unacknowledged participation in her deception of others and in her own deception, Brown attacks not only the evils of imposture in *Wieland* but also the evils of credulity; he places just as much responsibility on the audience to detect sophistry as he does on the rhetorician who creates it. Brown is squarely within the rhetorical tradition in this respect. Blair urged the importance of critically scrutinizing rhetoric, arguing that "the more that Eloquence is properly studied, the more shall we be guarded against the abuse which bad men make of it, and enabled the better to distinguish between true Eloquence and the tricks of Sophistry" (2:5).

But *does* the study of rhetoric offer an antidote to sophistry? Does Brown imply that all rhetoric—in essence all human communication—is to be feared because sophistry is undiscoverable? Two opposing views are offered in the novel's concluding chapter. Clara suggests that "the double-tongued deceiver would have been baffled and repelled" if "Wieland had framed juster notions of moral duty" (244) or if she had had more foresight—although she seems unaware of her psychological impulses that marred her insight. Maxwell, a potential seducer of Louisa Conway's mother, believes that "the impulses of love are so subtle, and the influence of false reasoning, when enforced by eloquence and passion, so unbounded, that no human virtue is secure from degeneracy" (241).

One resolution of this issue, which seems embedded in the subplot of *Wieland*, might be that the virtue of the audience provides its own shield against sophistic intentions. Clara notes that "all arts being tried, every temptation being summoned to his aid, dissimulation being carried to its utmost bound, Maxwell, at length, nearly accomplished his purpose. The lady's affections were withdrawn from her husband and transferred to him. She could not, as yet, be reconciled to dishonor. All efforts to induce her to elope with him were ineffectual" (241). Although Mrs. Stuart is in effect seduced by Maxwell's sophistry, she is only "nearly" seduced; her own virtuous sense of commitment to her husband proves an implacable shield.

Clara also relates herself as having had the benefit of such a shield. The genesis of Carwin's temptation to corrupt Clara's virtue, as he tells Clara, was his sight of her "just as tranquil and secure in this lonely dwelling, as if you were in the midst of a crowd" (201). Described thus, Clara could be Dante's Beatrice or the Lady in Milton's *Comus*. Clara's virtue, however, is imperfect because it was not combined with experience and because it was qualified by her own concentration on self-gratification; the first test of Clara's virtue occasioned her "abrupt and precipitate flight" (202). Brown seems to suggest by intimating Clara's unacknowledged emotional motivations throughout her narrated discourse that Clara's willful isolation bred for her own selfish reasons left her unprepared to defend her virtue.

But a *proper* study of eloquence may be the key to the epistemological questions in *Wieland*. Without this proper study, the problematics of human communication become a vicious circle. Since human communication is the necessary source of human knowledge, an inability to believe in the possibility of truth isolates the individual within his distrust of emotional relations. Equally, an innocent unaware of the potential dangers of human communication and unaware of how his or her own emotional needs may lead to self-deception will find himself or herself similarly isolated and also in moral danger. Proper rhetorical judgments, then, seem to be a matter of balance; one judges rhetoric, admittedly imperfectly, from one's store of experience and on the basis of one's emotional concern for others — not by lawless, selfish passion — and also upon one's moral principles. Axelrod claims that the American wilderness is symbolic of the inevitable limits to man's knowledge and places Wieland's judgments about the voices he hears in that context. Thus in Axelrod's view, Clara's return to Europe represents a false catharsis, "due largely to the influence of the European 'spectacle of living manners and the monument of past ages' which Clara contemplates 'with ardour.' The 'ancient world' reinstates in Clara's heart 'its ancient tranquility.'" He believes, therefore, that Brown "pictures a Europe in which forgetfulness approaches innocence, and an America made guilty by its discovery of the frontier of knowledge itself." [24]

But the living manners and monuments that Clara discovers in Europe hardly imply forgetfulness, and Clara's presence in Europe may at least provide her some protection from her own emotional vulnerability to deception. The balanced judgments made in the context of the inherited human knowledge symbolized by Europe enable a more integrated empirical approach to knowledge. Clara remarks significantly at the beginning of her tale, "We were left to the guidance of our own understanding, and the casual impressions which society might make upon us" (22). Europe's tradition and history literally provide the test of time and human verifiability which Blair proposes as the true standard for critical judgment in his *Lectures*. In other words, then, Wieland's fanatical interpretation of the voices should have been submitted for verifiability to the judgment of educated others, if his own sense of moral duty to his family had not already checked his inspired slaughter.

Brown goes to pains to explore the power of rhetoric in *Wieland*, not, however, to reject it, or to express, consciously or unconsciously, a fear of its power. Instead, he suggests that rhetoric is only as good or as evil as the intentions of the orator and that both the audience and the orator must assume responsibility for determining and judging its use. Brown's American gothic shows the consequences of *not* taking responsibility—the epistemological chaos that ensues.

3

"I Take the Shame Upon Myself": Ethical Veracity in *The Scarlet Letter*

SOCRATES: "Now tell me this: you say that we should not repress our desires if we're going to live the way we ought to; we should let them grow as great as possible and procure their satisfaction from any source we can; and that this, in fact, is virtue?"

CALLICLES: "That's what I say.". . .

SOCRATES: "But life would be terrible as you put the matter, too. . . . And perhaps we are really dead. At any rate I once heard a wise man declare that we are, in fact, dead here and now: the body is really our tomb, and the part of the soul in which the desires are located is such that it easily yields to persuasion and shifts back and forth."

—PLATO, *Gorgias*

The current link between literary criticism and Derridean, Lacanian, and Saussurian philosophy has made literary interpretation an act of philology. Deconstructive criticism has inevitably found its place in the interpretation of *The Scarlet Letter*, whose very title suggests that the theory of language implicit in the novel is the key to the novel's meaning. Modern analyses of language in *The Scarlet Letter* have proliferated within the last ten years, engaging implicitly in a shared discourse about what *The Scarlet Letter* means in relation to the Western metaphysical tradition of language, or *logos*, in relation to a closed teleological system which reinforces tacit values. In the Western metaphysical tradition, the "letter" has a supposed stability; its meaning derives from its reference to a divinely transcendent system of ideas, more specifically, to Christian theology. Today, the stability of the text is deconstructed by critics who believe that the authority of the letter derives from a social system of tyranny masking itself as divine transcendence. Accordingly, modern interpretations of *The Scarlet Letter* often find stable language in the novel to be synonymous with law, with something patriarchally or ideologically determined rather than transcendentally derived. In opposition to language and its origin in law, human desire in *The Scarlet Letter* is seen as personal and existentialistically free, healthily erosive of the stability of the sign since desire exposes any system of law that would control it as artificial and tyrannizing.

This dialectical opposition between law and desire in *The Scarlet Letter* is observed and expressed by critics in a variety of ways not restricted to deconstructive terminology. Nina Baym, for example, argues eloquently that the theme of *The Scarlet Letter* is that of the traditional conflict in American literature between the private self and society. The Puritan society is, of course, complicit with the tyrannizing power of authoritarian language. Hester "is the pre-civilized nature goddess opposing Western civilization, the impulsive heart defying the repressive letter of the law." Hester is allied to "sex, passion, eroticism, flesh, and the earth." [1] Louise K. Barnett rephrases this conflict in *The Scarlet Letter* as one between autonomous, genuine selves and the deceptive public: the "primary social purpose of speech — to foster the mutual understanding and agreement that make society possible," is deformed by Puritan constraints, by the Puritans' use of language to "mask socially unacceptable personal motives with official rationales." Hence the only honest language is private, occurring notably in the forest encounter between Dimmesdale and Hester, and, despite Barnett's observation that this honest language involves "the meeting of hearts," Barnett also makes clear that this meeting of hearts is sexual. [2]

Although both Baym and Barnett deplore the conditions of a repressive society that would inhibit sexuality and tyrannize over the power of language, neither critic takes on the deconstructive project of suggesting that this conflict between law and desire is inherent within the nature of the word. Barnett's and Baym's readings are confined to observations about the repressive world fictionalized in *The Scarlet Letter* and speculate on the grimness of Hawthorne's vision. Fred G. See's *Desire and the Sign: Nineteenth-Century American Fiction*, which begins with a selective reading of Hawthorne, including *The Scarlet Letter*, suggests that the tension between erosive desire — the signifier — and sedimented meaning — the signified — is the inevitable drama of the linguistic sign. See follows Michel Foucault in determining that "the logic of desire," or "the sign of sex," incites "scandal," the collapse of meaning in language. Further, See assumes that this collapse is desirable because scandal "makes it possible to see the necessity and hidden structure of law, an outrage which undoes law and rhythm and calls forth an original clarity of regulation: the cadence of language." Language must resist "the immense pressure of inherited forms," giving in to the scandal of desire. See is disappointed with Hawthorne, who is too much of a traditionalist to give in to his desire for scandal. Hence in *The Scarlet Letter*, Hawthorne conforms "to those dogmatic literary signs which are the cold trace of presence" by allowing Dimmesdale's reverence for the law to triumph over Hester's revolutionary desire.[3]

See perceives an unhappy stasis in *The Scarlet Letter* that eludes other deconstructive critics quite pleased with the destabilized language in the novel. Millicent Bell and Evan Carton discover in the romance form a perfect medium for the "play with the idea of significance"[4] that typifies modern literature and criticism. Truthful language in *The Scarlet Letter* "is present only through and as representation, as promise, as absence";[5] both Bell and Carton interpret the complicated symbolism in *The Scarlet Letter* to be Hawthorne's way of overdetermining meaning, of expressing a "loss of confidence in the sacred grounding of signs."[6] The narrator both offers and withdraws meaning, equivocating, contradicting, offering moral judgment on the characters in *The Scarlet Letter* and then withdrawing it, suggesting signs of a Divine Providence and then undermining them. Despite the more metaphysical intent of Carton's and Bell's criticism, their readings retain the sense of dialectical opposition noted by other critics between law/static meaning/dead form on one hand and passion/indeterminacy/spontaneity on the other in *The Scarlet Letter*. Hester is still Carton's imaginative "deviant" despite her more complicated participation also as conformist, and Dimmesdale is still connected with "the rigidity and predictability of the community's interpretive conventions"[7] despite his complicity also as a passionate rebel. For Carton and Bell, it is still the same dialectic of opposition, but the opposition, hence determinant language, collapses: all are both guilty and free from taint of judgment,[8] and language is appropriately indeterminant.

These critics seem right to perceive that if there is a dialectic in *The Scarlet Letter* between authority and passion, then it is inevitably implicating of itself; as Mark Seltzer has suggested in his Marxist reading of Henry James's fiction,[9] power by its very nature requires a complementary deviancy by which to define itself. Nina Baym suggests that witchcraft in *The Scarlet Letter* is the deviancy that "indirectly validate[s] the social structure" of Puritan society,[10] hence, that Hester by avoiding witchcraft escapes being implicated by power. But this reading does not take into account that passion in *The Scarlet Letter* is also inevitably implicated by power; adultery *is* the inevitable engendering act for law in *The Scarlet Letter* because adultery is the necessary antagonist against which law can define itself. Indeed, within this dialectic there would seem to be no possible transcendence; freedom from power and likewise from sexual passion would seem impossible. Hawthorne suggests this point by entrapping Hester's desire for escape from law within a seemingly irreducible system of codes. When Hester stands on the scaffold at the beginning of *The Scarlet Letter* thinking longingly of her European past free of legalistic taint (and sexual desire?), she herself is unaware that the incarceration of her identity began long before her life in Salem. Her original marriage to an elderly Hawthornian character of the intellect was prescribed by the patriarchal European conventions, possibly of arranged marriages, certainly of the financial necessities so often limiting to the James heroine. Hester's rebellion against legal marriage seems inevitably inscribed within this original act.

But is it possible that there is a third meaning system in *The Scarlet Letter* to challenge the supposed dialectical opposition between law and desire, a third human impulse both transcendent and spontaneous to which language in the novel is conjoined both more freely and more determinantly? That component can be identified as human morality, or ethics, as a sense of personal responsibility within the individual—a desire of the heart which is informed by a compassion for others as well as for oneself and which accordingly introduces the possibility of self-lessness as a component of human ethics. Lester Hunt comes closest to this understanding of *The Scarlet Letter* in his reading, which interprets the novel in light of Adam Smith's moral philosophy. But Hunt believes that Smith links sympathy for others with morality as a socially regulating force, while *The Scarlet Letter* illustrates that sympathy and morality are two incompatible virtues. Hunt aligns moral regulation with law in *The Scarlet Letter;* the "moralistic religion" of the Puritans "is competent to regulate all matters of conduct" and therefore shares with the law "the same sweeping omnipotence." [11] Hence morality becomes rigidified within an institutionalized form that by its regulative nature breaks down sympathy.

Hawthorne, of course, pointedly tells his reader that the Puritans were "a people amongst whom religion and law were almost identical." [12] Hawthorne emphasizes this point to alert his reader to a deplorable and not necessarily inevitable state of affairs. A sense of compassion and a sense of self-regulating personal responsibility equally compete against law and institutionalized morality in *The Scarlet Letter* as arbiters of human passion. Truthful language in *The Scarlet Letter* does not come from the institution. It comes from one's spontaneous and intuitive sense of what is ethically right, virtually, from one's sympathetic apprehension of the potential consequences of one's actions upon another. One might wonder why Hawthorne would feel it necessary to exhort against the skewed morality of a Puritan culture at such apparent distance from the democratic nature of his own. The answer is suggested in Hawthorne's Preface to *The Scarlet Letter*.

"The Custom-House" Preface not only conjoins law and passion in opposition to the regulative forces of personal responsibility and human compassion, or sympathy. The Preface also rejects Hawthorne's contemporary world, where power is wedded to passion and a sense of self-reflectiveness, or personal responsibility, seems completely absent, so that the modern world is actually less potentially able to escape the dialectic of power and passion than the society in *The Scarlet Letter*. Hawthorne himself escapes this world in the Preface in a variety of ways: he expresses a sense of personal responsibility by linking himself to a historical tradition of guilt; and he expresses compassion and rejects his own temptation to authority, first, by refusing to wield political power over the fellow occupants of the Custom House, and then by intuitively sympathizing with Hester through his experience with the scarlet letter. He also symbolically dies within the world of contemporary institutionalized fiction, where morality is wedded to a formal code, and resurrects himself within the world of romance, possibly within the oral tradition of the epic, where he hopes that he and his readers can unite in a mutual environment of sympathy.

Throughout the Preface, Hawthorne expresses a lack of ease with his position of authority as Surveyor of the Custom House. Because most of the officers in the Custom House are Whigs in political persuasion, Hawthorne knows that in his own incoming position as Democrat, "according to the received code in such matters, it would have been nothing short of duty, in a politician, to bring every one of those white heads under the axe of the guillotine." Hawthorne says that this thought "pained him" and that despite his further knowledge that these elderly officers were now barely functional in their position, "I knew it too, but could never quite find in my heart to act upon the knowledge"

(130). Hawthorne accordingly tempers justice with mercy, and he also implies that he avoids implementing institutionalized justice because he knows it to be arbitrary and because he wishes to avoid being an instrument of institutionalized power. He suggests that compassion rather than legal judgment is the appropriate basis for man's relations to others: "Unless people are more than commonly disagreeable, it is my foolish habit to contract a kindness for them" (131).

Authority in "The Custom House"—which was the basis upon which all individuals in the Custom House obtained their positions— is equated with life-denying images of death and stasis. Hawthorne suggests that living by authority is death-in-life, constitutes an authoritative artfulness—what one might call living by "company" art, which is the employment of morality as an institutionalized arm of political power, as an "official conscience." Hawthorne characterizes this artful deadening to life much in the same way that Murray Krieger describes formal art in his descriptions of lyric poetry in *The Play and Place of Criticism*. In lyric poetry, according to Krieger, the formal quality of art triumphs over the poem's temporal progression: "That is, through all sorts of repetitions, echoes, complexes of internal relations, it converts its chronological progression into simultaneity, its temporally unrepeatable flow into eternal recurrence; it converts its linear movement into circle." In a similar conversion of temporality into the eternal, the old men in Hawthorne's Custom-House "bore one another with the several thousandth repetition of old sea-stories." Just as this description of Hawthorne's implies the deadening property of formal art, Krieger also observes that formal art lends itself dangerously to stasis, and he warns "against the deadening of life, the freezing of movement" in poetry and adds that "time, in its unique empirical particularity, must always be celebrated in its flow even as we arrest it. . . . Or else poetry is hardened into static, Platonic discourse that has lost touch with—indeed that disdains to touch—our existential motions." [13] The old men in the Custom-House do not celebrate the flow of time but simply go through "the various formalities of office" (131), engaging in "the frozen witticisms of past generations." They are evacuated souls who have deadened themselves to gathering anything "worth preservation from their varied experience of life," instead carefully storing "their memories with the husks" (132), replacing real life with the deadened form of authority. They therefore replace spontaneous response to experience with the ineffectual response of authority, proceeding "to lock, and double-lock, and secure with tape and sealing wax, all the avenues of the delinquent vessel" (81) only *after* a smuggling mishap has occurred.

In "The Custom-House," displacement of personal identity by authority is linked to an unreflective life. This lack of reflection is in turn tied to a sensual life, for which Hawthorne expresses barely concealed contempt. Hawthorne connects his images of authority, physical passion, and unreflectiveness in his portrait of "a certain permanent Inspector" (132), whose "voice and laugh . . . perpetually re-echoed through the Custom-House" (133). Hawthorne appropriately identifies this embodiment of formal stasis as "the father of the Custom-House — the patriarch, not only of this little squad of officials, but, I am bold to say, of the respectable body of tide-waiters all over the United States" (132). By suggesting that this Inspector is representative of an entire system of authority, Hawthorne extends his criticism to the entire body of contemporary government. This man has such a "trifling admixture of moral and spiritual ingredients," accompanied by "the rare perfection of his animal nature," that Hawthorne wonders how he can keep "from walking on all-fours" (133). Hawthorne makes it clear that this constitution is not admirable. The Inspector "had vastly the advantage over his four-footed brethren" only in "his ability to recollect the good dinners which it had made no small portion of the happiness of his life to eat." The Inspector's animal nature is suggested not only by his husbanding of three wives and fathering of twenty children but also by his sense of "no higher moral responsibilities than the beasts of the field" and his "blessed immunity from the dreariness and duskiness of age" (134). His unreflectiveness results in an insensitivity to those events in his life that should have provoked sorrow — in particular, to death. And "power of thought" and "depth of feeling" have been replaced by apotheosization of himself as "authority"; he "did duty very respectably, and to general acceptance, in lieu of a heart" (133). One cannot mistake the implied ramifications of this portrait: authority and passion lead downward to animality while moral reflection on human mortality and other sorrowful experiences leads to spiritual evolution, to renewed life.

In "The Custom-House," these intimations about the relationship between authority and selfish passion also take on a sharp political edge. Hawthorne, a Democrat, lost his office upon the incumbency of a Whig government, and it is the Whig government that Hawthorne associates with institutionalized authority. After watching both parties' distinctive uses of authority, Hawthorne comments, "If, heretofore, I had been none of the warmest of partisans, I began now at this season of period and adversity, to be pretty actively sensible with which party my predilections lay." Hawthorne suggests that authority for Democrats is functional—"Democrats take the offices, as a general rule, because they need them"—but Whigs exercise authority out of a lust for power, a "fierce and bitter spirit of malice and revenge" (154). Hawthorne's Preface is a specific political indictment of the Whigs placed within the more universal context of authority and its abuse.

Surprisingly, it may be this specific political view of the Whigs as institutionally corrupt that suggested to Hawthorne a connection between his own contemporary political situation, when Whigs were dominant, and the Puritan society of *The Scarlet Letter*. This perceived link between the Whigs and the Puritans in terms of their abuse of power may have been suggested to Hawthorne by an essay entitled "Mr. Forrest's Oration," which appeared in the September 1838 *Democratic Review*. The *Democratic Review*, which first appeared in 1837, was the magazine in which Hawthorne's periodical contributions were most prolific,[14] and Hawthorne contributed a "Biographical Sketch of Jonathan Cilley" in the *Democratic Review* for September 1838, the issue in which "Mr. Forrest's Oration" appeared. Hawthorne's sketch appeared on pages 69 through 76;[15] the essay on Forrest's oration just barely anticipated it on pages 51 through 57. It seems possible that given Hawthorne's comments about the Whigs in "The Custom-House," he had read "Mr. Forrest's Oration," indeed, that it suggested to him the connection between his own political climate and that of Puritan society.

Praise of oratory was one of the most common periodical entries in America throughout the nineteenth century so what distinguishes "Mr. Forrest's Oration" is that a great deal of the essay is devoted to Forrest's politics rather than his eloquence. The polemical nature of the essay may be due to its appearance in the *Democratic Review* and its political agenda. The writer wishes to praise the Democrats for their ethical politics and to criticize the antidemocratic party, the precursors of the Whigs, for their abuse of power. He does so by suggesting that though Democrats practice self-government motivated by ethics, antidemocrats (Whigs) seek to control others, driven by a passion for power. The antidemocrats' "desire for political power is one of the strongest passions of man, civilized, or savage, and it may be called the natural enemy of a practical administration of a republican form of government."[16] The writer accuses antidemocrats of greed,

"embracing the largest private fortunes that have ever been accumu-
lated in this country" (52), and, just as Hawthorne views Whigs and
Democrats with divergent spirits in "The Custom-House," the writer
of "Mr. Forrest's Oration" endows Democrats with spiritual natures
and describes antidemocrats as barely evolved. It is by virtue of his
ethical self-government that the democrat "is only 'a little lower than
the angels,'" but the antidemocrat who abuses power "is but 'little
higher' than 'the least erected spirit that fell from heaven.'" There is
no affinity, the writer concludes, "between the intellectuality of the
democratic principles of the one, and the sensuality of the pride of the
other" (53–54).

Curiously, the writer opens his article by distinguishing between the
state of America before and "at the time our experiment as government
commenced" (51). In the process he links the sensuous pride of the
antidemocrats with that of the Puritans and suggests that the enabling
mechanism of authoritative tyranny is a conspiracy between religion
and law. "The clergy," the writer comments, "showed themselves not
exempt from the desire of power; indeed, it may be said, that a love of
temporal authority as an adjunct of ecclesiastical prerogative, was their
besetting sin, if not their ruling passion" (31). Since men "had so little
confidence in man's moral qualities, they did not conceive it possible to
sustain religion without the patronage, protection, and coercion of the
civil power in a government. It is no wonder that the clergy . . . attached
themselves politically to those who were of congenial sentiments with
them" (51).

The writer feels in contrast that his own Democratic party replaced
the institutionalized morality of a tyrannizing religious-legal state with
the self-motivated religion of personal ethics so that "the influence
of the clergy is now confined to the appropriate sphere of their vocation, and they are no longer the representatives of the religious feelings
of others. With the reform that we established, came also truer motives of man's individual accountability, and religion is now viewed
as an individual concern, and each man thinks and acts for himself"
(52). But this writer is assuming that the days of the Puritans — and
antidemocrats — are gone. It seems possible that with the Democrats
deposed through their contemporary representative Nathaniel Hawthorne, Hawthorne thought back to this article and contemplated the
connection between reinstated Whig tyranny and the religious tyranny
of the Puritan state.

Hawthorne also seems to perceive a connection between Whig/

Puritan tyranny and "the law of literary propriety" (142), and he pays rueful obeisance to this connection in "The Custom-House." The writer in "Mr. Forrest's Oration" is relieved that "the power of wealth, all-powerful as it is, has not had sufficient strength, to draw the literature of the country wholly into its sordid grasp" (53). But in "The Custom-House," Hawthorne takes advantage of a specific political situation to make the point that literature ground through the mill of Custom-House ethics is no different from literature ground through the mill of the Puritan marketplace. Hawthorne's Preface nods to the conventional expectations so well known in the time of Charles Brockden Brown that fiction must present both a moral and be "true" — that is, be based on a genuine historical event or incident. It is with this tradition in mind that Hawthorne comments that "the main facts" of *The Scarlet Letter* "are authorized and authenticated by the document of Mr. Surveyor Pue" (146–47). The historical basis for his tale brings it "a certain propriety, of a kind always recognized in literature" (122). But Hawthorne probably did not intend his audience to believe in this "germ" for his tale. He seems instead to be countering official expectations with defensive irony. In the Preface to the second edition of *The Scarlet Letter*, Hawthorne defends his first Preface against attack by using this very language of authority; his sketch was done with "frank and genuine good-humor," "general accuracy," conveying "sincere impressions," and could not have been done "with a livelier effect of truth" (119). Hawthorne seems to be responding to a tyrannizing audience with official expectations; truth under the wing of authority can only be doublespeak, and Hawthorne responds with his own.

Although Hawthorne scoffs at that part of his audience for whom thoughts will always be "frozen, and utterance benumbed," he still hopes to establish "some true relation" with a part of his audience. To search for "the one heart and mind of sympathy" seems to Hawthorne unrealistic. Given his sense of the strong prohibitory nature of official conscience that practices a tyranny of judgment, Hawthorne can at best imagine "a kind and apprehensive" friend who would "thaw" native reserve by "genial consciousness" (121). According to John Bayer, Hawthorne attempts to create a sympathetic audience in his Preface by making the Preface an "exordium for the romance proper, an atavistic reminder of oral modes of composition."[17] Bayer suggests that Hawthorne may have derived the inspiration to do this from the rhetorical tradition, specifically from his knowledge of Hugh Blair's *Rhetoric* that Hawthorne read while at Bowdoin, where he also, incidentally, studied and boarded with his rhetoric professor, Samuel P. Newman, who wrote the first American rhetoric text for colleges.[18] Bayer emphasizes that rhetoric is primarily an oral tradition and that Blair's description of persuasive tactics emerges in Hawthorne's attempts to create with his audience a bond of sympathy. This "bond between narrator and narratee is centered on sympathy and tolerance."[19]

Hawthorne's emphasis on speech in his Preface almost certainly derived also from his familiarity with the popularity of oratory during his own time. As we shall see, Hawthorne draws on contemporary descriptions of pulpit eloquence in his portrait of Arthur Dimmesdale. Oratory was for Hawthorne's contemporaries and for many of his close friends a consuming passion. But despite the undeniable source that contemporary rhetoric was for Hawthorne, Hawthorne's view of the rhetorical movement was probably not as simple as Bayer intimates. It was Hugh Blair, after all, who contributed to "the law of literary propriety" by insisting in his *Rhetoric* that literature be based on "what may actually occur in life; by means of which what is laudable or defective in character and in conduct, may be pointed out, and placed in an useful light."[20] Blair was a Presbyterian minister; rhetoric, in America, was a discipline studied primarily for the practice of religion and law. In *The Scarlet Letter*, Hawthorne expresses ambivalence about rhetoric as a public practice, possibly because of its great ability to induce sympathy—and then to exploit this sympathy for "company" purposes, promoting power/passion rather than personal accountability.

"The Custom-House" is a symbolic rejection of the world of substitutive authority within which Hawthorne has been entombed in the Custom-House, a world that has, because of its lack of connection with "a heart and sensibilities of human tenderness" (150), killed "the word." Hawthorne's Preface is a memoir from the underground—a very popular genre during Hawthorne's time, as J. Gerald Kennedy has persuasively demonstrated in his discussion of Edgar Allan Poe's use of the form.[21] Since the life of a Custom-House officer is such that "he does not share in the united effort of mankind" (151), Hawthorne takes advantage of his political deposition to exit this world. By employing "the metaphor of the political guillotine" (156), Hawthorne "decapitates" himself in his contemporary world, a world he must reject because of the shallowness of the modern age, and resurrects—redeems—himself within the world of living speech or oral tradition, specifically perhaps, of the epic. Hawthorne exits the world of the Custom-House, where he is "within the control of individuals who neither love nor understand him" (153). By doing so, he hopes to elicit the sympathy of his modern readers about whom he has expressed such apprehension at the beginning of the Preface. These readers, who would probably find Hawthorne's Preface "too autobiographical for a modest person to publish in his lifetime," will readily excuse it "in a gentleman who writes from beyond the grave." "Peace be with all the world!," Hawthorne writes. "My blessings on my friends!" My forgiveness to my enemies! For I am in the realm of quiet!" (156).

What a curious collection of remarks for Hawthorne to gather in his underground memoir. Apart from the Christlike nature of the benediction, there is a sentimental au revoir within the lines, a playfully melodramatic request for sympathy. Kennedy explains that in the nineteenth century "ritual of farewell, all that was sacred in bourgeois, middle-class culture — innocence, love, piety, and death — commingled in a moment of idealized beauty"; one might imagine, also, in mutual forgiveness. More interesting is Hawthorne's connection between death and the realm of quiet — the realm where there is no language. That Hawthorne is writing about his own absence from speech emphasizes the paradox of inscription, since "writing carries within it 'the principle of death' in its transformation of the verbal sign from a living utterance to a fixed mark on a lifeless page," and yet, at the same time, a writer discussing his own death suggests a "compensatory fantasy of escape," suggests "the idea of reclaiming life by a sheer act of will." According to Kennedy, "if death marks the forefeiture of language, a memoir of one's interment is always an unwritable record," but the writer who resurrects himself from the tomb indulges in "the aeolist fantasy par excellence": "His deliverance thus cancels the threat of corruption and converts his experience into a fable of resurrection." In doing so, the writer participates in the "great monomyth of ancient cultures . . . the agon of survival, the archetypal triumph of life over death."[22]

Hawthorne's "resurrection" occurs by virtue of his political decapitation, this "remarkable event of the third year of his surveyorship" (153). This reference to "three" as potential resurrection gains resonance as it is used throughout *The Scarlet Letter*. *How* resurrection of life and language occurs for Hawthorne is equally as important as the fact that it does. In *The Aeneid*, Aeneas recounts that the ghost of Hector came back to him in a dream to exhort him to leave Troy and found Rome. In *The Divine Comedy*, Dante the pilgrim discovers from Virgil that Dante has been divinely exhorted to undertake his journey. In both epics, also, the poet acknowledges his divine inspiration from the gods, or God, to tell his tale, a process that infuses his poetic language with a spiritually transcendent value. Hawthorne taps into this tradition by imagining "the ghost of Mr. Surveyor Pue":

> In his port was the dignity of one who had borne his Majesty's commission, and who was therefore illuminated by a ray of splendor that shone so dazzlingly about the throne. How unlike, alas! the hang-dog look of a republican official, who, as the servant of the people, feels himself less than the least, and below the lowest, of his masters. With his own ghostly voice, he had exhorted me, on the sacred consideration of my filial duty and reverence towards him,—who might reasonably regard himself as my official ancestor,—to bring his mouldy and moth-eaten lucubrations before the public. "Do this," said the ghost of Mr. Surveyor Pue, emphatically nodding the head that looked so imposing within its memorable wig, "do this, and the profit shall be all your own! You will shortly need it; for it is not in your days as it was in mine, when a man's office was a life-lease, and oftentimes an heirloom. But, I charge you, in this matter of old Mistress Prynne, give to your predecessor's memory of the credit which will be rightfully its due!" And I said to the ghost of Mr. Surveyor Pue,— "I will!" (147)

Just as in the ancient epics, Hawthorne is not only impelled to take on the responsibility of telling the tale; his own future is predicted by the now-ghostly oracle!

It is essential to realize, however, that the resurrection of the word does not take place for Hawthorne by the power of any external authority. The inspiration that impels Hawthorne to the responsibility of writing his tale comes from within Hawthorne's imagination—from the "as if" part of himself that can imagine a real link with his past—a sense of continuity with the world of experience that can invest Hawthorne's actions with a moral authority, that becomes part of a universal tie with like-minded individuals who pursue the same eternal verities, but in a self-engendered way. Entombed within the deadening influence of his "official conscience" (131), Hawthorne discovers that his "imagination was a tarnished mirror. It would not reflect, or only with miserable dimness, the figures within which I did my best to people it. The characters," Hawthorne writes, "would take neither the flow of passion nor the tenderness of sentiment, but retained all the rigidity of dead corpses, and stared me in the face with a fixed and ghastly grin of contemptuous defiance" (148). Hawthorne fears that if he remains too long entombed within an "official conscience" that estranges him from his own experience he will lose "the capability of self-support" and that "his forfeited powers" may not be "redeemable" (152). Given the context of Hawthorne's observations about the other characters in the Custom-House, it seems that the self-support being referred to is moral rather than financial. The revitalizing process for dead speech and death-in-life is the rejection of external authority as a substitutive stand-in for one's own conscience and then an assumption of responsibility for one's actions, a process that inevitably leads to an internalization of sin. In the Preface, this action occurs when Hawthorne establishes a link between himself and his Puritan ancestors and proclaims that "I, the present writer, as their representative, hereby take shame upon myself for their sakes" (127). Disgusted with the predominant lack of moral awareness that he senses in Custom-House modern humanity, Hawthorne resurrects himself through a vital link with his past into a time when sin was a vital, although skewed, force. Sin, for Hawthorne, is not something determined by law, but something affirmed through individual intuition. Hawthorne does not view the potential guilt that arises from a sense of sin as a destructive emotion or as an emotion valuable within itself; indeed, guilt implies a process of self-inflicted suffering after the fact that Hawthorne would not advocate, although he intimates that kind of suffering is inevitable. Hawthorne seems to believe that taking responsibility for one's own actions will be a prohibitory check on one's future actions that might cause others pain, and the causing of pain, for Hawthorne, seems to be constitutive of "sin." One's assumption of responsibility checks one's temptation to judge the sin of others. The appropriate response to the sin of others is to see it as an emblem of one's own sin, as Hawthorne takes the shame of his ancestors upon himself. And because of our mutual complicity in sin, the appropriate reaction toward others should be compassion and mercy. But toward oneself, a sense of our capability to wound others through a contemplated action and a sense of the consequent suffering it will cause both ourselves and others should act as a self-regulatory force to check the impulse to sin. The operative principle is the inevitability of human suffering balanced against the human desire to abate it.

Hawthorne seems to imply in *The Scarlet Letter* that sexual passion can be a selfish emotion most likely to be constitutive of sin—of the power to wound others. For Hawthorne, passion cannot be regulated by law—only by ethics. In *The Scarlet Letter*, passion is seen to be complicit with law, and, just as in the Custom-House, characters who relinquish self-regulation for the substitutive regulation of the law remain stagnant within the realm of their passion and dead to the changing world of experience, of redemptive possibility. In *The Scarlet Letter*, Hester Prynne and Arthur Dimmesdale are very like Dante's doomed lovers, Paolo and Francesca, who evade self-understanding and allow their passion to be ruled through eternity by the external force of the law. But through the course of powerful events in the novel, Hester and Dimmesdale effect their own redemptions, escape their entrapment within the powerful dialectic of passion and law.

The difference between Dante's adulterous characters in Hell and Hawthorne's adulterous Dimmesdale and Hester Prynne is that Dimmesdale and Hester can change; they are in a temporal world where fate remains unfixed and spiritual redemption is possible. Among all the recent plausible theories suggested for why Hawthorne never articulates *adulterer* in *The Scarlet Letter*, one more might be added. Hawthorne does not articulate *adulterer* because he does not want to fix Hester and Dimmesdale within this static position. If he were to do so, he would be guilty of assuming the same legal authority as the Puritan magistrates in the novel. Authoritative language in *The Scarlet Letter* is infected by law; it can only be equivalent to death.

Nevertheless, there seems no question that Hawthorne assumes the authoritative position of an epic poet in rendering ethical judgment on his characters. Passion in and of itself is not judged by Hawthorne in *The Scarlet Letter*, but adultery is. First, adultery has that inextricable complicity with law; passion in *The Scarlet Letter* exists only as a resistance to law and, thus, in a homeostatic system, is a necessary deviancy inscribed by law. Second, Hawthorne seems to condemn adultery on ethical rather than legal grounds. Despite the many instances of narrative indeterminacy in *The Scarlet Letter* so commonly noted by critics, Hawthorne offers unambiguous ethical judgments on Hester's relationship to her passion, on the selfishness implicit within it, and on its potential to wound others, Roger Chillingworth, Arthur Dimmesdale, and her daughter Pearl. These ethical judgments gain spontaneity from their origin in experience and in spontaneous and intuitive apprehension of what is morally right.

Most readings of *The Scarlet Letter* suggest that Hester Prynne is an artist. In addition, they see this artistry as a positive force in the novel and admire Hester's ability to transform the meaning of her symbol given the social constraints that limit her.[23] "The Custom-House" suggests, however, that art can be a deadening influence over life if art

is complicit with legal authority. The Custom-House officials are described as entombed within a formal stasis, which implies a consciously
artful resistance to the changing experiences of life. The Puritan society imposes on Hester a legal sentence, but Hester works artfully in
complicity with the law so that she will *not* be transformed, so that she
can entomb her passion within a stasis resistant to change and to redemption. Hester's "passion," Hawthorne writes very late in the novel,
"once so wild," is "even yet neither dead nor asleep, but only imprisoned within the same tomb-like heart" (273). In fairy-tale-like fashion, Hester petrifies her passion rather than submit it to the forces of
change, biding her time for the kiss that will reawaken it in its original
"unadulterated" form. As Krieger suggests, such artistry is a befouling
of life, since "time, in its unique empirical particularity, must always
be celebrated in its flow even as we arrest it."[24]

Puritan law, of course, complicitly induces Hester to nurse her adultery. The Puritan "sentence" stills Hester's "existential motions":

> To-morrow would bring its own trial with it; so would the next day, and
> so would the next; each its own trial, and yet the very same that was
> now so unutterably grievous to be borne. The days of the far-off future
> would toil onward, still with the same burden for her to take up, and
> bear along with her, but never to fling down; for the accumulating days,
> and added years, would pile up their misery upon the heap of shame.
> Throughout them all, giving up her individuality, she would become the
> general symbol at which the preacher and moralist might point, and in
> which they might vivify and embody their images of woman's frailty and
> sinful passion. (185)

"Company" art resists the changing content of life; it rigidifies one moment in life into a tyrannizing form. The one moment "A" of Hester's
life becomes "the undying, the ever-active sentence of the Puritan tri-
bunal," and the sentence into which Hester's potentially changing life
has become rigidified broadens out into the tyrannizing "text of the
discourse" (191). It only stands to reason that "the scarlet letter had
not done its office" (261) because the legal sentence does not reform; it
preserves: by privileging the adulterous moment of Hester's life over
all other moments, the legal letter reduces Hester's significance to
"passion" and preserves that passion in an unchanging magical state.

Law is therefore a preserver rather than a mediator of passion. The
problem with Puritan society is that the potential mediator of passion, ethics, has also been tyrannized over by law. This was a period,
Hawthorne relates, "when the forms of authority were felt to possess

the sacredness of divine institutions" (172–73). Linked to law, ethical judgment loses its spontaneity and origin in intuition, "the mildest and the severest acts of public discipline were alike made venerable and awful" (160). And ethics, which should unite men in a common bond of sympathy and impulse for self-regulation, are instead alienating. The imposed scarlet letter "had the effect of a spell—taking her out of the ordinary relations with humanity, and inclosing her in a sphere by herself" (164). We can see the contrast between how law and ethics regulate in their separate spheres in the scene in which Hester ascends to the scaffold for public display. The town-beadle, who "prefigured and represented in his aspect the whole dismal severity of the Puritanic code of law," appears "with a sword by his side and his staff of office in his hand" (162). The sexual imagery here conspires with the legal in a mutual complicity. Hester perceives that the rigidity of this law has collapsed her multitudinous experiences into the adulterous moment of the recent past, hence that she has been cut off from her mother's face, "with the look of heedful and anxious love which it always wore in her remembrance, and which, even since her death, had so often laid the impediment of a gentle remonstrance in her daughter's pathway" (168). It is curious that Hawthorne implies here that Hester has required an inhibitory check on her behavior in the past, perhaps that we all do, that people must always mediate within themselves against their lesser instincts. Such mediation, however, cannot be legislated by law but emerges out of our personal experience with "heedful and anxious love" and "gentle remonstrances," which, despite their mild link to judgment, suggest equally a sympathy and compassion.

Hawthorne's narration partakes of this heedful and anxious love and gentle remonstrance. Indeed, his repetitive use of *three* in reference both to Hester and to Dimmesdale suggests the possibility of imminent life changes, redemption, that they would deny themselves.[25] But Hawthorne also suggests in *The Scarlet Letter* that Hester's passion works in collusion with the law to stave off changes in her life that would bring about redemption. Hester uses the legal sentence as a means of escaping responsibility for her own sin. She accepts the legal sentence as a static judgment on herself; the sentence allows her to remain in a state in which her passion is unaltered. By giving herself over to the external authority of the law, she abdicates her own responsibility to regulate her passion. In a perverse way, also, the forced repression of her passion by the law also preserves it, and the law therefore allows for the inevitable resurfacing of the sublimated passion.

In her need to keep her passion alive, Hester actually suppresses a

potentially transformative type of art that would mediate it. As Hawthorne tells us, "Women derive a pleasure, incomprehensible to the
other sex, from the delicate toil of the needle. To Hester Prynne it
might have been a mode of expressing and therefore soothing, the
passion of her life." This "soothing" of her passion would imply an
alteration of and diversion from it. Hawthorne intimates that this rejection of pleasurable needlework "as sin"—an outward conforming to
the "sentence" of the Puritans—is actually a willful act on Hester's
part to preserve her passion in a static state: "This morbid meddling
of conscience with an immaterial matter betokened, it is to be feared,
no genuine and stedfast penitence, but something doubtful, something
that might be deeply wrong, beneath" (190). With no hint of narrative indeterminacy, Hawthorne frankly tells the reader that Hester is
harboring hopes of resuming her passionate relationship with Dimmesdale, hopes that arbitrate against her potential for redemptive change.
"What she compelled herself to believe," Hawthorne reveals, "what,
finally, she reasoned upon, as her motive for continuing a resident of
New England—was half a truth and half a delusion. Here, she said
to herself, had been the scene of her guilt, and here should be the
scene of her earthly punishment; and so, perchance, the torture of her
daily shame would at length purge her soul, and work out another
purity than that which she had lost; more saint-like, because the result of martyrdom" (187). The truth in Hester's reasoning is her desire to remain in stasis, in the scene where guilt and punishment are
mutually complicit in hypostatizing passion. The delusion is Hester's
rationalization that she is remaining in this scene for the purpose of
redemption; Hawthorne relates that Hester has a "loss of faith" (193).
She wanders "in a dismal labyrinth of doubt" (202). "Shame, Despair,
Solitude," Hawthorne writes. "These had been her teachers,—stern
and wild ones,—and they had made her strong, but taught her much
amiss" (298).

Despair is the opposite of hope, and doubt the opposite of faith,
terms meant in *The Scarlet Letter* as in *The Divine Comedy* to be taken
in a spiritual sense. Despair is the state of spiritual cowardice in which
Dante the Pilgrim originally finds himself at the beginning of the
epic. Hope is what Dante's doomed creatures condemned to Hell have
lost—the possibility of spiritual change, of redemption. In *The Inferno*, the logic is such that the damned cannot even know to hope for
redemption; they are absorbed with the emotions that have damned
them. In the circle of the Carnal, Francesca is absorbed with her adul-

terous passion, passion preserved for eternity in a perfect state. The irony is clear. Francesca would prefer a state of unaltered passion to spiritual redemption, and that is a part of her damnation. Hawthorne suggests that Hester imagines such an eternity for herself and Dimmesdale, "although she hid the secret from herself," the feeling that "there dwelt, there trode the feet of one with whom she deemed herself connected in a union, that, unrecognized on earth, would bring them together before the bar of final judgment, and make that their marriage altar, for a joint futurity of endless retribution. Over and over again, the tempter of souls had thrust this idea upon Hester's contemplation, and laughed at the passionate and desperate joy with which she seized and then strove to cast it from her" (186–87).

Hester conspires with the legalistic Puritans to create of her life a formal stasis resistant to change. The elaborate form of her embroidered letter is really no different from "the studied austerity of her dress" (258), which Hester deliberately wears; they are both consciously artful ways of excluding herself from the world of change:

> On this public holiday, as on all other occasions, for seven years past, Hester was clad in a garment of coarse gray cloth. Not more by its hue than by some indescribable peculiarity in its fashion, it had the effect of making her fade personally out of sight and outline; while, again the scarlet letter brought her back from this twilight indistinctness, and revealed her under the moral aspect of its own illumination. Her face, so long familiar to the townspeople, showed the marble quietude which they were accustomed to behold there. It was like a mask; or rather, like the frozen calmness of a dead woman's features; owing this dreary resemblance to the fact that Hester was actually dead, in respect to any claim of sympathy, and had departed out of the world with which she still seemed to mingle. (313)

As Krieger suggests, the appropriate figure of formal stasis is the circle. Hester stands in a "magic circle of ignominy, where the cunning cruelty of her sentence seemed to have fixed her forever" (331). But this circle is cocreated by Puritan law and by Hester; the "magic circle" which "formed itself about her. . . . enveloped its fated wearer; partly by her own reserve, and partly by the instinctive, though no longer so unkindly, withdrawal of her fellow-creatures" (320). Hester is distinct from the frozen Custom-House officials in Hawthorne's Preface because of her potential awareness that her harboring of her passion is a temptation and her moral awareness that her acceptance of formal stasis is a choice. In a crucial passage, Hawthorne describes Hester in a moral and geographical landscape similar to the one in which Dante the Pilgrim finds himself at the outset of *The Divine Comedy*. Hester,

> whose heart had lost its regular and healthy throb, wandered without a clew in the dark labyrinth of mind; now turned aside by an unsurmount-able precipice; now starting back from a deep chasm.[26] There was wild and ghastly scenery all around her, and a home and comfort nowhere. At times, a fearful doubt strove to possess her soul, whether it were not better to send Pearl at once to heaven, and go herself to such futurity as Eternal Justice should provide.
>
> The scarlet letter had not done its office. (261)

Put another way, law cannot mediate passion. Instead, law exacerbates it. Medea-like, Hester risks having her passion supplant her affection for her child.[27] Acceptance of that affection promises a change in Hester's homeostasis; it threatens the artful constraint of her formal art.

The insights in Donna Przybylowicz's study of the spectral in Henry James's fiction can be instructively applied to our understanding of Hester's relationship to Pearl. Przybylowicz's basic approach to the late fiction of Henry James is psychoanalytical and deconstructive. She suggests that a variety of late James protagonists attempt to achieve an inauthentic sense of plenitude through an artful approach to life in which a sense of inner difference is projected onto an other and then destroyed. Przybylowicz explains that

> the central consciousness is not only dissatisfied with his present iden-tity but is also involved in the symbolic recapture and reconstruction of accomplished facts or in the creation of a suppositional past never experienced. This situation is manifested in the objectification of self, which becomes an increasingly obsessive concern. The figure of the other is either concrete, in that the hero or autobiographical persona narcissistically identifies with an actual individual in the external world, or abstract, in that the subject projects his inner desires onto a purely hypothetical self, positioned in the past or present.

The James artist is seeking a "plenitude, a unity of being, never achieved in life," and the repressed internal difference that needs to be projected, hence expunged, is more often than not sexual desire.[28]

This formula takes on a different dimension in the instance of Hester, who projects her own passion onto Pearl as a means of obliterating the difference Pearl would potentially represent in Hester's controlled external universe. Hester subconsciously implicates Pearl as an extension of her own passion so that Pearl can have no counteractive effect on Hester's formal stasis, on Hester's passion preserved by the legal judgment of the scaffold, so "that her whole orb of life, both before and after, was connected with this spot, as with the one point that gave it unity" (328).

Most critics follow Hawthorne's suggestion that Pearl is Hester's opportunity for redemption,[29] but there is a lot of disagreement about the intelligibility in the child.[30] The mistake would be to share in Hester's misapprehension that the child has a preternatural ability to interpret beyond the limits of Hester's guidance. It is exactly this problem of a child's knowledge and its dependence on the adults in her world that is examined by Henry James in the Preface to *What Maisie Knew*, a novel that seems an expanded exploration of Pearl's dilemma in *The Scarlet Letter*. James centers his story on the consciousness of a child, whereas most of the impressions that we receive about Pearl derive from Hester. James's narrative ambition is therefore certainly different. But the dilemma of both children in their coming to understand the world is the same. Maisie is invested "with perceptions easily and almost infinitely quickened"; Pearl is described as acute (202). This ability to pick up hints and intensely interpret is nevertheless hindered by the way adults block knowledge in Maisie's and Pearl's worlds, and it stands to reason that "the infant mind would at the best leave great gaps and voids" in their grasp of meaning. As James points out, "small children have many more perceptions than they have terms to translate them"; Pearl as well as Maisie often gropes literally after the lead of her parents in interpreting the world. For James, Maisie retains "her undestroyed freshness, in other words that vivacity of intelligence by which she indeed does vibrate in the infected air, indeed does flourish in her immoral world," for she eventually transcends the tyranny of misinterpretations that adults in her world force upon her, though it costs her her childhood.[31] For Hawthorne, Pearl is a captive of her mother's interpretations, but she is thus also a potential instrument of her mother's redemption.

The clue to Hester's tyrannizing analysis of Pearl and her conversation is Hester's comment that in Pearl "was visible the tie that united" Hester and Dimmesdale. Pearl was "the living hieroglyphic, in which was revealed the secret they so darkly sought to hide, — all written in this symbol, all plainly manifest, — had there been a prophet or magician skilled to read the character of flame! And Pearl was the one-ness of their being. Be the foregone evil what it might, how could they doubt that their earthly lives and future destinies were conjoined, when they beheld at once the material union, and the spiritual idea, in whom they met, and were to dwell immortally together?" (296). Hester is that artist-magician, rigidifying her daughter's significance into passion, embalming her daughter's identity within a "destiny that had drawn an inviolable circle round about her" (198). There is irony in Hester's thinking that Pearl's identity and actions are autonomous, when they actually offer back to Hester a spectral image of herself. "Day after day," Hawthorne writes, Hester "looked fearfully into the child's expanding nature; ever dreading to detect some dark and wild peculiarity, that should correspond with the guiltiness to which she owed her being," only to discover that "throughout all . . . there was a trait of passion, a certain depth of hue, which she never lost" (194–95). Hester finds what she looks for. She even artfully constructs Pearl's dress "forcibly" to remind the world "of that red symbol which sears her bosom" (215). And Hester looks into Pearl's eyes as if "looking at her own image in them" only to see Arthur Dimmesdale's face "fiend-like, full of smiling malice . . . as if an evil spirit possessed the child, and had just then peeped forth in mockery" (201). Hester sees in Pearl a reflected image of her own and Dimmesdale's guilty passion, and she subconsciously suppresses the affection present in her child so that Pearl will conform to her mother's image of herself.

Hester assumes that it is some force external to herself and out of her control that isolates her daughter from other children; Pearl is full of "enmity and Passion . . . by inalienable right" (198); Hester is "heart-smitten at this bewildering and baffling spell" and "felt like one who has evoked a spirit, but, by some irregularity in the process of conju-ration, has failed to win the master-word" (197). The master-word is *sympathy*, which Hester has repressed in herself so as to maintain her passion and which she has subconsciously suppressed in her daughter. The mother does great disservice to the daughter by imagining an au-tonomous spirit in Pearl that Hester has herself in great part evoked. Hester at one point asks Pearl what she is, and Pearl responds with the simple literal fact as she knows it: " 'Oh, I am your little Pearl.' " Hester asks again, " 'Art thou my child, in very truth?' " Pearl again simply reveals what she has been taught by her mother to be true, " 'Yes; I am little Pearl!' " Hawthorne comments that Hester did not "put the question altogether idly . . . for such was Pearl's wonderful intelligence, that her mother half doubted whether she were not acquainted with the secret spell of her existence, and might not now reveal herself" (201). Hester at this moment projects her own thoughts onto a spectral other, investing Pearl with a supernatural ability to provide answers, while, in reality, Pearl is actually Hester's echo, although she struggles to find the master-word to her own identity from Hester's words. Hester then makes a startling revelation. " 'Thou art no child of mine!' " a comment that could unsettle the very basis of Pearl's identity as she knows it, and it is interesting that Hester offers this comment "half-playfully," with an impulse eerily reminiscent of the inconsistency that Hester has possibly engendered in her daughter: "It was often the case that a sportive impulse came over her, in the midst of her deepest suffering" (202).

Hester proceeds to confront Pearl as if she were a spectral other, asking Pearl as if she were an autonomous spirit the very questions about Pearl's identity that she as Pearl's mother should be providing. Pearl establishes her separate identity by claiming her own lack of knowledge and her dependence on her mother for that knowledge: " 'Tell me, mother,' said the child seriously, . . . 'Do thou tell me!' " Hester answers with the conventional catechismic response that Pearl has a heavenly father, but Pearl notices her mother's hesitation, and, on the basis of this hesitation, picks up the hint and experimentally denies this origin. Acute Pearl is groping after her mother's lead; her reply is based on her mother's hesitation. But Hester responds to Pearl as if Pearl were again offering autonomous replies from a supernatural source. She asks again about Pearl's origin, and Pearl again replies, " 'It is thou that must tell me!' " (202).

Pearl's refusal to say the catechism in the succeeding chapter, "The Governor's Hall," results from her mother's destabilization of Pearl's identity in this previous conversation. Hester cannot resolve her daughter's query, Hawthorne suggests, because she was "herself in a dismal labyrinth of doubt" (202). Hester inculcates this doubt in her daughter and then interprets the doubt parroted back as evidence that Pearl is a demon. In the Governor's Hall, Hester sees herself in a convex mirror in which the scarlet letter is "the most prominent feature of her appearance. In truth, she seemed absolutely hidden behind it." Hester's imagination is that convex mirror that has repressed all elements within her but the scarlet letter, which is evidence of her passion, and that must therefore also see, instead of the image of her child, the image of "an imp" (208). Hawthorne likewise finds his imagination in "The Custom-House" "a tarnished mirror" (148) because the frozen stasis of the officials in the Custom-House has suppressed the affection within him.

Roger Chillingworth and Hester make the mistake, in their final meeting together, of denying their own responsibility to exercise ethical authority and abdicating this responsibility instead to fate. Chillingworth, involved himself in repressing passion (264), decides that the "black flower" of "fate" has been the "dark necessity" motivating his torture of Arthur Dimmesdale. This black flower connects with the prison, the black flower of civilization; the link implies that the punishment Chillingworth is attributing to a supernatural force is instead of human devise. Hester also relinquishes her responsibility to the force of fate. She tells Chillingworth that neither she nor the law can alter the significance of her letter: " 'Were I worthy to be quit of it, it would fall away of its own nature, or be transformed into something that should speak a different purport" (263). Such magical thinking assumes that life is subject to external forces over which people have no control.

Hester's denial of responsibility explains her subsequent response to her daughter. When Pearl transforms the scarlet letter on her own bosom from scarlet to "freshly green" (271), Hester avoids the implication that the letter can be transformed. She once more reverts to the language of the law, to catechism, although her query shifts to the origin of the letter. Pearl again responds to her mother's question literally; she mentions her acquaintance with the letter as she has been dutifully taught to learn it in the hornbook. But Hester professes what Hawthorne calls "a morbid desire" to push her daughter to deeper interpretations. The daughter's epistemological growth can be witnessed by her ability to draw an analogy between her mother's letter and the minister's hand over his heart, but when the mother proceeds to invest her daughter with preternatural discernment, Pearl replies, " 'I have told all I know' " (272). Hester suddenly seems to see in her daughter a dignity and a difference. She suddenly wonders whether telling her daughter the truth would help her "overcome the passion" that is "imprisoned" in her "tomb-like heart" (273). But instead of seizing this opportunity for redemption by revealing the truth, Hester is "false to the symbol on her bosom"; she cannot pay "the price of the child's sympathy" (274).

For Hester, the price of subjecting her passion to the truth of Pearl's ethical authority, of her "spiritual instinct," would be the unwelcome transformation of her passion. If Hester recognizes her daughter's ethical authority, she allows Pearl to be different, not captive to the suppressive letter of the law. Hester "knew that there was love in the child's heart, although it mostly revealed itself in passion" (216). But by submitting the truth of the scarlet letter to the authority of Pearl's compassion rather than to Puritan law, Hester could potentially overcome her passion, and this is not something she wants to do, as we see in her succeeding scene with Dimmesdale. In that scene, Hester envelops Dimmesdale within her own sacred circle, and she claims, as Charlotte Stant does to Prince Amerigo in *The Golden Bowl*, that their union will have a consecration of its own. This scene must be read in light of Hester's denial of her daughter's autonomy. Hester calls Pearl "silly" as the obfuscating adults in Maisie's world call her "stupid," deliberately obscuring the moral realities that the children are coming to comprehend, these children "drawing some stray fragrance of an ideal across the scent of selfishness, by sowing on barren strands, through the mere fact of presence, the seed of the moral life." [32]

Hester wishes to consecrate her passion, and she can do so only by denying her own sense of ethics and by rejecting it equally in her daughter. Only by ignoring her own ethical sense can she compel Dimmesdale by a magical sort of rhetoric—"fixing her deep eyes on the minister's, and instinctively exercising a magnetic power over a spirit so shattered and subdued"—to ignore the ethical consequences of a real historical moment in time. Hester claims that Dimmesdale is "free" and should "exchange this false life of thine for a true one" (288–89), but to affirm the law of passion as true is arbitrary just as it is to derive "truth" from the law. "Real" truth—ethical truth—cannot deny the legitimacy of the historical moment of Hester and Dimmesdale's adulterous act and the sorrow that issued from it, as well as the daughter. Pearl is the only one who can escape the consequences of this historical moment. "'There is no law, nor reverence for authority'" in Pearl, as Roger Chillingworth remarks (233). Since Pearl's fate is not inscribed by law, she can potentially escape the entrapment of passion. "'Will it not come of its own accord, when I am a woman grown?'" asks Pearl of her mother about the scarlet letter. Hester should acknowledge to Pearl that the scarlet letter came to her as a result of choice; Pearl must realize that passionate action is a choice and therefore not inevitable.

Hester accepts the consequences of historical moment when she returns to "a more real life" in New England at the end of the novel. After a period of time abroad, leaving Pearl in Europe, "Hester Prynne had returned, and taken up her long-forsaken shame" (343). This phrase recalls Hawthorne's move in the Preface to take shame upon himself;

both decisions indicate a more real life than would be possible through the acceptance of external authority as the arbiter of one's actions. Hawthorne emphasizes that Hester's return to America marks a significant behavioral change from her initial actions there. Hester formerly experienced "her sin" and "her sorrow" through the arbitration of external law; she now returns to this scene "yet to be her penitence." The "yet" indicates that her acceptance of responsibility for her own actions is still to come. In addition, Hawthorne emphasizes that Hester returns "of her own free will" (344) to point out that Hester is only now taking responsibility for her own behavior. Will to regulate their own behavior is what the doomed Paolo and Francesca in the damned circle of Dante's Hell lack. And it is only when an individual accepts the responsibility for self-regulation in place of the substitutive external authority of the law that that individual can be truly "real" or truly "free" in any sense.

Hawthorne's conviction that ethics should be a matter of self-regulation guides his complex dramatization of the dynamics of public rhetoric in *The Scarlet Letter*. This view of the rhetorical process suggests that Hawthorne was responding directly to the movement of rhetorical enthusiasm popular during his own time, something no critic of the novel has observed to date.[33] That Hawthorne was intimately acquainted with the contemporary rhetorical movement is indisputable. Not only did Hawthorne study and temporarily board with the prominent American scholar of rhetoric Samuel Newman at Bowdoin, but Hawthorne's transcendentalist acquaintances were either influenced by or prominent within the mainstream of contemporary rhetorical instruction. William Ellery Channing II (1818–1901), whom Hawthorne identifies in "The Custom-House" as one of the transcendentalist group with whom he engaged in conversations, was the nephew of William Ellery and Edward Tyrell Channing. Edward Tyrell was the third Boylston Professor of Rhetoric and Oratory at Harvard from 1819 to 1851 and also founding editor of the *North American Review*. E. T. Channing taught many of America's great literati who came within Hawthorne's ken: Emerson, James Russell Lowell, Oliver Wendell Holmes, and Thoreau were taught by Channing, to name a few,[34] and Hawthorne may have known of Emerson's popular lecture "Eloquence," which extolled the virtue of oratory.[35] Hawthorne also was familiar with William Ellery Channing I (1780–1842), for whom Hawthorne's future sister-in-law Elizabeth Peabody was a secretary for a time.[36] The first William Ellery Channing was a Unitarian minister, who was praised in the periodicals for his virtuous rhetoric, the type that his brother Edward preached about at Harvard. Hawthorne could not have missed the constant periodical praise for William's eloquence or the ever-present praise for and faith in public oratory that had swept his own culture: one need only turn to the pages of the periodicals in which Hawthorne published in the 1830s and 1840s to find such praise and to discover the source for Hawthorne's description of Arthur Dimmesdale's eloquence.

One of the prominent features in columns of rhetoric in the periodicals of Hawthorne's time was an analogy drawn between rhetorical eloquence and music. This analogy was new, and it seems to have had its origin about 1827 with the publication of a book on rhetorical elocution by a Philadelphia doctor, James Rush. Its lengthy title began *Philosophy of the Human Voice* and concluded *a brief Analysis of Song and Recitative*. It is given lengthy coverage in the *North American Review* of July 1829, a periodical that Marion L. Kesselring notes Hawthorne checked out from the Salem Atheneum in the late 1820s, although this particular volume is not noted.[37] It is nevertheless a strange coincidence that the author of the article begins by taking "all shame to ourselves." He expresses regret that Rush's work had heretofore gone unmentioned in the periodical and praises Rush's work as both "novel" and "a pretty serious matter."[38] By the 1830s, connections between music and eloquence in periodicals became standard. In the December 1835 issue of the *New England Magazine*, in which Hawthorne published "Sketches from Memory, by a Pedestrian. No. II," the writer describes the statesman and orator Edward Everett as touching "the heart with the power of a master who draws music from a many-stringed instrument." Here the orator is described as the music master who elicits music, but the orator himself is described equally as an instrument, although as "no oaten pipe," and "no iron trumpet," but instead as a "sweet voice."[39] If Hawthorne read the essay "Mr. Forrest's Oration" in the *Democratic Review* as this chapter on *The Scarlet Letter* suggests, he would also have seen "immortal eloquence" described as a "heaven-drawn song" (54). In *The Scarlet Letter*, Hawthorne clearly makes this connection between eloquence and music. Dimmesdale's voice is described as an instrument "sweet, tremulous, but powerful" (215). In fact, Dimmesdale's voice is the thing most emphasized about him. After making his pact to leave America with Hester, Dimmesdale wonders whether "Heaven should see fit to transmit the grand and solemn music of its oracles through so foul an organ-pipe as he" (312).

Hawthorne also compares "the minister's very peculiar voice" to "all other music" (327).

Hawthorne makes a point also in *The Scarlet Letter* of emphasizing Dimmesdale's pulpit eloquence as unusual and tacitly criticizes the Puritan ministers who cannot adapt their discourse to their audience. Even the friendly Reverend John Wilson subordinates his "kind and genial spirit" to "his intellectual gifts" (173). Dimmesdale's reverend elders have "soberer reputations" because of their isolation from manhood in "abstruse lore." Their concern with the "doctrinal" and "weary toil among their books" has isolated them from human emotion so that they do not have "tongues of flame," the ability to address "the human brotherhood in the heart's native language" (239–40). Hawthorne's distinction between Dimmesdale's rhetorical eloquence and the lesser abilities of his peers seems likewise inspired by the proselytizing nature of articles on rhetoric in contemporary periodicals. The *Knickerbocker* ran a series for several decades beginning in the late 1830s on pulpit eloquence. Its major intent was to point out a lack in ministerial eloquence and to praise and define eloquence through portraits of eloquent ministers, thus encouraging more of it. As the gregarious editor of the *Knickerbocker* Lewis Gaylord Clark remarked in one of his popular Editors' Tables, "How can the preacher hope to influence his hearers, when, to adopt a theatrical phrase, he merely 'walks through his part?' No matter how important his inculcations, or how clear his arguments; if both be not enforced by a *manner* bearing some proportion to the nature of the lessons or principles set forth, many hearers must be utterly indifferent to them. They have not been made to feel, by the earnest eloquence of the speaker—that true eloquence which springs from feeling, and without which all attempts to catch the *aura populuris* will prove unavailing." [40]

Striking also is the resemblance between contemporary descriptions of rhetoric as inspirational and magnetizing and Hawthorne's similar descriptions of Dimmesdale's speeches. In both instances rhetoric is analogized to magic. Descriptions in contemporary periodicals are often rhapsodic and awash with purple prose. The congregation of a certain Reverend Daniel Sharp "have seen him turn from his manuscript, first to one side of the pulpit, then to another, revealing to all, eloquence kindling in his eye, flashing on his cheek, burning through every vein, vitalizing every muscle, enlarging and beautifying his noble and graceful form with preternatural splendor, while his long speaking arms, obedient to his intense conviction and harmonious with the mellow thunder of his tones, waved an awful majesty of thought into his spell-bound audience."[41] When a Dr. Bascom speaks from the pulpit, "what a cataract of jewells, flashing and pouring with inexhaustible gorgeousness, do we behold!" His words seem to the congregation "like repeated bolts of irresistible power."[42] The eloquence of the Reverend Sylvester Larned operates "as by an invisible wand," and in Daniel Webster's rhetoric "touch and demolition, as if magic were employed, seem indissolubly associated in the progress of the work."[43]

Hawthorne replicates this tone of rhapsody in his description of Dimmesdale's eloquence and its effects. Hawthorne seems purposefully to render this description from the perception of Dimmesdale's congregation, hence from the viewpoint of the effect of such rhetoric on a rhetorical audience. Dimmesdale's congregation responds to his eloquence as to a "high spell." Hawthorne writes that "according to their united testimony, never had man spoken in so wise, so high, and so holy a spirit, as he spake that day; nor had inspiration ever breathed through mortal lips more evidently than it did through his." As Reverend Sharp turns from his manuscript and out of inspiration speaks extemporaneously, so, too, the influence of Dimmesdale's inspiration is seen as "descending upon him, and possessing him, and continually lifting him out of the written discourse that lay before him" (332). As Sharp's form is perceived to have preternatural splendor, to Dimmesdale's congregation "it was as if an angel, in his passage to the skies, has shaken his bright wings over the people for an instant" (333) — such "was the enthusiasm kindled in the auditors by that high strain of eloquence which was yet reverberating in their ears" (334).

In his description of Dimmesdale's features, Hawthorne also replicates the typical periodical convention of addressing the speaker's countenance as a part of his eloquence. We have already read of the Reverend Sharp's "noble and graceful form" and "long speaking arms." The Reverend Larned has a "face of blended sweetness and intellectual nobleness. 'His body,'" says his biographer, "'was the appropriate habitation of his mind, combining in just proportions, dignity, grace and strength.'"[44] In particular, a description of William Ellery Channing I that appeared in the May 1843 issue of the *Democratic Review*, which also featured Hawthorne's "Celestial Railroad,"[45] recalls, in part at least, the phrenological description of Arthur Dimmesdale. "The upper part of his face," according to the essayist on Channing, was eminently characterized by intellect, while his mouth gave indications of a heart profoundly tender. His eye, with its overhanging brow, shone in gentle light, clear and beautiful, yet strong and forcible. The forehead, remarkably expanded, seemed filled with thought. His hair was thrown off on one side, and he uniformly wore it long; it was very graceful and waving. The whole expression of the face breathed a mild benignity, a gentle charity, and a profound sympathy with the joys and sufferings of man. It was a countenance that affected you with perfect confidence: it was trusting and humble, yet full of freedom.[46]

Dimmesdale is described as "a person of very striking aspect, with a white, lofty, and impending brow, large, brown, melancholy eyes, and a mouth which, unless when he forcibly compressed it, was apt to be tremulous, expressing both nervous sensibility and a vast power of self-restraint" (174). There is an interesting similar note of implied repression in the description of Channing: "Chiefly was he noted by the imperturbableness of his life, engrafted upon a constitution nervously sensitive, but subdued into an incomparable moderation."[47]

The most significant underlying feature of all these contemporary periodical descriptions of rhetoric is the expressed confidence that all eloquence will of necessity be truthful. This precept can be referred to as the Quintilian principle, which was revived by eighteenth-century Scottish rhetoricians George Campbell and Hugh Blair from classical times and which accordingly became a persistent feature of American popular rhetoric, a derivative and often simplified version of Scottish rhetoric. The Quintilian principle, as discussed in the several preceding chapters of this book, implied that only virtuous rhetoric could be eloquent. As one contemporary periodicalist expressed it, "no master in any department of mental greatness can be graceful, imaginative, or original, except so far as he is truthful."[48] Dimmesdale, of course, is agonized by public confidence in his truthfulness and likewise by his own deceitfulness because of "his genuine impulse to adore the truth" (241).

One of the more critical and elusive issues to resolve, then, concerning rhetoric, is the exact constitution of what these contemporary periodicals so confidently assumed to be truth. Rhetorical scholar Barnet Baskerville has observed of the era that "closely allied to the concept of eloquence as arising from the character of the speaker is the idea that truth is essential to eloquence." Baskerville also confirms that the periodicals unswervingly assumed that "truth, if given free currency, will always beat out falsehood and error." More important,

Baskerville observes that periodical remarks imply "that truth is readily ascertainable and has the same appearance to all men." His speculation about how this can be is of particular significance. For Baskerville, "a possible explanation of this certainty about the nature of truth is that these writers are using the term in a metaphysical sense. They are talking not about probability or demonstrable fact, but about external verities, intuitively perceived." [49]

From Baskerville's observations, one can infer that the period revitalized classical rhetoric in a very particular way. In the rejection of probability for eternal verities, these theorists assumed a Platonic absolutism rather than an Aristotelian probabilistic basis for rhetorical truth. Plato explains in the *Gorgias*, one of the two Platonic dialogues that attacks rhetorical sophistry, that "the moral artist, the true orator. . . . will always fix his mind upon this aim: the engendering of justice in the souls of his fellow-citizens and the eradication of injustice, the planting of self-control and the uprooting of uncontrol, the entrance of virtue and the exit of vice." [50]

American periodicalists writing on rhetoric, however, seemed to revise the Platonic absolutism mentioned in the *Gorgias* in favor of the eternal verities of Christianity. These were charity, which in a sense implied a tempering of justice, and sympathy, which suggested an emotional bonding between humans rather than intellectual reason as the basis for self-regulation. This American view of rhetoric seems to imply an uneasiness with the intellect that could too easily be subverted into the logic of authority instead of used in the regulation of self. Instead, intuitive emotions as the basis for ethics were perceived to turn one inward toward self-regulation out of the compassion engendered by feeling. As one essayist writes in his definition of eloquence, "He who would stir up the soul must have a calm, sympathizing heart. The man whose sympathies are with common humanity, whose heart is moved by pure benevolence, breathes thoughts that will never die. Like the silent dews, they descend in the bosom to cheer, to bless and to save. The breath of true life is thus felt in the heart. Such a writer blends genius with humanity, and is destined to sway the multitude and urge them on to deeds of mercy and unending glory." [51]

Reason also seems subordinate to emotion as the eternal verity motivating the force of eloquence in *The Scarlet Letter*. Hawthorne writes that Dimmesdale's "voice was tremulously sweet, rich, deep, and broken. The feeling that it so evidently manifested, rather than the direct purport of the words, caused it to vibrate within all hearts, and brought the listeners into one accord of sympathy" (175). Hawthorne notes that it is the emotional undertone in Dimmesdale's oratory rather than the logic of its words that gave the minister "his most appropriate power." It was "the complaint of a human heart, sorrow-laden, perchance guilty, telling its secret, whether of guilt or sorrow, to the great heart of mankind; beseeching its sympathy or forgiveness, — at every moment, — in each accent, — and never in vain!" (327).

Dimmesdale's rhetoric, nevertheless, is a very problematic instance of American eloquence. It is in fact a subtle perversion of the rhetoric described in the contemporary periodicals, for Dimmesdale's rhetoric is motivated by selfishness rather than selflessness, and it therefore only mimics — although with dangerous success — the genuine emotional ethos of benevolent rhetorical truth. Michel Small's essay on the subtle manipulativeness of Arthur Dimmesdale's rhetoric portrays with penetrating accuracy the way that Dimmesdale uses language "to manipulate rather than genuinely to master potentially dangerous internal and external situations." Small implicitly suggests that Dimmesdale's danger is his passion. When Dimmesdale uses language to recover self-esteem and to prevent being exposed as an adulterer, he and his language become "temporarily enslaved to desire." Although Small is apparently unaware of the expectations for ethical rhetoric dominant during Hawthorne's time, he apparently intuits that Hawthorne intends us to see emotional ethos as a potential for rhetoric, since he suggests that Dimmesdale's rhetoric has features that should be able to "break down the isolation of others and lead them to recognize their own brotherhood." And we do. We have already seen the variety of ways in which Dimmesdale's pulpit eloquence resembles the ethical prescriptions of Hawthorne's time. It is adapted to its audience, it is musical, inspirational, magical, and addressed to the heart of the congregation with the truthful message of Christian sympathy. But at this point Dimmesdale's rhetoric deviates from contemporary expectations because "the gift of eloquence does not lead him into fruitful connection with others, but rather, like Chillingworth's intellectual gifts, comes to serve those fears and wishes that isolate him." [52]

Again, the fear and wish that isolates Dimmesdale is his passion. Small shrewdly perceives that Dimmesdale unconsciously uses language "to release impulses from . . . the minister's 'strong animal nature.'" [53] Just as Hester's red letter functions as an authoritative punishment that allows her secretly to harbor her passion, Dimmesdale's eloquence, by aligning itself with the authority of religious law, both enables passion and allows Dimmesdale to avoid accepting personal responsibility for his adulterous sin. Dimmesdale's religious language articulates that sin only in a vague and general sense. Dimmesdale "has spoken the very truth, and transformed it into the veriest falsehood," by "making the avowal of a guilty conscience," but in the form of a "vague confession" (242) that he knows will be interpreted by his audience as external to him, as part of a codified religious form, the confession of sin. Dimmesdale uses the "iron framework" (223) of his religious creed as a shield to avoid public censure. This is obviously an external shield; Hawthorne's Dantesque pilgrim is paralyzed in "Cowardice which invariably drew him back, with her tremulous gripe, just when the other impulse had hurried him to the verge of a disclosure" (245).[54]

Plato discloses in the *Gorgias* that virtuous eloquence should compel from the audience "the planting of self-control and the uprooting of uncontrol, the entrance of virtue and the exit of vice." Ironically, Dimmesdale's eloquence promotes passion rather than compassion. Since Dimmesdale's language is riveted to law, it implicates itself within the dialectic of law/passion and, within this dialectic, it will be passion rather than emotional ethos that is inevitably compelled. Thus, on hearing Dimmesdale's eloquence, "the virgins of his church grew pale around him, victims of a passion so imbued with religious sentiment that they imagined it to be all religion, and brought it openly, in their white bosoms, as their most acceptable sacrifice before the altar" (241). The antecedent for the pronoun *it* in this passage is curiously complicating for the reference ambiguously alludes on first reading to both religious sentiment and passion; it is the fusion between the two that suggests how passion thrives within religious repression but in a perverted and repressed form. This response to Dimmesdale's eloquence is hardly what Hawthorne's contemporary rhetorical theorists had in mind.

The reason that Dimmesdale's eloquence is so dangerous is that it provokes the emotion so valued by Hawthorne's contemporary rhetorical theorists, but in the service of law and passion. It makes total sense that Hawthorne would portray the dangerous potential of an emotionally charged rhetoric to mystify its audience, for, in doing so, he would have warned against the facile assumptions of the Quintilian principle, a principle that could be understood to place responsibility for self-regulation on the audience rather than on the orator. This was the way E. T. Channing interpreted the principle in his Harvard lectures. He thought that he could coerce honest rhetoric from his

students by portraying Americans as a shrewd audience with the un-
canny ability to penetrate sophistry. Channing felt that Americans, in
contrast to the gullible Greeks, could not be seduced by flattery or
diverted from sound judgment: "No festival eloquence will do then,
no vain mockery of art, no treacherous allurements from a close and
sober inspection of the truths upon which we are to act. We want then
the orator who feels and acts with us; in whom we can confide even
better than in ourselves; who is filled with our cause, and looks at it
with solemnity and wisdom." [55] This faith in the discernment of the
contemporary audience carried over in the popular periodicals. In the
December 1834 *New England Magazine*, a brief essay with this point appeared only thirty pages removed from an installment of Hawthorne's
"Story Teller." [56] "A modern audience demands better eloquence," the
periodicalist emphatically states, and a "greater refinement of argument is required," although "the heart is as liable to be moved now, as
it was two thousand years ago." [57] It is ironic, given Hawthorne's portrayal of the complicity between institutionalized religion and law in
The Scarlet Letter, that the periodicalist goes on to say that this superior
alacrity on the part of the audience and orator is brought about in large
part by Christianity.

Hawthorne treats this contemporary faith in audience in *The Scarlet
Letter* with irony and warns of its potential danger. As we have seen,
Dimmesdale's initial faith in his congregation's ability to discern his sin
is one that Hawthorne's contemporary audience would have shared.
But it is Dimmesdale's faith in the ability of his audience to regulate
his actions that allows him to rationalize his own evasion of responsibility. He cannot believe that his audience does not discern his falsity
and punish him. He is bemused although relieved when they do not.

Hawthorne's comments about the American community as rhetorical audience in *The Scarlet Letter* are dichotomous. On one hand, the
contemporary valorization of emotional ethos as the way to truth is
confirmed, for when the community "forms its judgment, as it usually
does on the intuitions of its great and warm heart, the conclusions thus
attained are often so profound and so unerring, as to possess the character of truths supernaturally revealed" (226). But when the community
is called upon to make law, to regulate the behavior of others rather
than to sympathize, it succumbs to flattery rather than reason, and it
becomes "despotic in its temper; it is capable of denying common justice, when too strenuously demanded as a right; but quite as frequently
it awards more than justice, when the appeal is made, as despots love

to have it made, entirely to its generosity" (257). For Hawthorne as for Plato, the rhetorical audience seems incapable of regulating the orator. Further, although Plato entertains the possibility that the audience may perhaps be capable of being brought to virtue, Hawthorne finds this point questionable in the society described in *The Scarlet Letter*. Certainly Dimmesdale's eventual confession of adultery does not bring his audience to virtue. Beyond the truth of their initially sympathetic response, the audience's judgmental interpretations of Dimmesdale's confession begin to splinter, and the audience mystifies Dimmesdale's act so as to evade responsibility for their own regulation by perpetuating the version of Dimmesdale as authority and thus Dimmesdale/ religious law as external regulator.

Even so, the ideal result of rhetorical eloquence for Hawthorne *should* be the compelling of emotional caritas, which in turn would impel the audience toward ethical self-regulation. It is on the basis of this ideal for public rhetoric that Dimmesdale fails his congregation, because by orating under the external regulation of the law, Dimmesdale imprisons the language of emotional truth within the suffocating grip of passion, which aborts the ameliorative process that an emotion elicited free of passion might promote. But Hawthorne even more emphatically wants to suggest that Dimmesdale's vague rhetoric fails Dimmesdale most of all, for, by evading the responsibility for self-regulation which would be assumed from honest confession, Dimmesdale lives the dead life of the company men in the Custom-House; he finds his life " 'all falsehood!—all emptiness!—all death!' " (283). He also fails his family, for Hawthorne at least extends the regulatory purview of rhetoric to a familial sphere of influence. Dimmesdale's confession of adultery catalyzes both Hester's and Pearl's transformations. They cannot mystify Dimmesdale's confession because they know it to be true, Hester, of course, for the obvious reason of shared experience, Pearl from the conclusions she has drawn from a pattern of observation, perhaps, but also from emotional intuition. " 'So let me make haste to take my shame upon me,' " Dimmesdale declares (337), and, when he does so, Dimmesdale compels from Hester the virtue of self-control and self-regulation by his own example, and he also frees emotion from passion so that his daughter is free to see that there is an ethical choice to be made between sympathy and selfish passion.

Small is dubious that Dimmesdale is ultimately converted, since he believes the conversion to be represented by Dimmesdale's last sermon, a sermon which "in one stroke . . . symbolically gains" for Dimmesdale an obfuscating amalgam of "sexual and spiritual love."[58] But this is to mislocate Dimmesdale's conversion, which actually takes place when Dimmesdale accepts his responsibility for self-regulation by taking the shame of his actions upon himself. It is irrelevant to our understanding of Dimmesdale's confession that the larger community willfully misinterprets it. Instead, we are to see this confession in light of what it does for Dimmesdale. Hawthorne suggests that we hurt mostly ourselves when we are not truthful to ourselves and also those intimate to us who are engaged with us in relationships of mutual trust. Regulation of our behavior should begin at home. Public rhetoric is easily subverted, and only by accepting responsibility for our own behavior can we escape the prison-house dialectic of repressive law and selfish, isolating passion and set in motion the ethical process of regulating our behavior through our emotional apprehension of the common bond of humanity.

4

No More in This World: An Instance of Moral Rhetoric in *Adventures of Huckleberry Finn*

❧❧

"When you lie, it makes you feel in charge of your life. Telling lies is very seductive to orphans. I know," Dr. Larch wrote, "I know because I tell them, too. I love to lie. When you lie, you feel as if you have cheated fate—your own, and everybody's else's."

—JOHN IRVING, *Cider House Rules*

Two novels in this study about the truth-telling capacity of language begin in first-person narration, Brown's *Wieland* and Mark Twain's *Adventures of Huckleberry Finn*, but perhaps no two major American novels told in first person begin with such apparently dissimilar views of truthful language as do these two. On one hand, the Advertisement in *Wieland* promises a novel that will illustrate "some important branches of the moral constitution of man" (3). The frontispiece in *Adventures of Huckleberry Finn*, on the other, promises to banish any person "attempting to find a moral in it."[1] Clara Wieland begins her tale with a statement of didactic purpose, to "inculcate the duty of avoiding deceit" (5). Huck begins his tale with a stoic acceptance that practically everybody lies. Whereas Clara has clear reason for telling her story, which is purportedly to indict lying, Huck is ostensibly given none.

But the difference between these openings is perhaps one of narrative technique, not of perspective on truthful language, and Brockden Brown's more didactic preface is simply replaced by Mark Twain's more comic indirection. Huck does indeed share Clara's absorption with deception, but the concern is expressed more obliquely, betraying itself subconsciously. Beginnings of novels give the reader a first important glimpse into an author's or character's central thoughts. In the opening paragraph of *Adventures of Huckleberry Finn*, Huck ponders the subject of deception, which is all the more striking because Huck is apparently unaware that he is preoccupied with the subject:

> You don't know about me, without you have read a book by the name of "The Adventures of Tom Sawyer," but that ain't no matter. That book was made by Mr. Mark Twain, and he told the truth, mainly. There was things which he stretched, but mainly he told the truth. That is nothing. I never seen anybody but lied, one time or another, without it was aunt Polly, or the widow, or maybe Mary. Aunt Polly—Tom's aunt Polly, she is—and Mary, and the widow Douglas, is all told about in that book—which is mostly a true book; with some stretchers, as I said before. (1)

Some readers assume that Mark Twain is standing behind Huck in this passage and throughout the book with only the pretext of a thinly veiled persona. Henry Nash Smith contributes his important claim that "Mark Twain's satiric method requires that Huck be a mask for the writer, not a fully developed character."[2] This may be why Huck's remarks about lies in the beginning of the novel have seldom been taken seriously. If it is Mark Twain's muffled voice in the opening, Huck's reference to truth and lies can be brushed aside as part of the conventional humor that Mark Twain uses to ingratiate his new book with his audience, *Adventures of Huckleberry Finn* placed alongside its popular predecessor, *The Adventures of Tom Sawyer*, the mention of stretchers placing both books within the comic convention of the tall tale. In addition, the Mark Twain who chats with his audience through Huck can be imagined as the garrulous storyteller who likes "to swap lies" with his lifelong friend, the Reverend Joe Twichell,[3] and who sees lies as a delightful reprieve from the usual run of social hypocrisy.

But it is equally plausible that Twain intended Huck to have a separate fictional integrity. If so, Huck's words in this instance reflect seriously on his character. And Huck's first words are about truth and lies. He mentions truth three times, stretching the truth twice, and lying once, in the pivotal sentence of the paragraph: "I never seen anybody but lied, one time or another." Thus Huck appears to have an abiding concern for the ethos of language. There are recent critics who have addressed and judged this possibility, and they do so in one of several ways: they either analyze Huck's skeptical views on truthful language as a type of skeptical realism, or they determine that Huck actually betrays a longing for and belief in truthful language which Mark Twain undercuts as a false romantic delusion. Forrest Robinson suggests, for example, that Mark Twain is certain that "all people lie all the time, but they lie first in denying this law of their nature." People's great self-deception is that "they actually imagine themselves honest."[4] Thus in Robinson's view, Huck shows himself one step ahead of his culture when he observes that everyone lies, and Huck continues to be so until he himself is unaware of his own dishonesty.

Arguably, however, Huck is not just aware of the ubiquity of the deception of others, but he unwittingly reveals himself to be disturbed by it as well. In this view, he can be interpreted in the novel's opening commentary to be going out of his way to vindicate Mark Twain by suggesting that Twain at least mainly "told the truth." It is true that Huck's conscious, conventional self—that is, the part of him that has been trained and structured by his cultural environment—accepts lies with matter-of-fact braggadocio. But the sheer presence of the opening comments on language suggests that Huck is troubled on a subconscious level by the prevalence of liars in his culture. Lee Mitchell is one recent critic who has noted Huck's concern about lying. He concludes, however, that Huck is suffering from romantic delusions because of it. Mitchell claims that Huck's " 'romantic' faith in a unique being somehow independent of behavior—of an inner self untouched by its expression—remains steadfast right through to the closing 'Yours Truly,' " and he views this assumption as patently absurd. In Mitchell's view, Twain clearly shows in the novel that language creates rather than reflects reality. Huck errs greatly when he assumes "that words mirror reality rather than constitute the way things are."[5]

Critics like Mitchell and Robinson differ radically about the nature and legitimacy of Huck's feelings for language in the novel, but they converge, oddly, in their assumption that Twain as author implies that lying is an inevitable social and existential condition. In Mitchell's view, Twain implies in *Adventures of Huckleberry Finn* that language creates reality, and for Robinson, Twain's theme in the novel is that it is in the nature of human beings that their language must inevitably diverge from that reality. Both assume that Twain suggests that honest language is impossible.

The rhetorical idealism that implies the possibility of honest language is also no doubt antagonistic to current thoughts on the novel. J. Hillis Miller claims, for example, that the novel can appeal to no transcendent value. The epic, "with its eternal repetition of celestial archetypes," can "put human time in relation to the end of time or to an escape from time." But the novel marks "a turning to relations between persons as the chief, if not exclusive, source of authentic life for the individual." And human relations are "unable to escape the necessary defects, disturbances, indistinctions, and confusions of any subjective mirroring of reality." Honesty in human relations is therefore impossible, and the novel form which reflects human relations marks a corresponding "fading of faith in celestial models or archetypes which would give a narrative stability and ground it in the transcendently real."[6]

Yet just such a rhetorical philosophy grounded in the "transcendently real" and in the ethos of honesty was popular in nineteenth-century America at the time when Twain was writing *Adventures of Huckleberry Finn* and at the time when Twain was good friends with one of its most ardent spokespersons.[7] Eighteenth- and nineteenth-century rhetorical idealism, which had filtered into American popular culture as demonstrated in the Introduction to this study, asserted that human communication could approach the level of the transcendently real. It asserted that individuals could transcend the boundaries of self-interest and unite in a communion of truth. Human relations could, in essence, transcend the limits of human relations. One of the principal transmitters of this rhetorical philosophy to nineteenth-century America was Twain's friend Henry Ward Beecher. Beecher found a celestial archetype for honest communication in Christianity, as one can see from his sermons. He claimed a dichotomy in man between his animal and spiritual nature, and he suggested that man's animal nature was a "pain-giving power" but that his spiritual nature, as he evolved into a " 'new man' in Christ Jesus," would cause him to interact in the world with "kindness and love."[8] Beecher thus implied that truthfulness is synonymous with Christian-inspired benevolence. Christianity "spares the weak," "pardons the guilty," is "long-suffering," but, most important, demands that "there shall forever be a difference between truth and lies, between right and wrong." In Beecher's view, truth in a metaphysical sense was thus equivalent to benevolence, and lies, to selfishness. Denouncing lies amounted to a promise that "forever and ever selfishness shall be painful, and benevolence shall be blessed; and I will maintain that which is high and noble."[9]

Beecher's plea for honest language that would transcend the bounds of human selfishness was actually a plea for humanism, which is probably why Beecher was so popular during his time, since even secular humanists could appreciate his message. The context of benevolence in which Beecher placed his definition of truth also helps to explain why a noted skeptic such as Mark Twain might be found endorsing so suspect a word as *truth*. Additional light may be shed on this seeming paradox by noting a reverence for the quality of truthfulness in Twain's time, a truthfulness that Twain might have endorsed, that can be distinguished from the problematics of universal truths, of which Twain probably would have been critical. When John Henry Newman wrote *Apologia Pro Vita Sua* in 1864, Newman claimed that his principal reason for writing it was to defend himself against the charge of untruthfulness.[10] Most reviewers of Newman's work responded in kind by generally rejecting Newman's religious views but putting a premium on his sincerity.[11] Response to Beecher also demonstrates this same fine distinction between the validity of his religious doctrine and the idealistic ethos implicit in his truthfulness. Even though one *Atlantic Monthly* reviewer found in Beecher's sermons "doctrines assumed to be true which have become incredible to us," he lavishly praised Beecher because "during the whole evening not a canting word nor a false tone had been uttered."[12]

The reviewer makes clear that it is Beecher's "complete extirpation of the desire of producing an illegitimate effect; it is his sincerity and genuineness as a human being" that made the difference. This enthusiasm for Beecher's candor was apparently a large-scale cultural phenomenon, expressive of a culture's love of the truth:

> We have a fancy, that we can tell by the manner and bearing of an inhabitant of the place whether he attends this church or not; for there is a certain joyousness, candor, and democratic simplicity about the members of the congregation, which might be styled Beecherian, if there were not a better word. This church is simply the most characteristic thing of America. If we had a foreigner in charge to whom we wished to reveal this country, we should like to push him, hand him over to one of the brethren who perform the arduous duty of providing seats for visitors, and say to him: "There, stranger, you have arrived; *this* is the United States, the New Testament, Plymouth Rock, and the Fourth of July, — *this* is what they have brought us to."[13]

There seems to be no question, as this chapter on *Adventures of Huckleberry Finn* will suggest, that Mark Twain in *Adventures of Huckleberry Finn*, like Herman Melville in *The Confidence-Man* before him, rejected the imposition of codified or institutionalized truths by one power structure upon a weaker on the basis that such institutionalized truths result in thinly disguised excuses for tyranny. Twain the skeptic often commented on the relativistic status of doctrinal truth, quipping in one instance that "the affirmative opinion of a stupid man is neutralized by the negative opinion of his stupid neighbor—no decision is reached; the affirmative opinion of the intellectual giant Gladstone is neutralized by the negative opinion of the intellectual giant Newman—no decision is reached." [14]

Yet, despite Twain's problematizing of the truthful status of a person's doctrinal opinions, which certainly seems to have a moral impetus, the author of *Adventures of Huckleberry Finn* seems to address in this novel the possibility that one can judge sincerity because even in Huck's remark that all men lie it is implicit that deception is something that can be discerned. Huck's remark that all men lie raises the question, How does he know? (If all men's deception is impenetrably deceptive, then how can a person discern lies?) A partial answer is that Huck is not referring to the uncertain truth values of religious opinions but to the world of human relations, where one man judges another's deception. But, again, the question might be asked, How is such judgment possible? The world of human relations also, as one can see in Melville's *Confidence-Man*, can be determined to be problematic. Yet, counter to the way that various characters are gulled by the Confidence Man in his various guises in Melville's novel, in *Adventures of Huckleberry Finn*, when Huck meets the Duke and King, he is able to penetrate their disguise immediately: "It didn't take me long to make up my mind that these liars warn't no kings nor dukes, at all, but just low-down humbugs and frauds" (165). The predominance of lying in *Adventures of Huckleberry Finn* explains the amount of critical attention devoted to deception, but such a simple passage as this should not be slighted; this passage tacitly assumes an element of knowing of which the human being is capable, an all-important possibility of clarity and certainty.

It seems that, akin to the measure for judgment implied by the rhetorical idealism of Twain's age, the measure for judging sincerity in *Adventures of Huckleberry Finn* is a matter of a shrewd mind and good intentions. The 1874 *Presbyterian Quarterly* claimed that rhetoric "postulates a full mind and a full heart." [15] These credentials were equally applied to the audience in the matter of taste and discernment: "A good head and a good heart are essential to the full enjoyment of the moral beauties and glories of composition." [16] The rhetoricians consistently located the source of judgment in one's experience, Beecher claiming that "what a man has not known personally or experimentally he cannot understand."[17] Yet they argued equally that a good heart was essential to clear judgment, since "there are realms of knowledge which cannot be reached by vision, and which must be reached by the spirit."[18] Since truth in the late nineteenth century was connotatively linked to benevolence, it makes sense that a bad heart would be linked to lies.

What Robinson calls "bad faith" in *Adventures of Huckleberry Finn* is consistently linked both to liars and to the rhetorical audience that cannot penetrate the lies. Robinson asserts that the largest source of bad faith in *Huckleberry Finn* is "the unbearable significance of race slavery."[19] This presence of bad heart in the audience seriously impairs its judgment of rhetoric. Although an unwillingness to face the moral implications of slavery is not the only reason why characters in the novel are both willing to be deceived and/or to deceive, Robinson is certainly accurate in judging slavery as the most potent impetus for hypocrisy in the novel. Actually, Twain can capitalize in his novel on the ironically schizophrenic split between his audience's need to consider itself truthful according to the current standards of morality for the day and its own bad faith, which causes it, Twain implies through his satirical although distanced portrait of American society in the novel, to embrace what is false as true. Not coincidentally, Twain's friend Beecher warned similarly against the debilitating effect of slavery upon national judgment in an 1850 sermon, "Shall We Compromise?" Indeed, there is a similarity between the way Twain made slavery the great metaphor for social hypocrisy in his novel and Beecher's earlier identification of slavery as the nation's most vulnerable point to deception: "We can bear much, but we cannot and will not bear the guilt of Slavery. We regard it as epitomizing every offense which man can commit against man. It takes liberty from those to whom God gave it as the right of all rights. It forbids all food either for the understanding or the heart. It takes all honesty from the conscience."[20]

Characters in *Huckleberry Finn* who exhibit bad hearts find their judgments of deception seriously impaired. Nowhere is this more clear than in the incident involving Judith Loftus, who can see right through Huck's disguise so long as her conscience does not impair her judgment. When Huck first tries to trick Judith into believing that he is a girl, she has no difficulty penetrating Huck's false disguise. Her own experience with the way of young ladies helps her establish that Huck is not a girl. Judith puts Huck through a series of tests, and because she knows that no girl would have such a deft arm for throwing stones, and that no girl would thread a needle the way Huck does, she knows Huck is lying.

The problem in detection comes with Judith's own bad heart, which explains why she provides Huck with his alternative alibi about being a runaway apprentice and then hastily believes in the story that Huck builds upon it. She tells Huck, " 'You just tell me your secret, and trust me. I'll keep it; and what's more, I'll help you. So'll my old man, if you want him to' " (73). Ironically, Judith's statement alludes to the rhetorical transaction of good faith popular during her time. Judith is convinced here of her own good heart, and so perhaps may be the reader because of the sympathy she extends to Huck. Yet it seems suggestively implicit in the text that Judith leaps to the invention of this story to hide from herself her own bad faith on the issue of slavery. At the time that Huck is discovered by Judith, Judith and her husband are actively seeking the runaway slave Jim for their own profit. It seems that Judith's subconscious guilt about her complicit participation in slavery impels her to retreat into this self-created fiction of benevolence in her dealings with Huck. (At the least, the discrepancy between Judith's imagined benevolence and her callous cruelty in regard to the runaway slave Jim is suggested by Twain to the reader through his juxtaposition of Judith's two reactions.) Judith and her husband will risk nothing by aiding a runaway slave; hence, weaving this fiction about Huck as a runaway apprentice is a safe way of convincing herself of her own benevolence and of avoiding her own immoral view of slavery. As Robinson points out, "The readiness to be deceived is an integral component of the culture of bad faith, in which credulity is almost always in the service of unacknowledged, often unconscious ends." [21]

Undeniably, the issue of slavery in *Adventures of Huckleberry Finn* is the largest metaphor for the overall unpleasant truths that the community is avoiding, but one remembers that slavery in Twain's contemporary time is supposedly no longer an issue. The concluding paradox in the novel concerning how to set free a runaway slave who has already been set free seems to suggest, though, that for Twain, slavery and forms of tyranny exercised by one person or group over another in the name of truth are an implicit, ever-present reality not obliterated by the supposed legal abolition of race slavery. Because of the institutionalized tyrannies enabled by hypocritical society, but also because of other realities of human experience, such as death, that are inevitably

unavoidable, the genuine truth of human reality and of experience that
Twain seems to imply in *Adventures of Huckleberry Finn* is the inevitability of human suffering, and, further, Twain's moral in the novel
seems to be that facing this reality is absolutely crucial because of the
ethos of caritas that a bold-faced encounter with suffering would promote. This ethos of caritas compelled by suffering is the essential truth
of the novel, for facing that truth compels empathy—that great ability
to feel for others by virtue of participation in one's own and the witnessing of others' misery. Empathy in *Adventures of Huckleberry Finn* is
that great moral reservoir of compassion that serves to restrain man's
crueler, more selfish survivalist instincts that will cause him to lie. And
awareness of the suffering that is not only defended against but in the
process inflicted by deception is the awareness necessary to combating
deception itself: this need to acknowledge suffering is a mutual theme
in Brown's *Wieland*, Hawthorne's *The Scarlet Letter*, and Twain's *Adventures of Huckleberry Finn*, and in all three novels this awareness serves
as the impetus for the acceptance of ethical responsibility (although
this acceptance occurs in *Wieland* only in the subplot). In inventing
the fiction of Huck as a runaway apprentice, Judith in essence substitutes an instance of lesser human suffering for the greater. And in many
instances in the novel, Twain portrays people inventing similar mock-
eries of suffering which will allow them similarly to deny the reality of
suffering. Twain makes the point in *Adventures of Huckleberry Finn* that
it is people's concerted avoidance of suffering that allows suffering to
continue and that it is only by attending to suffering that there can be
some relief from it. An awareness of human suffering is the truthful
underside to institutionalized conventions of benevolence that actually
obscure the reality of suffering.

One of Mark Twain's inspirations for such a view of truth and its
relation to suffering may have been the sermons on this issue by Henry
Ward Beecher. Mark Twain knew and clearly admired Beecher. He
owned copies, for example, of all Beecher's published sermons between
1868 and 1884, and he read them.[22] Mark Twain also stood by Beecher
when this minister, beloved for his truthfulness, went on trial for adultery in 1875. According to Kenneth R. Andrews, Elizabeth Tilton, one
of Beecher's married parishioners, apparently confessed her infidelity
to fellow suffragists Susan B. Anthony and Elizabeth Cady Stanton.
These women then passed on the information to Victoria Woodhull,
an advocate of free love, spiritualism, and feminism, who published an
accusation against Beecher in *Woodhull & Claflin's Weekly* in Novem-

ber 1872.[23] In a scandal that shocked the nation, Beecher was named in the Tilton divorce suit of 1874. Subsequently put on trial by his own ministry, Beecher was acquitted in 1875 by a verdict of nine to three, but his sister Isabella Beecher Hooker was convinced that he was guilty, despite Beecher's own steadfast proclamation of his innocence. Isabella at one point demanded to take over her brother's pulpit so as to denounce him.

Mark Twain was very close at this point to the whole Beecher family; in fact, he and his family were renting their home from Isabella. Mark Twain adamantly supported Beecher in the family split, informing his wife that they would move out of their home and refuse the social company of Isabella Beecher Hooker. In 1887, after Beecher's death, Twain wrote of the misfortune that Elizabeth Tilton " 'could clip the locks of this Samson and make him as other men, in the estimation of a nation of Lilliputians creeping and climbing about his sole shoes.' "[24]

Andrews observes that Twain's "whole life is a record of extreme sensibility. He was outraged by the smallest breach of ethical decency."[25] Yet Twain apparently believed in the practice and preaching of Henry Ward Beecher. It seems odd that an ethical man would speak so sympathetically on the issue of Beecher's adultery, yet Twain's inclination to connect in his mind the apparently larger image and mission of Beecher with imagery evoking a famous social satirist might suggest that Twain's admiration for Beecher rested primarily on the quality of Beecher's ameliorative rhetoric. Twain's use of the image of Samson may even be an unconscious recollection of the power of Beecher's rhetoric. Beecher, in his Thanksgiving Day sermon in 1861, had written, "Samson was on an errand of love. He was interrupted by a lion, which he slew; for love is stronger than any lion. He gained his suit; but, alas! everything went by contraries thereafter. The woman whose love was at first sweeter to him than honey, betrayed him. She was his lion."[26] At any rate, the overwhelming verdict and lingering national reputation of Beecher centered on his truthfulness and on his message as it related to suffering, and it would seem that Beecher's mission and message of truthfulness put him above other men in Twain's estimation.

One finds in Beecher's sermon "The Moral Teaching of Suffering," for example, the suggestion that a truthful approach to suffering in life, which involves risks to the self, would decrease the suffering of others. Beecher asserts that "a hundred men who could not be made to sacrifice truth, who could not be made to fall from duty, who would cheerfully accept suffering, a hundred men who should be as heroic as Christ was, would lift the world, at one impulse, clear through a hundred degrees of excellence. We need again, not only the Sufferer, Christ, in us, the hope of glory, but Christ in us glorious by making us willing to suffer." Significantly, Beecher urged "suffering as an interpreter of moral *truth*, and as a great moral force acting through the imagination and the affections." Suffering brought about "the heroic forms of moral *truth:* "*truths* of fidelity and love and self-sacrifice and faith and hope" (italics added).[27] In Beecher's view, anyone who could "contrive to maintain [himself or herself] inviolate from suffering," was living by means "inconsistent with our fundamental notions of *true* manhood" (italics added). And in his Christianized recasting of Darwinism, Beecher argued that natural evolution merely reflected in paler form spiritual evolution; suffering was the prime motivating force for this spiritual evolution for it made a person Christlike, with a "heart and soul that feels for sin, for infirmities, for sorrows, for mistakes."[28] Finally, Beecher not only claimed the necessity for suffering in a general sense; he also urged that the acceptance of duty, even if it involves risk to self, is especially important in the relationship between the child and the adult. The community, suggests Beecher, should be particularly willing to suffer in its benevolent consideration of the child. In the sermon "The Debt of Strength," Beecher reminds his congregation about the proper role of parent to child within a community, warning that children are "objects on which the great can exercise their disinterested benevolence. Father and mother, according to the great law of love, or of disinterested benevolence, owe the children all that there is in them."[29]

In Twain's *Adventures of Huckleberry Finn*, there seems to be a negative echo of Beecher's message, in that the novel demonstrates how the community falters in its responsibility to the child, failing to exercise benevolence, ironically, in the supposed name of benevolence, in fact, using institutionalized benevolence (an institutionalized convention of truth) to disguise its own failure to take responsibility for a child's suffering. In an important sense, Huck is just as much a helpless ward of the state as the slave Jim. Huck is a child, subject to the whims of adults, and even worse than an orphan, for his hapless father is the horrible embodiment of a child's worst irrational fears (and a symbol of those crueler survivalist instincts against which the acceptance of ethical reponsibility in the larger community is supposed to defend). In fact, Pap as the embodiment of the cruel survivalist ethos is described as a mortal who has practically evolved back into the sea. In terms of Beecher's spiritualized Darwinism, Pap has evolved backward into his selfish animal nature: "There warn't no color in his face, where his face showed; it was white; not like another man's white, but a white to make a body sick, a white to make a body's flesh crawl—a tree-toad white, a fish-belly white" (23). Pap's white face is the face of death, of unmediated violence. As the representative of all that humanity is not supposed to be, Pap tries in his first encounter with Huck to take away the very symbol of nineteenth-century civilization, Huck's education. Pap rips up Huck's book and offers him violence instead: " 'I'll give you something better—I'll give you a cowhide' " (24).

Huck does about as much as he can to protect himself. As he indicates in the novel's opening paragraph, Huck knows that the community lies—that the community shares Pap's predominant self-interest and will not likely protect him. So Huck, distrusting the inclination of the community to protect him, takes matters into his own hands, giving his money to Judge Thatcher so that he can tell Pap that he has no money. True to Huck's prediction, the community does not protect him. The community consigns Huck back to Pap, in the name of benevolence. But it is an institutionalized benevolence with codes that do not require genuine interpretation but instead eliminate the ethical responsibility of interpretation itself and actually obscure the reality of suffering. When the St. Petersburg community consigns Huck back to Pap, it is done in the name of benevolence. The legal verdict is rendered by a new judge, one certain to base his decision on the platitudes of parent-child relationships rather than on true benevolent judgment, which would require that this new judge become familiar with the actual horror of Huck and Pap's relationship. That would embroil the judge in a difficult issue of ethical responsibility. The new judge is predictably swindled by Pap's sentimental rhetoric because Pap tells the judge what he wants to hear. The judge allows himself to be deceived rather than facing potential responsibility for the situation.

The communities along the river in *Huckleberry Finn* mark a similar refusal to take responsibility for suffering. Their retreat into self-deception seems to chart a continuing regression down the evolutionary scale. But the principle of disintegration in these communities is implicit in the more ostensibly civilized St. Petersburg in which Huck grew up; the veneer of civilization is simply less subtle and the animalistic state more progressed. One sees in the river communities parallel instances of the judge's moral blindness in evaluating Pap: the same discrepancy between the actual horror of a situation and the sanctimonious platitudes that accompany it.

Given Twain's well-known view of institutionalized religion, one might wonder about his fondness for Beecher's religious rhetoric. Thus Beecher's indictment of institutionalized religion and its corrosive nature is significant. He believed that "there never was so little of anything on earth as peace, and among those things that have destroyed it nothing has done more than organized religion. Religion as a creed or system has been one of the most ruthless or destructive of the influences that have ravaged human society." [30] The Grangerford episode in *Adventures of Huckleberry Finn* dramatizes Beecher's point that institutionalized religious creeds can give one a false sense of moral virtue that allows one to be morally blind to his or her immoral acts. Religious rhetoric has lulled the Shepherdsons and Grangerfords into a false sense of moral complacency that allows them to avert their eyes from their own heinous acts. The river communities collectively form one large rhetorical audience that is willingly responsive to deceptive rhetoric that abates its own sense of suffering. Thus the rhetorical artists who thrive along the river are those who offer catharsis, those who offer, through the imitation of human suffering, the notion that all human suffering is fictive, which is the great lie that culture and its entertainments seem desirous of perpetuating.

Huck's experience with the circus immediately following the Sherburn incident reveals the dynamics of this rhetorical process and its dangers. The circus, described by Huck, begins as a seductively beautiful evasion of the realities of life. "It was a real bully circus," Huck rhapsodizes. "It was the splendidest sight that ever was . . . every lady with a lovely complexion, and perfectly beautiful, and looking just like a gang of real sure-enough queens, and dressed in clothes that cost millions of dollars, and just littered with diamonds" (191–92). The reality of paste diamonds and questionable ladies, of which Twain's audience, but not Huck, is aware, only emphasizes the inevitable collision between human vanity and human suffering reminiscent of Hardy's "Hap." Yet the suffering that is portrayed in Huck's circus is accompanied by the cathartic reassurance that such suffering is only a fictive illusion.

The imposture occurs when a supposedly drunk man insists on climbing in the ring and imperiling his life by riding the circus horse. Significantly, the crowd laughs at the man's danger; be it imaginary *or* real, they have ceased distinguishing. Through similar deceptions in which they have cooperatively participated, they have learned to distance themselves emotionally from the reality of pain. Huck's reaction to what he perceives as the genuinely perilous situation of the drunk is far more authentic: he is disturbed for the man: "It warn't funny to me, though; I was all of a tremble to see his danger" (193). This is a genuine, human response to genuine, human pain. When Huck realizes that the man is only feigning, however, he feels sheepish, and it may be partially his pride that prompts him to begin privileging the illusory over the real. His emotion debunked, he concludes that "there may be bullier circuses than what that one was, but I never struck them yet" (194). But Huck's eager endorsement of this parody of suffering suggests the danger in such parody, the temptation to distance oneself from the reality of suffering.

The rhetorical artist who panders to his audience's self-interest by fabricating such catharsis is in a precarious position, for, in doing so, he loses his own soul. Just as Brown focused in *Wieland* both on the moral responsibility of the rhetorical audience and of the rhetorician, Twain is greatly concerned with the moral responsibility of the rhetorician in *Huckleberry Finn*. Robinson asserts quite the contrary in his analysis of Twain's own rhetoric in the novel. Robinson believes that in Twain's exposure of the "righteous, self-serving delusion" of the rhetorical audience, Twain shows himself as a "secular Jeremiah, the righteous showman who assures his audience that the conditions of life in a fallen world are remote from mortal influence and utterly resistant to change." Such a showman feels "enormous prestige and authority" [31] while his comedic exposure simultaneously entertains the members of his audience and reassures them that they are inherently depraved and cannot change. Twain is thus a rhetorician capitalizing for his own reward on his audience's need for evasion, just like all the flimflam rhetoricians in his novel.

But the desire for social change lies at the very heart of Twain's novel. Significantly, not every rhetorical transaction is deceitful, and those that are are heartily condemned. Further, these transactions are not only condemned by a "secular Jeremiah," but the differing motivations for deception are carefully discriminated between. In *Adventures of Huckleberry Finn*, Twain's scrupulous attention to and judgment on the various reasons for deception show a careful social theorist at work trying to explain a culture's weaknesses to itself for the purpose of social change.

There are four types of rhetorical artists in *Huckleberry Finn*, and each is judged differently. On the negative side, there are those who exploit the emotions of others for profit, like the Duke and the King, and they are unquestionably doomed. There are also those who invent artful deceptions as a form of cathartic entertainment to avoid the reality of suffering. More positively, there are those who lie to protect their own emotional vulnerabilities against those who would exploit them, and, finally, there are those who risk telling the truth. Those who lie to protect their own emotional vulnerabilities would seem to have some justification for doing so in a survivalist community. By far the greatest danger to the rhetorician and to his audience is the temptation afflicting Brown's Carwin in *Wieland*—the practice of deception for the sake of self-entertainment. This is a great temptation because the rhetorician in a survivalist environment is thrown back on himself for support against his feelings of existential dread; and game playing allows both egotistical amusement and an evasion of his own feared emotions. Such deception constitutes danger both to himself and to his audience because his entertainment evades the emotional realities of life; he discounts both his audience's genuine emotions and his own.

Huck's reaction to the circus implies that a rhetorical artist in a survivalist culture is perpetually in danger of seeking a welcome evasion from the reality of suffering. Huck's knowledge of suffering is the source both of his virtue and of his greatest temptation. While his recollection of his own suffering makes him empathetic to the suffering of others, it also invests him with the desire to escape further suffering through evasive art. In *Adventures of Huckleberry Finn*, only a rhetorical deception that fictively mocks suffering and also engages others in this process allows the artist to escape from his own. The community consensus allows the artist the illusion that he is actually reordering the nature of reality—or that he can be indifferent, at least temporarily, to an alternate "real" experience.

Of course, the most portentous reality of suffering in human experience is death. It was in the nineteenth century that death became the greatest source of existential angst, according to J. Gerald Kennedy. And one of the ways that death as reality was avoided was by cloaking it in a cult of sentimentality, a literature of consolation, a " 'domestication of death.' " Emmeline Grangerford's death poetry in *Adventures of Huckleberry Finn* bears much resemblance to the cult poems appearing in the ladies' magazines and gift books in America's early nineteenth century. Emmeline's entitled pictures, "And Art Thou Gone Yes Thou Art Gone Alas" and "I Shall Never Hear Thy Sweet Chirrup More

Alas" and her "Ode to Stephen Dowling Bots, Dec'd" are obviously products of a highly conventionalized formula. The artificiality of this tradition is suggested by Emmeline Grangerford's unfinished gothic picture of a willowy young lady about to exit the bridge with a few too many legs and arms. The image called forth of this Arachne left by Emmeline's own untimely death is extremely funny. But underlying this humor is a canny portrayal of the architectonics of consolation literature, the calculatedly mediatory intent implicit in portraying death by means of a highly formalized art, which in its very formulaic nature points to itself as unreal. Kennedy concludes that "whatever its underlying intentions," consolation literature "turned grief into a commodity and dying into an increasingly unreal phenomenon." [32] One might say that artificial grief was sought in a sentimentalized artistic form so that real grief could be avoided. The moral point behind Twain's satirizing of Emmeline's sentimentalized poetry of suffering seems clear.

This desire to escape suffering in its most irrevocable form, death, explains Tom's evasive artistry in *Adventures of Huckleberry Finn* and why it is so seductive to Huck. Robinson claims that Tom's artistry "involves belief in the objective existence of its own conscious fabrications." [33] But Tom's artistry does not really involve belief so much as a haughty indifference to reality. He is caught up in the existentialistic energy of game playing not as a corrective to reality but as an alternative to it. It is no coincidence that Lee Mitchell posits Tom as the genuine hero of the novel, since Tom can "acknowledge how fully language creates the self." [34] Tom is the quintessential deconstructionist, whose artistry George Carrington feels to be the necessary response to life which Huck must eventually learn. Tom's drama, according to Carrington, is the necessary response to a lonely world that provokes existential nausea: "The destruction of solidity, the creation of 'squishiness,' that is, the celebration of random activity and the denial of stasis and finality—these are at the heart of the world of *Huckleberry Finn* as it presents itself to the characters and to the readers." [35] Tom's roleplaying, according to Carrington, is a celebration of random activity, a denial of finality, of suffering. Strikingly, Tom enlists his fellow playmates in hackneyed chivalric games whose major feature is that they play out suffering on an imaginative level; those games also imaginatively resolve it. The conventionalized hero of the romance gets out of his scrape.

It is no wonder, then, that after Huck's bout with existential nausea, in the beginning of the novel, he seeks out Tom Sawyer's companion-ship: "Then I set down in a chair by the window and tried to think of something cheerful, but it warn't no use. I felt so lonesome I most wished I was dead. The stars was shining, and the leaves rustled in the woods ever so mournful; and I heard an owl away off, who-whooing about somebody that was dead, and a whippowill and a dog crying about somebody that was going to die. . . . I got so down-hearted and scared, I did wish I had some company" (4). Robinson identifies this passage as an instance of Huck's "anticipatory, or proleptic, guilt,"[36] illustrating it as one of many instances in Twain's fiction and prose when the guilty passage precedes a guilt-provoking incident. Robin-son anticipates the passage as a foreshadowing of Huck's participation in the diminishment of Jim as a human being. But one may also in-terpret this passage in a counter sense as symbolic of the more all-encompassing existential feeling of aloneness and awareness of suffer-ing of which Huck as an abused child has more than a little. Depending on one's interpretation, Huck's seeking out of Tom Sawyer can be read either as an attempt to evade responsibility for slavery or as an attempt to find in the concept of community a mutuality that would abate the feeling of being alone. There seems to be evidence that Huck is seeking the latter. It should come as no surprise that the characters with moral potential in *Adventures of Huckleberry Finn* are almost unbearably aware of human suffering. It seems morally significant that while sneaking off with Tom for a night of adventure, which Huck is attracted to as a means of escaping his aloneness, Huck still retains his hold on human reality and cannot find in Tom's adventures a sense of catharsis. When Huck and Tom reach the edge of the hilltop overlooking town, for example, Huck sees "three or four lights twinkling" and speculates, "there was sick folks, may be" (8). He also resigns from Tom's band of robbers because they "only just pretended" (14). He tests Tom's myth about the powers of a magic lamp empirically: "I thought all this over for two or three days, and then I reckoned I would see if there was any-thing in it. I got an old tin lamp and an iron ring and went out in the woods and rubbed and rubbed till I sweat like an Injun, calculating to build a palace and sell it; but it warn't no use, none of the genies come. So then I judged that all that stuff was only just one of Tom Sawyer's lies. I reckoned he believe in the A-rabs and the elephants, but as for me I think different. It had all the marks of a Sunday school" (17).

There is a paradox in Huck's reaction to Tom. Huck is impatient with Tom's inventions for their lack of resemblance to reality, but, at the same time, Huck admires Tom, even after Tom's stories are not borne out by fact. Huck's admiration for Tom may be the result of a tragic flaw in Huck's character. By not living according to the rules of reality, Tom is, Huck sees, the quintessential soul of convention. Huck's need for company, for community, renders him vulnerable to community and therefore, in the special terms of the novel, vulnerable to a survivalist community, whose ethics he has intellectually absorbed. Tom Sawyer is the master rhetorician of the survivalist community, whose capability to entertain himself by making a mockery of genuine suffering through his mock tales of suffering puts him in a position of survivalist invulnerability. Huck admires Tom as king of the survivalist jungle, and, when he finds himself in potentially threatening situations, he imagines how Tom would escape them. In a sense, though, Huck has transferred the values of the community onto himself, and it is with the gaze of the community that Huck looks approvingly on Tom. It is Huck's desire to be conventional, so as to link himself with community, that provokes his admiration of Tom. This attempt is almost a self-taught primer lesson to absorb the rules of the conventional community.

Seduced by Tom's rhetoric, Huck apprentices himself to Tom briefly, playing the same rhetorical tricks of make-believe on Jim that Tom plays on Huck. Huck's lies to Jim sometimes occur in the form of tricks, when, for example, Huck places the snakeskin on Jim's bedding, subsequently attracting a deadly snake, and when Huck convinces Jim that their separation in the storm is a dream. Robinson claims that Huck's pranks at Jim's expense are "designed to expose the gullibility and superstition which manifest what is assumed to be Jim's racial inferiority,"[37] but this is rather a puzzling assessment. The fact that Huck does consider Jim inferior very likely makes Huck think that he can fool with Jim in the same subservient manner that Tom treats Huck, but it is not clear why Huck would in turn need to expose Jim's inferiority to some invisible audience as if Jim's inferiority were in question. The pranks both make a mockery of suffering and imply that danger is not real. Huck experiments with Tom's form of catharsis on a vulnerable audience, his principal goal self-entertainment, egotistical amusement, at the expense of the emotions of a vulnerable other. After this point, Huck abandons the use of rhetoric for catharsis, the process of exploiting the emotions of others for entertainment. Jim teaches Huck that pain results from such egotistical rhetoric; Huck learns that cathartic rhetoric is destructive. After the storm episode, Jim chides Huck for taking advantage of his emotions: " 'When I got all wore out wid work, en wid de callin for you, en went to sleep, my heart wuz mos' broke bekase you wuz los', en I didn' k'yer no mo' what become er me en de raf.' En when I wake up en fine you back agin, all safe en soun', de tears come en I could a got down on my knees en kiss' yo' foot I's so thankful. En all you wuz thinkin 'bout wuz how you could make a fool uv ole Jim wid a lie. Dat truck dah is *trash;* en trash is what people is dat puts dirt on de head er dey fren's en makes 'em ashamed.' " Huck rejoins: "It was fifteen minutes before I could work myself up to go and humble myself to a nigger—but I done it, and I warn't ever sorry for it afterwards, neither. I didn't do him no more mean tricks, and I wouldn't done that one if I'd a knowed it would make him feel that way" (105).

Huck plays no more tricks on the emotions of others for the sake of gratuitous entertainment. Huck may lie, but it is never the lie of Tom's rhetoric. Tom's rhetoric makes language a meaningless convention that mislabels the real world and promotes the user's self-interests and self-indulgent imagination. It is the language of a cynic who plays on the naïveté and gullibility of his audience and who views that audience with a cold detachment from its emotional welfare. Tom's game playing is thus an attitude as well as a form of language, an attitude of cold disdain for one's fellow man, not of community feeling. Although much is made of the ethnic prejudice implicit in Huck's tricks on Jim, one sees in Tom's behavior and in the behavior of the townspeople along the river that cold indifference to one's fellow man is not limited in *Adventures of Huckleberry Finn* to the issue of color.

Nevertheless, Huck does remain self-deceived, as Robinson points out, about the greatest truth that *Adventures of Huckleberry Finn* presents: the truth of the suffering implicit in slavery and the concomitant truth that "truth" in the nineteenth-century ethical sense could not imply the tyranny of one race or one group of people over another. As Robinson convincingly suggests, Jim's suffering does not serve as an ameliorative example for Huck, although I would qualify this by suggesting that since Huck abandons deceptive tricks after witnessing the suffering they cause Jim, Jim does serve as a strong ethical influence nevertheless. But Robinson suggests that Jim tries to get himself recognized by Huck as a human being through the parable he presents Huck of his own insensitive cruelty to his deaf daughter, which is supposed to suggest to Huck Huck's insensitivity to Jim since he refuses to challenge the presence of the Duke and the King on the raft. Robinson is right, of course, that Huck does not let this message sink in, nor is he able to defend Jim's rights as a human being when Tom plays out his final drama of dehumanization on Jim at the novel's conclusion.

Serious ethical questions can be and have been raised about the ethical validity of *Adventures of Huckleberry Finn*. These questions obviously involve the narrative architectonics of an author who would present an issue as morally reprehensible as slavery from a point of view that is problematic in one or more ways. Grave concern about whether the novel is covertly racist has been expressed most recently in a powerful reading by Wayne Booth, who suggests that the novel promotes some of the worst stereotypes of racism. One of Booth's concerns is that Twain portrays Jim with a patronizing benevolence. In the sections in which Jim is portrayed as "an ideally generous, spiritually sound, wonderfully undemanding surrogate parent," for example, this characterization still perpetuates the stereotype of blacks as "infinitely grateful people who will cooperate lovingly with their former masters . . . in trying to combat the wicked white folks." Worse, the beginning of the novel and its prolonged conclusion present another racial stereotype which Booth finds morally questionable: "Jim is portrayed as simply a comic butt, suitable for exploitation by cute little white boys of good heart who have been led into concocting a misguided adventure by reading silly books." Booth discovers in such stereotypes "Twain's full indifference to what all this means to Jim, and his seeming indifference to the full meaning of slavery and emancipation."[38]

Questions about Twain's own ethical reliability in telling his tale shift the field of attention, temporarily, from questions about the ethical reliability of his narrator, but objections to Huck as an ethical character have also been recently raised, and not only regarding the often cited fall from moral grace that critics note occurs to Huck at the conclusion of the novel, when he conspires with Tom to set Jim free with little regard for Jim's dignity. James Kastely, for example, has suggested that Huck fails an ethical test when he first tells himself early on in the book that his basis for not betraying Jim is doing "whichever come handiest at the time." Kastely claims that Huck's "corrupt conscience," inherited from his father, "prevents him from acknowledging his true and praiseworthy motive," and he thus "adopts the morally corrupt interpretation that understands the world solely in terms of self-interest and that defines it only as an arena in which people meet as combatants. Such a world is finally one in which community, and, hence, meaningful freedom are not possible."[39] In Kastely's view, Huck's decision to affirm an ethics of self-interest ushers in the violent middle chapters of the novel that show the pernicious effects of a doctrine of self-interest.

I mention these two issues concerning Twain as ethical storyteller and Huck as ethical narrator simultaneously because, for many readers who find *Adventures of Huckleberry Finn* to be racist, in this instance Wayne Booth, the distinction between Huckleberry Finn as first-person narrator and Mark Twain as author seems to have been to a great extent collapsed. It would seem that any moral ambiguity that we might see in Huck inevitably rubs off on the imputations of authorial motive; that is, if Huck is blind to the racial stereotypes that he is implicitly revealing, then Twain participates equally in this same blindness, since it is only through Huck's point of view that we can arrive at Twain's message. I shall expand a little further on Booth's implied use of this ethics of narration in a moment, but first it might be useful to point out how the choice of a first-person narration inevitably involves an author in using irony to deliver his moral message.

In relation to the ethical necessity of truth as a moral message in nineteenth-century American literature, one might ask several questions about the methods of the two authors, Charles Brockden Brown and Mark Twain, who choose to deliver that message through first-person narration. It is interesting that in the novels of both, the authors' message about the moral necessity of telling the truth is imparted by a first-person narrator who is herself or himself at least partially deceived. As Chapter 1 of this study suggests, for instance, Clara Wieland, who imparts the message of the importance of truth in Brown's novel, remains self-deceived about some of her own responsibility for the past deceptions she is narrating. In Twain's novel, Huck Finn also is deceived about the moral rightness or wrongness in the issue of slavery, yet I have suggested thus far that Twain implicitly suggests through this narrator the moral necessity, also, of telling the truth.

From a reader's point of view, it might seem strange that an author choosing to impart a moral message would risk compromising that message by presenting it through a narrator misled in some important way. And yet, from an author's point of view, the issue of imparting any ethical meaning through a first-person narrator might seem to have other risks. An author using a first-person narrator might well ask how one *does* advocate such a thing as the moral necessity of telling the truth through the persona of a first-person narrator without being didactic.

Let me go back to Brown's use of Clara as both naive and retrospective narrator to illustrate what I mean. Clara is recounting those experiences with her family that caused the Wieland family to be un-wittingly taken in by the clever hoaxes of the sophistic Carwin, and she also recounts the disaster that arose when her brother is misled into thinking that he hears voices and slaughters his immediate family. Clara tells this story for the purpose of warning her audience against gullibility, but she shows no clear awareness, even in retrospect, of the emotional dynamics within herself that caused her initially to be deceived. Why, one might ask, would Brown risk compromising his message about truth by imparting it through a narrator with only par-tial awareness? But let one assume, for a moment, that Brown had chosen to create a fully enlightened Clara, who presented the tale of past deception with full enlightenment. *This* retrospective Clara would recount her tale leaving no implications to be deduced by the reader; when she discussed how she started thinking about death shortly after becoming suspicious of Carwin's eloquence, for example, rather than narrating these events impartially and disconnectedly, she would say, "there, reader, it is obvious to me now that my thoughts of death were spawned by my dawning fear of the deceptive capabilities of language." How many more such instances of intrusive interpretation would the intelligent reader tolerate?

With a first-person narrator, the author has to ask himself whether he wants the narrator to do all the interpretive work for the reader. Imparting the message in such a straightforward way implies moral didacticism, not the subtlety of art. It may even be that in *Wieland*, Brown actually intended no part of Clara's past self-deception to com-promise her present narrative role as clear seer. Clara's compromised position as retrospective narrator may actually be a result of Brown's desire to concentrate on those elements in Clara's personality that allowed her to be deceived in the past, not to characterize the present Clara so much as to suggest the dynamics involved in the process of deception itself. And, in my view, for purposes of narrative subtlety, Brown chose to illuminate the true bases for being undeceived only in the subplot.

In *Adventures of Huckleberry Finn*, it is easier to see the distance between the ethical point of view of the author and the narrator, be-cause Huck can never be seen to narrate from the enlightened ethi-cal position of the author; whereas Clara openly advocates telling the truth, Huck is never privileged with an intellectual awareness of its importance. Of course, some readers do not accept that Mark Twain *is* advocating the importance of telling the truth, or, articulated more specifically, that Mark Twain is advocating the importance of discerning the moral reprehensibility of one person calling any other person a "slave." But even those readers who equate Mark Twain with Huck and in some way problematize Twain's message must acknowledge that in significant instances, such as when Twain shows Huck Finn expressing the sentiment that he will go to hell when he decides not to incriminate his friend Jim, Mark Twain is detached from Huck Finn, because Mark Twain knows that no person making such an ethical decision would go to hell.

I think that it is of maximum significance to retain the impression *throughout* the narrative of *Adventures of Huckleberry Finn* that Huck Finn never reaches the ethical stature of the author of the novel, because it is through retention of that fact that one can recover both the aim of the satire in the novel and the ethical intent of the author. Wayne Booth, referring specifically to my reading of the novel and quoting my words, calls this method of morally justifying the book as

> the simplest: the attribution to Huck, not to Mark Twain, of all the ethical deficiencies. Since Twain is obviously a master ironist, and since we see hundreds of moments in the book when he and the reader stand back and watch Huck make mistakes, why cannot we assume that *any* flaw of perception or behavior we discern is part of Twain's portrait of a "character whose moral vision, though profound, is seriously and consistently flawed." . . . In this view, the problems we have raised result strictly from Twain's use of Huck's blindnesses as "an added indictment against the society of which he [Huck] is a victim."

Although Booth suggests that "this defense will work perfectly" because "if we embrace it in advance of our actual experience line-by-line" we can "explain away any fault," assuming "in advance an *author* of unlimited wisdom, tact, and artistic skill," he feels equally that this approach nevertheless does not solve the more complex problems of the text.[40]

These problems, for Booth, relate to his ethical concerns about the novel's implicit racism that have been summarized here, but it is useful for my argumentative purposes also to point out the underlying premises of Booth's ethical objections to *Adventures of Huckleberry Finn*. Since Booth's ethical objections are addressed most closely to the ending of Twain's novel and also explicitly challenge the reading of the novel's conclusion with which I will close this chapter, I wish to defend, in turn, my own reading of the novel by analyzing and then questioning the assumptions and expectations about narrative upon which Booth's objections to the novel, and to my reading, are based. Essentially, I believe that implicit within Booth's ethical standards for fiction is a golden measure for an ethically sound narrative. Booth's golden measure is that ethical narrative delivers a rhetorically democ-ratized recoverability of meaning; in other words, Booth believes that a narrative is ethically sound only if it delivers an ethical meaning that is clearly obvious to the majority of readers. In rejecting a reading such as mine, Booth thus asks, "What then happens to the great un-washed, for whom so much of the book has proved totally deceptive?" And he rejects the possibility that comedy in the novel's final section is clearly subordinate to social satire by pointing out that "surely the most common reading of this book, by non-professional whites, has always been the kind of enraptured, thoroughly comfortable reading that I gave it when young, the kind that sees the final episodes as a climax of good clean fun." In sum, Booth rejects the notion that Twain may be a master satirist, a "real author" above all the disturbing com-edy that the book engages in at expense of Jim, and he believes that positing an author who writes for "a few discerning readers" may be of "maximum fairness to Twain, but it doesn't work at all for the critic who cares about what a book does to or for the majority of its readers, sophisticated or unsophisticated." [41]

I am uncertain how to respond to this implicit ethics of narrative, which in principle is reminiscent of Booth's earlier *Rhetoric of Fiction*, in which he decides that "the moral question is really whether an author has an obligation to write well in the sense of making his moral or-derings clear, and if so, clear to whom." [42] Booth, of course, decides in the instance of both these profound critical works that, yes, the author *does* have the obligation to make his moral orderings clear, and my suspicion is that one reason that Booth has ethical reservations about *Adventures of Huckleberry Finn* is that Twain's use of first-person nar-ration to tell his tale—and the necessary way that his tale is veiled by ironies in the telling so as to avoid the tyranny of moral didacticism—makes Twain's moral orderings, for Booth, less than clear. All I can say is that I never found the conclusion of *Adventures of Huckleberry Finn* to be remotely humorous, and neither have any of the first-time readers of the novels in any of my classes. What age level—what level of awareness—determines the common denominator for a clear but subtle narration?

Twain's moral orderings *are* clear, I believe, if one views with care the way that Twain consistently depicts his narrator Huck as sensitive but inevitably self-deceived, and if one holds a firm grasp on the fact that Twain does not endorse all of Huck's actions or views. It is also significant to be aware that Twain does not blame his own narrator for his moral failings; rather, Twain blames his narrator's self-deception about the nature of slavery on the culture in which Huck was raised, which tyrannized over Huck's interpretation of meaning and intellectual understanding of truth. How do we know this? Partly because the reader can employ his or her own moral norms as a way of judging the portraits of selfish and self-deceived behavior that are seen through Huck's naive and sometimes unreflective eyes. And in a sense, also, Twain encourages moral standards in us by dramatizing the human suffering that results from this selfish and deceptive behavior, and, further, Twain gives us the opportunity to see through Huck's eyes one instance when a virtuous rhetorical transaction occurs that can be applied as an ethical standard.

Huck's moment of truth does not occur, however, with Jim. If it did, this might be Twain's lie, for to depict a white boy of his time as capable of a virtuous rhetorical transaction would be to sentimentalize the realities of real race relations. Even though Huck is blessed in this novel with an extremely heightened sensitivity to suffering, Twain allows him only marginal awareness of the suffering of a black man, and this closure to the suffering of Jim prohibits Huck from participating in a fully honest relationship with him. Ironically, it is Huck's perceived dependency on the larger community as a form of support that gives him the rhetorically proverbial "bad head"; the community tinctures his perception of experience. Robinson observes that "physical distance from civilized folk is for Huck the absolutely essential condition for the achievement of the freedom and comfort and satisfaction he so craves," but Huck's experience *outside* the community with being alone and with the fearful forces of nature actually impels him back toward the community, convincing him that he is in need of it. Through depicting Huck's dependency on the community, Twain does not seem to suggest that this need of Huck's to establish his identity through the community is wrong in principle. Rather, Twain implies that the community is at fault for subverting Huck's healthy need for community into a tragic character flaw. As Robinson notes, Huck "is the victim of a wrenching ambivalence which finds its epicenter at the intersection of totally irreconcilable attitudes toward Jim."[43]

Because Huck intellectually absorbs the conventional truths of society, he never consciously grants Jim his equality as a human being on an intellectual level. Twain shows Huck's belief, then, in two irreconcilable truths, and, unfortunately, Huck can be seen to perceive both as transcendently real, as permanent, unchanging. One truth is the truth of human emotion, of human suffering and the corresponding caritas one should extend toward one's fellow human being. The other is the truth of social convention. Stephen Mailloux defines such convention as ideological "sets of ideas serving specific political interests in a political context."[44] One such convention present in *Adventures of Huckleberry Finn* is the fallacy of white supremacy. Conventions are arbitrary, environmentally conditioned, and subject to change. But Huck's cultural indoctrination has suggested to him that they are static truths. Ideologies instead should be tested to determine whether experience bears them out. Henry Ward Beecher supported this view. "I have sometimes said that life was a test of truth," Beecher commented, "that that which men believe on philosophical principles, being carried into outward life, will very soon show whether it is harmonious or at discord with it. Life is, in an important sense, the test of truth."[45] Huck, however, drawing connections between institutionalized religion and slavery, and the conventional behavior that Tom exhibits which is divorced from the reality of emotion, has been educated by his community that a matrix of social conventions together comprises the religiously sanctioned, unchanging truth. It is the link that an individual like Miss Watson makes between the transcendent "good place" *beyond* life and institutionalized religion *in* life that convinces Huck of the unchanging nature of such truths. And for Huck, with his feelings of helplessness and loneliness, such an image of eternity must be potent. Even the bad place, to which Huck tells Miss Watson he would rather go in preference to heaven, is tied up with a transcendent reassurance of something permanent beyond life.

As I have mentioned, Huck has recently come under attack for his existential cowardice in the face of social corruption. James Kastely has suggested that Mark Twain implies that but for Huck's faulty ethics, he and Jim could have built an alternative ethical community to the corrupt, larger community around them. Given the reality of Huck's character as Twain presents him, however, such an existential leap into an ideal ethics seems impossible for Huck. Because of his belief in the permanence of conventional truths, Huck is paralyzed and unable to acknowledge any support of Jim in an unambiguous way. Huck does not consider himself and Jim as an alternative community—although

Twain and the reader might—but as recreant members of the community at large. Kastely's point, therefore, seems essentially moot;
Huck has no realistic chance to initiate such a community. Nevertheless, Huck does not participate in situational ethics, as Kastely suggests. He is radically different from Pap, certainly, and from the rest
of the survivalist community. The adults in the survivalist community
of the novel consciously pursue self-interest for the sake of genuine
self-interest, but Huck never actually pursues self-interest; he pursues
a complex reconciliation of his split ethos. His emotional honesty is at
odds with his intellectual awareness and certainty about the truth of
the social codes. When Huck says he will "always do whichever comes
handiest at the time," he is referring to his complex ambivalence. What
is handiest for Huck at the time is what is most ethically compelling to
his conscience within an immediate situation involving his two incompatible truths. Huck's unresolvable ambivalence is the reason for his
usual passivity. When committed to truth, in a world where any action
seems to be both a truth and a lie, one's only recourse is inaction.

A good example of his suspended action is his handling of Jim's escape in the novel's troubling final chapters. As I have noted, critics
have long been dissatisfied with the narrative consistency of these final
chapters in which Huck defers to Tom. Leo Marx, for example, claims
that "in the end Huck regresses to the subordinate role in which he
had first appeared in *The Adventures of Tom Sawyer*. Most of those traits
which made him so appealing a hero now disappear . . . now, in the
end, he submits in awe to Tom's notion of what is amusing. To satisfy
Tom's hunger for adventure he makes himself a party to sport which
aggravates Jim's misery."[46] Henry Nash Smith suggests that *Adventures
of Huckleberry Finn* "is forced back into the framework of comedy" because "Mark Twain's portrayal of Huck and Jim as complex characters
has carried him beyond the limits of his original plan," and "the writer
has on his hands a hybrid—a comic story in which the protagonists
have acquired something like tragic depth."[47]

Critical dismay is based on critics' perception of Huck's moral
growth in chapter 31, in which Huck determines to go to hell rather
than betray Jim. Kastely, for example, is convinced that in this instance Huck abandons the ethics of self-interest for the sake of a friend
because his "only possible motive is one rooted in a genuine ethical
community of fellow feeling in which one freely chooses responsibility
for another."[48]

The final chapters of *Adventures of Huckleberry Finn* are consistent, though, with Huck's behavior in chapter 31 because Huck's intellectual awareness in the passage remains unswervingly constant with his former beliefs. Huck's motive is rooted in genuine feeling for Jim, but Huck still addresses his conventionally conceptualized God. He just defers one type of hell to avoid the immediate possibility of another, the hell of betraying his friendship with Jim: "It was a close place. I took it up, and held it in my hand. I was a trembling, because I'd got to decide, forever, betwixt two things, and I knowed it. I studied a minute, sort of holding my breath, and then says to myself: 'All right, then, I'll go to hell'" (270–71).

Huck's moral awareness perpetually coexists with his incompatible faith in social convention. It is true that on one hand Huck decides to steal Jim out of slavery after Jim has just been sold down the river to the Phelps's farm by the Duke and the King, but this is an act, on the other hand, to which Huck's moral paralysis has been largely contributive. It is significant that Huck successfully removes these two vile carpetbaggers from the company of Mary Jane, but he cannot seem to oust them from the raft. As Mailloux and Robinson point out, Huck retains his conviction about white supremacy throughout his relationship with Jim. Thus it is consistent with Huck's ambivalent character that he responds the way he does to Tom in the novel's final chapters. Huck retains all aspects of his complex ambivalence, both his fondness for Jim and his awareness of how Tom's conventions contradict it. He is, at the same time, paralyzed by his own respect for convention. From the outset of Tom's involvement in Jim's escape, Huck is paralyzed from aggressively helping Jim by his own fears of community rejection: "And then think of *me*! It would get all around, that Huck Finn helped a nigger to get his freedom; and if I was to ever see anybody from that town again, I'd be ready to get down and lick his boots for shame" (268).

Huck practically does lick Tom Sawyer's boots at the end of *Adventures of Huckleberry Finn*, which is foreshadowed by the above-quoted segment of a passage normally considered as evidence of moral enlightenment. If Huck acts in awe of Tom Sawyer at the novel's end, his awe is not for Tom's improbable antics, and it is not for Tom's imaginative rhetoric, but because this paragon of social convention is breaking the social rules. Huck feels bound to orchestrate Jim's escape out of deference to Tom's great sacrifice, Tom's tremendous fall—in helping Jim —from the truths of social convention. Tom's offer of help astonishes Huck: "Well, I let go all holts, then, like I was shot. It was the most astonishing speech I ever heard—and I'm bound to say Tom Sawyer fell, considerable, in my estimation. Only I couldn't believe it. Tom Sawyer a *nigger stealer*!" (284). It seems clear at least to me that in passages such as this, Mark Twain is not implying that *he* shares a similar shock based on *his* feeling that those who aid blacks in slavery fall in estimation. But *Huck* feels beholden to any conceptualization of the escape that Tom wishes to form, and, predictably, of course, when Tom Sawyer and Huck Finn thus conspire to liberate Jim "heroically" from the Phelps's farm, Tom informs Huck that "when a prisoner of style escapes, it's called an evasion" (333). Huck's helplessness to act counter to his culture's conventional truth that slavery is justified makes Huck and Jim Tom's prisoners of style—a style that is the antithesis of moral rhetoric, a conventionalized style devoid of substance—but I think that it would be a serious error to mistake Tom's convention of evasive style as equally Mark Twain's.

Twain seems to reveal a great deal of tension in this supposedly comic scene because he implies that his narrator Huck is as exasperated with the impracticality of Tom's plans as he has always been. Huck mutes his frustration with understated irony, observing that "I see in a minute [Tom's plan] was worth fifteen of mine, for style, and would make Jim just as free a man as mine would, and maybe get us all killed, besides." Some readers might interpret Huck's comment as admiration, but Huck's response must be read in the consistent context of his reaction to Tom's Sunday school lies, and a note of impatience seems implicit in Huck's further observation that "I knowed he would be changing it around, every which way, as we went along, and heaving in new bullinesses wherever he got a chance" (292).

Despite mounting exasperation, venting itself in phrases like "Consound it, it's foolish, Tom" (304), Huck is nevertheless subdued, not by the comic delight of Tom's imagined antics but by his sense of complicity in Tom's downfall:

> That was the thing that was too many for me. Here was a boy that was respectable, and well brung up; and had a character to lose . . . and yet here he was, without any more pride, or rightness, or feeling, than to stoop to this business, and make himself a shame, and his family a shame, before everybody. I *couldn't* understand it, no way at all. It was outrageous, and I knowed I ought to just up and tell him so; and so be his true friend, and let him quit the thing right where he was, and save himself. And I *did* start to tell him; but he shut me up. (292–93)

Twain thus makes it clear that Huck never relinquishes his obedience to the god of convention throughout the novel, and now his fear that he has brought about the downfall of a youthful paragon of conventional virtue (Twain presents it as conventional virtue; Huck sees it simply as virtue) literally paralyzes him with a guilt that forces him to acquiesce to all the actions of his fallen idol. The final pages of *Adventures of Huckleberry Finn* excise Huck's source of guilt so that Huck is free to "light out for the Territory ahead of the rest" (362). And why is Huck so eager to leave? When Huck discovers Tom's secret knowledge of Jim's freedom, he says, "I couldn't ever understand, before, until that minute and that talk, how he *could* help a body set a nigger free, with his bringing-up" (358). The way his decision to leave follows closely on the heels of his discovery of Tom's perpetration of one more hoax suggests Huck's disgust with the way he was duped by Tom and his continual exasperation with the incompatibility between the truths of his emotions and the truths of his culture.

In presenting Huck's moral dilemma, Mark Twain attempts to educate his audience, to correct its hackneyed misprision of rhetorical truth, its confused substitution of ideological truth for the rhetorical truth of benevolence. *Adventures of Huckleberry Finn* demonstrates that much harm comes when conventional truths are considered as invariable and used to evade the genuine truth of human suffering; why should Twain's often noted attacks on conventionalized sentimentality, or religion, be any different than his implied attack on slavery? In one instance of what must have been tremendous optimism for Twain, however, the rhetorical formula is righted in *Adventures of Huckleberry Finn*; a coalescence between good heads and good hearts produces an instance of rhetorical communication that is transcendently real.

Deception meant self-interestedness and truth meant benevolence — those were the connotations of *truth* and *deception* in nineteenth-century American rhetorical idealism. Beecher and other rhetoricians also communicated to the culture that "lying disintegrates society" by corroding the basis for all potentially positive social contact. Just as eighteenth-century rhetorician George Campbell believed that "the clear representations of memory" must be true in order to move a single step in the acquisition of knowledge, Beecher and others believed that faith in one's fellow man was necessary to advance a single step in human relations. Men "are united together in the great interests of human life by trust. On an average they believe when a man says a thing; when he says he has done a thing they take it for granted. We could not live if we could not believe in men."[49]

Trust is a rare commodity in the dramatized world of *Adventures of Huckleberry Finn*. This novel seems to throw a gauntlet in the face of Beecher's claim that "the progress of all human life begins with the belief that all men substantially tell the truth." According to this reasoning, what chance does Huck have to progress spiritually or morally within his culture when he begins with the belief that all men substantially lie? What chance has his society given Huck since it is responsible for Huck's belief? Beecher expressed himself dumbfounded that people might "have faith in the Transfiguration and faith in immortality" but not have "faith in the safety of telling the truth everywhere and always."[50] In Twain's fictional society, where expectations are completely inverted, Huck acknowledges that "a body that ups and tells the truth when he is in a tight place is taking considerable many resks" (239). Telling the truth, in Huck's survivalist culture, is definitely not safe. Lie perpetuates lie. No one can be trusted.

Twain appears to satirize his own culture by deliberately inverting Beecher's well-known social picture — not for the purpose of discrediting Beecher's values but to discredit what Twain perceived to be his hypocritical culture. As an affirmation of Beecher's values, Twain gives Huck a rare gift — an instance of trust and an instance of truth — and he even manages to do so realistically within the framework of his novel and the limitations of his protagonist. Huck is able to find one transcendently real instance "where I'm blest if it don't look to me like the truth is better, and actualy *safer*, than a lie," so that he decides to "chance it," to "up and tell the truth this time, though it does seem most like setting down on a kag of powder and touching it off, just to see where you'll go to" (239). He finds it no thanks to his culture, Twain seems to imply, but in spite of it.

That Huck cannot find such a moment with Jim is because of Huck's social indoctrination. Indeed he does have honest moments with Jim, but he cannot generalize universally from them because of his feeling that he and Jim are apart from society. Huck has a "bad head" about Jim. If Huck is to change his thoughts about lying, he must do so through culture. It is through culture, according to Beecher, that one's perceptions change.[51] Since Mary Jane Wilks is a part of the conventional society that Huck has been taught to revere, she provides Huck with a metaphorical bridge to a new experience of the social universe, one where he can act on emotional truths without the con-flicting truths of convention because he perceives himself still to be acting within the accepted social code.

As a passive part of the Duke and King's scam to rob Mary Jane and her sisters of their inheritance, Huck improvises wildly in response to Joanna Wilks's questions about his life as an English servant. Joanna Wilks notes the improbability of Huck's answers and suggests that he is telling "a lot of lies." Joanna makes Huck swear on a book, to Huck's relief, "nothing but a dictionary," and about this time Mary Jane Wilks steps in and chides Joanna for her disbelief. The important distinction between Mary Jane's belief and the ready credulity of those previously self-deceived in the novel is that Mary Jane's belief is based on dis-interested benevolence. She tells Joanna that she must believe Huck because " 'if you was in his place, it would make you feel ashamed; and so you oughtn't to say a thing to another person that will make *them* feel ashamed' " (225).

Mary Jane is one of a series of nineteenth-century American fic-tional women — Milly Theale in *The Wings of the Dove*, Maggie Verver in *The Golden Bowl* are others — who compel a man's virtue through her own example of honesty and benevolence.[52] Mary Jane's trust in Huck is the pivotal experience for his rejection of the King and the Duke's plan, which now made him "feel pretty bad. About an hour or two ago, it would a been a little different, but now it made me feel bad and disap-pointed" (227). Huck's compunction increases as the scam continues, feeding off the Wilks sisters' good-natured faith: "Them poor things was that glad and happy it made my heart ache to see them getting fooled and lied to, so, but I didn't see no safe way for me to chip in and change the general tune" (234).

But Huck decides he must tell Mary Jane the truth, though he "ain't had no experience" in doing so. Significantly, it is Mary Jane's concern for her black servants that motivates her promise to do whatever Huck tells her to. The honesty implicit in Mary Jane's concern for others — notably the most conventionally abused and ignored — causes Huck to trust her: " 'I don't want nothing more out of *you* than just your word — I druther have it than another man's kiss-the-Bible' " (239). Huck real-izes Mary Jane " 'ain't one of these leather-face people. I don't want no better book than what your face is. A body can set down and read it off like a coarse print' " (242). Here is one instance when honesty is safer because trust and honesty are certain features in the rhetorical relationship.

The instance of rhetorical truth becomes transcendently real when Huck's great risk in trusting Mary Jane is confirmed. Huck asks Mary Jane to flash a light in her window as part of their scheme. Metaphorically, this becomes the rhetorical light of truth, invested for Huck with all the symbolic value of truthful eloquence. Huck seeks this light with all his invested faith: "When I struck the town, I see there warn't nobody out in the storm, so I never hunted for no back streets, but humped it straight through the main one; and when I begun to get towards our house I aimed my eye and set it. No light there; the house all dark—which made me feel sorry and disappointed, I didn't know why" (258). Huck's disappointment shows the risk involved in investing faith and being deceived, and Huck's great consuming passion, although on a subconscious level, for rhetorical truth. Twain suspends the confirmation of Huck's faith so as to make it seem the more splendid when it comes and to show also the fragility and importance of reciprocal human emotion.

When the light does finally come, Huck responds to it with all the heartfelt emotion the rhetoricians predicted would be inspired by truth: "But at last, just as I was sailing by, *flash* comes the light in Mary Jane's window! and my heart swelled up sudden, like to bust, and the same second the house and all was behind me in the dark, and wasn't ever going to be before me no more in this world. She *was* the best girl I ever see, and had the most sand" (258). A moment of rhetorical truth—and gone, to be seen "no more in this world," and again this seems because Twain's honesty as author must force him away from a romantic, idealized conclusion. *How* could Huck and Jim have transcended the limits of their culture? How can a child in a corrupt culture take on the world all on his own? Equally, if Twain were to suggest that Mary Jane were representative of her culture, he would be letting his uncomfortable readers off the hook. As it is, Huck's honesty with Mary Jane synchronously exists with his "honor-bright" lies to the Duke and King to protect her. Although Mary Jane is a conventionally acceptable character, she is much like Jim and Huck in being a minority member of society; she is a woman, and she is emotionally vulnerable. Mary Jane's faith within a survivalist world constitutes a danger both to herself and to Huck. Huck must protect her from her own innocence and honesty. To do this, Huck must resort to lies; they are lies of benevolence, not self-interest, lies that function pragmatically in an inverted culture to help protect and promote the greater truth. Huck promises Mary Jane falsely that he will not give her love to the Duke and King because "it was well enough to tell *her* so—no harm in it. It was only a little thing to do, and no trouble; and it's the little things that smoothes people's roads the most, down here below; it would make Mary Jane comfortable, and it wouldn't cost nothing" (242–43).

"Down here below" is certainly the imperfect world of deception in *Adventures of Huckleberry Finn*, but the ideal of rhetorical truth is also presented as something for which to strive. Although Huck never rids himself on an intellectual level of the lie of slavery, he hardly seems to blame for his lack of cultural awareness, which remains claustrophobically locked within the limits of what his culture has taught him to see, although Twain does not lock his reader claustrophobically within the limits of Huck's view to see beyond it, since we perceive the ironies in Huck's view that he does not see. Ethically, Huck seems to go about as far as a child can go toward moral awareness, without guiding examples within his conventional culture. He learns not to lie exploitatively and he learns, on guarded terms, to tell the truth, in a culture where the norm is that everybody lies. The fact that praise was lavished on contemporary nineteenth-century figures for their capacity to tell the truth intimates that in Mark Twain's nineteenth-century America, truth-telling was not only valued but probably rare. *Adventures of Huckleberry Finn* seems to be Twain's clear warning to culture of the dangers of that rarity.

5

James's *The Bostonians:*
Love and Discourse
in the American Marketplace

☙❧

He was as warm as the south wall of a garden or as the flushed fruit that
grows there. Of all consummate artists he was the most natural. Every
impression he gave out passed through the imagination, but only to take
from it more common truth.

—HENRY JAMES ON DAUDET,
Literature, December 25, 1897

Henry James's *The Bostonians* has been explored for its topical references to the Civil War, to transcendentalism, and to the nineteenth-
century feminist movement in America,[1] but there is a yet more striking intensity of social realism in *The Bostonians*. James depicts the
nineteenth-century Bostonians' love affair with public rhetoric. He
draws from his own experience and observation an accurate portrait of
the marriage of rhetorical idealism to political ideology that was playing to sell-out audiences in the American cultural marketplace in the
1870s and 1880s. Huck Finn guilelessly informs his *Century Magazine*
audience in the novel's opening paragraph that everyone lies. During
the same period, in the same magazine, glib Mrs. Luna in *The Bostonians* tells her southern cousin Basil Ransom that her sister Olive is, as
all Bostonians, " 'very honest.' " In fact, " 'nobody tells fibs in Boston;
I don't know what to make of them all.' "[2]

James accurately portrays in *The Bostonians* the feeling that public
oratory was the appropriate vehicle for "new truths of the age." These
truths in fact gained sanction through eloquent oratory, which Ameri-

cans generally believed to be divinely inspired. Henry Ward Beecher proclaimed at the opening of the National School of Oratory in Philadelphia in 1876 that "nowhere is training nobler than in preparing the orator for the great work to which he educates himself—the elevation of his kind, through truth, through earnestness, through beauty, through every divine influence."[3] Here was the Quintilian principle sentimentalized by the American populace, the assumption that every orator trained for the purpose of elevating mankind.

James accurately sets his tale of rhetorical enthusiasm in Boston, 1870s (161) because perhaps nowhere, and in no other time period, was the eagerness for public rhetoric so prevalent.[4] C. E. Grinnell rhapsodized in *American Law Review* in 1882, "Of what is old or new Boston more justly proud than of its public spirit? And to whom is it more indebted for its development, in its present generous and noble proportions, than to the orators of old and of new Boston."[5] Grinnell's expression of faith in the vitality of Bostonian oratory is not surprising inasmuch as the first university school of oratory was established at Boston University in 1872 headed by Lewis Baxter Monroe. This school admitted women and men impartially, which makes it plausible that James's fictional female orators, such as Verena or Mrs. Farrinder, might exist or be so well received.

One of the more memorable oratorical personages of the time was James Steele MacKaye. MacKaye, who subsequently lectured in Brooklyn at the invitation of Henry Ward Beecher, popularized the elocutionary work of French music teacher François Delsarte, which emphasized "harmonic gymnastics," or "primarily a system of physical training." MacKaye lectured for the first time at the St. James Hotel in Boston on March 21, 1871, a lecture repeated twice subsequently at Boston's Tremont Temple and then delivered at Harvard in April, under the patronage of Henry W. Longfellow.[6] Boston in the 1870s to 1890s was fervently involved in public oratory. The *Boston Herald*, in 1879, observed that there were five thousand students of oratory and elocution in Boston.[7] Monroe's school prompted the establishment of private schools of speech in the 1880s and 1890s, whose judgments on elocution and preferred delivery techniques are echoed in *The Bostonians* by the various characters who comment on Verena's oratory.

James's personal experience with rhetoric may also have influenced his decision to set his American tale about rhetoric in Boston. In 1862–63, James pursued an experimental year studying law at Harvard. "The forenoon lectures at Dane Hall I never in all my time missed," James relates in "Notes of a Son and Brother." Despite his demurring remark that it was "quite prodigious that I should have been so systematically faithful to them without my understanding the first word of what they were about,"[8] James inevitably came into contact with classical and eighteenth-century rhetorics in his bout with Harvard forensics—his fellow companion in such studies, for example, his brother William, quotes George Campbell in his later psychological studies.[9] Even more suggestive is James's mention of his fellow boarder at Miss Upham's for whom he felt great admiration, Francis J. Child. "The image most vividly restored," James relates,

> is doubtless that of Professor F. J. Child, head of the "English Department" at Harvard and master of that great modern science of folk-lore to his accomplishment in which his vast and slowly-published collection of the Ballad literature of our language is a recognized monument; delightful man, rounded character, passionate patriot, admirable talker, above all thorough humanist and humorist. He was the genial autocrat of that breakfast-table not only, but of our symposia otherwise timed, and as he comes back to me with the fresh and quite circular countenance of the time before the personal cares and complications of life had gravely thickened for him . . . I see that *there* was the American spirit . . . of a quality inbred, beautifully adjusted to all extensions of knowledge and taste.[10]

James's description of Child is interesting in its omission: in 1862–63, when James was at Harvard, Child was not head of a department of English but serving as the fourth Boylston Professor of Rhetoric and Oratory at Harvard, a chair he apparently held, reluctantly, from 1851 to 1876. A newspaper report of Child's assumption of this chair announced that " 'he was—God knows why!—Boylston Professor of Rhetoric and Oratory.' " "The personal cares and complications of life" that James alludes to as troubling Child may well have been his altercations with the Board of Overseers at Harvard in 1873, who apparently accused Child of negligence. A sympathetic Charles W. Eliot, who came to Harvard as president in 1869, eventually created a separate chair of English for Child. According to one scholar, Child's disdain for rhetoric was instrumental in turning his department away from that discipline.[11]

Undoubtedly, a main topic James would have heard addressed as part of Child's socratic symposia was his grave reservations about public oratory. Child shared the opinion of his former teacher and third

Boylston Professor of Rhetoric and Oratory E. T. Channing that ancient orators were sophistic and classical audiences were ignorant and
easily swayed. Channing believed, however, that "the splendor that
surrounds" the modern orator "must be the natural light of truth,
not the false brilliancy that startles and blinds," [12] affirming faith in
the democratic public's unsusceptibility to sophistry. Child adopted a
thoroughly consistent cynical view of all orators and all audiences. As
a senior at Harvard, he had written a prize-winning essay, "The Moral
Views of Plato as Unfolded in the *Gorgias*," which reiterated Plato's
warning that the orator panders "to the worst inclinations of man" [13]
and encourages man in the pursuit of self-gratification rather than self-
knowledge. James's failure to mention Child's obligation to rhetoric
during the time of James's intimacy with him suggests James's own
complex psychological reaction to the ideals of rhetoric. A complex
panorama of the American rhetorical landscape is portrayed in *The Bostonians*. It is one accompanied by a certain ambivalence of attitude on
James's part about American rhetoric.

One particular type of American rhetorician is unconditionally condemned in *The Bostonians*. This is the rhetorician who lives only for
public acclaim. Matthias Pardon, Selah Tarrant, and Mrs. Farrinder are
all public rhetoricians suggestive of Plato's concern in the *Gorgias*—
which James certainly knew through his association with Child—that
rhetoricians in a profit-oriented society are inevitably corrupt. Irving
Howe observes that "James registers a certain impatience with the idea
or the need for politics" and "an uneasy contempt for the very idea
of 'public life,' which for him would always be at odds with private
values." [14] One important discrimination consistently made by the various morally sentient characters in *The Bostonians* is between "public"
and "personal" rhetoric. Verena's rhetoric is immediately distinguished
by Olive and Basil as "an intensely personal exhibition" (61). Mrs. Farrinder, in contrast, "the great oratress" (45), was "a mixture of the
American matron and the public character. There was something public in her eye, which was large, cold, and quiet" (30).

  Mrs. Farrinder's profit-oriented rhetoric is suggested as corrupt. She
is described by Olive Chancellor as an "eloquent woman" (32), and yet
Olive discerns "a false note when she spoke to her young friends about
the ladies in Beacon Street"; Olive detects a telltale envy of "worldly
glory" (34). When Mrs. Farrinder is bested at her own game by Verena,
James puts the self-interested, competitive nature of Mrs. Farrinder's

rhetoric in a comical light: "By this time Mrs. Farrinder was in a condition of overhanging gloom; she greeted the charming suppliant with the frown of Juno" (57). Olive finally concludes that "Mrs. Farrinder was not weak, of course, and she brought a great intellect to the matter; but she was not personal enough—she was too abstract" (86).

In *The Bostonians*, the consequence of being too abstract, too public, is the loss of conscience and of soul. E. L. Godkin, in the *Nation* in 1875, claimed that rhetorical study is "productive of fatuous conceit and self-worship. It is almost certain to produce, too, love of notoriety; and when once this takes possession of a rhetorician, it consumes him utterly." [15] Plato makes the point in the *Gorgias* that a rhetorician must first know himself before he can presume to teach others.[16] Matthias Pardon and Selah Tarrant surrender to and gain identity from "the great bourgeois blankness," [17] and in doing so each becomes a moral vacuum—large, cold, and quiet—becomes, as Olive damningly describes Selah Tarrant, "a moralist without a moral sense" (111). Ransom labels Tarrant "false, cunning, vulgar, ignoble; the cheapest kind of human product" (58). James actually establishes a phenomenological reason for Tarrant's falseness; by abdicating his responsibility for a reflective life, Tarrant forfeits his opportunity for any meaningful interaction with the outside world. Mrs. Tarrant knows that Tarrant "was an awful humbug, and yet her knowledge had this imperfection, that he had never confessed it." She acknowledges that "even in the privacy of domestic intercourse he had phrases, excuses, explanations, ways of putting things, which, as she felt, were *too* sublime for just herself; they were pitched, as Selah's nature was pitched, altogether in the key of public life." Tarrant's comical fate is that, for all his love of public notoriety, he "didn't know how to speak. That was where the shoe pinched—that was where Selah was slim. He couldn't hold the attention of an audience, he was not acceptable as a lecturer. He had plenty of thoughts, but it seemed as if he couldn't fit them into each other" (74). Mrs. Tarrant thinks it "a poor consolation" that Selah instead possesses "the eloquence of the hand" (75). Tarrant's lack of rhetorical success is amusing, but it also implies that Americans may be more discerning than one might suspect.

Selah exemplifies the hypocrisy underlying moral pretensions and the way that rhetorical idealism can be exploitatively used in a society whose ethos is profit. Tarrant sanctimoniously remarks to his wife "that the only refreshment *he* ever wanted was the sense that he was doing some good" (106). This moral pretension covers the fact that he is bedding and boarding with his "spiritual clients" while Mrs. Tarrant is "sustaining nature with a hard-boiled egg and a doughnut" (105). More important, Tarrant has very little conscience; he adopts the reforming zeal only as a means to an end: "In reality he had one all-absorbing solicitude — the desire to get paragraphs put into the newspapers." For Tarrant, "the vision of that publicity haunted his dreams, and he would gladly have sacrificed to it the innermost sanctities of home. Human existence to him, indeed, was a huge publicity, in which the only fault was that it was sometimes not sufficiently effective" (103). Tarrant, in this culture where money and notoriety seem equally a form of profit, interchangeable commodities productive of each other, is understandably ambivalent about which he most desires, publicity or receipts. He knows, however, that the rhetorical ideal is to deny the desire for either; as Plato suggests in the *Gorgias* and the *Apology*, the only truly disinterested and thus virtuous orator is the one who does not speak for money.[18] Selah considers that Verena's speeches in the West "had brought in no money; they had been delivered only for the good of the cause. If it could only be known that she spoke for nothing, that might deepen the reverberation." Selah fulfills Plato's prophecy that the orator desires to appear virtuous rather than to be so.[19] He concludes that "the only trouble was that speaking for nothing was not the way to remind him that he had a remunerative daughter. It was not the way to stand out so very much either." Not only does free oratory bring no public acclaim, but "disinterestedness, too, was incompatible with receipts; and receipts were what Selah Tarrant was, in his own parlance, after" (104).

Matthias Pardon is also after receipts, but he predictably denies it. Pardon tells Olive that he does not want to make money by publicizing Verena. " 'What do you want to make, then?' " Olive asks. " 'Well, I want to make history!' " Pardon replies, " 'I want to help the ladies' " (146). He considers the emancipation of women " 'the great modern question' "; however, he assesses Verena's appeal with the eyes of the stock market: "She had charm, and there was a great demand for that nowadays in connection with new ideas" (128). He murmurs upon first hearing Verena, " 'There's money for someone in that girl; you see if she don't have quite a run!' " (64). Pardon obviously holds equal reverence for the exchange commodities of money and notoriety.

Pardon also obscures the boundaries between the public and the personal and in doing so loses the personal altogether. Pardon "regarded the mission of mankind upon the earth as a perpetual evolution of telegrams; everything to him was very much the same, he had no sense of proportion or quality." In his "cultivation of the great arts of publicity," Pardon weds himself to a "state of intimacy with the newspapers" (125). James's oxymoron suggests that Pardon has no possibility of intimacy with or reverence for another. Pardon believes "that he himself was in love with Verena, but his passion was not a jealous one, and included a remarkable disposition to share the object of his affection with the American people" (126). His supposed benevolence is undercut by this possible allusion to Plato's remarks in the *Phaedrus* about disinterested love. Plato refutes the argument that a nonlover is best because of his benign indifference by pointing out that missed intimacy is a missed opportunity for spiritual growth.[20] Pardon, in substituting his lust for the great bourgeois public for genuine intimacy, avoids this opportunity.

Indeed, Pardon's and Tarrant's love of notoriety has become their substitute religion. The religious symbolism in *The Bostonians* implies that rhetoric has replaced religion as the religion of the democracy. The name of Matthias Pardon's newspaper is the *Vesper*, and Tarrant looks "like the priest of a religion that was passing through the stage of miracles" (102).

In *The Bostonians*, there is also a sharp implicit criticism of the infringement of the publicity-seeker on the privacy of others. The word *familiar* appears in the text of *The Bostonians* to condemn those who use language in blatant disregard for the private lives of others. Pardon, James explains, abounds in "familiar reference": "For this ingenuous son of his age all distinction between the person and the artist had ceased to exist; the writer was personal, the person food for newsboys, and everything and everyone was everyone's business." Thus Pardon "poured contumely on their private life, on their personal appearance, with the best conscience in the world" (125). Clearly, for one whose approach to others is to see them as commodities and not as individuals, the best conscience is no conscience and the best self-awareness is no self-awareness.

Mrs. Luna is also perceived by Basil Ransom as "intolerably familiar" (5). Miss Chancellor describes Mrs. Luna as "that woman of many words" and decides that Mrs. Luna has made Olive's own natural shyness worse "by becoming instantly so personal" (10). Despite the neuroses of Olive's guarded protectiveness, *The Bostonians* ultimately defends the idea that human personality and identity are fragile and human intercourse a risk to the individual psyche not to be taken lightly. An assumption of instant intimacy poses an immediate threat to the other in its suggestion of insincerity. Carl Rogers has described human intercourse as a bridge forged through mutual respect and compromise between two differing individuals.[21] Basil listens in dismay as Mrs. Luna too facilely traverses that bridge in her discussion of her sister: "She had as many ways as possible of marking the gulf that divided them; but she bridged it over lightly now by saying to Basil Ransom: 'Isn't she a dear old thing?' This bridge, he saw, would not bear his weight, and her question seemed to him to have more audacity than sense. Why should she be so insincere?'" (95). Basil concludes that Mrs. Luna "was a tremendously familiar little woman—that she took, more rapidly than he had ever known, a high degree of intimacy for granted" (198).

Just as Carwin intrudes on Clara's psychological as well as physical privacy in *Wieland* by hiding in her closet, Basil "disliked extremely the way in which, in spite of her love of form and order, she attempted to clamber in at the window of one's house when one locked the door" (199). One may be reminded of Hawthorne's perception of the greatest sin—the violation of the sanctity of the human heart. An intimacy carelessly acquired and cavalierly used fits this classification. Ironically, Mrs. Luna is self-deceived about her own excessive familiarity: "In all Mrs. Luna's visions of herself, her discretion was the leading feature" (212). Adeline is obviously the victim of her own sophistry. "In reality," Basil realizes, "Olive was distinguished and discriminating, and Adeline was the dupe of confusions in which the worse was apt to be mistaken for the better" (199). Again, there is the reference to Plato, this time to the *Apology*, where Socrates is on trial for being a sophist who makes "the worse appear the better cause."[22] This expression—making the worse appear the better—also runs consistently through nineteenth-century periodical references to rhetoric.

Mrs. Burrage's rhetoric is also described by Basil Ransom as being familiar, but her familiarity is more the social type that eases people off rather than exposing their vulnerabilities. Ransom notes that when she cannot discover the reason why Basil has been invited to her evening soiree, she "faded into vagueness": "Basil Ransom could see she was a woman who could carry off an awkwardness like that, and he considered her with a sense of her importance. She had a brisk, familiar, slightly impatient way, and if she had not spoken so fast, and had more of the softness of the southern matron, she would have reminded him of a certain type of woman he had seen of old, before the changes in his own part of the world—the clever, hospitable proprietress, widowed or unmarried, of a big plantation" (281).

Olive mistakenly assumes that Mrs. Burrage's rhetoric was formed through European influence. This is not surprising because Mrs. Burrage handles conversations with a good deal of form. She handles them adroitly and with seeming impartiality and indifference to achieve her purpose. Her purpose is to procure Verena for her son and to handle what she obviously feels to be the difficult situation with Olive and with Verena's work with great aplomb. The heights of Olive's self-deception are revealed in her scene of collusion with Mrs. Burrage's sophistry. The scene also reveals the finesse of Mrs. Burrage's rhetoric. James expresses Olive's reactions to Mrs. Burrage in such a way as to indicate that Mrs. Burrage indeed is the sophist flattering her audience's deceptive self-image for the accomplishment of her own ends. Olive, faced with the greater evil of Basil as a potential suitor to Verena rather than Burrage, decides that "she liked her hostess better this morning than she had liked her before; she had more than ever the air of taking all sorts of sentiments for granted between them; which could only be flattering to Olive so long as it was really Mrs. Burrage who made each advance, while her visitor sat watchful and motionless" (311).

Olive waits to see if Mrs. Burrage can present her son as a suitor to Verena on terms reassuring to Olive while at the same time flattering Olive's need to perceive herself as definitely disinterested. "People like Mrs. Burrage lived and fattened on abuses, prejudices, privileges, on the petrified cruel fashions of the past," Olive observes. Yet Olive's need to keep Verena from Basil, while convincing herself that she is not controlling Verena's life, causes her to decide "that if her hostess was a humbug, Olive had never met one who provoked her less; she was such a brilliant, genial, artistic one, with such a recklessness of perfidy, such a willingness to bribe you if she couldn't deceive you. She seemed to be offering Olive all the kingdoms of the earth if she would only exert herself to bring about a state of feeling on Verena Tarrant's part which would lead the girl to accept Henry Burrage" (313). To Mrs. Burrage's implication that Olive controls her friend, Olive responds, " 'She is absolutely free; you speak as if I were her keeper!' " Mrs. Burrage willingly participates in Olive's self-deceit to accomplish her own ends, explaining "that of course she didn't mean that Miss Chancellor exercised a conscious tyranny; but only that Verena had a boundless admiration for her, saw through her eyes, took the impress of all her opinions, preferences" (314).

Mrs. Burrage blithely admits that she is "excellent at taking up a cause. I haven't renounced, I have only changed sides. For or against, I must be a partisan. Don't you know that kind of nature?" (315). Her nature is that of a sophist, who manipulates language to achieve her own end, who also falsely implies that reality is constituted by what is stated rather than referred to by language. Mrs. Burrage's rhetoric is not American in the sense that the quintessential American in *The Bostonians* is shown to strive for and to believe in honesty; even Mrs. Luna, except on certain occasions threatening to her pride, offers bitingly honest observations that are typical of the candid American. Indeed, Mrs. Burrage's manipulations of language recur as a central theme in James's later works *The Wings of the Dove* and *The Golden Bowl*, and the dangers of such language to human integrity are explicitly exposed. James simply suggests those dangers in *The Bostonians* when he reveals the contempt and coldness that Mrs. Burrage really feels for Olive underlying her rhetorical warmth: "If we were this moment to take, in a single glance, an inside view of Mrs. Burrage (a liberty we have not yet ventured on), I suspect we should find that she was considerably exasperated at her visitor's superior tone, at seeing herself regarded by this dry, shy, obstinate, provincial young woman as superficial. If she liked Verena very nearly as much as she tried to convince Miss Chancellor, she was conscious of disliking Miss Chancellor more than she should probably ever be able to reveal to Verena" (319).

Despite this brief foray into the subtleties of European rhetoric, the focus in *The Bostonians* is primarily on American rhetorical enthusiasm, on the supposed American adoration of honesty and the American faith that rhetoricians "have received, fresh from heaven, the divine afflatus and inspiration." [23] It is on this concept of rhetoric that hypocritical rhetoricians such as Selah Tarrant feed. One can determine clearly how such a character as Tarrant should be judged. But James's view of American rhetoric becomes more difficult to judge when one considers the rhetoric of Tarrant's daughter. In the consideration of Verena's rhetoric James's portrait of the American rhetorical landscape becomes more complex.

Verena is an important commodity in the American marketplace because she confirms American faith in the virtue of rhetoric. Elizabeth Allen has provided James scholars with a convincing image of what the young woman was supposed to represent in nineteenth-century America. She was to symbolize "piety, purity, submissiveness, and domesticity," and yet, also, paradoxically, to represent America's sense of independence. This conflict in symbolic value was resolved by granting the young American woman a tenuous hold on her independence from the time she left her father's home until she got married. Allen's point is that James dramatizes the existential plight of this young woman, who recognizes herself not first as a person but as a symbol. The young American girl's "innocence and openness thus becomes the very essence of the idealist illusion of the untouched, blank materials of signification waiting to be shaped and formed by the external (male) subject." "In the world of *The Bostonians*," according to Allen, "the young girl is a devalued commodity, able to be manipulated by anyone who can gain control over her and direct what she signifies. There are no 'real' values or meanings, only those assigned by the expediency of the moment." [24] Interestingly, Allen could just as well be referring to the symbolic value of rhetoric in nineteenth-century America. In *The Bostonians*, James intertwines the significations of rhetoric and of the young American girl so that they are one and the same; the issue of the exploitability of the young American girl's innocence is inter-changeable with the issue of the exploitability of rhetorical idealism. These intertwined issues and James's continuing faith in and ambivalence toward the moral value of both rhetorical idealism and the young American girl are continuing concerns in his novels.

It is not surprising that James originally intended to title his novel *Verena* rather than *The Bostonians:* both titles refer to the topic of American rhetoric that the book explores. James goes to pains to re-iterate repeatedly, in his portrait of Verena and her rhetoric, the typical catchwords and catchphrases used to describe American rhetorical eloquence during the latter part of the nineteenth century. Although rhetorical and elocutionary theory were often studied separately during the third quarter of the century, their ideals were interchangeable in suggesting a moral rectitude for the eloquent speaker, and James develops Verena's portrait and people's response to her with attention to both. One of the major principles of elocutionary training was an emphasis on "the natural expression of thought by speech and gesture." [25] This philosophy may have been influenced by the rhetorical innovations of Richard Whately, whose 1828 *Elements of Rhetoric* retained strong popularity toward the end of the nineteenth century.[26] Whately was the first to suggest that elocution be "natural"; it should be "stripped, as it were, of the sheltering veil of a conventional and artificial delivery." [27] According to J. W. Shoemaker's 1880 *Practical Elo-*

cution, "all speech style should be based on that of conversation," and all "reading and public address should be 'noble conversation.' "[28] True to these contemporary standards, Verena informs Basil that "they tell me I speak as I talk" (232–33).

Another characterization of elocution during this time was its analogy drawn from singing: François Delsarte, for example, was a music teacher whose popularized theory emphasized vocal harmony. James E. Murdoch's 1884 *Analytic Evolution* stressed "that training the voice was the most important part of elocution" and "that the speaking voice may be developed in the same strength, beauty, and flexibility as the singing voice."[29] This notion was compatible with rhetorical theory, which, in blending with aesthetic theory toward the century's end, was progressively describing rhetoric in aesthetic terms: "Eloquence is not mechanical nor artificial, but spontaneous and natural. Of course we are speaking of that highest and sublimest form of speech which fills the heart with emotion and impassioned feeling, and which trembles on the tongue as the thrilling notes of inspiring and uplifting song."[30] The comparison between Verena's eloquence and singing is made in *The Bostonians*. Basil Ransom thrice refers to Verena's eloquence by comparing it to singing. When he first hears Verena, he regards her "as a vocalist of exquisite faculty, condemned to sing bad music" (62). He later discovers his impulse to ridicule Verena "charmed into stillness by the fear of losing something" since "she speechified as a bird sings!" (232). When he finally implores Verena to leave the public circuit for his vision of domestic bliss, he consoles her, "you will sing to me; you will sing to everyone who knows you and approaches you" (402).

Verena's eloquence is also connected with one of the principal terms relating to the source of rhetoric in late nineteenth-century rhetorical theory, *inspiration*. According to the 1863 *National Quarterly Review*, "Eloquence is an art which cannot be acquired in the schools. All mere institutes are powerless to teach it—to confer this divine degree. They are without the genius and inspiration that give it soaring force and lend it wings. It will not obey the barest of rules. If it come at all, it must come as the lightning that flashes along the southern sky, making a track for the hoarse notes of muffled thunder."[31] That same essay uses a form of the word *inspire* six different times. The 1863 *Universalist Quarterly Review* describes Christ as a rhetorician, who, as "lord of life and Truth," came to Earth "to inspire and to teach."[32] Beecher also uses the term repeatedly in his 1876 lecture "Eloquence and Oratory."

Eloquence is "now a living force that brings to itself all the resources of imagination, all the inspirations of feeling, all that is influential in body, in voice, in eye, in gesture, in posture, in the whole animated man, is in strict analogy with the divine thought and the divine arrangement." [33]

James first uses *inspiration* in *The Bostonians* to describe Olive's response to Mrs. Farrinder's suggestion that she make donations to a women's fund: Olive felt "this bold, rapid sketch had the vividness which characterized the speaker's most successful public efforts. It placed Olive under the spell; it made her feel almost inspired" (37). The 1863 *National Quarterly Review* explains that "great orators are magicians; we cannot resist their incantations; we are controlled by their power; we are under their magic spell." [34] Verena also alludes to inspiration when she describes the rhetorical effect that Olive has upon her: "I can tell you, she kindles me; she does, mother, really" (101). Beecher asks of orators, "Are we never to study how skillfully to pick the lock of curiosity, to unfasten the door of fancy, to throw wide open the halls of emotion, and to kindle the light of inspiration in the souls of men?" [35]

In the main, however, people attach the term *inspirational* to Verena. Mr. Tarrant first calls Verena's gift "inspirational" (47). Matthias Pardon explains Verena's gift to Olive Chancellor. "They call it inspirational. I don't know what it is — only it's exquisite; so fresh and poetical. She has to have her father to start her up. It seems to pass into her" (53). Later, Olive decides that Verena's gift could not have come from her corrupt parent but must have "dropped straight from heaven" (84). After Verena's first speech, Ransom observes, "then memory, or inspiration, returned to her, and presently she was in possession of her part" (61). To Olive's mind, it becomes "more and more clear that her eloquence, when she stood up that way before a roomful of people, was literally inspiration" (85).

The blurred boundary between art and nature in the characterization of Verena's eloquence is a dominant feature also of late nineteenth-century rhetoric. This rhetoric was increasingly involved with late nineteenth-century aesthetics. T. Hunt's 1874 essay "Rhetorical Science" sheds light on what the time period meant by "personal" and how this was related to the connection between nature and art. "The Rhetorician in the highest sense is the man himself," according to Hunt, "in full possession of his powers and acquisitions, writing out the full expression of his nature, in the most natural forms." For the highest rhetorical art, "more of the writer's personality is what we need in our writing, a more unreserved utterance, i.e. out-terance of the inner man, self revelation; and then who read us; the transfer of personal feelings into the most central experience of others." [36] One recalls that Basil perceives Verena's first speech as "intensely personal" (61). It is in this vein of expecting art to express nature that Olive quizzes Verena, wanting to know "how I can speak the way I do unless I feel" (102).

Just as the rhetorical artist was to be intensely personal in the natural expression of himself, it was felt that his natural self could be expressed only through art. Hunt suggests that "art is the very Nature of man, or the outward portraiture of his inner self" and that "it is verily impossible for nature properly to express itself without Art." [37] James maintains such an intriguing balance between the possible artistry and innocence of Verena's rhetoric in *The Bostonians* that it often emerges as oxymoron; Verena is called "naturally theatrical" (53). To Olive, "Verena had the disposition of the artist, the spirit to which all forms come easily and naturally" (117). She has "some natural light, some divine spark of taste" (118). Basil decides "he had never seen such an odd mixture of elements; she had the sweetest, most unworldly face, and yet, with it, an air of being on exhibition, of belonging to a troupe, of living in the gaslight, which pervaded even the details of her dress, fashioned evidently with an attempt at the histrionic" (58–59). It is the artistry of Verena's rhetoric, despite her innocence, that provokes scientific Doctor Prance to intimate "that she was a deceiver" (59). "And yet," Basil notices, "there was a strange spontaneity in her manner, and an air of artless enthusiasm, of personal purity" (53). In Olive's view, "she had kept the consummate innocence of the American girl, that innocence which was the greatest of all" (124). Verena, apparently, has both natural spontaneity and a self-awareness of her artistry, a combination qualifying her as the quintessential model of rhetorical eloquence that was being touted during her time.

Verena also has the accompanying honesty that causes Basil and Olive to cherish her and to covet her as the genuine American article. Both Basil and Olive ethically transcend the casual sophistry of the American public rhetoricians with their insistence on honesty as the underlying prerequisite of any acceptable rhetoric. "Olive," James relates, "had a standing quarrel with the levity, the good-nature, of the judgments of the day; many of them seemed to her weak to imbecility, losing sight of all measures and standards, lavishing superlatives, delighted to be fooled" (127). Verena, in contrast, has "extraordinary candor and confidence" (52). "Verena," James notes, "wanted to know the truth" (153). When Olive first discovers there is a history to Verena and Basil's relationship of which she is unaware, James writes, "It was Olive's plan of life not to lie, and attributing a similar disposition to people she liked, it was impossible for her to believe that Verena had had the intention of deceiving her" (287). Verena's innocence is important to Basil and Olive primarily because it signifies her honesty. Basil, for example, is cautious about his attraction to Verena until he is certain that she measures up to his standard of honesty. "He understood her now very well," he reassures himself; "he saw she was honest and natural" (253).

Despite Basil's and Olive's admiration for Verena's rhetorical style and honesty, they hold no such respect for her logic; both feel they have the necessary "truth" that will complement Verena's rhetoric. In assuming that ideal rhetoric implies a lack, a necessary accompanying logic, Basil and Olive reiterate one of the issues debated by nineteenth-century rhetorical theorists: did rhetoric imply its own logic, as George Campbell very nearly suggests in *The Philosophy of Rhetoric*, or did rhetoric exist apart from logic, as Richard Whately adamantly claims in *The Principles of Rhetoric*. One can clearly see in the statements of moral rhetoricians during the period that the eloquent rhetorician was perceived to have some mysterious hold on the truth, whatever that might be. The assumption that the truth was absolute was definitely implied. Plato's *Gorgias* had of course warned against naively accepting that the eloquent orator had a hold on virtue, claiming that the orator's "truth" was often selfishly and politically motivated. And yet the rhetoricians who urged the truth on their audiences in the nineteenth century were liberal in tolerance and ameliorative; their truth implied apolitical qualities like Christian compassion, love, and charity extended to all. Their message was more often than not antipolitical, not infused with dogma. Thus it might be that the nineteenth-century rhetorician's conception of truth was close to Plato's definition of *virtue*.

Irving Howe claims that "if James meant Verena as the one 'positive' moral force, the one figure toward whom our response should be more sympathetic than ironic, he failed." If instead "she is intended mainly as a charming creature over whose imperilled innocence a violent battle of ideologies is being fought, he brilliantly succeeded."[38] Other critics have thought also that Verena is "an empty cipher who can receive meaning from only one of the two antagonists."[39] The problem for James in *The Bostonians* is this tendency on the part of his audience to devalue the moral cogency both of Verena's logical argument and of moral rhetoric because of their slightness in formal logic. Instead,

Verena's argument is based intuitively upon benevolent emotion and upon an optimistic interpretation of experience, much like the message of the rhetorical idealism of her day. Contrary to the opinion of many James scholars, Verena does actually offer her own rhetorical argument, constituted out of her good faith and innocence. Her message of "truth" is close to the Christian message of truth argued by nineteenth-century rhetorician Henry Ward Beecher. She argues for the emancipation of women out of the logic of conciliation and love: "I am not here to recriminate, nor to deepen the gulf that already yawns between the sexes, and I don't accept the doctrine that they are natural enemies." Verena's message is instead one of conciliation and possible redemption: "I should like to press home to each of you, personally, individually—to give him the vision of the world as it hangs perpetually before me, redeemed, transfigured, by a new moral tone. There would be generosity, tenderness, sympathy, where there is now only brute force and sordid rivalry" (273–74).

Just as Howe remarks, Basil and Olive do fight ideological battles over Verena but that they can do so is not James's failure—or Verena's—but theirs. Basil and Olive, out of their own ideological blindness, fail to "see" Verena, to help her "realize" her loving approach to the world. Instead, they ignore her very essence—while at the same time they are sure that they have seen it—by imposing on her their own visions of the world, visions that involve a competitiveness and hatred exactly opposite to her vision of benevolent love. They both do so certain that they are acting in the name of honesty and in the name of truth. In the characterizations of Basil and Olive—Olive, particularly—James warns about the ease with which idealism can be perverted into self-serving ideology and about how tempting it is for the tyrant to rationalize his oppressiveness by seeing it as a form of idealism. James does this in his portrait of Olive, for Olive devoutly believes she is pursuing the Platonic ideal of virtuous rhetoric.

Henry Ward Beecher and the other moral rhetoricians of his time believed that they were Platonic Aristotelians, that they consistently found the Christian truth inspired by their faith verified by practical experience. Beecher believed that man's evolution through increasingly sophisticated cultural forms would bring about man's spiritual evolution, a notion confirmed, in Beecher's view, by Darwin's discovery of the principle of evolution. Beecher asserted that man's exposure to experience would promote a continuing dialectical movement upward:

"The relations of the ideal and the practical, of the visible and the invisible, of the real and the imaginative, are of transcendent importance. It has been said that everybody in the world is either a Platonist or an Aristotelian — Plato standing for ideal philosophy, and Aristotle for the real and practical." In Beecher's view, "the perfect man unites them both" with "his heart the balance between them."[40]

The irony of Olive's dogmatizing is that she clearly perceives herself to be a rhetorical idealist. She feels that she knows the highest spiritual truth, but, as she informs Mrs. Farrinder, "I have no self-possession, no eloquence; I can't put three words together. But I do want to contribute" (36). Olive decides that, between them, Verena and she will be the perfect union of Plato and Aristotle: the truth will be embodied in a real form. George Campbell had described sound rhetoric as a marriage of logic and style: "If then it is the business of logic to evince the truth; to convince an auditory, which is the province of eloquence, is but a particular application of the logician's art. As logic therefore forges the arms which eloquence teacheth us to wield, we must first have recourse to the former."[41] A dialogue between Verena and Olive, in which they discuss their rhetorical union, echoes Campbell's words. Verena calls Olive her "conscience," and Olive calls Verena her "form," her "envelope," which implies the organic union between eloquence and argument that Campbell describes:

> To Olive it appeared that just this partnership of their two minds — each of them, by itself, lacking an important group of facets — made an organic whole which, for the work in hand, could not fail to be brilliantly effective. Verena was often far more irresponsive than she liked to see her, but the happy thing in her composition was that, after a short contact with the divine idea — Olive was always trying to flash it at her, like a jewel in an uncovered case — she kindled, flamed up. . . . Then Olive perceived how fatally, without Verena's tender notes, her crusade would lack sweetness, what the Catholics call unction; and, on the other hand, how weak Verena would be on the statistical and logical side if she herself should not bring up the rear. Together, in short, they would be complete, they would have everything, and together they would triumph. (160)

In line with the rhetorical idealists of her day, Olive sees herself involved in the discourse of love, as Plato defines it in the *Phaedrus:* she sees herself as the spiritual teacher who will help Verena evolve to a higher form of spiritual truth through the more sophisticated forms of cultural experience that Olive can provide her. In line with Plato's definition of genuine love, Olive believes that she is not coercing Verena, but, rather, helping her to become further enlightened about her own innate spiritual essence. Thus Olive believes that her discourse of love aimed at Verena is of the highest nature, that she does not take away, but rather enhances, Verena's freedom. Plato, in the *Phaedrus*, relates that every human soul unknowingly follows a particular spiritual truth and in so doing inspires others to follow that similar truth through example. That soul exhibits "no jealousy or pettiness toward the loved one; rather, every act is aimed at bringing the beloved to be as much as possible like themselves, that is, like the god they honor."[42]

Franz Theremin's *Eloquence a Virtue*, popular in the United States in the mid-nineteenth century, is strongly derivative of Plato's dialogue. It pursues the implications of Plato's dialogue for rhetoric and helps to explicate Olive's rhetorical motives. Theremin states that "eloquence strives to produce a change in the sentiments and conducts of other men." Eloquence asks "what are the laws according to which a free being may exert influence upon other free beings?" Rhetorical eloquence responds that the orator must respect human freedom and that he can do so only by arguing for something that his audience "must will, from their moral nature; from the fact that the true freedom of man is constantly striving after the realization of certain ideas." According to Theremin, man despite his possibly superficial desires actually wishes to realize the idea of his own moral virtue. Hence, Theremin writes, "the orator must address man as he came from his Creator, and not as he has made himself." The orator eloquent on the subject of his audience's virtue therefore "not only respects the freedom of the hearer, but while he seems to overpower and utterly subject him, raises him, through the enlivenment of his ideas, to the very highest good of an independent self-consciousness."[43]

Olive thinks that she is proceeding in her rhetorical pursuit of Verena with a constant vigilance of her own ethics and consideration of Verena's freedom. She thinks that she is eloquent in pursuit of Verena's virtue. Her "sense that she found here what she had been looking for so long—a friend of her own sex with whom she might have a union of soul" is immediately checked by her ethical consideration of Verena's freedom in the matter since "it took a double consent to make a friendship" (80). When Olive bursts out, " 'Will you be my friend, my friend of friends, beyond everyone, everything, forever and forever?' " she notes Verena's cautious response, " 'Perhaps you like me too much.' " Olive confirms Verena's suspicion, but she also recognizes the fear of compulsion expressed in it. She quickly adds, " 'But of course it's another thing, your liking me.' " She hastily reassures that " 'we must wait—we must wait. When I care for anything, I can be patient' " (81). The important ethical point for Olive is that she is very certain that she is enhancing Verena's spiritual growth and thus freedom by responding to Verena's moral essence. When Olive visits Verena's home and sees her flirting with young men, she discounts the possibility some "might have . . . fancied" that "Verena's vocation was to smile and talk with young men who bent toward her." Olive decides instead that she has "reason to know that a 'gifted being' is sent into the world for a very different purpose" (22). Verena also appears to confirm that she is being spiritually enhanced. She feels that "Olive had taken her up, in the literal sense of the phrase, like a bird of the air, had spread an extraordinary pair of wings, and carried her through the dizzying void of space" (78). Plato similarly observes that "when a man sees beauty in this world and has a remembrance of true beauty, he begins to grow wings."[44]

Nevertheless, Olive's desire to extract a pledge from Verena not to marry is completely at odds with her ethics because it is such a restriction of Verena's freedom. Hence her dilemma of what James calls "feminine" inconsistency: "She wished to extract a certainty at the same time that she wished to deprecate a pledge" (140). Olive retracts her request with a subtle sophistry that causes Verena to exclaim, " 'Why, Olive, you are quite a speaker yourself!' " (139–40) and well she should, for Olive attempts to deceive herself and Verena into believing she is practicing ethics:

> "Don't think me capricious if I say I would rather trust you without a pledge. I owe you, I owe every one, an apology for my rudeness and fierceness at your mother's. It came over me—just seeing those young men—how exposed you are; and the idea made me (for the moment) frantic. I see your danger still, but I see other things too, and I have recovered my balance. You must be safe, Verena—you must be saved; but your safety must not come from your having tied your hands. It must come from the growth of your perception; from your seeing things, of yourself, sincerely and with conviction, in the light in which I see them; from your feeling that for your work your freedom is essential, and that there is no freedom for you and me save in religiously *not* doing what you will often be asked to do—and I never!" (140)

Olive resorts to another ideal of the day as a sort of subscription to ethics. Olive actively seeks suffering—or at least she thinks she does—

as a means of further assuring herself that she is virtuous. Henry Ward Beecher's ethics of suffering revealed in a sermon such as "The Moral Teaching of Suffering" implied that suffering was morally ameliorative. Beecher stated in that sermon, incidentally, that "there is nothing more beautiful in the world than the story of Joan of Arc,"[45] a figure to whom Verena blithely alludes in an early discussion with Olive, having absorbed the popular references of the feminist movement. Later, the idea of Verena as Joan of Arc "lodged itself in Olive's imagination" (147). When Olive faces the prospect of visiting Verena's vulgar mother, "her only consolation was that she expected to suffer intensely; for that prospect of suffering was always, spiritually speaking, so much cash in her pocket" (113).

Olive's need to perceive herself as suffering is part of a complex defense mechanism that she constructs in an attempt to rationalize her own personal feelings. These feelings are based on vindictiveness, not virtue. Theremin notes that the difference between virtuous and spiritually destructive emotions is that "instead of *Enthusiasm*, there very easily arises blind *Adoration*, and instead of *Displeasure*, raging *Hatred*; and these political Passions, which presuppose a great obscuration of the rational idea of Happiness, are the more frightful, because it is easy for every man to justify to himself, and to others, his own selfish efforts, under the appearance of a patriotic disposition."[46] Olive's tragic flaw is her personal prejudice, her hatred and fear of male sexuality, and her resultant contempt for a large portion of humanity. Her need to perceive herself as ethical leads her to become a political tyrant who attempts to turn her private convictions into public dogma. Ironically, also, part of Olive's profile as feminist reformer—the public stance that allows her to sanction her hatred of men—involves her perception that she must deny her own aesthetic sense so as to be part of the democratic movement to which she has pledged faith. James betrays not only Olive's aesthetic sense, but also her covert attention to it as one of his means of pointing out Olive's self-deception.

Olive knows that, ethically, she should not hate, but, rather, pity anyone to whom she takes a dislike. As one recalls from the discussion of *Adventures of Huckleberry Finn*, the ethics of suffering, as advocated by Beecher, promoted compassion, not hatred. Olive resorts, nevertheless, to a public sanction of ideology based on the notion of women's suffering as a way of rationalizing her own ill feeling. One discovers, in chapter 1, that Olive avoids hating her sister because she had "forbidden herself this emotion as directed to individuals" (10). Yet Olive allows herself to dislike Basil Ransom because "she had, however, a moral resource that she could always fall back upon; it had already been a comfort to her, on occasions of acute feeling that she hated men as a class anyway" (22). "Men as a class" is a social, not personal, condemnation in line with her feminine dogmatism. One perceives that even Olive's bid for political power for women has a strong underlying motive of hatred and contempt. Olive believes that her attempt to educate Verena is solid ethical rhetoric, that she will be enhancing a spiritual ideal through cultural education. Yet Olive's account of "real" history, her attempt to prove her version of the "truth" to Verena by providing "a parallel from the facts of history"[47] is compromised by feminist ideology, as Verena gently intimates. Olive selects for study innumerable instances of cruelty and social inequities sponsored by men. James describes these ladies' studies in cozy progress:

> There were some nights of deep snowfall, when Charles Street was white and muffled and the doorbell foredoomed to silence, which seemed little islands of lamplight, of entangled and intensified vision. They read a great deal of history together, and read it ever with the same thought — that of finding confirmation in it for this idea that their sex had suffered inexpressibly, and that at any moment in the course of human affairs the state of the world would have been so much less horrible . . . if women had been able to press down the scale. Verena was full of suggestions which stimulated discussions; it was she, oftenest, who kept in view the fact that a good many women in the past had been intrusted with power and had not always used it amiably. . . . These ladies were easily disposed of between the two, and the public crimes of Bloody Mary, the private misdemeanors of Faustina, wife of the pure Marcus Aurelius, were very satisfactorily classified. If the influence of women in the past accounted for every act of virtue that men had happened to achieve, it only made the matter balance properly that the influence of men should explain the casual irregularities of the other sex. (179)

The facile sophistry of Olive's argument — and the biased way in which she depicts human suffering — is emphasized by the narrator's use of the phrases "easily disposed of," "very satisfactorily classified," and "casual irregularities" and by the subtle way that James introduces into this argument a countergeneralization about the cruelty of women and then supports it with specific examples.

If the Platonic Aristotelian is supposed to be able to "go from the real to the ideal, and then come back,"[48] then he should also be able to integrate private with public. The disharmony between Olive's personal self and the public ideal she supposedly espouses explains why she can find no voice of her own to address the public. To begin with, the public ideal in *The Bostonians* is seen to be politically, not spiritually, motivated, so, in exploiting Verena as a vicarious voice through which to spread her public dogma, Olive gravely endangers Verena's spiritual growth. Olive has simply refined the public ideal of the Matthias Pardons and Selah Tarrants privately, rationalizing her own doctrine based on animosity. Appropriately, Olive's fashioned ideology, which hides from her her hating self, also forces her to renounce the personal and loving part of herself, which is primarily expressed through her aesthetic sense. James says that Olive's "most poignant sufferings came from the injury of her taste" (29), a sense James betrays in her. Olive attempts to renounce aesthetics to illustrate women's triumph over vanity. Miss Birdseye's lack of vanity, Olive decides, is proven by the fact that she will "go down into the grave" having nothing "but the clothes on her back" and leaving "nothing behind her but her grotesque, undistinguished, pathetic little name." Olive's dubious and melodramatic praise for Miss Birdseye is amusing because Olive, who secretly abhors the grotesque and pathetic, strains so to appreciate these traits. The irony intensifies when James betrays Olive's own eye for aesthetics: "While Miss Birdseye stood there, asking Mrs. Farrinder if she wouldn't say something, Olive Chancellor tenderly fastened a small battered brooch which had half detached itself" (38).

Despite the gentleness with which James for the most part depicts Miss Birdseye, her avoidance of anything personal (28) causes her stunted spiritual growth. James calls her "a confused, entangled, inconsequent, discursive old woman, whose charity began at home and ended nowhere, whose credulity kept pace with it, and who knew less about her fellow-creatures if possible, after fifty years of humanitary zeal, than on the day she had gone into the field to testify against the iniquity of most arrangements" (27). James's suggestion that "it would have been a nice question whether, in her heart of hearts, for the sake of this excitement, she did not sometimes wish the blacks back in bondage" (28) provides a chilling echo of the concluding antics of Tom Sawyer. In denying the personal, the very artistic forms through which one sees life, one cannot dynamically interact with the public, and one cannot grow.

Actually, by loving Verena, Olive has the opportunity for spiritual growth herself. The wings that are sprouted in the pursuit of true beauty, alluded to earlier in this chapter, are clearly not Verena's but Olive's: "Olive had taken her up." Olive "had spread an extraordinary pair of wings" (79). Olive's true spiritual course would be to follow Verena in the discourse of love, gaining tolerance, and growing out of her personally destructive feelings of hate. Instead, Olive tries to compel Verena to follow her false ideal, one clearly not responsive to Verena's essence. Verena "also had dreamed of a friendship, though it was not what she had dreamed of most" (83), a perception Basil quickly intuits and capitalizes on. From the start, Verena fears for her essence: "Verena wondered afterward why she had not been more afraid of her—why indeed, she had not turned and saved herself by darting out of the room. But it was not in this young woman's nature to be either timid or cautious; she had as yet to make an acquaintance with the sentiment of fear" (82–83). That Verena would wonder in retrospect at her initial ease with Olive suggests Verena's growing fear.

Olive is a self-deluded sophist who practices on Verena a dangerous rhetorical charm: "Verena was completely under the charm. The idea of Olive's charm will perhaps make the reader smile; but I use the word not in its derived, but in its literal sense. The fine web of authority, of dependence, that her strenuous companion had woven about her, was as dense as a suit of golden mail" (170). Through Olive's inversion, then, of the spiritual journey as one toward hate rather than love, there is an accompanying inversion of the Quintilian principle. Olive uses her suffering as a type of rhetorical eloquence, but her end is political enmity and division, and thus she compels Verena not through moral rhetoric but through the eloquence of sophistry. Thus in the characters of Verena and Olive, James represents two types of eloquence—moral rhetoric and sophistry—and he challenges the notion of the workability of the Quintilian principle's assumption that the "good" man will be the most compelling in a realistic world where the will of the sophist is stronger. It is not Verena who compels Olive but Olive who compels Verena to renounce her essence. Ironically, Olive does so by appealing to that very essence of generosity in Verena which makes Verena a virtuous rhetorician. True to her own virtue, Verena tries very hard to believe in Olive's ideal, not for the sake of the ideal but for the sake of the more meaningful ideal of friendship.

Verena's "necessary ideas," in true Platonic fashion, are never political but always based on love. When Olive asks Verena to pledge abstinence from marriage, "the effect of that quick, violent colloquy was to make her nervous and impatient, as if she had had a sudden glimpse of futurity. That was rather awful, even if it represented the fate one would like" (137). The young lady who "at the beginning" decides that she "would have liked to resemble Mrs. Luna" (110) shows sufficient indexes of her personality to convince anyone not so willingly self-deluded as Olive that Verena's full zest for life, including men, is not just a "phase." But Verena decides terms on which she can pledge to Olive's ideal so that she can "give her so much pleasure" (137). Verena responds personally, in the context of the immediate suit of Matthias Pardon, that, as "she came to think of it, she didn't want to marry any-one" (81). Verena responds only on the limited basis of the experience she has already had, but she intuitively fears that Olive may have a stultifying effect on her future experience, thus on her future growth.

James's descriptions of Verena's supposed communion of soul with Olive always gravely qualify the extent to which Verena's essence is being enhanced by Olive. Verena, for example, "was not always think-ing of the unhappiness of women; but the touch of Olive's tone worked a spell, and she found something toward which at least a portion of her nature turned with eagerness." Verena's ideal of friendship is being exploited by Olive for Olive's own selfish ends, and the exploitation is made even more grievous by Olive's employment of her own sham ethics as an argument: "Verena wished to please her if only because she had such a dread of displeasing her. Olive's displeasures, disap-pointments, disapprovals were tragic, truly memorable; she grew white under them, not shedding many tears, as a general thing, like inferior women (she cried when she was angry, not when she was hurt), but limping and panting, morally, as if she had received a wound that she would carry for life" (141).

Olive's "fearful power of suffering" (298), as Verena calls it, does not obscure from Verena's maturing sight the latent hypocrisies in Olive's behavior: "It was nothing new to Verena that if the great striv-ing of Olive's life was for justice she yet sometimes failed to arrive at it in particular cases" (302). When Olive attempts to banish Ransom from Verena's mind with a sweeping dismissal of their whole New York stay, Verena uses Olive's words ultimately to chide her gently. " 'Well, you know, Verena, this isn't our *real* life—it isn't our work,' " Olive exclaims. Verena's immediate response shows her spiritual difference from Olive: " 'Well, no, it isn't, certainly,' said Verena, not pretend-ing at first that she did not know what Olive meant" (296). Olive later proposes to Verena that she stay in New York with Mrs. Burrage. "Verena," James writes, "broke into a laugh. 'You know it's not our real life!'" (307). Verena's early remark that she feels as far as she realizes (102) reminds us that Verena's growth is contingent on received care. Paul Armstrong, in discussing Maisie's plight in *What Maisie Knew*, writes that care "is the founding structure of existence."[49] Adults in Maisie's life block her knowledge; Olive, by delimiting the perimeters of Verena's experience, indeed, by structuring Verena's "real" upon a bogus ideal that does not conform to her essence, takes away the personal freedom that in Olive's delusional ethics she believes she is trying to give.

Basil Ransom also appeals to Verena on the basis of her personal freedom, convincing Verena that in his expansive presence she will be "standing forth in [her] freedom as well as in [her] loveliness!" (346). Even Basil's physical voice, with its "elisions and interpolations which were equally unexpected" and "his discourse . . . pervaded by something sultry and vast . . . something that suggested the teeming expanse of the cotton field" (5) seems to suggest this freedom. Basil continually pleads with Verena to come away, "'a little way from the house; beyond it, outside the village'" (395) or out "'to the water, where we can speak'" (377), as if by physically expanding the narrow perimeters of Verena's enslaved enclosures with Olive, he can exorcise Olive's alternative structuring of reality from her spirit. "'You always want me to come out!'" Verena at one point complains (395), although, strangely enough, it is Verena who first suggests to Basil an outing in Cambridge, as if Verena herself desires freedom from Olive's repressive world.

Whether or not Basil enhances Verena's personal freedom is an interesting question. Olive once observes that Verena is "free from private self-reference" (176) and, when one recalls how the absence of a private life has made Miss Birdseye vague and inconsequent and Selah Tarrant downright immoral, the private life that Verena discovers with Basil must be seen in one sense at least as a sign of freedom. Verena, under Basil's influence, "commits her first conscious indiscretion" (239). In James's fiction, the sharing between two persons of a secret truth that excludes the rest of the world initiates intimacy and also a heightened sense of self. As one perceives the difference between oneself and the rest of the world—in other words, the discrepancy between perception of self and the way the rest of the world perceives one—consciousness becomes more defined. Verena gains independence from Olive by withholding part of her identity from Olive through the secret. She "ended by keeping the incident of Basil Ransom's visit to Monadnoc Place buried in unspoken, in unspeakable, considerations, the only secret she had in the world—the only thing that was all her own . . . the moment her secret was threatened it became dearer to her" (295).

Despite Judith Fetterly's claim that Verena is essentially passive,[50] Verena's withholding of a secret resists a parental—even masculine—influence because Olive's aggressiveness is essentially masculine. As James reveals, "it was a curious incident of her zeal for the regeneration of her sex that manly things were, perhaps on the whole, what she understood best" (122). Olive has asked Verena to "renounce, refrain, abstain!" (87). Carren Kaston's perceptive observation that in James's fiction "renunciations are a matter of emotional obedience to characters who function as parents in the text"[51] applies here to the all-consuming parental function that Olive attempts with Verena. Prior to her secret with Basil, Verena had "but one little secret, namely, that if she could have chosen at the beginning she would have liked to resemble Mrs. Luna," and if this choice does not seem particularly felicitous to us, to Verena, with her minimal experience, the selection is simply a rebellion against the present "aridity of her life" (110) of renunciation. Verena favors her private meeting with Basil in Central Park over her public drive with Mr. Burrage because "it was more free, more intense, more full of amusing incident and opportunity. She could stop and look at everything now, and indulge all her curiosities" (333). In a sense, Central Park is a metaphor for Verena's consciousness, which she is allowed only to skim over with Mr. Burrage, but which she is allowed to explore more fully and intensely in the presence of Basil, so that she ends up "not knowing why she had come" but that "it made her happy" (334).

So Basil replaces Olive as the person to compel Verena through his rhetoric. Basil indeed liberates Verena from her parental tie through his language—his use of wit and sarcasm. It is Basil's amused and irreverent attitude toward the feminist movement that makes Olive instinctively apprehensive about the possible deadliness of this unexpected opponent. Her apprehension solidifies when Basil declares war on Olive in front of Verena by taunting her, " 'My dear cousin, your truth is a most vain thing!' " (94), and when Basil utters this challenge, one sees that both Basil and Olive claim victory by virtue of the assumptions of the Quintilian principle. They both claim to have the truth and assume therefore that their rhetoric will be most compelling.

When Basil calls Olive's truth "vain," he probably puns here, insinuating that *vain* can mean personal vanity as well as uselessness.

Indeed, Basil's tactic is to convince Verena of the absurdity of Olive's maxim about a woman's "true" destiny; he attempts a "reduction ad absurdum"—the very tactic he suggests Verena uses in her own speeches (91). He mocks and refutes Olive's demands upon Verena by extracting them from the narrow context of Olive's dogmatism and holding them up to the mirror of accepted social behavior. Verena's plea to Ransom that his presence at Marmion makes Olive angry is countered by Ransom's request "to know since when it was more becoming to take up with a morbid old maid than with an honorable young man; and when Verena pronounced the sacred name of friendship he inquired what fanatical sophistry excluded him from a similar privilege." When Verena responds that Olive believes "his resolute pursuit of Verena [to be] a covert persecution of herself," Basil responds to Olive's reflections by "making them the subject of much free laughter" (403). Basil, in other words, determines, through his refuting wit, to relegate Olive's rhetoric "to the land of vapors, of dead phrases" (339).

He succeeds. He compels Verena's conviction through his alternate version of truth. Olive had conceived of her union with Verena as organic, but, by contrast, Verena decides through Basil's influence that "Olive's earnestness began to appear as inharmonious with the scheme of the universe as if it had been a broken saw" (304). Verena startlingly concludes:

> It was simply that the truth had changed sides. . . . Formerly she had been convinced that the fire of her spirit was a kind of double flame, one half of which was responsive friendship for a most extraordinary person, and the other part for the sufferings of women in general. Verena gazed aghast at the colorless dust into which, in three short months—such a conviction as that could crumble; she felt it must be a magical touch that could bring about such a cataclysm. Why Basil Ransom had been deputed by fate to exercise this spell was more than she could say—poor Verena, who up to so lately had flattered herself that she had a wizard's wand in her pocket. (396–97)

The puzzle in *The Bostonians*, and the sadness, is the victory of the sophists through the exploitation of the Quintilian principle over the moral rhetorician, Verena, who really *does* have the virtuous wizard's wand. Ironically, the disinherited Basil Ransom uses the same Beecherian precepts about suffering to refute Olive's feminism and thus to serve in his version of truth. In contrast to Olive's perception of a new truth, Basil claims to "have never yet encountered in the world any but old truths—as old as the sun and moon" (21). Basil's truth counter to Olive's is that "what is most agreeable to women is to be agreeable to men! That is a truth as old as the human race" (345). Basil's attitude about suffering constitutes a part of his rationalizing stoicism. He subscribes to an ecclesiastical fatalism about suffering, but he applies the principle in a sophistically self-interested way that allows him to justify the inequality of women, since women's past suffering, he argues, suggests that their future suffering is inevitable. " 'The suffering of women is the suffering of all humanity,' " Basil argues. " 'Do you think any movement is going to stop that—or all the lectures from now to doomsday? We are born to suffer—and to bear it, like decent people' " (238). But Basil's "we" is suspicious. The irony is that Basil excludes men from his stoic acceptance of the obligatory burden of suffering that he says is the necessary predestined role for women. Indeed, Basil's response to the suffering of men does provoke the benevolent emotions that, according to Beecher's philosophy, an awareness of suffering should provoke—the conciliatory benevolence that is implied by an awareness of suffering in *Adventures of Huckleberry Finn*. For Basil, the effect of the war memorial at Harvard was "singularly noble and solemn, and it is impossible to feel it without a lifting of the heart. It stands there for duty and honor, speaks of sacrifice and example, seems a kind of temple to youth, manhood, generosity. . . . He was capable of being a generous foeman, and he forgot, now, the whole question of sides and parties" (248).

As Judith Fetterly points out, Basil's reactions at Harvard demonstrate his "conviction of the absolute primacy of the male point of view." Basil's response to suffering, like Olive's, actually constitutes an avoidance of the responsibility for suffering; they use the fact of human suffering in the service of their own ideological struggles for power, as the competitive edge in their battle of the sexes. Fetterly notes that Basil's "code of chivalry is consistently accommodated to his self-interest." [52] That chivalry is actually a form of benevolent control. According to John Carlos Rowe, "Basil's defensive projection is the displacement of his cultural authority over the black slave to domination of the New England woman." [53] Fetterly points out the violence implicit in Ransom's thoughts about Verena, in such statements as "if he should become her husband he should know a way to strike her dumb" (329).

There is also a rapidly progressive degeneration of happiness in

Verena's response to Basil and an air of perversity in their relations that does not spring entirely from Verena's guilt about betraying Olive. Basil's cynicism about other people disheartens Verena so that she "hoped that something really bad had happened to him—not by way of gratifying any resentment he aroused in her nature, but to help herself to forgive him for so much contempt and brutality" (336). Basil makes Verena feel "cold, slightly sick" (343), and "the ugliness of her companion's profession of faith made her shiver; it would have been difficult to her to imagine anything more crudely profane" (344).

There does seem to be, then, a dark treatment of suffering in *The Bostonians*, since both Olive and Basil exploit the rhetorical ethos implicit in suffering to promote their own ideological versions of truth. And James's depiction of Olive's and Basil's manipulative uses of suffering certainly casts a curious light on recent information that has been uncovered about the relationship between Beecher and James's family. When Henry Ward Beecher was publicly accused of adultery with his parishioner Elizabeth Tilton in 1874 by feminist, spiritualist, and free-love advocate Victoria Woodhull in *Woodhull & Claflin's Weekly*, Henry James, Sr., wrote a letter in Beecher's defense to the *Saint Paul Daily Press* in Minnesota.[54] This letter became a source of embarrassment to the James family when it resurfaced in 1879 in *Woodhull & Claflin's* when Beecher became involved in the Tilton divorce case. According to Alfred Habegger, Henry James, Sr., had been an advocate of free love doctrine in the 1840s—free love suggesting, in the main, that love between the sexes should not be bound by the laws or obligations of marriage but allowed to develop freely. But this doctrine could extend to a sanction of sexual promiscuity, which was not a direction that Henry James, Sr., wanted to endorse. Habegger reveals that Henry, Sr., eventually backed off from this position because of the potential public embarrassment it might cause him and became instead a staunch attacker of free love doctrine. James, Sr.'s, position became antifeminist; he maintained that there were distinctions between the sexes and that the role of women was to suffer as a spiritualizing example for men. Indeed, James's position bears affinity to that of Basil Ransom in *The Bostonians*.

Habegger provides proof that Henry James, Jr., staunchly defended his father's position on the role of women. But Henry, Sr.'s, letter defending Beecher was an embarrassment to the family. According to Habegger, Henry, Sr., appeared to defend Beecher while also implying Beecher's guilt. James's unconscious identification with Beecher and his testimony that as for himself he would " 'abide in my chains' " meant that "Henry Sr.'s radical ghosts were out of the closet with a vengeance."[55]

Habegger's discovery of this Beecher connection with the James family can only render Henry James, Jr.'s, treatment of suffering in *The Bostonians* more problematic. Given James, Sr.'s, position on the ameliorative power of women's suffering, and the loyal defense of his father's position by James, Jr., one would expect that the idealization of suffering in *The Bostonians* would be endorsed. But the one thing that emerges from *The Bostonians* is the immorality of polemicizing suffering for political use, which subordinates the moral ethos of virtuous rhetoric to the tyrannous letter of the law. Olive Chancellor, Basil Ransom, and Henry James, Sr., all manipulate the concept of feminine suffering so as to justify power for one privileged group.

Curiously, this is something that Henry Ward Beecher in his preachings on suffering did not do. Suffering, in Beecher's vision, was not gender-based but was an equal possession of all human beings and thus not a force of division but one that unifies all people in a common bond of compassion, thus compelling them to be persuaded by and to embrace the virtuous truths of compassion, kindness, mercy, and love. There *is* one character in *The Bostonians* who would seem to represent Beecher's view. Verena Tarrant advocates a community of forgiveness and love based on the principle that all suffer. Despite the implication in *The Bostonians* that Verena's speeches are empty, one must remember that the one who harangues her speeches is the polemical Basil. So it is just possible that in this novel written so soon after his father's death, Henry James, who no longer had to append "Jr." to his name, wanted to expose the perniciousness of any politically motivated notion of suffering, perhaps also, in Verena, to present a more positive idealized notion.

Verena's virtuous rhetoric does at least to a certain extent compel. Verena makes inroads into Basil's ideological code of chivalry and into compelling honest relations on a personal level with him. Ransom compliments Verena honestly, "feeling himself now, and as if by a sudden clearing up of his spiritual atmosphere, no longer in the vein for making the concessions of chivalry, and yet conscious that his words were an expression of homage" (272). " 'I have been joking; I have been piling it up,' " Basil at one point confesses to Verena, "making that concession unexpectedly to the girl" (341). But unfortunately, although Verena may compel honesty from Basil on a personal level, she cannot compel him to change his political ideology, and Basil's honesty with Verena simply consists in admitting his own unchanged political views. When Basil admits to Verena that it is the *male* sex that he wants to save, "Verena saw that he was not piling it up satirically, but saying really and a trifle wearily, as if suddenly he were tired of much talk, what he meant" (343).

Thus in the political world of *The Bostonians*, the Quintilian principle fails, for the message of ethical truth embodied by Verena becomes enslaved to the tyrannous rhetoric of political dissension. In this bleak picture of America, James cannot see beyond the helplessness of a spiritually conceived notion of truth to transform a corrupt world.

Yet in his picture of Verena, James implicitly embraces the original ideals of democracy as a part of rhetorical idealism. The difference between the politics of rhetorical ideology and rhetorical idealism can be seen in the differing opinions of the public held by Olive, Basil, and Verena. Olive considers the democratic public en masse in a romantic sense, yet she secretly harbors an apprehension about their vulgarity and thinks the age morally lax. Basil similarly doubts "the stupid, gregarious, gullible public" (328) and considers them "senseless brutes!" (461). Verena, on the other hand, believes mightily in the goodwill of her audience, in "the great good-natured childish public" (457). Her belief implicitly suggests Theremin's claim that the "necessary idea" of the public is moral virtue. James's final word about the audience in *The Bostonians*, the suggestion of its apparent tolerance for Olive as a last-minute speaker, is a vote for the optimism expressed by Verena. Verena believes that she can bring her audience to virtue — as did Henry Ward Beecher — by the discourse of love; Olive's and Basil's discourse is politically premised upon hatred and contempt. Rowe suggests that the difference between Verena's and Basil's approach to the public can be seen in their differing views about publication. Verena, Rowe observes, "judges publishing to be a measure of public opinion, some indication of democratic consensus. As ideal as such a view might be in this patriarchal culture, Verena's notion remains true to *James's* ideals. In Basil's far more cynical terms, publishing is merely at the whim of fashion, an expedience and entertainment, driven by an insatiable public need for novelty and variety, and deadly afraid of any *true* 'originality.' " [56]

In *The Bostonians*, in the communion between Verena and the larger American audience, one sees a tentative intimation of the plausibility of the Quintilian principle, that a virtuous speaker might, indeed, be more persuasive. And yet James's portrayal of public discourse also has a darker underside; James reports that by the time of Verena's final speech, "inspiration, moreover, seemed rather to have faded away" (404). The young, inexperienced woman who possesses rhetorical goodness, James seems to imply, will lose her inspiration if it is not enhanced by positive experience, nurtured on the personal level. She will also lose moral awareness—witness Miss Birdseye—if she is not allowed to cultivate a sense of personal self.

The Bostonians is one of only several instances when James ventured in his fiction explicitly into the political world, and the failed inter-action between that world and the transformative power of virtuous rhetoric may be one reason that James ventured into that world rarely. In two later novels, *The Wings of the Dove* and *The Golden Bowl*, James changes the battleground for the argument of the Quintilian principle, retreating from the world of the public into the personal, so that the truth is not tied to any ancillary political ideology. Instead, James alters the odds for victory of the Quintilian principle in several ways. First, in Milly Theale and Maggie Verver, James reconstitutes the virtuous American girl as a rhetorical argument in herself, as she presents her own honesty as a moral persuasion to engage the honesty of others. Second, he gives his heroines better odds with their audience by cre-ating two male protagonists who value an ethical definition of *truth*. James seems very much to want to urge the moral necessity of the Quintilian principle—that a good man's (or woman's) eloquence will be most convincing, and, in these later two novels, where the battle-ground is honesty versus dishonesty in human relations rather than combative political ideologies, James finds a way to insist on the moral transcendence of the Quintilian principle.

6

The Light That Cannot Fail:
The Ideal of Truth in *The Wings of the Dove*

ᚠᚷ

> He would make a try for Paradise, whatever might be the result. He
> would be happy, by the Lord, if it cost all honesty of statement, all
> abandonment of truth.
>
> —THEODORE DREISER, *Sister Carrie*

In *Sister Carrie*, Theodore Dreiser suggests in one philosophical passage that mankind is in an intermediate stage of evolution, "moved
by every breath of passion, acting now by his will and now by his instincts." Dreiser implies that will is "good" and that passion is "evil,"
and he optimistically concludes that there will come a time "when this
jangle of free-will and instinct shall have been adjusted, when perfect
understanding has given the former the power to replace the latter entirely." There will come a time, Dreiser concludes, when "the needle
of understanding will yet point steadfast and unwavering to the distant pole of truth."[1] Dreiser's Platonic implication that reason leads to
spiritual truth while passion leads to spiritual deception explains why
he conceives of his protagonist George Hurstwood in *Sister Carrie* as
tragically doomed. Hurstwood's "passion," Dreiser tells us,

> had gotten to that stage now where it was no longer coloured with rea-
> son. He did not trouble over little barriers of this sort in the face of so
> much loveliness. He would accept the situation with all its difficulties;
> he would not try to answer the objections which cold truth thrust upon
> him. He would promise anything, everything, and trust to fortune to
> disentangle him. He would make a try for Paradise, whatever might be
> the result. He would be happy, by the Lord, if it cost all honesty of
> statement, all abandonment of truth.[2]

The irony in Hurstwood's belief that he can "try for Paradise" is that it is undercut by his decision to evade the truth in favor of his passion.

George Hurstwood is only one of the characters in late nineteenth-century fiction to purchase his or her passion with the coinage of dishonest statement and the abandonment of truth. In Henry James's canon, a prominent example is Kate Croy. Kate Croy's abandonment of all truth in Henry James's *The Wings of the Dove* is caused by the "strange enough" fact that Kate believes, "or at all events began to act, as if she might work them in [Densher's long looks] with other and alien things, privately cherish them and yet, as regards the rigour of it, pay no price."[3] Penniless, beautiful Kate Croy, yoked to the will of her wealthy Aunt Maud by Kate's perceived obligation to her "bond of blood. . . . Her haunting, harassing father, her menacing aunt, her portionless little nephews and nieces" (19:32), is indeed the naturalistic heroine, as many readers have noted.[4] Kate's actions are also often justified as inevitable, since they are set within the naturalistic framework. Elizabeth Allen notes that "Kate's potential for integrity is eroded by the sheer economic squalor of her circumstances."[5] Interestingly, this decision to forfeit moral judgment on the basis of environmental determinism is not subscribed to initially by Kate, who admits to Densher, in the opening throes of their predicament with Aunt Maud, that "I do see my danger of doing something base" (19:72). It seems that baseness, in *The Wings of the Dove*, involves an insensitivity to others which is intimately connected with a lack of linguistic integrity, as Kate herself suggests in the opening chapter in her judgment of her father. Kate supports her feeling that her father is heinous, that "no relation with him could be so short or so superficial as not to be somehow to your hurt" (19:6) with the conviction that "there was no truth in him. . . . he dealt out lies as he might the cards from the greasy old pack for the game of diplomacy to which you were to sit down with him" (19:7). Telling lies, Kate clearly implies, will somehow be to the hurt of the other person. Telling lies has all to do with destructive human relations.

Most modern critics of Henry James's later works would find that the implied distinction Kate makes here between truth and falsity is archaic and epistemologically invalid. Indeed, John Carlos Rowe claims that Kate's hopes for linguistic salvation are misplaced: "Kate Croy longs to act in a salvatory manner" through meaningful words that would "bring about a harmony that would shield man from his fundamental isolation. Yet, built upon the 'lies' of 'another man's truth,' neither society in general nor intersubjective relations can ever hope to bridge the abyss of human differences."[6] James's narrative, the modern critic suggests, undercuts the presumption that distinctions can be made between truth and falsehood. Ruth Bernard Yeazell's fascinating scrutiny of metaphor in James's later novels asserts that "when the characters in James's late fiction talk, the reader suffers from a kind of epistemological vertigo, for he is granted no secure position from which to judge the novel or even the factual truth of what is being said."[7] Yet characters in *The Wings of the Dove* not only judge others by the nature of their truth or falsity but seem assured that they can discover what is true or false: if they find language evasive, they assume a deliberate deception which itself reveals a truth about the character or incident they are trying to assess. The novel's great lies, Kate's withholding of her feelings for Densher, and what James openly calls Milly's great lie, her pretense of life in the face of impending death, reveal themselves as lies because they are fielded so evasively.

A primary theme in *The Wings of the Dove* is a concern for the underlying moral determinacy of language. Maud Lowder's surroundings appear to Densher as a language that reveals her inner character: they imply a literalness that threatens him because of the lack of imagination thus revealed. He muses that "the message of her massive florid furniture, the immense expression of her signs and symbols . . . so almost abnormally affirmative, so aggressively erect, were the huge heavy objects that syllabled his hostess's story" (19:76). This paraphrasing of Densher's thoughts is not simply a line of Jamesian metaphor. Maud's house bespeaks her personality because it is a rhetorical tool that utters the language of the material. There is an expected organic relationship between language and the reality it reveals. This does not mean, however, that honest language cannot be intentionally persuasive and combative: "It was the language of the house itself that spoke to him. . . . the solid forms, the wasted finish, the misguided cost, the general attestation of morality and money, a good conscience and a big balance. These things finally represented for him a portentous negation of his own world of thought" (19:78–79).

Aunt Maud functions much as the public and vacuous American rhetoricians such as Mrs. Farrinder in *The Bostonians*, since the excessively public language of the house functions as a persuasion. Language in *The Wings of the Dove* is not only truthful or false; it is also inevitably rhetorical. And the truth that Aunt Maud's rhetoric presents about itself is one infused with the ideology of materialism — "the great glaze of her surface" (82)—that entitles her to the epithet "Britannia of the Marketplace." This rhetoric of the marketplace is the language of conventional morality which itself can constitute a form of environmental determinism in nineteenth-century American fiction. Edith Wharton at least intimates that Ethan Frome's conventionally bound ties to his cruel wife are stifling and ludicrous; Kate's bonds to a cruel father and to a selfish, insipid sister seem equally unimaginative and conventionally conceived, resulting from a servitude to bourgeois ideology and to a sense of bourgeois rather than genuine emotional bonding. Because Kate can see more deeply than the surface of conventional morality, she can perceive her aunt as "unscrupulous and immoral" (19:31). But it is in Kate's nature also to see "as she had never seen before how material things spoke to her" (19:28) and to become bound, by her reverence for the surface, to the forces of environmental determinism.

The cage that Kate, in a sense, creates for herself is not a prison that she can accept; Kate, like Oedipus, determines to avoid her own fate: "I shall sacrifice nobody and nothing, and that's just my situation, that I want and that I shall try for everything" (19:73). Kate's tragic flaw, her denial of the reality of human suffering, which results from her use of deceptive language, takes form in her try for paradise at the expense of all honesty, in her manipulative attempts to get what she wants without paying a price. Kate attempts to obscure reality for Milly, Aunt Maud, and even Densher, through the power of deceptive language, so that she can manipulate characters into performing her will. She determines to disregard the underlying moral determinacy of language, to see it as a little barrier in the face of so much loveliness. Even early on, the narrator relates, "Densher . . . found himself moved to wonder at her simplifications, her values" (19:61). But Kate is not alone in her use of language to a persuasive end. Little American heiress Milly Theale becomes locked in a rhetorical battle with Kate for the affections of Merton Densher. *The Wings of the Dove* rearranges the rhetorical triangle in *The Bostonians*, in this instance reconstituting the rhetorical battle between two principal heroines for the love of a man. Both Kate and Milly use language to their own persuasive ends. But despite Kate's great beauty and intellect, her great attraction for Densher, it is Milly, oddly enough, who will finally win the rhetorical battle. This time, the virtuous rhetor will win. The outcome of their battle reveals that for rhetorical eloquence, the truthful and persuasive functions of language must be compatible, in fact, interchangeable: the most persuasive language is one that does not violate the truths of human emotion, for linguistic truth promotes both trust—the basis for meaningful relationships—and epistemological growth. In *The Wings of the Dove*, James celebrates the inevitable victory of the Quintilian principle.

As we recall from the previous chapter on *The Bostonians*, James was not only aware of but fascinated by American nineteenth-century rhetorical idealism. He also almost certainly was familiar with one of the most influential rhetorical studies underlying that movement, George Campbell's *Philosophy of Rhetoric*, which his brother William quotes in "The Stream of Thought" and which was a compulsory part of beginning course work while Henry spent his experimental year at Harvard. Campbell's *Philosophy of Rhetoric* was an undisguised moral treatise that emphasized the necessary relationship between rhetorical eloquence and sincerity. As David Potter observes in an introduction to Campbell's works, "the most prominent feature in his moral character was his love of truth. No man was ever more strict in speaking truth; and the least deviation from it was accompanied with the strongest mark of his disapprobation."[8] Campbell asserts that "the sense of the discourse ought to have its source in the inevitable nature of truth and right,"[9] and he suggests invariable sources of truth against which the veracity of language can be judged. These sources of truth can be found in *The Wings of the Dove* as the basis against which characters discern the difference between truth and deception. Significantly, this discernment is of paramount importance to the novel's male protagonist, Merton Densher. It is no coincidence that James creates in *The Wings of the Dove* and *The Golden Bowl* two male protagonists whose primary quality is a reverence for honesty not only in others but in themselves as well. James endows these heroes with this unusual reverence so that the Quintilian confidence in rhetorical virtue will triumph, so that, in effect, in the face of Milly's rhetoric, the thinness of Milly's American girl argument can become to Densher the fullness of her American girl virtue.

John Goode's penetratingly subtle reading of *The Wings of the Dove* suggests, among other things, that "Densher's conversion is to be seen as the intercourse between his flawed plastic consciousness and Milly's stylistic power (which is her wealth),"[10] but it is important to remember that Densher first falls in love with a beautiful but poor young Englishwoman—there is no suggestion that he feels anything but aversion for Aunt Maud's money—and that he virtually forgets the phenomenally wealthy young American heiress after his brief encounter with Milly in New York. It is important to remember that Densher is *in love* with Kate; he values her beauty and intellect, in specific, "the immediate air of life" (19:51) that she brings to his thought. And she does that, for him, through language, "something that banished the talk of other women, so far as he knew other women, to the dull desert of the conventional" (19:70). It is Kate's fall from rhetorical grace through her determination to have it all, her language being ground in the mill of the conventional, that causes Densher to fall out of love with her, but not before he tries hard not to. Densher's primary pull is toward the power of language, which Kate proves can be a powerful tool in the manipulation of surfaces. Ever the mistress of appearances, she creates the appearance of reality by manipulating its surface — language — to make reality appear other than what it is. If we do experience epistemological vertigo in the novel, it occurs as we watch characters like Milly and Densher juggling their notions of reality against the ways they are being told to perceive the world by Kate.

Elizabeth Allen claims that it is Kate and Milly who, as women, are conjoined as opposed to the male subject in having to assert their identities, if they can, through a sign function imposed on them by society.[11] Yet it is Kate, as a representative of conventional society, who attempts to subdue Milly's and Densher's vital functions as subjects by assigning them the static significations of "dove" and "gentleman." None of these three is deceived, however, about the underlying reality being denied. As a matter of fact, the reader in *The Wings of the Dove* is usually a witness in the midst of a conversation that is a verbal performance in which all characters involved, as well as the reader, know the underlying reality that language is attempting to deceive.

According to Campbell's theory, the language governing human relationships usually has two underlying realities, or, as Campbell calls them, logical evidences. One of these — the evidence of human experience — Kate attempts to obfuscate, and the other — the evidence of analogy — she tries to harness for her own purposes, performing a sort of black magic with her sophistic language. Densher and Milly experiment with her scheme; her rhetoric conforms to their own needs, but, also, it seems seductively "fun" to play games with the relationships between reality and language. Densher's experiments with sophistry are reminiscent of Huck's exploratory tricks played on Jim; both betray a nervous dis-ease with sophistry. When Densher considers his false position with Milly, he expresses himself as launched in an experiment: "In default of being right with himself he had meanwhile, for the one thing, the interest of seeing—and quite for the first time in his life—whether, on a given occasion, that might be quite so necessary to happiness as was commonly assumed and as he had up to this moment never doubted" (19:183). Densher confides that he has always equated "happiness" with "being right with himself," a comment evocative of Plato's definition of happiness in the *Gorgias*.[12] Densher's "never doubted" faith in truthfulness falls prey to the purely seductive nature of Kate's rhetoric: "There were moments again—we know that from the first they had been numerous—when he felt with a strange mixed passion the mastery of her mere way of putting things. There was something in it that bent him at once to conviction and to reaction" (19:196).

Campbell's description of experience as an epistemological source of truth shows how Kate plays fast and loose in language with experience. Campbell states in *The Philosophy of Rhetoric* that "the proper province of rhetoric is . . . moral evidence" because "it is principally to the acquisitions procured by experience, that we owe the use of language." Further, experience, or moral evidence, is directed by "the clear representations of . . . memory," which "in regard to past events, are indubitably true."[13] Such a close relationship in *The Wings of the Dove* is established between language and the empirical reality to which it refers that characters experiment with the possibility that language can create meaning rather than refer to it. Kate, however, attempts to reconcile incompatible tensions in her environment through the "simplifying" force of a language that simply covers inconvenient facts or evades them. Kate's rhetoric thus fails because of its deceptive features.

Milly's rhetoric does not triumph in *The Wings of the Dove* so much as Kate's rhetoric defeats itself. Densher falls in love and out of love with Kate because of what happens in his verbal intercourse with her. He revels in Kate because "they could think whatever they liked about whatever they would—in other words they could say it" (19:65). He loves Kate because "of those deep and free interchanges that made everything but confidence a false note for them" (19:90). Indeed, as the fledgling relationship between Densher and Kate illustrates, truthful language is the basis for trust in their relationship. It is important to Kate, when she affirms her love to Densher, that she speak the words: "And I pledge you—I call God to witness!—every spark of my faith; I give you every drop of my life" (19:95). Yet in this very scene, after her pledge, Kate's language slides into evasion. Densher, on his way to America, shows his typical respect for truthfulness when he requests that he be allowed to send his letters to Kate at Aunt Maud's because "it's straighter." Kate, on the other hand, reveals her intention to post her letters independently of Aunt Maud. Densher is impelled to ask whose responsibility it will be to lie to Aunt Maud about their relationship. His very question implies his unease with deceit. Yet his decision that Kate will bear the responsibility for deception, which comes as a consequence of Kate's deceit in letter posting, proves his first attempt to deny responsibility for the conspiratorial nature of their deceit:

> His discrimination seemed to mark . . . a difference in the air—even if none other than the supposedly usual difference in truth between man and woman; and it was almost as if the sense of this provoked her. . . . She appeared to take up rather more seriously than she need the joke about her freedom to deceive. Yet she did this too in a beautiful way. "Men are too stupid—even you. You didn't understand just now why, if I post my letters myself, it won't be for anything so vulgar as to hide them" (19:99)

Kate deceives other characters about the reality of their mutually shared social universe by the evasive and misleading tactic of silence, as in this previous instance. She simply removes the action of posting letters to Densher from Aunt Maud's view, a symbolic silence that implies, in its absence of concrete words, that she is not posting letters to Densher at all. Yet Densher is not fooled. Kate could often more easily deceive if she were to lie outright, to tell Milly, for instance, that she does not love Densher, yet Kate chooses the path of evasion because of its rhetorical subtlety and possibly also out of concern for her own moral well-being. Kate comes to believe so much in appearances that she sometimes seems to believe that the appearance of morality is morality itself. She evades moral responsibility not only through her own silence but also by transferring the responsibility for her sophistry to Densher. It is Densher who is bound by Kate's lie to Milly, as Kate points out: "It's not *I* who am responsible for her, my dear. It seems to me it's you" (19:91).

Kate's remark strikes Densher "as making light of a matter that had been costing him sundry qualms; so that they couldn't both be quite just" (19:91). Kate is not so much callous as incognizant; she assumes that Densher's language of evasion will give him a sense of moral straightness equal to her own. Densher is a character, however, of some moral subtlety, who rejects his temptation to rationalize when faced with

the good faith of Milly's benevolence. . . . It didn't take him far to remember that he had himself as yet done nothing deceptive. It was Kate's
description of him, his defeated state, it was none of his own; his responsibility would begin, as he might say, only with acting it out. The sharp
point was, however, in the difference between acting and not acting: this
difference in fact it was that made the case of conscience. He saw it with
a certain alarm rise before him that everything was acting that was not
speaking the particular word. (19:76)

Densher views honesty as the hallmark of his relationship with Kate,
yet their different reactions to the situation with Milly cause him to
think back upon early imperfections in their communication that anticipate their present estrangement. He remembers that "there were
certain of his remarks—those mostly of the sharper penetration—that
it had been quite her practice from the first not formally, not reverently
to notice" (20:18). As this linguistic rupture becomes more noticeable,
Densher's sexual need for Kate becomes fused with, if not subordinate
to, his verbal need for her, so that he actually makes the sexual act
an antidote for her linguistic evasion. Densher's realization that "he
had already suffered Kate to begin finely to apply antidotes and reme-
dies and subtle sedatives" to his sexual desires (20:7) is a simultaneous
allusion to Kate's verbal manipulation of him. Densher determines
that "what it amounted to was that he couldn't have her—hanged if
he could!—evasive. . . . He didn't want her deeper than himself, fine
as it might be as wit or as character; he wanted to keep her where
their communications would be straight and easy and their intercourse
independent" (20:19).

The blend between sexual and verbal intimacy continues as Densher
tries to use his accomplished sexual intercourse with Kate as an "historic truth" (20:236) to counteract his compromised conscience. "I'll
tell you any lie you want, any your idea requires, if you'll only come
to me" (20:200), he simply tells Kate. He has previously denied himself knowledge of Milly's illness so that he can rationalize, "in what
therefore was the duplicity? . . . He was acting for Kate and not, by the
deviation of an inch, for her friend" (20:204). He has refrained from
telling Milly that he loves Kate, and "the proof of the truth in question
was precisely in his silence; resisting the impulse to break out was what
he *was* doing for Kate" (20:85). Densher hopes that by creating a personal little world of honest intimacy he can cancel out his dishonesty
in the larger public realm.

But Densher is far from insulated. Maud, Susan Stringham, and

Milly constitute claims on his conscience and make him feel the extent of his deceit. This deceit causes a rift in Kate and Densher's communication, so that even in "remoteness from earshot, with solitude and security," they discover "it was as if, being in possession, they could say what they liked; and it was also as if, in consequence of that, each had an apprehension of what the other wanted to say. It was most of all for them moreover, as if this very quantity, seated on their lips in the bright historic air, where the only sign for their ears was the flutter of the doves, begot in the heart of each a fear" (20:193). Both are absorbed with "the flutter of the doves," with the intervening fact of Milly, the irrepressible recollection of whom causes Kate and Densher to consider their own duplicity. Kate, however, does not fear her own deceit so much as Densher's uneasy conscience. Densher, on the other hand, sees his private world crumbling as he apprehends that Kate will lie even to him. "She balanced an instant," the narrator writes, "during which Densher might have just wondered if pure historic truth were to suffer a slight strain" (20:195–96).

The popular rhetorical theory of James's day suggested that we judge what is true or false on the basis of memory. Such a theory would explain why Densher concentrates so determinedly on his sexual experience with Kate as his one "historic truth. . . . It played for him — certainly in this prime afterglow — the part of a treasure kept at home in safety and sanctity, something he was sure of finding in its place when, with each return, he worked his heavy old key in the lock" (20:236). He determines to live authentically only in his room, to avoid the fact of his larger deception so that "never was a consciousness more rounded and fastened down over what filled it" (20:237). Determining that "Kate was *all* in his poor rooms (20:238)," he gives himself up "to the general feeling of his renewed engagement to fidelity" (20:237). Densher fixes his memory on one historical fact so as to avoid his own deceit.

The room scene toward the end of the novel, where Densher mourns the fact that "he should never, never know what had been in Milly's letter" and guards the possibilities of what Milly might have said "like the sight of a priceless pearl cast before his eyes . . . or rather even . . . like the sacrifice of something sentient and throbbing" (20:396), is a deliberate inversion of the earlier room scene; here is "the sound," representing Milly, that "he cherished when alone in the stillness of his rooms" (20:396). Milly's "beautiful little eloquence" (20:81) ultimately constitutes a stronger claim for Densher. Densher chooses to validate Milly's trust in him, thus restructuring his own emotions so that they conform to the emotional estrangement from Kate that his discourse with Milly has implied. He responds, in other words, to the moral imperativeness of honest language.

Yet there is a perplexing question concerning the honesty of Milly's discourse which must be addressed to justify Densher's conversion. The question remains whether or not Densher is duped by just another fabric of lies that he perceives as honesty. The text does seem to show Milly's tentative knowledge, at one point, in Book Fifth, of Kate's affection for Densher. The issue raised, therefore, is whether Milly's supposed innocence, which so impresses Densher, is not really after all simply a part of what Kate calls "their common duplicity" (20:140). Is Densher, one might ask, simply a quixotic fool in an absurdist world, whose reverence for truthful language is derided by Milly's deceit, her posture of innocence, upon which her rhetoric is based?

The answer resides partially in the much more complex relationship with "pure historic truth" that Milly has in comparison to Kate. Kate employs a consciously deceitful language that denies, as Densher is aware, the pure historic truths of which she is certain. Milly, on the other hand, seems poised on the brink of discovering pure historic truths which it would be better, for her own welfare, not to know. In the Preface to *The Wings of the Dove*, James discusses the revelation of "Milly's now almost full-blown consciousness" in Book Fifth: "I note how, again and again, I go but a little way with the direct—that is with the straight exhibition of Milly; it resorts for relief, this process, whenever it can, to some kinder, more merciful indirection: all as if to approach her circuitously, deal with her at second hand, as an unspotted princess is ever dealt with; the pressure all round her kept easy for her, the sounds, the movements regulated, the forms and ambiguities made charming."[14] James seems especially scrupulous in retaining a paradoxical balance between Milly's self-consciousness and her nature as an unspotted princess, her innocence. In *The Bostonians*, Verena is perceived as a paradoxical combination of self-conscious artistry and innocence. In *The Wings of the Dove*, Milly is granted enough knowledge to be aware of her innocence in the face of probable undesirable knowledge and enough faith in the virtue of her innocence to attempt to recreate the world in her own image through a rhetoric that advertises that virtue. In *The Bostonians*, Verena's rhetoric is admired either for the money it will bring or for its potential exploitability by ideological dogma. In *The Wings of the Dove*, as John Goode points out, most characters admire Milly, again, for her money.[15] Susan Stringham perceives, for example, that it was "the truth of truths that the girl couldn't get away from her wealth . . . that was what it was to be really rich. It had to be *the* thing you were" (19:121). But Merton Densher admires Milly for her virtue, or, put another way, for her appeal to his. James gives Milly the opportunity to make something of her innocence and a male protagonist to appreciate it.

To do this, Milly must not only remain unclear about the probable state of Kate's affection for Densher; she must also retain a paradoxical balance between innocence and awareness of other harsh realities. Besides historic truth, which forms the basis for moral judgment, Campbell states that another invariable source of truth is the truth of science. This is a truth which Milly, initially, actively seeks in the novel, with as much aggressiveness as she initially seeks the truths of experience. She finds herself, with Sir Luke Strett, in the "brown old temple of truth," where "she accepted such an interest as regular in the highest type of scientific mind . . . she could at the same time take it as a direct source of light upon herself" (19:241, 240). Although we never hear Sir Luke Strett tell Milly she is dying, James establishes potent evidence of Sir Luke's invariable sentence. Strett, a busy man, desires to see Milly repeatedly and puts restrictions on her travels. Susan, after seeing Sir Luke, breaks down in tears before Aunt Maud. James, by not having Sir Luke Strett directly utter the verdict of death, arrests Milly's awareness of her own death just short of certain knowledge. Strett, whose scientific genius approaches the metaphysical, recognizes that the sentence itself would conclude even an abbreviated life prematurely. And living life—keeping at bay the knowledge of imminent death—is a necessary deceit.

James suggests the paradox that death, although man's ultimate reality, is also a lie violating the truth of human life. As Densher observes, "in presence of the truth that was the truest about Milly," during the conclusion of his stay in Venice, "[death represents] the great smudge of mortality across the picture, the shadow of pain and horror, finding in no quarter a surface of spirit or of speech that consented to reflect it. 'The mere aesthetic instinct of mankind—!' our young man had more than once, in the connexion, said to himself; letting the rest of the proposition drop, but touching again thus sufficiently on the outrage even to taste involved in one's having to *see*" (20:298–99). Milly's condition, James seems to imply, is simply an exaggerated attenuation of the general human condition. Death to the living person must seem an absurdity. Milly, in order to live at all, must live as if she were not to die. Thus Milly's lie is, in a sense, not a lie because her life, while she is living, is a countermand to death. John Goode writes that what Milly "has to create is something which can assimilate both lies and truths, which has its own inner logic and is immune to the law of natural selection which Kate is seeking to operate." [16] Milly's tentative art of living temporarily escapes the law of natural selection because she operates in a realm of contingency, subject either to verifiability by future life or by death. In *The Wings of the Dove*, James distinguishes, then, between human lies and an existentialistically deceitful evasion of death that makes it in fact possible to live.

Relations with others, then, who can provide such verifiability, are a matter of enormous trust. One may recall that Milly's first gesture of trust in her friend Kate was to allude to the possible fact of her fatal illness. That trust disintegrates, however, and Milly chooses to withhold from Kate the more crucial second interview with her doctor. Milly senses the careless inquisitiveness in Kate's manner, especially as it is contrasted with Milly's own troubling pilgrimage to Regent's Park: "The contrast between this free quantity and the maze of possibilities through which, for hours, she had herself been picking her way, put on, in short, for the moment, a grossness that even friendly forms scarce lightened: it helped forward in fact the revelation to herself that she absolutely had nothing to tell" (19:257–58). Having "nothing to tell" directly contradicts what both the reader and Milly know to be true; however, Milly's motivations for lying are existentialistically valid and complex. On one hand, truth in the novel is portrayed as a precious investment that one gives only to those one can most definitely trust. Milly's linguistic evasion with Kate is a form of withdrawal and self-protection from the already known-to-be deceitful other who might do her harm.

More crucially, however, the narrator tells us that Milly speaks "with no consciousness of fraud, only as with a sudden flare of the famous 'will-power' she had heard about, read about, and which was what her medical adviser had mainly thrown her back on" (19:258). A key suggestion here is that Milly is operating on the doctor's advice and that her language will henceforth be impelled by the premises of pragmatism. Sir Luke instructs Milly to live as if she *could*, on the premise that any known fact about the universe, even one ascertained by science, is always contingent. According to pragmatic tenets, one may posit and hold a belief until it is contradicted by concrete experience. With astonishing willpower, Milly has been able to banish from her consciousness, we are told, the sense of her impending death through a pragmatic recognition that death is contingent upon the act of death itself. In the true spirit of American pragmatism, Milly has adopted a belief, most useful to herself, that she *can* live, as her thoughts imply when she considers "the more earnest of the lady-copyists" in the National Gallery: "Two or three in particular, spectacled, aproned, absorbed, engaged her sympathy to an absurd extent, seemed to show her for the time the right way to live. She should have been a lady-copyist—it met so the case. The case was the case of escape, of living under water, of being at once impersonal and firm. There it was before one—one had only to stick and stick" (19:288). Milly's apprehension that this truth of science—her inevitable death—is contingent on her ability to "stick and stick" but ultimately incontrovertible nonetheless allows her to identify with the universal nature of human suffering. Human suffering is an instinctive truth in this poetic work that underlies the truth of science. Milly apprehends that the center of Regent's Park "was the real thing; the real thing was to be quite away from the pompous roads, well within the centre and on the stretches of shabby grass. Here were benches and smutty sheep; here were idle lads at games of ball, with their cries mild in the thick air; here were wanderers anxious and tired like herself; here doubtless were hundreds of others just in the same box" (19:250). We seem to discover here that Milly's future actions and language will be based on faith, a faith in life and in other people that is paradoxically born of a sense of community in suffering. Milly will soon act on Sir Luke Strett's advice that she find a young man to love, acting out the pragmatic assumption that she *could* be loved if she would *act* as if she could be loved, linking together inextricably her act of love with her act of life, her act of faith in Kate and Densher with her faith in her ability to live. Her language will operate on that premise and express that faith. Milly's Christlike apprehension of human suffering, her equation of the smutty sheep and the idle lads who bleat like lambs, foreshadows her eventual sacrifice to the flock, as the suspense surrounding Milly's imminent death resembles the scene before Christ's crucifixion. The allusions filtering through Milly's perception of Regent's Park foreshadow that someone will indeed abuse her faith through deception, undermining the sacred trusts upon which human relationships are constituted. Those relationships are man's only comfort given his inherent tragic condition.

A subtle but crucial distinction seems to exist, then, between Kate's and Milly's language that marks the difference between artistic lie and poetic truth. The key to the distinction lies in the pivotal scene in which Kate offers Milly a metaphor by which to live: "It was moreover, for the girl, like an inspiration. . . . She met it on the instant as she would have met revealed truth" (19:283).

Kate's suggested dove metaphor gives Milly a pragmatic stance from which to view the relationship between Kate and Densher in the way most pleasing to Milly. Indeed, Milly launches from this point a pragmatic attempt to validate her innocence (which is constituted on the basis of her belief that Kate and Densher's relationship is innocent) through experience, much as she wills herself to live until thwarted by death. Her relationship with language within this process becomes a fascinatingly contingent one; it is a language posited on the belief that anything is possible until experience proves otherwise, which is one reason, perhaps, why her crucial conversation with Densher is in the form of questions, not statements. Although, as we shall see, Milly is quite aware of the initial problematic nature of her innocence, she works to create an environment in which her innocence can be realized sincerely. Milly's rhetoric addresses the issue of how language can be persuasive instead of simply referential; her rhetoric involves a dynamic relationship between language and reality. Kate's language, on the other hand, involves dead convention, unreflective of reality and simply manipulative in function, neither referential nor creative. Kate's recourse to deceitful language reveals her naturalistic definition of human relations and her belief that an individual cannot defend his own identity against the pressure of an oppressive environment. Milly's exploratory use of metaphor suggests that an individual can change the underlying essential truths of his world through a dynamic linguistic response to his environment.

Symbolically significant in this regard is Kate and Milly's diverse exploration of the dove metaphor in Book Fifth that Kate offers up as a fiat to compel Milly's innocence in the face of "Milly's now almost full-blown consciousness." Maud Lowder, one remembers, convinces Milly to discover from Kate whether Densher has returned to London from America. For Milly, this is both a feat and a dilemma, since she has been engaging in intricate self-inquiries about her own secretiveness, and Kate's, concerning this knowledge of Densher. Paul Armstrong's splendid phenomenological studies of the relationship between Jamesian characters and knowledge certainly could be applied to Milly's mental explorations at this point.[17] Yet the essential role of language in the struggle of such characters to achieve identity and foster commitment needs emphasis.

Central to Milly's pursuit in this scene is her attempt to goad Kate out of silence into conversation about Densher. Milly has heretofore determined that Kate's "silence succeeded in passing muster with her as the beginning of a new sort of fun. The sort was all the newer by reason of its containing measurably a small element of anxiety" (19: 189). Milly's attempt to rationalize away Kate's deceit as "fun" is not successful; nor is her attempt to redeem Kate from charges of duplicity on rhetorical principles: "She should never know how Kate truly felt about anything such a one as Milly Theale should give her to feel. Kate would never — and not from ill will nor from duplicity, but from a sort of failure of common terms — reduce it to such a one's comprehension or put it within her convenience" (19:190–91). Milly's need to reassure herself that her friend Kate is not duplicitous can be likened to Densher's valuation of honesty as the foundation of a relationship. Milly wants Kate to be honest with her because she wants to retain a friend.

In Book Fifth, Milly desires both a reinstitution of her faith in her relationship with Kate and knowledge for her own sake about the relationship between Kate and Densher, desires that both demand verbal sincerity. Kate, on the other hand, eludes Milly's advances, indicating to Milly the relative insignificance, to Kate, of Kate and Milly's friendship, a potentially damaging lack of caritas. Under the guise of dazzling Milly with untold confidences, Kate clearly attempts to silence Milly through the sheer force of her verbal energy. Neither character, however, is puzzled about the intent of the language she uses. Milly recognizes in Kate's verbal virtuosity "the quality of a rough rehearsal of the possible big drama. . . . If Kate moreover, quite mercilessly, had never been so good, the beauty and the marvel of it was that she had never really been so frank: being a person of such a calibre . . . that, even while 'dealing' with you and thereby, as it were, picking her steps, she could let herself go, could, in irony, in confidence, in extravagance, tell you things she had never told before" (19:275–76). Milly discerns that Kate, under the guise of her supposed frankness, has devised an "alibi," a red herring to avoid discussion of Densher: "Lord Mark was substantially what she had begun with as soon as they were alone; the impression was even yet with Milly of her having sounded his name, having imposed it, as a topic, in direct opposition to the other name that Mrs. Lowder had left in the air and that all her own look, as we have seen, kept there at first for her companion" (19:279).

As she raises this false issue, Kate also attempts to shift the burden of proof from herself to Milly. She claims that Kate's failed involvement with Lord Mark is the result of Mark's affection for Milly. Milly, with a combative irony of her own, denies Lord Mark, claiming, in all apparent good faith in what Kate is saying, to leave the path open for Kate. Yet it is with a profound sense of the violence being done to language that Milly pursues her verbal counterattack, asking Kate if she would like her to swear, knowing full well how deceitful a vow it would be. Although Milly tries to enjoy the verbal game, she senses the lack of moral honesty underlying it. She is distressed by the lack of care that Kate's intentional deceit displays. The encounter is too much for Milly, who "tried to be amused, so as not—it was too absurd—to be fairly frightened" (19:282). Milly's fear has been most immediately incited by Kate's subsequent threat to abandon her social nurturance of Milly under pretense of protecting Milly's social interests.[18] Yet when Milly later reflects that "she had felt herself alone with a creature who paced like a panther" (19:282), her fear is also a recognition of the predatory nature of Kate's language. In James, characters prowl and pace through the civilized instrument of words. This is why Milly's outburst, with its "small solemnity of remonstrance" (19:282), is phrased, "Why do you say such things to me?" instead of "why do you do such things to me?"

Kate's response, "Because you're a dove," is a brilliant stroke. The dove metaphor responds most immediately to the dependency Milly is feeling and suggests a graceful exit that Milly can take from her aggressive confrontation with the facts of Densher and Kate's relationship. Kate wishes Milly to be passive and to adopt a pose of innocence about Kate's feelings for Densher. She extends the dove image to Milly as a metaphor for Milly's existence, not seeking to express through language what she perceives as the invariable truth of Milly's identity, rather suggesting through persuasive imagery what it would be most expedient to consider as Milly's truth. Kate simply cashes in on the potential of the analogy to go far afield of the logical truth. She does not attempt to alter the facts of her relationship with Densher, simply to cover them.

As a means of describing "what is," therefore, as Campbell claims, "analogical evidence is at best but a feeble support, and is hardly ever honored with the name of proof." Interestingly, Campbell observes that the analogy "is generally more successful in silencing objections than in evincing truth, and on this account may more properly be styled the defensive arms of the orator, than the offensive. Though it rarely refutes, it frequently repels refutation, like those weapons which, though they cannot kill the enemy, will ward his blows."[19] Kate uses her analogy defensively, to ward off Milly's aggressive inquiry and to refute, deceitfully, the world that "is."

Kate's use of the dove metaphor corresponds to the classical rhetorician's definition of metaphor, according to experimental psychologist and rhetorician Gertrude Buck, who sought to amend that traditional misconception in her 1899 tract "The Metaphor: A Study in the Psychology of Rhetoric." Buck's tract was published in a series on rhetoric edited by Fred Newton Scott, and, although it is perhaps improbable that James ever saw it, Buck's ideas reflect how the metaphor would logically have been rethought within the atmosphere of experimental psychology that James did know. According to Buck, Quintilian, Cicero, Aristotle (and Campbell on down the line) joined "in affirming the writer's anticipation of the effect of his figure upon the reader as the motive of his employment of it." This assessment of the metaphor "makes the act of metaphor so mechanical, so crude, so essentially cheap and tawdry that the sensitive reader of literature can hardly suffer serious consideration of its truthfulness." Seeing the metaphor as a devious form of persuasion—as, indeed, Kate uses it, creates a "metaphoraphobia."[20]

Buck's consideration of the more likely origin and use of the metaphor has interesting reverberations for the instance of Milly's use of the dove image. Original metaphors, according to Buck, are either radical or poetic, differing primarily in the degree of consciousness involved in the process of image-making. Radical metaphors are a function of primitive consciousness, in which two objects of thought are part of "a perception as yet homogenous and undeveloped" and there is no discrimination "between the two situations to which the same term has been applied . . . psychologically a survival from a primitive stage of perception, a vestige of the early homogenous consciousness." What occurs, then, in what Buck interestingly calls "the old tragedy of progress," is an eventual realization of the discrete elements in the metaphor, of "a tension within the expression itself which brings to light . . . a gradual movement in the direction of limiting this word to one of its tugging significations, and remanding the other meaning to a different phase."[21]

The poetic metaphor versus the radical one, according to Buck, is marked by the difference between art and artlessness. Buck seems to suggest that the poet continually recaptures the state of primitive consciousness, "when the two elements in the perception are just emerging from the primitive mass, and both, therefore, appear in the figure. . . . Poetic metaphor, like radical, is a straightforward attempt to communicate to another person the maker's vision of an object as it appeared to him at the moment of expression, not at all to carry out a dark design of persuading the reader that this object is something which the writer knows it is not." [22] Sources cited for examples of poetic metaphor are Emily Dickinson, Alfred Lord Tennyson, John Milton, John Keats, and Henry James.

It is important, finally, that in Buck's scheme, three stages of progressive estrangement from the homogenousness of the metaphor mark increasing epistemological sophistication. First, there is the radical metaphor, where two objects remain undifferentiated. Second, there is the poetic consciousness, where "two objects or images are just beginning to disentangle themselves from this homogenous sensation." [23] Finally, there exists the language of the simile, where a consciousness of distinction is explicitly acknowledged and referred to.

The stages of this process are shifted in the encounter between Kate and Milly. Kate uses the language of the radical metaphor, a linking form of *to be* to simulate a fusion between the dove and Milly. But Kate's use is insincere. Milly, on the other hand, receives the image "like" an inspiration and "as she *would have* met revealed truth" (19: 283) (italics added). *Inspiration*, as one recalls from the previous chapter on *The Bostonians*, was the most common term of nineteenth-century rhetorical idealism to describe reception of the revealed truths of love and fellowship. Milly cannot be inspired by Kate because of her knowledge of Kate's insincerity; there is a distance, an estrangement, from the proferred image; Milly has a reserve about the spontaneity of the image and a consciousness of the distinction between herself and the dove. But she can accept this image contingently. Milly, in accepting the dove metaphor as an apt description of herself, attempts to recapture the homogenous world of radical metaphor, or at least of poetic consciousness, where the discrete elements of her personality—her previous innocence and good faith versus her fledgling knowledge—are fused. Elizabeth Allen suggests that Milly mystifies her own function as sign—as dove—to fascinate Densher into paying attention to her and to give Densher the protection he requires from the reality of suffering.

Allen suggests that Milly consciously manipulates a sign function that she knows to be artificial.[24] Yet it seems equally likely that she adopts a role of innocence in the same experimental manner that she accepts from her physician the edict that she might live, possible that Milly is attempting to transform both contingent hypotheses into living realities through the use of her imagination. Milly's interpretation of the dove metaphor is the interpretation of the artist; it is based on her imagination. As Densher comments, "It was neither Kate nor he who made his strange relation to Milly, who made her own, so far as it might be, innocent; it was neither of them who practically purged it—if practically purged it was. Milly herself did everything—so far at least as he was concerned—Milly herself, and Milly's house, and Milly's hospitality, and Milly's manner, and Milly's character, and, perhaps still more than anything else, Milly's imagination" (20:239). Milly's will to believe both in her own innocence and in that of her friends is fortified by her pragmatic courage to make a leap in faith, a leap made possible because of her imagination and then stabilized by her knowledge that her faith will either be validated or invalidated by the test of future experience.

Milly decides, after assuming a "most dovelike" innocence with Maud Lowder about anything she has learned of Densher and Kate, that "she should have to be clear as to how a dove *would* act" (19:284). Her next step is to shift information of her illness from her own person to Susan Stringham. Milly is attempting to become an artist on the canvas of her own destiny. As the rhetorical artist Verena in *The Bostonians*, Milly retains a paradoxical balance between innocence and artfulness. She strives to *become* the dove, yet she must constantly intuit with each new situation just how a dove would act, and she must hope that future events will justify her behavior. One must assume that, as with her past pragmatic behavior, Milly is operating with no consciousness of fraud. She is simply launching a pragmatic experiment that she hopes to verify through experience. And she is launching that experiment through an imaginative leap in faith.

We cannot really know, with full assurance, the assumptions Milly holds about Kate and Densher's relationship after the incident between Milly and Kate; Milly's thoughts are inscrutably withheld from us as we perceive her through the filtering perception of Densher's point of view. We do know that she backs off from an aggressive pursuit of her instincts with Kate to an acceptance, on faith, of Kate's word. We have seen how James explains that he has decided to "deal with her at second

hand, as an unspotted princess is ever dealt with." The artistic purpose of James's indirection, however, seems to be to back away from
Milly's knowledge, to grant her her faith and its transformative power.
If there is a great instance of self-deceit in the novel, it is perhaps at
this point, when Milly backs away from a growth into knowledge and
consciously affirms instead a position of ambivalence in regard to that
knowledge. Milly's "deceits," however, differ radically from Kate's because they are existential in nature; they involve the issue of how one
creates freedom and identity within the boundary of restrictions; not
how one denies those restrictions but how one dynamically interacts
with them to alter the undesirable aspects of one's future such as impending death or thwarted love interests. Milly does not believe Kate
for purposes of self-delusion. She does so with the pragmatic intent of
validating her faith in the future possibilities for her life.

Milly's faith is the spiritual faith described by Henry Ward Beecher
in many of his sermons, including one entitled "The Naturalness of
Faith." It seems likely that James had read the most popular published
sermons in America in the nineteenth century; the stress on Milly's
imagination as a kind of faith in *The Wings of the Dove* finds complement in Beecher's theory. Beecher comments that there are "men
who realize invisible truths," who do so "by the imagination; and this
imagination is called faith." When men act on faith, they do so "not
from a knowledge of things in the present which they could see, and
hear, and smell, and taste, and handle, but from a large consideration of
the future, from a consideration of things that lay above the ordinary
sensuous perceptions of men." Yet such faith is not to be considered
foolhardy or blind: "Believing that things are true which every part of
you instinctively feels are not true—that has been taught to be faith.
. . . Faith is the use of reason, and not the abuse of it. Faith is the employment of reason along the line of analogy, not the suppression of
it." [25] Faith also can be expected to be validated by experience: "I have
sometimes said that life was a test of truth; that that which men believe
on philosophical principles, being carried into outward life, will very
soon show where it is harmonious or at discord with it." [26] Milly accepts
the analogy of the dove which she hopes can be carried into outward
life and borne out by experience.

John Auchard has interpreted Milly's adventure in *The Wings of the
Dove* as a sojourn into mysticism, into the Via Negativa: "No handsome journalist rests at the heart of Milly Theale's vitality." [27] Yet Milly
actively, although carefully, descends from the retreating heights of

her Venice palazzo to gain validation for her faith. Her very presentation of herself as having faith in Densher and Kate is an inducement to Densher to validate it. She also actively pursues Densher to gain validation for her faith.

Milly inquires of Densher his reasons for remaining in Italy. She phrases her questions in the language of contingency, based on her pragmatic decision to believe that what Kate and Densher tell her will be proven true. Her questions are both exploratory and persuasive. She is seeking to confirm her belief that, given what she has been told, Densher is open to the affections of others besides Kate, and also, at the same time, she is attempting to ensure this fact by expressing to Densher her faith in him and asking him to verify it.

In a sense, Milly's questions seem closely akin to the rhetorical device Campbell calls "interrogation," which is effective in its subtlety:

> It . . . appears difficult to account for the effect of interrogation, which, being an appeal to the hearers, though it might awaken a closer attention, yet could not, one would imagine, excite in their minds any emotion that was not there before. This, nevertheless, it doth excite. . . . Such an appeal implies in the orator the strongest confidence in the rectitude of his sentiments, and in the concurrence of every reasonable being. The auditors, by sympathizing with this frame of spirit, find it impracticable to withhold an assent which is so confidently depended on.[28]

Despite the suspicion, engendered by Campbell's explanation of the device, that Milly's discourse with Densher is perforce self-conscious and perhaps manipulatively duplicitous, one must consider also that Milly is genuinely trying to verify the present state of Densher's emotions. There is a certain timidity and humility in the way she first assumes that Densher has remained in Venice to write a book. Indeed, Densher does become increasingly remorseful simply by responding to her questions in his own guileful way. But Densher's remorse is caused by his *own* deceit, not Milly's. Pressed finally into giving Milly concrete reasons for remaining in Italy, he admits he stays behind for her. He utters this and his conscience smites him; he is certain she believes him. We only know for certain that she gives the impression of believing him, but it seems to me that Milly's statement of faith in Densher, which goes beyond the grave, emphasizes the extent of her own pragmatic project and "will to believe." Milly makes an appeal to Densher to verify her own faith by showing him the strongest confidence in her innocence and thus in his motives. Milly perpetuates the reality of her innocence through the linguistic force of her argument, and succeeds: "It was amazing what so brief an exchange had at this point done with him. . . . What had taken place for him, however— the drop, almost with violence, of everything but a sense of her own reality—apparently showed in his face or his manner" (20:246–47). Lord Mark's vengeful insistence on informing Milly of the actual facts about Kate and Densher's relationship provides concrete evidence that undermines Milly's pragmatic belief. The fact that she "turns her face to the wall" and dies reveals how closely her two pragmatic assertions of faith are intermingled. Her project to live, her capability to imagine herself living, determines her other tenuous flight, her ability to imagine herself innocent, which allows her the possibility of a future in which to establish a relationship with Densher. Milly's persuasive language was an attempt to compel the moral character, Densher, to choose to recreate his own emotional nature. At the point when Lord Mark reenters the scene, Densher was in the process of sorting through his emotions and shifting his perspective so that his actions would become commensurate with his words. In responding to Milly's faith that he is honest, he is responding to his own moral sense that honesty and trust in a relationship bear priority over emotions. Unlike Kate, Milly is not asking Densher to lie but to become truthful in a higher, more spiritual way than he had heretofore been. In Beecher's spiritual terms, Milly has been Christlike, not only in her eventual sacrifice but in her active presence on earth. Christ, according to Beecher, presents atonement

> which draws men out of themselves, which is long-suffering, but which says, "There shall forever be a difference between truth and lies, between right and wrong;" which says, "Forever and ever selfishness shall be painful and benevolence shall be blessed; and I will maintain that which is high and noble, and will bring the race up to it by stripes, by chastisements, by suffering, by long trial; and I will bear and forbear with them, never forgetting that I am striving for the glorious enfranchisement of the animal into manhood."[29]

Milly draws Densher out of himself to acknowledge the difference between truth and lies.

Lord Mark, however, transforms Milly's creative sphere from one of white magic to necromancy. Milly does not actually die "for" language but as a result of her profound recognition of what language bespeaks about life. Milly must acknowledge Lord Mark's concrete facts because of her pragmatic reverence for referentially truthful language that, in expressing the facts of experience, can alter the nature of pragmatic belief. She must acknowledge death because the possibility of life and of love was part of the same experimental impulse in her pragmatic stance of innocence. *The Wings of the Dove*, then, concludes with the intimation that in certain instances literally truthful language can be potentially the most damaging. Lord Mark serves as an ironic parody of the care in human relationships that truthful language normally implies. Thus, *The Wings of the Dove* goes beyond an examination of language itself to an evaluation of the human impulses that guide it. One primary prerequisite of language is that it be truthful, but primarily because the impulse to speak truth to another shows reverence and care for another human spirit. Language, as the basis of trust, is thus sacred in the Jamesian world. This is something which Merton Densher, in *The Wings of the Dove*, comes to realize fully.

Merton Densher is a dilettante journalist at the beginning of *The Wings of the Dove*. This has to be a warning signal about him, since journalism as an art form is concerned with surface appearances and impressions and usually looked down upon as such by James. Nevertheless, as Oscar Cargill notes, "Merton Densher possesses little of the cynicism we have come to associate with a career in journalism, and in particular with other journalists whom James has created, for example, George Flack and Matthias Pardon."[30] Instead, as we have noted, Densher's admiration for Kate is a result of ethics as well as of his journalistic love of style. It is their shared truths which Densher cherishes, but it is Kate's ability to live, to adopt a style, that Densher admires: Densher admires Kate's ability to live life by envisioning forms through which desire can be gratified. Densher recognizes, for example, how Kate acts out a form to appease her aunt. He "now recognised in it something like the artistic idea, the plastic substance, imposed by tradition, by genius, by criticism, in respect to a given character, or a distinguished actress. As such a person was to dress the part, to walk, to look, to speak, in every way to express, the part, so all this was what Kate was to do for the character she had undertaken, under her aunt's roof, to represent" (20:34).

At the risk of suggesting a parallel that to some may seem invidious, I would suggest that Kate's rhetorical capabilities hold for Merton the same fascination and seductiveness that Tom Sawyer's do for Huck; both Kate and Tom "do" something versus Merton's and Huck's paralyzing passivity; both Kate and Tom suggest that appearances constitute reality and refuse to accept that their evasions will have ethical consequences and might cause harm. "Woe to him whose beliefs play fast and loose with the order which realities follow in his experience," to quote William James, "they will lead him nowhere or else make false connexions."[31] That one can have everything without paying a price defies reality as Kate or any Jamesian character knows it. The lure of the sophistic rhetorician who plays fast and loose with truth is the suggestion that action can be free from responsibility. Merton, by deferring his point of view to Kate, lets her be the artist of his subjective vision; he absents himself from the world as much as possible by temporarily subscribing to Kate's sophistry. He attempts to avoid responsibility for his own sense of what he knows to be true about the world and to avoid the possible consequences of his own actions in it.

James adroitly conceives in Densher a person who might decide in favor of rhetorical virtue rather than rhetorical style. Densher, at the outset, is a mixture of strengths and weaknesses. In his journalistic stance as passive observer, he is weak-willed, an artist-voyeur who experiences life vicariously rather than through action for which he would have to accept some consequence. He therefore has only a shallow conception of what would constitute fine style. He cannot initially appreciate, for example, any inherent strength in the argument of the virtuous American girl: "Little Miss Theale's individual history was not stuff for his newspaper; besides which, moreover, he was seeing but too many little Miss Theales. They even went so far as to impose themselves as one of the groups of social phenomena that fell into the scheme of his public letters" (20:10). That Miss Theale seems both "little" as an argument for Densher's affection and blurred in identity among a group of similar others is both a result of Densher's exclusive concentration on Kate as a subject and of his devaluation of virtue and overvaluation of superficial style as the determinant of rhetorical excellence. Densher does, however, possess a strong sense of as yet untested ethics. He will test that sense when he becomes involved, much like Huck Finn, in an experiment with sophistic rhetoric. He will come, through that experience, to a different awareness of Kate's and Milly's rhetoric.

Densher's critical dependency on Kate seems to be the result of a weak will; he is listless professionally and unable to supply Kate with any way to circumvent their mutual poverty. Gaining money is not Densher's desire, however; his wish is to gain Kate. To have her, Densher must go along with Kate's attempt to get money so that she will feel able to marry him. Out of love for Kate rather than greed, Densher responds eagerly yet nervously to the role Kate assigns him in their money-making scheme. Immediately, Densher's ethical sense warns him that in adopting a point of view alien to his own he is not "being right with himself," but he rationalizes his sophistic pose as an adventure, "he who had never thought himself cut out for them, and it fairly helped him that he was able at moments to say to himself that he mustn't fall below it" (20:183).

Densher's adventure is his adoption of a point of view alien to what he knows to be true of the world. Densher apprehends that "the single thing that was clear in complications was that, whatever happened, one was to behave as a gentleman—to which was added indeed the perhaps slightly less shining truth that complications might sometimes have their tedium beguiled by a study of the question of how a gentleman would behave" (20:183–84). Both Milly and Densher wonder at the roles Kate gives them, but, whereas Milly attempts to reify hers, Densher is only too aware that his role as gentleman is only a duplicitous cover. Even though Densher's thoughts lead him initially "to a degree of eventual peace, for what they luminously amounted to was that he was to do nothing" (20:252), Densher will finally object to his sense of false position.

Densher accepts the role of gentleman because he perceives this role as one consonant with his own experience of himself as relatively passive and compatible with the satisfaction of his desire for Kate. The amoral pragmatism of such a movement echoes Kate's purely pragmatic manuevers, but with the notable exception that for Densher his amorality is such a decided posture, an outright adventure. Densher's initial state is one of moral ambivalence because, although he has the potential capacity for making moral decisions, he does not want to take responsibility for doing so. Moral scruples, however, plague him from the outset. He concentrates for a long while on the relatively passive nature of his response so that he can negate responsibility for his co-operation in Kate's scheme and on the do-nothing nature of his task so that he can rationalize his own participation in a conscious deception. The way Densher thus interprets *gentleman* reflects ironically on the term.

Densher does desire to absolve himself from responsibility in the deception of Milly. Within himself, he has the capacity for recognizing the dire implications of deception for healthy human relations. Accordingly, he rationalizes that his silence should indicate to Milly his lack of feeling for her, which is why he even ignores the state of her health:

> He hadn't even the amount of curiosity that he would have had about an ordinary friend. . . . In what therefore was the duplicity? He was at least sure about his feelings — it being so established that he had none at all. They were all for Kate, without a feather's weight to spare. He was acting for Kate — not, by the deviation of an inch, for her friend. He was accordingly not interested, for had he been interested he would have cared, and had he cared he would have wanted to know. Had he wanted to know he wouldn't have been purely passive, and it was his pure passivity that had to represent his honour. (20:204)

Unlike Kate, Densher is clearly preoccupied with morals. His attempts to deny moral responsibility are only temporarily successful and even then obstructed by his unerring sense that abstention from truth is itself morally reprehensible. His knowledge that "it was false that he wasn't loved" by Kate is tempered by his self-reassurance "that he had himself as yet done nothing deceptive," but immediately checked by his continued speculation: "It was Kate's description of him, his defeated state, it was none of his own; his responsibility would begin, as he might say, only with acting it out. The sharp point was, however, in the difference between acting and not acting: this difference in fact it was that made the case of conscience. He saw it with a certain alarm rise before him that everything was acting that was not speaking the particular word" (20:76). Densher is alarmed because he knows that there are particular words that could be said to conform to truth or to have their frame of reference in the truth of experience. Just as Milly's higher artistic sense causes her to be preoccupied with the truth or morality of metaphor, Merton's active conscience causes him finally to recoil from his own deceptive behavior. His eventual transferral of loyalties from Kate to Milly is consistent with his mental and emotional development throughout the latter half of the novel.

Consistently throughout the novel, the moral question of truthful rhetoric is inextricably bound up with the artistic definition of truth. In *The Wings of the Dove*, James implies that conforming to the truths of experience and to the truths of the human heart not only constitutes the best moral decision; it also makes for the higher art. Kate's attraction for Densher is always articulated in terms of her artistry and, conversely, Milly's understated presence causes Densher initially to ignore her. By the end of the novel, however, this situation has turned around and the reader not too bedazzled by Kate's initial brilliance can carefully follow Densher's transformation under the spell of Milly's imagination. As Nicola Bradbury remarks, "It is because Milly's is the more comprehensive imagination that she achieves a paradoxical success, while Kate, with all her manipulative vigour, fails utterly." [32]

Densher's aversion to "too many little Miss Theales" changes to awe by the time Mrs. Stringham describes to him her mistress' establishment in Vienna:

> "She's lodged for the first time as she ought, from her type, to be; and doing it—I mean bringing out all the glory of the place—makes her really happy. It's a Veronese picture, as near as can be—with me as the inevitable dwarf, the small blackamoor, put into a corner of the fore-ground for effect. If I only had a hawk or a hound or something of that sort I should do the scene more honour. The old housekeeper, the woman in charge here, has a big red cockatoo that I might borrow and perch on my thumb for the evening." (20:206)

Densher's response is to feel his own art inadequate: "What part was there for *him*, with his attitude that lacked the highest style, in a composition in which everything else would have it?" (20:206). Striving for definition now in Milly's composition instead of Kate's, not co-incidentally in the same meditative passage, Densher recognizes that, with his behavior in Italy, "he had incurred it, the expectation of performance" (20:208). (In the unrevised edition, James wrote "conscious responsibility.") Milly makes him feel this; the highest style involves an expectation of performance, a recognition of conscious responsibility.

The adoption of Kate's point of view eventually wears both morally and artistically on Densher's astute intelligence. Densher, as a moral being with a strong sense of the sacredness of human emotion, sees the discrepancy between the deceptive way he presents himself to Milly and what he truly is. He also becomes disenchanted with Kate, seeing how, even given their eventual physical relation, she can still place pragmatic considerations above her love for him. When he suggests that they announce their marriage instead of continuing in their scheme with Milly, she demurs, at which point "he could but stand there with his wasted passion . . . his horror, almost, of her [Kate's] lucidity. They made in him a mixture that might have been rage, but that was turning quickly to mere cold thought, thought which led to something else and was like a new dim dawn" (20:350). Densher eventually falls away from Kate, detaches from her because of her own emotional detachment, which implies to him that there is something illicit in their relation, something causing "the need to bury in the dark blindness of each other's arms the knowledge of each other that they couldn't undo" (20:392).

To square his conscience after Milly's death, Densher sees one of two choices: to deny the entire deceptive structure upon which Milly's faith in him is built through giving up Milly's money, the result of his deception; or to reinvest his past with meaning differently apportioned so that he can affirm the form he has adopted, claiming love for Milly and interiorizing this as a truth. He appeals to Kate one last time to shed the hypocritical veil of their past behavior by denying the money. That Kate is stunned by Densher's suggestion and thus fails him both as artist and as human being is a tragic instance of how estranged Kate has become from the noble emotions that once inspired her. When Densher does not deny Kate's accusation that he has fallen in love with the idea of Milly, he reveals the impossibility of going back to Kate.[33] Densher travels a long journey ethically from the point at which he perceived his adventure to be discovering if "being right with himself" was necessary to his happiness, from the point at which he chose to abandon momentarily his own established moral rules—that inherent aspect of his personality—in light of an apparently more useful scheme with Kate.

Densher rejects his moral sojourn into Kate's culture as a result of a rigorous self-investigation into who has the greater claim on him, Kate or Milly. Milly has mere numbers on her side; the pressure of her claim is made known by Maud, Susan Stringham, and, ironically, even by Kate herself. More profoundly, by recognizing Milly's higher art and being moved by her sacrifice in death, Densher is deeply penetrated by the higher fidelities, sacrificing easy gratification to higher claims because he senses the need for what William James would call the search for divinity: "In the interests of our own ideal of systematically unified moral truth, therefore, we, as would-be philosophers, must postulate a divine thinker, and pray for the victory of the religious cause." Even before her death, Milly, in her relations with Densher, represents a Christ figure, "divine in her trust, or at any rate inscrutable in her mercy" (20:292). She does indeed seem to appeal to Densher's sense of the sacred. William James, when arguing as in the previous passage for what we *ought* to be, comes close to Campbell's claim, in his assertion of the Quintilian principle, for what we are: we will listen, Campbell claims, and be most persuaded, by virtue. In both cases, the truth lies within, as James asserts, our "interior characters." The potential to listen to the higher claims "is not in heaven, neither is it beyond the sea; but the word is very nigh unto thee; in thy mouth and in thy heart, that thou mayest do it." [34]

That Densher "does it" disturbs many exasperated readers who discount him as simply another misguided American idealist too inept to deal with the given conditions of the world, safely in love with a woman who is obviously impossible to attain. [35] Undoubtedly, Densher's loss of the beautiful Kate and her own loss of her essential inner beauty casts a somber twilight in the novel. But the magnitude of what Densher sacrifices when he accepts that fact and makes his decision makes his choice seem all the more courageous. With both Kate and Milly off the stage, the reader must finally focus on Densher and celebrate the timely birth of a creative consciousness, the birth of a rhetorical being, the birth of an ethical artist. What we have finally witnessed in *The Wings of the Dove* is the evolution of Densher's consciousness as an active force that constantly readjusts its form to the content of experience even, at crucial times, working with its memory of past events and reshifting them to incorporate a more ethical apprehension of experience. Densher's next relationship with an individual will be based on moral certitude and unwavering ethics.

Milly and Densher are soul mates finally because their inherent rhetorical idealism encourages them to employ their consciousnesses creatively to transform the world into an ethical reality, both concerned with the ethical quality of their ideas, but equally concerned that those ideas conform to the facts of experience as they know them. Whereas Milly assumes provisionally that her innocence will some day be validated in the future if she can win Densher's love from Kate, Densher turns to his own past to reinterpret the quality of his emotion for Kate. Won over by Milly's insistent innocence, shown in "Milly herself, and Milly's house, and Milly's hospitality, and Milly's manner, and Milly's character, and, perhaps still more than anything else, Milly's imagination" (20:239), Densher evolves as an artist; his consciousness reinvests his past with a shifted significance which incorporates past and present into a synthetic unity. He wills a reevaluation of his past to honor the feelings Milly has for him and to honor the mutual reverence both he and Milly hold for the relationship between experience and language. He looks to his past to enact the change of focus. Riding in Venice with Milly, Densher reflects:

Her [Milly's] welcome, her frankness, sweetness, sadness, brightness, her disconcerting poetry . . . his renewed remembrance, which had fairly become a habit, that he had been the first to know her. . . . It had worked as a clear connexion with something lodged in the past, something already their own. He had more than once recalled how he had said to himself even at that moment, at some point in the drive, that he was not *there*, not just as he was in so doing it, through Kate and Kate's idea, but through Milly and Milly's own, and through himself and *his* own, unmistakeably—as well as through the little facts, whatever they had amounted to, of his time in New York. (20:184–86)

This is a clear dramatization of William James's thoughts on how the mind works. "The mind, in short," writes James, "works on the data it receives very much as a sculptor works on his block of stone. In a sense the statue stood there from eternity. But there were a thousand different ones beside it, and the sculptor alone is to thank for having extricated this one from the rest." The sculpting mind may extricate at any given time any element of its past, present, or anticipated future. It may extricate one piece of data to sculpt, as Densher does when he initially decides to focus on Kate, but the mind can also choose to sculpt any other state from the eternity of mental experiences composing its past and present. As James explains, "A mind which has become conscious of its own cognitive function, plays what we have called 'the psychologist' upon itself. It not only knows the things that appear before it; it knows that it knows them. This stage of reflective condition, is, more or less explicitly, our habitual adult state of mind." [36]

In the world of Henry James, the successful individual must inevitably be an artist, taking the responsibility to create his own meaning from what he knows of himself and of the world and taking the consequences for it. Densher, freeing his mind from Kate's rigid dictates, adopts a point of view more in harmony with his own ethical sense. Paul B. Armstrong has observed that "for James, the pursuit of the moral life is an often ambiguous, always perilous, never ultimately completed activity because it is a constant epistemological and existential challenge." [37] For the child who takes all in, this would be true. But the mature individual takes a great deal of responsibility for the choice of his own meaning and, although always in pursuit of that meaning, his mental activity is often more deliberate than perilous. Densher's positive response to Milly's rhetorical virtue arises out of his sense of moral ethics and from listening to the ruby vault of his own human heart.

7

Maggie's Unfortunate Virtue: Rhetorical Responsibility in *The Golden Bowl*

๙๔

"May not one's affection for her do something more for one's decency, as you call it, than her own generosity— her own affection, *her* 'decency' — has the unfortunate virtue to undo?"

— HENRY JAMES, *The Golden Bowl*

As we have seen, the ideal of nineteenth-century rhetorical virtue implied that truthful language was a tangible manifestation of caring human relationships. Henry James endows American young women with this contemporary ideal of rhetorical virtue in notable fictional instances. He then charges these special fictional women with the task of compelling rhetorical virtue, or caring behavior, in the opposite sex. In *The Wings of the Dove*, Merton Densher undertakes the adventure of discovering whether "in default of being right with himself he had meanwhile, for one thing, the interest of seeing— and quite for the first time in his life— whether, on a given occasion, that might be quite so necessary to happiness as was commonly assumed and as he had up to this moment never doubted" (20:183). Through Milly's influence, Densher discovers that being right with himself is the only means of achieving personal happiness, and he consequently tries to change his "deception" into truth. In *The Golden Bowl*, the hero is again engaged in an adventure, although Prince Amerigo's experiment is the exact opposite of Densher's. At the opening of the novel, Amerigo perceives himself to be seeking an ethical sense that he has never had. His moral sense is like "the tortuous stone staircase— half-ruined into the bargain! — in some castle of our *quattrocento.*"[1] This adventure is difficult and problematic; the first several chapters of *The Golden Bowl* reveal the subtleties of the Prince's conscience, his vacillating and imperfect ethical sense. And again, the Prince's ethical behavior is metaphorically described in the popular rhetorical terms of deception and truth.

There is evidence in the opening chapters of *The Golden Bowl* that Amerigo has been sexually promiscuous and that he is now struggling to overcome that habit through the compulsion of his commitment to a future caring relationship with Maggie. Nicola Bradbury sympathetically observes that "Amerigo is not a figure who can eventually be left behind. He must be worthy of Maggie's devotion, yet capable of entering a position so false as to justify her measures to set it right."[2] Elizabeth Allen quite differently characterizes "Amerigo's controlled, civilized, quasi-brutality in his relations to women."[3] Neither of these critics is wrong. A sexually promiscuous way of thinking is so much a part of Amerigo's background that he is helpless to it, although chapters 1 and 2 of *The Golden Bowl* reveal him fighting it in a state of frustrated isolation.

Amerigo feels "the gravity of the hour" (23:18) upon the approach of his marriage to Maggie. And despite his concerted sexual abstention, he still rues the fact that he is now shut off from life's seamier possibilities, that "his fate had practically been sealed, and that even when one pretended to no quarrel with it the moment had something of the grimness of a crunched key in the strongest lock that could be made" (23:4–5). But he is more frustrated because no one seems to be aware of or to appreciate the moral effort he is making in keeping faithful to his marital commitment to Maggie. He implies the effort again and again to Maggie, but she consistently refuses to acknowledge it. Amerigo is left to wonder whether the effort of fidelity is even necessary: "What was this so important step he had just taken but the desire for some new history that should, so far as possible, contradict, and even if need be flatly dishonour, the old. . . . He thought of these things — of his not being at all events futile, and of his absolute acceptance of the developments of the coming age — to redress the balance of his being so differently considered. The moments when he most winced were those at which he found himself believing that, really, futility would have been forgiven him. Even *with* it, in that absurd view, he would have been good enough. Such was the laxity, in the Ververs, of the romantic spirit" (23:16–17).

Futility, in chapters 1 and 2 of *The Golden Bowl*, is suggestively synonymous with sexual promiscuity, and, correspondingly, with rhetorical deception. Amerigo believes that his American marriage, with its good faith and bundle of money, will rectify both the "moral depravity" and pennilessness of his European tradition. He believes that his forthcoming marriage is a way out of a naturalistic dilemma, and he sees the part of the bargain he can make and the good he can provide as the gift of marital fidelity, so alien to his tradition and instinct and thus requiring immense effort. Interestingly enough, Amerigo conceives of this twofold transaction in the popular terminology of rhetorical idealism. He reminisces that his efforts, for six months, have been singled down to Maggie and decides that "success, as he would otherwise have put it, had rewarded virtue; whereby the consciousness of these things made him for the hour rather serious than gay" (23:4). Amerigo's virtuous and apparently effortful pursuit of one woman has resulted in the Ververs' "London lawyers" having "reached an inspired harmony with his own man of business" (23:5). *Inspiration* was the popular term for the effect of virtuous rhetoric. Amerigo connects the financial resurrection he is going to receive with his rhetorical virtue—or sexual fidelity—the ongoing virtue he expects to have compelled by the inspiration of his marriage. Amerigo appropriately considers that his "fate had practically been sealed" at three o'clock, and quantities of three recur in Maggie's narrative section, alluding to Maggie's ultimate role in Amerigo's spiritual resurrection.

True to the rhetorical ideal of the time, the beginning chapters blur the distinction between rhetorical and moral virtue; sexual promiscuity is linked with verbal deception, and Amerigo's fear of lying to his wife is a veiled way of expressing his fear of committing adultery and a foreshadowing of the given fact. Sexual temptation is inextricably of the texture and quality of Amerigo's mind, and this is made abundantly clear by the narrative innuendos James embeds in the description of his hero's contemplative walk through the streets of London. Amerigo is so preoccuped with his impending sexual faithfulness that

> the young man's movements, however, betrayed no consistency of attention—not even, for that matter, when one of his arrests had proceeded from possibilities in faces shaded, as they passed him on the pavement, by huge beribboned hats, or more delicately tinted still under the tense silk of parasols held at perverse angles in waiting victorias. And the Prince's undirected thought was not a little symptomatic, since, though the turn of the season had come and the flush of the streets begun to

fade, the possibilities of faces, on the August afternoon, were still one of
the notes of the scene. He was too restless—that was the fact—for any
concentration, and the last idea that would just now have occurred to
him in any connexion was the idea of pursuit. (23:3–4)

This passage which filters through Amerigo's mind is full of erotic
suggestiveness. Even though the Prince is otherwise absorbed, he has
been virtually "arrested" by "possibilities." There are tempting faces
shaded by parasols teasingly held at "perverse" angles, *tense* implying
also the sexual tension which is both a projection from the Prince's
mind and applicable equally to the women, provocatively contradicted
by the sensuous fluidity implied by *silk*. This is one of James's most
erotic passages, and he applies it to the quality of the Prince's mind.
But equally important is that its evocativeness has been deflected by
the Prince's concentration upon his marriage and its attendant duties.

But not obliterated. In fact, the Prince tacitly acknowledges that
"his crisis . . . of the immediate two or three hours" is one of sexual
temptation:

> He paused on corners, at crossings; there kept rising for him, in waves,
> that consciousness, sharp as to its source while vague as to its end, which
> I began by speaking of—the consciousness of an appeal to do something
> or other, before it was too late, for himself. By any friend to whom he
> might have mentioned it the appeal could have been turned to frank de-
> rision. For what, for whom indeed but himself and the high advantages
> attached, was he about to marry an extraordinarily charming girl whose
> "prospects," of the solid sort, were as guaranteed as her amiability? He
> wasn't to do it assuredly all for *her*. The Prince, as happened, however,
> was so free to feel and yet not to formulate that there rose before him
> after a little, definitely, the image of a friend whom he had often found
> ironic. He withheld the tribute of attention from passing faces only to
> let his impulse accumulate. Youth and beauty made him scarcely turn,
> but the image of Mrs. Assingham made him presently stop a hansom.
> (23:19–20)

This passage represents Amerigo's "pre-marital jitters" and impulse to
"sow his wild oats." It is important that again this sexual impulse is
arrested by his thought of someone who can inspire him to be virtuous
and, equally, appreciate his effort to be so.

The Prince at one point connects his sexual fidelity with his existentialistic escape from his past. He clearly links his past—and, thus,
sexual promiscuity—with naturalistic failure:

The Prince's notion of a recompense to women—similar in this to his notion of an appeal—was more or less to make love to them. Now he hadn't, as he believed, made love the least little bit to Mrs. Assingham— nor did he think she had for a moment supposed it. He liked in these days, to mark them off, the women to whom he hadn't made love; it represented—and that was what pleased him in it—a different stage of existence from the time at which he liked to mark off the women to whom he had. (23:21–22)

Within this context of Amerigo's conscious struggle with his tradition of promiscuity, he recollects asking his future American wife a veiled question ostensibly about rhetorical virtue: " 'You do believe I'm not a hypocrite? You recognise that I don't lie nor dissemble nor deceive? Is *that* water-tight?' " (23:15). This question about Maggie's faith in Amerigo's verbal fidelity might seem odd, as it does to Maggie, if it were posed out of the context of chapter 1, but the subtle innuendos about Amerigo's sexual temptations as he meditates in stream-of-consciousness fashion in his walk through London lead directly into the question so that the reader is led to connect verbal with sexual fidelity.

This may have been James's sly way of introducing the subject of adultery to his American readers. Anne T. Margolis has suggested that James wanted desperately to introduce the subject of adultery into his fiction for the purposes of literary mastery and experimentation. James felt frustrated in this effort by the prohibition of American critics wanting to protect the innocence of the predominantly female and adolescent American readers. His solution, according to Margolis, was to introduce the subject in covert form through the innocent perspective of his fictional innocent women.[4] Amerigo's frustration with Maggie's initial refusal to acknowledge even the possibility of her husband's potential for sexual deception—metaphorically represented here by her rhetorical innocence—parallels James's own frustration with the supposed moral obtuseness of the young American female reader in her response to adultery. In *The Golden Bowl*, the moral value of telling the truth and sexual fidelity make these two terms synonymous, and rightly so. The transactions of rhetoric and marriage both involve issues of sincerity and trust and can both involve a willful innocence on one side of the transaction. Adultery and linguistic deception become interchangeable issues in *The Golden Bowl*, adultery the metonym for rhetorical deception.

Amerigo's expressed hope that he not deceive his wife implies his hope that he not commit adultery. His anxiety about the possibility of adultery is revealed by his asking his future wife a question about her belief in him rather than stating a declarative intent. Amerigo actually implicates Maggie in his adultery through this attempt to shift responsibility from his own role as rhetorical actor to hers as audience. He implies that it is her belief in him that will compel him to be virtuous. He requires that his wife's belief in him be a conscious effort. He wants his own effort to be virtuous to be rewarded. Just as James must have felt frustrated by the idea of an audience of American female innocents, Amerigo comes to realize that Maggie is shielded within an invulnerability of rhetorical innocence, that she simply refuses to address the possibility of linguistic—thus marital—deception: "He had perceived on the spot that any *serious* discussion of veracity, of loyalty, or rather of the want of them, practically took her unprepared, as if it were quite new to her. He had noticed it before: it was the English, the American sign that duplicity, like 'love,' had to be joked about. It couldn't be 'gone into'" (23:15). As Mrs. Assingham aptly remarks, "Maggie was the creature in the world to whom a wrong thing could least be communicated. It was as if her imagination had been closed to it, her sense altogether sealed" (23:384).

Maggie Verver's rhetorical innocence qualifies her as Clara Wieland's literary sister; both fantasize an isolated community of idyllic innocence, and both have their fantasies finally shattered by their coming to awareness of deception. In both instances, deception is exacerbated by the rhetorical audience's unwillingness to address the possibility of deception. In both instances, then, there is a stress upon the responsibility of the rhetorical audience.

This was a responsibility implied to be negligible by the popular Quintilian principle. In 1806, John Quincy Adams refused to teach Hugh Blair's *Lectures on Rhetoric and Belles Lettres* in his position as Harvard Boylston Professor of Rhetoric because of the potential damage he saw implicit in the Quintilian principle Blair advocated. Adams feared that the "style" or "appearance" of the rhetoric might be misunderstood to imply the content.[5] Just as Clara Wieland cavalierly dismisses the need to judge the quality of the Ciceronian bust, Adam Verver in *The Golden Bowl* similarly cares only that "a work of art of price should 'look like' the master to whom it might perhaps be deceitfully attributed" (23:146–47). The Quintilian principle seems to have implied to the American mind that deceit is not even an issue if the style is fine.

It is not surprising that Amerigo predicts that his "futility" would be forgiven him and that he is frustratedly aware "that practically he was never to be tried or tested" (23:23).

Yet Amerigo demonstrates in his opening conversations with Charlotte a determination to remain "straight" and to take responsibility for his own virtue. Charlotte is his greatest fear because she presents the greatest temptation to Amerigo's virtue, to his conscious choice to renounce sexual promiscuity. Amerigo's own constitutional tendency would be to let appearance stand for reality as a means of moral evasion. Whereas the American's good-natured acceptance of appearance for fact suggests rhetorical innocence, the Europeans substitute appearance for fact with a Machiavellian sense of convenience, out of worldly cynicism, and with the desire to exploit. *The Golden Bowl* reveals that of the two forms of rhetorical irresponsibility, James would find the European form more culpable and the American one more potentially redeemable.

Mrs. Assingham, as she herself knows, is one of the more culpable characters in the novel because she refuses her responsibility for encouraging Amerigo to change from his sexually promiscuous ways. Although Mrs. Assingham has an inherited American reverence for truth, she has allowed her reverence to degenerate into a mere need to appease her conscience. From her acquired knowledge of the European obfuscation of appearance with reality, she consciously practices a sham art of self-deception. She is a hypocrite whose obvious reverence for the virtue of truth misleads Amerigo into thinking she can aid him and instruct him in his own efforts to be morally straight. Amerigo believes that looking at Fanny is like looking into the mirror of his own soul; it was *her* confidence in his virtue that initially allowed him to have confidence in his own: "You had it first. You had it most" (23:28). And instruction from Fanny should turn out to be instruction in finding his way toward the best part of himself. Yet instruction from Fanny turns out to be dangerous; in skirting responsibility for her faith in Amerigo, she causes him to question himself. Amerigo mentions to Fanny his fears about "the quantity of confidence reposed in him" (23:23), and he consciously attempts with her to give "his sincerity—for it *was* sincerity—fuller expression" (23:26). Amerigo's discourse with Fanny involves a great deal of trust because, in his risked honesty, in his candid revelation of who he is, Amerigo will see reflected back from Fanny's reaction his own self-image. Amerigo presses on with his "real honest fear of being 'off' some day, of being wrong, *without* knowing it. That's what I shall always trust you for" (23:30). Amerigo further expresses his anxiety that in "the moral" (23:31) sense he is "stupid. . . . Therefore it is that I want, that I shall always want, your eyes. Through them I wish to look—even at any risk of their showing me what I mayn't like. For then,' he wound up, 'I shall know. And of that I shall never be afraid' " (23:30).

In the main, Fanny responds by treating "him in fine as if he were not uttering truths but making pretty figures for her diversion" (23:27). Fanny refuses to take responsibility for her faith in Amerigo out of her own fear that he will fail her and prove her wrong. Amerigo sees this fear of himself in her eyes and is confirmed of his own moral stupidity rather than encouraged in his moral adventure.

Mrs. Assingham's fear fails Amerigo when he most needs her confidence: with the arrival of Charlotte from America. Mrs. Assingham's informed confidence would be infinitely more meaningful than Maggie's naive one, since Fanny's would be in a tried and tested and presumably successful virtue. Her faltering confidence at the sight of Charlotte throws Amerigo back on his fledgling moral resources. One of the things that critics neglect to consider when they celebrate either the epiphanic nature of Charlotte and Amerigo's love[6] or consider Charlotte and Amerigo as "gay, young parents, made into demons in childish imagination by their dimly divined sexual complicity"[7] is how fiercely Amerigo initially fights to counteract Charlotte's influence, "her presence in the world, so closely, so irretrievably contemporaneous with his own: a sharp, sharp fact" (23:45).

If Amerigo connects with Charlotte in any "collaborative experience,"[8] it is within the felt presence of his old self, the one from whom Amerigo is struggling to evolve. The word *evolve* has reference to nineteenth-century minister and rhetorician Henry Ward Beecher's spiritualized definition of evolution, to the idea that man could evolve from his animal nature to a more spiritualized realm of truth. Beecher would comment, for example, "that there is no other atonement but that everlasting nature of God . . . which says, 'There shall forever be a difference between truth and lies, between right and wrong,' which says, 'Forever and ever selfishness shall be painful, and benevolence shall be blessed; and I will maintain that which is high and noble . . . never forgetting that I am striving for the glorious enfranchisement of the animal into manhood.'"[9] As Maggie waits, at the conclusion of the novel, for evidence of change in Amerigo's "personal attitude," she muses, "What retarded evolution . . . mightn't poor Charlotte all unwittingly have precipitated" (24:282) in her husband. The evolution is retarded initially, however, by the reentrance of Charlotte into Amerigo's life. She literally haunts him from the past and tries to turn him into the ghost of his former self.

It is in Amerigo's struggle to resist Charlotte that he first begins to vacillate in and out of his old habit of conveniently taking appearance for reality. It is not only her sexual appeal that troubles Amerigo. It is that she might have a claim on him threatening to his new moral sense of responsibility. Charlotte's pronouncing that claim frightens Amerigo the most: "She was afraid of herself, however; whereas, to his gain of lucidity, he was afraid only of her" (23:50–51). In his panic to ward off responsibility for Charlotte's possible claim, Amerigo reverts to his old European sophistry, perceiving Charlotte both as his "huntress" and as his "muse," his inspiration for the covering language that will allow him to evade the chase: "And why couldn't he have dignity when he had so much of the good conscience, as it were, on which such advantages rested? He had done nothing he oughtn't—he had in fact done nothing at all" (23:37). Faced with his guilt, the Prince affects the full sophistry of an innocent appearance: "He looked younger than his years; he was beautiful innocent vague" (23:42).

Ironically, Amerigo relies on Charlotte to cover up her own claim for the sake of her pride and, with the "quasi-brutality" that Allen identifies in him, Amerigo perversely expresses contempt for the generic woman, for her need to practice such a deception. At least, this is one way to interpret a very complex passage in which Amerigo appears to be expressing such feelings:

> Once more, as a man conscious of having known many women, he could assist, as he would have called it, at the recurrent, the predestined phenomenon, . . . the doing by the woman of the thing that gave her away. She did it, ever, inevitably, infallibly—she couldn't possibly not do it. It was her nature, it was her life, and the man could always expect it without lifting a finger. This was *his*, the man's, any man's, position and strength—that he had necessarily the advantage, that he only had to wait, with a decent patience to be placed, in spite of himself, it might really be said, in the right. Just so the punctuality of performance on the part of the other creature was her weakness and her deep misfortune— not less, no doubt, than her beauty. . . . She always dressed her act up, of course, she muffled and disguised and arranged it, showing in fact in these dissimulations a cleverness equal to but one thing in the world, equal to her abjection: she would let it be known for anything, for every-

thing, but the truth of which it was made. . . . She was the twentieth woman, she was possessed by her doom, but her doom was also to arrange appearances, and what now concerned him was to learn how she proposed. (23:49–50)

Elizabeth Allen claims that it is the doom of all women in James to arrange and to interpret the world for men, to keep them "safe" from the fear of themselves they wish to avoid.[10] And, yet, true knowledge of himself, through Fanny's eyes, is something Amerigo claims he wants. The preceding lengthy passage yields a perplexing meaning because we would normally think that "the doing by the woman of the thing that gave her away" would be her utterance of the truth. But in Amerigo's perspective, it seems to be the truth of a woman's passion that is given away by her very need to dissimulate against it. She does this, rather than utter her grievance with a man, to save her pride; and it is the very excessive, baroque way in which appearances are arranged to disavow her own abjection (rejection from the male) that gives her away, but which also, through its disavowal of grievance, puts the man in the appearance of the right. A woman's passion, then, is her weakness; it robs her of her power to compel a man's virtue. Through her own pride, or need for the man, she will help him lie. Amerigo correspondingly does not expect this process from Fanny because he had not "made love the least little bit to Mrs. Assingham — nor did he think she had for a moment supposed it." As Gabriel Pearson has astutely observed, "James's abject women, driven by sexual passion, are one with the women victims of naturalism. Their own carnality is essentially of the same substance as the other impersonal forces that render down and demonically possess free will and consciousness."[11]

Charlotte talks quite often in *The Golden Bowl* about her and Amerigo's freedom. But freedom, within a James novel, is also a matter of accepting the limits imposed by one's choices. Charlotte certainly does not have to agree with the Prince's choice not to marry her. She needs, however, to respect the integrity and the reality of his choice. Fanny says that the Prince's and Charlotte's decision to give "each other up" was mutual: "It wouldn't have been a bit amusing, either, to marry him as a pauper — I mean leaving him one. That was what she had — as *he* had — the reason to see" (23:71). Granted, therefore, even with Fanny's characterization of the decision as mutual, the Prince's "quasi-brutality" surfaces again here with Fanny's implication that Charlotte's knowledge of the Prince's financial requirements constricted her own decision and made him inaccessible to her. Yet the Prince's decision seems based not only on the desire to gain money but also virtue, and Charlotte may represent a metaphor of the past relationships that Amerigo has perceived to be inadequate on both counts.

Charlotte reveals herself to be inadequate through the course of the novel because she is a sophist and indifferent to the way she or others may be compromised by playing fast and loose with appearances. Further, she preys on others' moral weaknesses, in the chink in their moral armor that they are somehow attempting to avoid seeing. In this way, she becomes an extortionist in moral blackmail rather than a positive force. Charlotte has two ethical choices when confronted with the Prince's behavior: she can confront him honestly with his obligation to her and risk the consequences; she can accept his decision and renounce him. Anne T. Margolis suggests as few critics do that Charlotte's return on the eve of the Prince's marriage is "expressly . . . to bear witness to her continuing passion for him and obliquely signify her willingness to resume their old relation where it left off, should he so desire." But Margolis still expresses Charlotte's motives too mildly: Charlotte's intent is not to follow Amerigo's desire but to manipulate it. Charlotte affects the form of renunciation, by going to America, only to return to exert pressure covertly on Amerigo to continue their relationship. She thus finds her wedge in by blackmailing his moral sense of obligation, while she gives him the surface impression that he is safe from her claim upon him: "He was *safe*, in a word—that was what it all meant; and he had required to be safe" (23:59). Margolis places the blame for the Prince and Charlotte's adultery on Maggie, asserting that "there is no conscious conspiracy in *The Golden Bowl*" and that "Charlotte and especially the Prince manage to restrain themselves admirably until Maggie unwittingly tempts them beyond their control,"[12] but this interpretation misses the careful way in which Charlotte has plotted from her return to engage the Prince in old desires that he is attempting to abjure.

Charlotte makes her claim upon the Prince covertly; she has come back from America to "ask" the Prince for an hour or so of his time, a price she exacts for his superficial sense of safety. (One may recall the hour Medea asks from the king of Thebes.) This request both threatens the Prince's sense of the integrity of the surface and binds him in agreement so as to preserve it: "He wonderfully smiled, but it was after all rather more than he had been reckoning with. It went somehow so little with the rest that, directly, for him, it wasn't the note of safety." Indeed, Charlotte's claim is a clever bit of sabotage; it serves as an insinuation of the larger claim she could make upon Amerigo, and she knows he must acquiesce to the smaller to avoid the larger. The Prince, further, attempts to diminish the reality of the claim by giving it "the note of publicity. Quickly, quickly, however, the note of publicity struck him as better than any other. In another moment even it seemed positively what he wanted; for what so much as publicity put their relation on the right footing? By this appeal to Mrs. Assingham it was established as right, and she immediately showed that such was her own under-standing" (23:61). Small as the claim might be, however, and however anesthesized by its attachment to appearance, to publicity, Charlotte has succeeded in making a claim by appealing to Amerigo's need to be self-deceived that there is none. Despite the Prince's ostensible dependence on Mrs. Assingham to keep him honest, he is himself obviously conscious on one level here that he is practicing self-deception. But his need to be virtuous cannot be satisfied in his situation with Charlotte because, to be so, he would have to satisfy Charlotte's claim on him. This he cannot do because of his prior commitment to Maggie.

Charlotte subverts a fundamentally positive activity of the James-ian consciousness for the purpose of ensuring a future intimacy with Amerigo. The preceding chapter of this book discusses how Merton Densher, in an effort to affirm Milly Theale's confidence in him, selec-tively recalls from his past an incident that links him to Milly and literally recreates the reality of their relationship. Charlotte's condition to the Prince, to "keep away from any place to which he had already been with Maggie" (23:100), is her attempt to obliterate the reality of his conscious ethical choice. Within a temporary suspension of time, Charlotte attempts to carve out a present intimacy with the Prince that will allow her to have an ongoing relationship with him despite his marriage to Maggie. Thus, the narrator writes, the Prince "had as a consequence—in all consistency—to take it for amusing that she reaffirmed, and reaffirmed again, the truth that was *her* truth" (23:96).

As Charlotte says, " 'What I want is that it shall always be with you— so that you'll never be able quite to get rid of it. . . . Giving myself, in other words, away—and perfectly willing to do it for nothing' " (23: 97–98). Amerigo is alarmed by "the sense of the resemblance of the little plan before him to occasions, of the past, from which he was quite disconnected, from which he could only desire to be" (23:94). Charlotte tyrannizes over Amerigo's consciousness. In James, helpless passion is rendered far below conscious effort on an ethical scale. Are we really to believe that the Prince is better off in finally succumbing to his passion for Charlotte than he would be in honestly living out the consequences of his ethical choice? If so, we must wonder at his struggle against Charlotte at this early point: "He clutched, however, at what he could best clutch at—the fact that she let him off, definitely let him off" (23:98).

So much critical attention has been devoted to the imagery of the golden bowl in chapter 6, Book First, that little if any attention is given to the discussion between Charlotte and Amerigo about Maggie that immediately precedes it. Critics who address the golden bowl scene usually interpret this expedition of the Prince and Charlotte's to buy a wedding gift as a mutually agreed-upon venture. Joseph Boone, for example, sees the scene as a "pretext," but in juxtaposing this scene with "Adam's calculating wooing of Charlotte," Boone interprets Charlotte in both instances to perform the passive role. Boone suggests that "Charlotte's victimization is inevitable" because she accepts roles "grounded in assumptions of female inferiority or capitulation to male whims and power." [13] Elizabeth Allen, on the other hand, takes note of Charlotte's contrivance of the expedition but suggests that although Charlotte does not simply want "her hour with Amerigo," all she wants from him is that he "understand, . . . hear—to be aware and see what she is doing and sacrificing." [14] And despite the distinction that Carren Kaston perceives between Amerigo's and Charlotte's superior intelligence exhibited in the scene, Kaston also suggests that the two characters function as a unit who in their unity are not actually responsible for their future actions because they "are virtually compelled to renew their intimacy by the pressure of Maggie and Adam's arrangements," which "makes it difficult to blame them." [15]

Nevertheless, more blame would devolve directly upon Charlotte if the golden bowl scene were perceived as one rife with ethical tension, with Charlotte attempting to maneuver the Prince into accepting her own ethical position. The scene involves one of the most significant conversations in the entire novel, and the discussion alludes, in its airing of ethics, to rhetorical principles. Chapter 5 begins with Charlotte's stated desire "to be absolutely honest" (23:89), which immediately sets the chapter within the context of rhetoric and virtue; the chapter will reveal what the terms of Charlotte's honesty are to be.

Charlotte tries to set the groundwork for her future relationship with Amerigo by subverting the logic of the Quintilian principle to her advantage. Maggie's weakness is her adherence to the Quintilian principle. Paradoxically, it will also be found, throughout the course of the novel, to be her strength, but Charlotte first uses the Quintilian principle to work around the Prince's ethical sense. Just as the Prince speculates, in chapter 1, that because of his fine style "futility" might be forgiven him, and just as he questions the reward in his attempts to be honest with Maggie when she refuses even to address the possibility of deception, Charlotte suggests that because of Maggie's dearness, " 'Anything of course. . . . *will* do for her' " (23:101). Ostensibly discussing Maggie's wedding gift, Charlotte quite obviously discusses the nature of future relationships with Maggie herself. Charlotte none-too-subtly implies, under the guise of characterizing Maggie's dearness, that because of Maggie's lack of responsibility as audience in the rhetorical transaction, it is Maggie's responsibility if she is deceived:

> "She lets everything go but her own disposition to be kind to you. It's of herself that she asks efforts—so far as she ever *has* to ask them. She hasn't, much. She does everything herself. And that's terrible."
>
> The Prince had listened; but, always with propriety, he didn't commit himself. "Terrible?"
>
> "Well, unless one's almost as good as she. It makes too easy terms for one. It takes stuff within one so far as one's decency is concerned, to stand it . . . not without help from religion or something of that kind. Not without prayer and fasting—that is without taking great care. Certainly," she said, "such people as you and I are not." (23:102)

Charlotte wishes to lay the groundwork for Amerigo's and her future adultery by placing the full burden of their deception on the temptation represented by a preternaturally innocent audience. She also tries to bring back Amerigo into the framework of her own naturalistic point of view by convincing him that "we happen each, I think, to be of the kind that are easily spoiled' " (23:102).

Amerigo's superior recognition of rhetorical ethics comes out in his resistance to Charlotte's logic. Amerigo objects, " 'May not one's affection for her do something more for one's decency, as you call it, than her own generosity—her own affection, *her* 'decency'—has the unfortunate virtue to undo?' " (23:102). This disclaimer is ethically sound; Amerigo rights the equation of the Quintilian principle. He places the responsibility for "decency" back upon the rhetorician and claims that a rhetorician should strive to be virtuous as a result of his goodwill and affection for his audience. Yet Amerigo's ethical clarity vacillates, as we have discovered. Charlotte has brought out a line of reasoning that is "all the same, interesting to him." (23:103). He cannot resist dwelling on the quality of Maggie's innocence: " 'What it comes to—one can see what you mean—is the way she believes in one. That is if she believes at all.' " Amerigo addresses the possibility that a lack of conscious will to believe may hardly qualify as belief. This allows him to follow Charlotte's point that Maggie must be pitied and to progress to his pursuant point that she must be helped. Giving in to his own subconscious resentment of Maggie's indifference to his efforts, Amerigo has already also here subconsciously committed the act of adultery and proceeded to consider the consequences of pitying and helping Maggie. The conversation concludes with Charlotte assenting that they must refuse to be spoiled, the Prince reasserting that this is the essence of decency, and Charlotte's final statement, " 'It's just what *I* meant,' she then reasonably said' " (23:103). One ends the chapter with the sense that Charlotte, somehow, has won. She has nurtured the seed of temptation in the Prince's mind and revised the terms of his ethics to be within *her* terms, *his* definition of decency reduced to a level of surface decency.

This same conversation and moral vacillation on the part of the Prince is replayed in the scene with the golden bowl. In a reversal of roles, however, the dealer in the antique shop becomes the rhetorician and Charlotte finds herself to be the audience. Contrary to how one would feel in the rhetorical transaction described by the Quintilian principle, Charlotte has a notable lack of faith in the shopman. This results in a corresponding inscrutability and subtle sophistry on the part of the shopkeeper, who has produced "My Golden Bowl" (23:112). As many critics have suggested, this shopkeeper seems certainly to be James himself.[16] If so, James seems to emphasize the sense in which authorship, and the rhetoric of it, is an impersonal force that gives back what the characters so imagined by the author would likely put into it. The shopman is seduced by the cleverness and charming appearances of the Prince and Charlotte to bring out his "Golden Bowl," but he can only give back to them that same seduction in his descriptive version of the bowl, can only give back the sophistic logic that he finds in the characters, at least in Charlotte. When Charlotte inquires of him whether the bowl is " 'cut out of a single crystal,' " the shopman responds in the terms that Charlotte would understand, " 'If it isn't I think I can promise you that you'll never find any joint or any piecing' " (23:113). When Charlotte asks what is the matter with the bowl that it can be had so cheaply, the shopman inscrutably replies, " 'What *is* the matter with it?' " Charlotte responds by trying to force the shopman into the logic of the Quintilian principle: " 'Oh it's not for me to say; it's for you honestly to tell me. Of course I know something must be.' " The shopkeeper does not answer honestly because he sees the irrelevancy of honesty with Charlotte. Instead, he speaks within her sophistic terms by urging on her the beauty of the bowl's appearance and the irrelevancy of the quality, because it will not likely be discovered: " 'But if it's something you can't find out isn't that as good as if it were nothing?' " (23:114).

Charlotte seems satisfied with this sophistry, convinced " 'that the more I looked at it the more I liked it, and that if you weren't so unaccommodating this would be just the occasion for your giving me the pleasure of accepting it' " (23:118). Her willingness to accept the bowl and to give it to Amerigo indicates her cynical indifference to the ethics of truth, to a convergence between appearance and reality, to the singly cut crystal of organic rhetoric. No inherent judgment of Charlotte's keeps her from buying the bowl. Only her perception of the Prince's reticence about the purchase serves to restrain her, and then because she is trying to adopt the Prince's discretionary tactics so as finally to disarm them. Carren Kaston claims that "in the midst of all the verbs of seeing and knowing on which he leans for Amerigo's advantage in this scene, James nevertheless celebrates a superior capacity for complexity in Charlotte. . . . Amerigo is a less genuinely moral character than Charlotte in the sense that morality, for James, depended upon 'the amount of felt life' . . . to which consciousness makes itself heir." [17] Yet Charlotte's indifference to the essence of the bowl shows her to be ethically bankrupt. As the novel progresses, Charlotte's attention to appearance becomes almost baroque, excessively lavish. This is because Charlotte's intelligent consciousness has devoted itself, not to real actions and their consequences, but to the art of a "too perfect competence" that may ultimately, Maggie speculates, wear "on the Prince's spirit, on his nerves, on his finer irritability" (24:143). This finer irritability is the Prince's ethical sense, evidenced, for example, when Amerigo tells Charlotte that the bowl has a crack: "It sounded, on his lips, so sharp, it had such an authority, that she almost started, while her colour rose at the word." Yet Amerigo's offer to Charlotte of a little "ricordo" reveals his own moral equivocation. And he corroborates with Charlotte in equating his "happiness" and his marriage with "safety" (23:119). As the preceding chapters on *The Bostonians* and *The*

Wings of the Dove suggest, happiness in James's fiction is a condition achieved by conforming to the Platonic conception of virtue. Safety, on the other hand, alludes to the sophistic logic of false appearances and thus is a moral equivocation of the concept of virtue. The Prince, in his "retarded evolution," vacillates between a finer apprehension of what it means to be virtuous and a winking sophistry that subordinates this concept to convenience.

What results, in the remainder of the Prince's section, is a subtle sophistry of consecrating the surface, a consecration frightening because, in its so perfect mimicry of the logic of ethics, it has managed to convince many readers of the blessedness of Charlotte and Amerigo's relationship. Indeed, in Book Third, after Charlotte's marriage to Adam, on the occasion of her being out with Amerigo in the eyes of the social world, Charlotte uses all the terms of moral rhetoric to sanctify her relationship. Each of those terms, however, is subtly perverted in Charlotte's rhetoric.

Charlotte describes herself as in the midst of a "crisis. For a crisis she was ready to take it, and this ease it was, doubtless, that helped her, while she waited, to the right assurance, to the right indifference, to the right expression, and above all, as she felt, to the right view of her opportunity for happiness" (23:246). Charlotte's crisis is parallel to the Prince's in the novel's beginning chapter; it is a crisis of discovering happiness or virtue. Charlotte, also, similarly seeks out Fanny Assingham to confirm her virtue. But Charlotte, counter to the Prince's wish to be virtuous, seeks to be indifferent to the reality of the Prince's marriage, seeks the happiness of a consummated passion, not of her own virtue. As would the most earnest rhetorical enthusiast, Charlotte describes herself as drawing "inspiration" from the "virtue" of the Prince's appearance (23:248), feeling "herself in truth crowned" (23: 246). Charlotte's "truth" is an appearance of virtue hoped to appease contemplated adultery. She hopes "that she might prove to herself, let alone to Mrs. Assingham also, that she could convert it to good" (23: 249–50). It is important that James notes that "for herself indeed particularly it wasn't a question; but something in her bones told her that Fanny would treat it as one" (23:250). Charlotte's concern is not with virtue but with the appearance of it, to serve as a cover, so that she and Amerigo are left alone. Charlotte discovers that Fanny does not want to acknowledge the real truth. This enables her to decide that

> her point was before her; it was sharp, bright, true; above all it was her own. She had reached it quite by herself; no one, not even Amerigo—

Amerigo least of all, who would have nothing to do with it—had given her aid. To make it now with force for Fanny Assingham's benefit would see her further, in the direction in which the light had dawned, than any other spring she should doubtless yet awhile be able to press. The direction was that of her greater freedom—which was all in the world she had in mind. (23:255)

Freedom, for Charlotte, means a denial of the truth of the genuine restrictions imposed by choices and a concentration instead on the truth of appearances. Charlotte relies on Fanny's guilty complicity in needing to ignore the truth and on Maggie and Adam's unwitting complicity as a naive rhetorical audience. Further, Charlotte again shifts responsibility for her adulterous act onto Maggie, whose failure to address her husband's complexity constitutes the real "truth of the matter— . . . that Maggie thinks more on the whole of fathers than of husbands. . . . What I say is that she doesn't think of him. . . . This is just *how* she adores him" (23:257). This abuse of the Quintilian principle, of placing the responsibility for virtue on the audience rather than the orator, is the basis of Charlotte's self-justifying logic. Yet there is a possibility, also, that this evidence of Maggie's irresponsibility as it appears to Amerigo and to Fanny has been arranged by Charlotte; Charlotte may have forced Maggie into a position of seeming indifference to the Prince by pressing Maggie harder, as a result of Charlotte's own negligence, into the role of caring for her father. Mrs. Assingham implies this when she asks Charlotte why Maggie has gone home to take care of her father while Charlotte has instead stayed at the party. Charlotte's evasion of this question leads Fanny to question silently Charlotte's failure to take care of Adam "'since by your account Maggie has him not less, but so much more, on her mind'" (23:262). Readers in essence accept Charlotte's version when they read Maggie's continued care of her father as self-initiated. They should remember Charlotte's suspicious claim for "the highest considerations. The highest considerations were good humour, candour, clearness and, obviously, the *real* truth" (23:256).

In contrast with Charlotte's sophistic ease, Amerigo's self-justifying discourse with Fanny is far more troubled. Fanny perceives that "there were moments positively, still beyond this, when, with the meeting of their eyes, something as yet unnamable came out for her in his look, when something strange and subtle and at variance with his words, something that *gave them away*, glimmered deep down, as an appeal, almost an incredible one, to her finer comprehension. . . . like a quintessential wink, a hint of the possibility of their *really* treating their subject" (23:271). Amerigo pleads for " 'a good kind hour' " (23:274) to have such a hypothetical discussion, and one sees, again, that Amerigo is seeking from Fanny the tutelage into virtue that he initially sought. Her abandonment of Amerigo at this point is unforgivable, an act worthy of her name. No wonder Charlotte can be through with Fanny. In her desertion of the Prince's evolution into ethics, she no longer poses a threat.

On her next visit to the Prince, Charlotte finds the opportunity to cash in on all the rhetorical groundwork she constructed in the golden bowl sequence. Once again, the Prince is feeling himself in a "dreary little crisis," having "looked into this room on the chance that he might find the Princess at tea" (23:294) and, finding himself unengaged, abandoned. This crisis of temptation is emphasized by "Charlotte Stant turning up for him at the very climax of his special inner vision." Significantly, Amerigo describes her as an "apparition" (23:295), and he discovers that "particular links and gaps had at the end of a few minutes found themselves renewed and bridged." As mentioned in the preceding chapter, William James had theorized the selective principle of the creative consciousness that could selectively engage itself with a past event in combination with the present to create a new truth. Amerigo has a similar "vision of alternatives . . . opened out altogether with this tangible truth of her attitude by the chimney-place" (23:297).

Amerigo's creation is spectral because he has already chosen marriage to Maggie. Thus Charlotte can only continue to inspire Amerigo with a false eloquence. Perversely, Amerigo's capitulation to Charlotte's rhetoric is to an "odd eloquence — the positive picturesqueness, yes, given all the rest of the matter — of a dull dress and a black Bowdlerised hat that seemed to make a point of insisting on their time of life and their moral intention, the hat's and the frock's own, as well as on the irony of indifference to them practically playing in her so handsome rain-freshened face. The sense of the past revived for him nevertheless as it had not yet done" (23:297–98). This passage reveals Charlotte's flaunting indifference to the reality of ethical choice and her rhetorical diminishment of ethics to a bad and boring revision of Shakespeare, her anachronistic implication that Amerigo's present ethical choice is outmoded and that his future is really in the past. In order to live this spectral truth, Amerigo and Charlotte must employ "the most independent, not to say original, interpretation of signs" (23: 288). Language must be independent and original — not representative of reality—if the reality of Amerigo's marriage to Maggie is to be de-nied. And any imputation of active effort must be denied this "perfectly passive pair: no more extraordinary decree had ever been launched against such victims than this of forcing them against their will into a relation of mutual close contact that they had done everything to avoid" (23:289).

There is surely a derogatory implication in James's description of Charlotte "so handling and hustling the present that this poor quantity scarce retained substance enough, scarce remained sufficiently *there*, to be wounded or shocked." Charlotte's "hustling" is aimed at suggesting that Maggie's rhetorical awareness is the scarcely negligible present that in its negligibility cannot be harmed. Maggie's present abdication of awareness places Charlotte and Amerigo "face to face in a free-dom that extraordinarily partook of ideal perfection, since the magic web had spun itself without their toil, almost without their touch" (23:298). Charlotte's denial of responsibility is amusing, considering how hard she has been hustling, and Amerigo still vaguely discerns the responsibility: "This came out so straight that he saw at once how much truth it expressed; yet it was truth that still a little puzzled him" (23:300).

Amerigo's claim that he does not understand the Ververs and that he had hoped Fanny Assingham would help him to do so (23:309) is to be taken seriously as James's formulation of the embryonic nature of the Prince's ethical consciousness. Amerigo's elision of the respon-sibility for his own virtue in favor of practicing toward the Ververs a "conscious care" of deceptive appearances is part of the vacillation seen to be constantly endemic to his Italianate consciousness. And the final passage of chapter 5, Book Third, where the Prince and Charlotte pronounce their union sacred, is to be read as a scandalous account of an unhallowed consecration. In the narrator's final lyrical rendering of this consecration, James risks engendering empathy for the sake of revealing the full extent of blasphemy in this union. James's rhetoric depends upon the subtlety of his audience for discernment.

In Book Fourth, Maggie subjects herself to this same sort of subtlety as she is moved to wonder at Charlotte, to "marvel afresh at the mystery by which a creature who could be in some connexions so earnestly right could be in others so perversely wrong" (24:289). Indeed, Maggie thought previously that Charlotte and Amerigo were "accompanied with that degree of earnestness which indicates sincerity."[18] This quotation is not from *The Golden Bowl;* it is from Charles Brockden Brown's *Wieland*, and it refers to Clara's description of the rhetorically adept Carwin. Both Clara and Maggie are described as "a creature of pure virtue," and each discovers what happens when she "suffers her sympathy, her disinterestedness, her exquisite sense for the lives of others, to carry her too far" (24:129). Both learn the dangers of the American romance with the Quintilian principle, the possibility of "criminal intrigue carried on, from day to day, amid perfect trust and sympathy" (24:119). Maggie describes her initiation into the possibility of deception as "moving for the first time in her life as in the darkening shadow of a false position" (24:6), just as Carwin's appearance precipitates in Clara a "dread of unknown dangers, and the future was a scene over which clouds rolled and thunders muttered" (*Wieland*, 83). "Why was my mind absorbed in thoughts ominous and dreary?" Clara asks. "Something whispered that the happiness we at present enjoyed was set on mutable foundations" (*Wieland*, 67).

Using the terms of American rhetorical enthusiasm, Maggie Verver explains the source for what had previously been "that ideal consistency on which her moral comfort almost at any time depended" (24:6). The source is the "inspiration" that Maggie and her father mutually share that Maggie can "marry without breaking, as she liked to put it, with her past. She had surrendered herself to her husband without the shadow of a reserve or a condition and yet she hadn't all the while given up her father by the least little inch" (24:5). Maggie and Adam discover this "truth had been distinctly brought home to them by the bright testimony, the quite explicit envy, of most of their friends." Further, the knowledge that the rhetoric of the situation could be deceptive had always been willfully shut off by Maggie by her "cutting down more or less her prior term" (24:6).

Many critics, such as John Carlos Rowe, accuse Maggie of a formalist reductiveness throughout the remainder of the novel: "Maggie's design involves a false idealism, which seeks to suppress the truth to preserve her father's dream of order 'without a flaw.'" And yet Maggie herself faces the less-than-ideal truth of her husband's adultery and reveals her awareness to her husband. Rowe asserts that, "fearing the failure of her marriage, Maggie tries to save it by preserving its form. Repeatedly, the characters choose the security of social appearance over the difficulties of personal relations."[19] Yet Maggie sacrifices her "pure virtue" as a forfeiture; she pays by embroiling herself within the difficulties of personal relations with her husband: Maggie implicates herself in the rhetoric of her husband's adultery for the sake of redeeming his virtue. Just as Amerigo must break from the adulterous deceptions of his passionate past through silence, Maggie must break from the platonically ideal consistency of her own passionless one through words. For language, in *The Golden Bowl*, is equivalent to passion.

John Auchard, in his engrossing study of silence in *The Golden Bowl*, points out that Maggie's final full conversation with Adam is "the novel's most complex unspoken conversation. It must be sufficiently explicit to prepare Adam to pack luggage, wife, and a mountain of art, and ship back to America. Yet it must be sufficiently quiet so that the fact of adultery—or even the suspicion—never breaks the surface and demands verbal recognition. Words can get too far out of hand too rapidly." Yet communication does occur; "through this intelligent, loving, trusting act of tense non-communication, they both are moved to understand the necessarily strong action which must be theirs."[20]

A similarly tense noncommunication is exchanged in the earlier parallel scene between Maggie and Adam which this later scene recalls. This earlier scene, in which Adam's marriage is plotted, involves a similar reticence about the mention of passion, Maggie's reluctance to discuss her passion for Amerigo with her father. Curiously, in this first instance, Adam even goes so far as to imagine his daughter as both a nymph and a nun (23:188). The power of Adam Verver, as well as his failure, is his inability to imagine sexual passion. As Charlotte implies, Adam is sexually sterile, and his seemingly eternal youth and purity—reminiscent of the Prince's feigning of a preternatural youth and beauty in his initial denial of his passion for Charlotte—seems to result from his refusal to engage himself in the world of language and passion. Maggie's own passionate relationship with the Prince clearly distinguishes her from her father, and her adroit ability to manuever for what she wants around this one coveted obscurity of her father's reveals her linguistic potential. What Maggie does appear to inherit from her father is the capacity for love and for good faith. Although Adam is ostensibly alluding to his new-found aesthetic interests in the following passage, he might just as well have been referring to Maggie: "His comparative blindness had made the good faith, which in its turn had made the soil propitious for the flower of the supreme idea" (23:144).

Maggie's good faith conversely inspires in Adam his love and the gift of anything, with the exception of an explicit knowledge of passion, that he can give her. When Maggie presents to him the idea, for example, that he should marry for her sake, "the idea shone upon him,

more than that, as exciting, inspiring, uplifting. . . . He really didn't
know when in his life he had thought of anything happier. To think of
it merely for himself would have been, even as he had just lately felt,
even doing all justice to that condition—yes, impossible. But there was
a grand difference in thinking of it for his child" (23:208–9). Adam's
definition of happiness, of virtue, can allow him to conceive of marriage only as a sacrificial act, not as one of passion. "Mr. Verver, blessed
man, all indulgent but all inscrutable" (24:105), as Maggie at one point
calls him, derives his inscrutability from his passionlessness. Maggie
is able to tap this source of passionless virtue in herself as she finally
engages in the world of language and of passion.

Maggie's quick passage into knowledge indicates that her innocence
was not so much willed as habitual. Assailed for the first time with
doubts about her husband, Maggie first enters a stage of epistemological uncertainty described with such frequent vividness in Brockden Brown's *Wieland*. Maggie "reflected that she should either not
have ceased to be right—that is to be confident—or have recognized
that she was wrong" (24:6). This either-or wishfulness for certainty
is reminiscent of Theodore Wieland's desire for a cause-effect logical certainty: " 'Your assurances,' said he, 'are solemn and unanimous;
and yet I must deny credit to your assertions, or disbelieve the testimony of my senses' " (*Wieland*, 41). But the gothic world of uncertainty
that undercuts Wieland's logic is not to be found in *The Golden Bowl*.
Although Maggie comes quickly in her phenomenological struggle to
an acceptance of "what she should never know" (24:14–15), she gains
many certainties about her world, as Paul Armstrong's brilliant reading
of the novel has shown.[21]

Essentially, Maggie gains her knowledge through the gathering
force of impressions: "That impression came back—it had its hours of
doing so; and it may interest us on the ground of its having prompted
in Maggie a final reflexion, a reflexion out of the heart of which a light
flashed for her like a great flower grown in a night" (24:41). Our subsequent reliance on Maggie's imaginative and empathetic perceptions for
much of the telling of the story is greatly strengthened by our initial
insight into how closely her progressive apprehensions of knowledge
fit with the real facts of the adultery as we know it. As L. A. Westervelt
has observed, Maggie also gains additional information through her
exploratory conversations with her husband;[22] and the shopkeeper also
presents Maggie with important corroborative facts that let her know
her world. What Maggie learns about her world is both the possibility

and the fact of deception in social relations, as it is metaphorized in *The Golden Bowl* by adultery. Her gain is the redemption of her world from the fact of deception. Her gain and loss is the uneasy awareness of its eternal possibility.

If language in *The Golden Bowl* represents passion, then the presence of deception indicates the presence of a wrongful passion. Just as deception violates the trust implicit in the rhetorical communication and subverts the representative nature of language, adultery violates the trust implicit in a marital commitment and subverts the inherent meaning of marriage. Passion—or the rhetorically persuasive force of language—can be either destructive of human relations or a positive means of creating a community, of fostering trust. In the Jamesian world, deception—wrongful passion—exists in such ominous surplus that communities of trust can at best only be established between two. Truth, or what one could call rightful passion, is a risk leaving one vulnerable to the exploitation of the possibly deceptive, because rightful passion involves one's soul, the essence of what one truly is. Paradoxically, since Amerigo makes love simultaneously to two women in *The Golden Bowl*, he leaves open the possibility of two competitive versions for what his truth really is.

Amerigo, however, makes a conscious choice at the beginning of the novel never to deceive Maggie, which suggests that his passion for Charlotte is harmful to his conscious, creative, and spiritual self. Charlotte's cynical indifference to the discrepancy between the appearance and reality of language suggests her equally cynical indifference to the discrepancy within herself and Amerigo between their conscious ethical commitments and their external actions. Maggie reminds Amerigo of who he really is by telling him the truth. John Auchard has written that "nothing of real value receives report through speech" in *The Golden Bowl*.[23] On the contrary, Maggie tells Amerigo that the golden bowl has "given me so much of the truth about you" (24:189). Her report is the single most important event in the novel. It signals to Amerigo her awareness of "the whole case—the case of your having for so long successfully deceived me," words spoken plainly, and simply, out loud. By pointing out to the Prince her awareness of the discrepancy between his appearance and his reality, Maggie literally becomes a rhetorical argument in herself to compel the Prince to recover his virtue. " 'You've never been more sacred to me than you were at that hour—unless perhaps you've become so at this one' " (24:199), declares the Prince, indicating that his desire not to deceive his future wife, which prompted his initial crisis, has been restored in the present crisis by his wife's moral awareness.

In Volume 23, Amerigo's passionate relationship with Maggie seems to be the wrongful one. It is initiated by Amerigo's desire to appease his wife's surface awareness beyond which he thinks she will not go. Paul Armstrong states that "Maggie's ambivalent reaction to the call of desire betrays an anxiety that reveals that she has not adequately examined or understood her own sexuality,"[24] yet Maggie's resistance to the passionate overtures of the Prince in Volume 24 is one of the great sacrificial efforts she makes to keep the truth present between the Prince and herself. If Maggie were to give in to her passion, she would be assenting, for the sake of it, to a relationship built on deception, giving in to the woman's fatalistic tendency to "do the thing that gives her away." Maggie "felt how the act operated with him *instead* of the words he hadn't uttered—operated in his view as probably better than any words, as always better in fact at any time than anything. Her acceptance of it, her response to it, inevitable, foredoomed, came back to her later on as a virtual assent to the assumption he had thus made that there was really nothing such a demonstration didn't anticipate and didn't dispose of" (24:28–29). Maggie's concern for her *own* spiritual integrity at the sacrifice of her passion lifts her above the level of naturalism:

> He could be on occasion, as she had lately more than ever learned, so munificent a lover. . . . She should have but to lay her head back on his shoulder with a certain movement to make it definite for him that she didn't resist. To this as they went every throb of her consciousness prompted her—every throb, that is, but one, the throb of her deeper need to know where she "really" was. . . . She was making an effort that horribly hurt her, and as she couldn't cry out her eyes swam in her silence. (24:56–57)

Silence in *The Golden Bowl* is the withdrawal of passion. Maggie would like to engage in language with the Prince, but not in the language of the surface but of genuine feeling. Maggie

> knew more and more—every lapsing minute taught her—how he might by a single rightness make her cease to watch him; that rightness, a million miles removed from the queer actual, falling so short, which would consist of his breaking out to her diviningly, indulgently, with the last happy inconsequence. "Come away with me somewhere, *you*—and then we needn't think, we needn't even talk, of anything, of any one else":

five words like that would answer her, would break her utterly down. But they were the only ones that would so serve. She waited for them, and there was a supreme instant when by the testimony of all the rest of him she seemed to feel them in his heart and on his lips; only they didn't sound, and as that made her wait again so it made her more intensely watch. (24:60)

Maggie realizes "the truth about his good nature and his good manners. . . . this demonstration of his virtue" (24:59), but she realizes that both are manipulatable appearances that cover deception.

Maggie insists on holding up to the Prince a mirror of truth; she works to effect her husband's evolution to virtue: "It had operated within her now to the last intensity, her glimpse of the precious truth that by her helping him, helping him to help himself, as it were, she should help him help *her*. Hadn't she fairly got into his labyrinth with him? — wasn't she indeed in the very act of placing herself there for him at its centre and core, whence, on that definite orientation and by an instinct all her own, she might securely guide him out of it?" (24:187).

Paul Armstrong, among a number of James critics, complains that "Maggie presents the Prince with a severely limited choice that she has carefully orchestrated." [25] Yet, as Carren Kaston points out, "Only Maggie's designs . . . wed personal emotion to authorial style, sincerity to artfulness, thereby giving them an unprecedented power and legitimacy." The Prince's initial struggle to seduce Maggie into a language of knowing deception is a holdover of his less ethical self, allowed to flourish, in the absence of Maggie's attention, through his union with Charlotte. Maggie's failure to act on her pity for Amerigo and Charlotte does not indict her. Maggie replies to Fanny's implication that she is cruel, " 'Ah there wouldn't be any terror for them if they had nothing to hide' " (24:116). Kaston concludes that "James demonstrates here the immense cruelties that can grow out of intending kindness." [26] But this subtle shifting of responsibility is an acceptance of Charlotte's version of the story. Should the rhetorical audience bear responsibility for the deceptions of the orator? Haven't the Prince and Charlotte fostered deceptions for which they must take responsibility?

If one follows the implied logic of many James readers, Maggie can only not be cruel and not present Amerigo with a severely limited choice if she offers him the double option of continued adultery and marriage. Instead, the Princess simply insists on the integrity of her husband's decision. There is textual evidence that she trembles for her own fate, fearing her husband will choose Charlotte. Instead, her gamble that the Prince will love most in the direction of his virtue wins out; and the Princess is not simply working for the reinstituted "form" of marriage. She has had that, after all, all along. She carefully gauges the truth of the growing emotion that the Prince feels for her; that growing emotion can be her only basis for a final acceptance of the marriage.

Maggie gets down into Amerigo's labyrinth with him by collaborating with him in deception. Now, it is important to note that her deception is far different from that in which Amerigo and Charlotte had participated. Just as Charlotte does, Maggie lies to protect the deceptive integrity of appearances. But when Maggie becomes what she perceives various loved ones want her and need her to be, she sees this collaboration in deception as a painful form of abjection. Maggie not only has to relinquish her untenable faith in the validity of the Quintilian principle; she has also had to compromise her own virtue as a rhetorician by artfully lying. Significantly, however, Maggie excepts her relationship with Amerigo from this collusion of lies; she has had to narrow down her world of truthful relationships to two. Despite Maggie's initial self-protective silence with Amerigo in the midst of her initial uncertainty, her ultimate revelation of the truth to Amerigo and her withholding of her passion as a witness to that truth in the midst of their external collaborative deceptions presents the remaining possibility for her, at least, of a truthful relationship. This opportunity is provided Maggie by—surprisingly—the successful intervention of the Quintilian principle.

Amerigo is astounded at how his wife has come to receive an honest report from the shopman about the quality of the golden bowl when Charlotte's more adroit conversational powers had failed to do so. This virtue has been elicited, Maggie's narrative reveals, by the extent of Maggie's good faith: " 'I did "believe in it," you see—must have believed in it somehow instinctively; for I took it [the bowl] as soon as I saw it' " (24:195). Rather than being repulsed by Maggie's innocence, as the Prince had been, the shopman, Maggie relates, " 'liked me, I mean—very particularly. . . . He gave me it frankly as his reason. . . . I can only think of him as kind, for he had nothing to gain. He had in fact only to lose. It was what he came to tell me—that he had asked me too high a price, more than the object was really worth' " (24:196–97).

The Prince later reverts to this mystery again, still mystified by this operation of the Quintilian principle, which does not, after all, operate by strict logic—rather, through a logic of love. Maggie's rhetoric is "lightning unaccompanied by thunder," which John Auchard remarks as an allusion to Eastern mysticism.[27] But the reference is reminiscent of contemporary descriptions of rhetorical inspiration: "Eloquence is an art which cannot be acquired in the schools. All mere institutes are powerless to teach it—to confer divine degree. They are without the genius and inspiration that give it soaring force and lend it wings. It will not obey the barest of rules. If it come at all, it must come as the lightning that flashes along the southern sky, making a track for the hoarse notes of muffled thunder."[28] Amerigo considers the rhetorical transaction between his wife and the shopman "remarkable," and "Maggie had felt her explanation weak, but there were the facts, and she could give no other" (24:222).

Nineteenth-century moral rhetorician Henry Ward Beecher questions, "Are we never to study how skillfully to pick the lock of curiosity, to unfasten the door of fancy, to throw wide open the halls of emotion, and to kindle the light of inspiration in the souls of men?"[29] Virtuous rhetoric, according to the Quintilian principle, unerringly does this. Maggie explains that the shopman's "'joy moreover was—as much as Amerigo would!—a matter of the personal interest with which her kindness, gentleness, grace, her charming presence and easy humanity and familiarity, had inspired him'" (24:226).

Nevertheless, despite the shopman's conversion via Maggie's rhetorical virtue, it is not surprising that Maggie's "straight little story . . . might very conceivably make a long sum for the Prince to puzzle out" (24:226). Her virtuous rhetorical innocence is the essence of Platonic friendship; for Maggie "truly" to marry the Prince, Maggie and the Prince must engage in a rhetoric of passion that entertains the possibility of deception. James's tribute here to the inviolability of virtuous rhetoric only in the world of Platonic alliances may be tied neatly to James the virtuous artist—passionless in the "real" world. Maggie's virtue, however, will "inspire" the Prince only if it shows itself tied to the real world. And in three alternate instances, Maggie sees that love in the real world involves compromise, a love and protection of weaknesses as well as strengths. In the Prince's case, Maggie realizes that, as she had speculated early on about Charlotte, "where there's a great deal of pride there's a great deal of silence" (23:186). Maggie helps the Prince to preserve his pride in the integrity of appearances, his vestige of self-deception about the equivalent value of surface truth and virtue: "'Leave me my reserve; don't question it—it's all I have just now, don't you see? so that, if you'll make me the concession of letting me alone with it for as long a time as I require I promise you something or other, grown under cover of it, even though I don't yet quite make out what, as a return for your patience'" (24:221).

Despite their shared knowledge of the truth, testified to continually by Maggie's withdrawal of passion, Maggie not only deceives others about her knowledge but, for the sake of the Prince and for herself accordingly also, retains temporarily the surface illusion of innocence: "As regards herself Maggie had become more conscious from week to week of his ingenuities of intention to make up to her for their forfeiture, in so dire a degree, of any reality of frankness—a privation that had left on his lips perhaps a little of the same thirst with which she fairly felt her own distorted, the torment of the lost pilgrim who listens in the desert sands for the possible, the impossible plash of water" (24:281). Maggie meets the Prince halfway in their rhetorical marriage of form and content by temporarily betraying her own integrity so that she can help her husband preserve the form of his integrity until he can transform it into content. She thus suffers with him the consequences of his deception, "essentially there to bear the burden, in the last resort, of surrounding omissions and evasions" (24:302). Just as Milly Theale backs away from her knowledge, Maggie does from hers, to give the Prince a chance to make her "innocence" true: "The heart of the Princess swelled accordingly even in her abasement; she had kept in tune with the right, and something certainly, something that might resemble a rare flower snatched from an impossible ledge, would, and possibly soon, come of it for her" (24:250). The privation of the "impossible ledge" is akin to the desert of deceptive language, but the "rare flower" would be the blossoming of Amerigo's love within it.

The preceding passage narrates Maggie's reaction to her terrace scene at Fawns with Charlotte. Maggie, of course, is not only protecting the Prince's superficial integrity when she lies, under pressure, to Charlotte. She is also protecting that passionless innocence of her father. Indeed, before Maggie first risked uttering the truth of her knowledge to the Prince, she included him also in her resolve of silence: "She couldn't—and he knew it—say what was true. . . . It would have translated itself on the spot for his ear into jealousy, and from reverberation to repercussion would have reached her father's exactly in the form of a cry piercing the stillness of peaceful sleep" (24:76–77). After the scene of "high publicity" (24:252) at Fawns, Adam finally acknowledges the adultery by acknowledging Maggie's passion for Amerigo:

The mere fine pulse of passion in it . . . his half-shy assent to it, her probable enjoyment of a rapture that he in his day had presumably convinced
no great number of persons either of his giving or his receiving. He sat
awhile as if he knew himself hushed, almost admonished, and not for the
first time; yet. . . . It could pass further for knowing—for knowing that
without him nothing might have been: which would have been miss-
ing least of all. "I guess I've never been jealous," he finally remarked.
(24:263–64)

The curious retraction implicit in "least of all" implies the power—
the lack of a feeling of absence—in passionlessness. Maggie has also
expressed her jealousy to Adam—the tip-off that she has something
to be jealous of—in the covering terminology of passionless passion:
"When you love in a deeper and intenser way, then you're in the very
same proportion jealous; your jealousy has intensity and, no doubt,
ferocity. When however you love in the most abysmal and unutter-
able way of all—why then you're beyond everything, and nothing can
pull you down" (24:262). This description seems an allusion to Plato's
Phaedrus, where the love arising out of virtuous passion surpasses the
naturalistic oppressiveness of jealousy bred from mere animal passion.
Maggie has managed adroitly both to tell her father and not to tell him,
articulating her sexual knowledge in Platonic terms. Maggie is told by
Adam that she will not sacrifice her father as long as she believes in
him. What she implies that she must continue to believe in is the ideal
of Platonic virtue: " 'Oh it's you, father, who are what I call beyond
everything. Nothing can pull *you* down' " (24:269).

The companion scenes in which Charlotte and Maggie engage in
conscious deception illustrate well the fundamental contrast between
the ethics of the two women. In the card game and gazebo scenes,
the situation of pursued and pursuer is reversed and one would expect, since Charlotte feels victorious in soliciting a false note of confidence in the first instance, that Maggie's eliciting of a similar type of
deception would be her triumph in the second. In both scenes, however, Maggie's avowed sense is of her own sacrifice. In the first scene,
full of sinister undertones, Charlotte approaches Maggie by literally
stalking her and forcing her will. This scene is followed up by the
somber tone of the second, in which Maggie approaches Charlotte out
of pity, voluntarily engaging in deception with the intention of allevi-
ating Charlotte's pain as best she can by corroborating with Charlotte
in Charlotte's system of ethics, in the structuralist ethics of appearance
as constitutive of reality.

It is important to note that Maggie suffers in both scenes, not because of what Charlotte says but because of what Charlotte forces Maggie to do, experience "the coldness of their conscious perjury" (24:251). The value of the spoken word and its role in naming reality is for Maggie a thing sacred. Charlotte's structuralist ethics suggestively create a scenario in which the reality of acknowledged adultery that Maggie has been fixed on in her scrutiny of the bridge players through the window will seem upended:

> Side by side for three minutes they fixed this picture of quiet harmonies, the positive charm of it and, as might have been said, the full significance — which, as was now brought home to Maggie, could be no more after all than a matter of interpretation, differing always for a different interpreter. As she herself had hovered in sight of it a quarter of an hour before, it would have been a thing for her to show Charlotte — to show in righteous irony, in reproach too stern for anything but silence. But now it was she who was being shown it, and shown it by Charlotte, and she saw quickly enough that as Charlotte showed it so she must at present submissively seem to take it. (24:243–44)

One needs to remember that the issue in question in this scene is adultery. Charlotte's exploitation of the pragmatic basis for knowledge is sophistic; the scene has been stabilized, for Maggie and Charlotte, by their shared perception of adultery. When Charlotte abandons the card game, in her immense prowling dignity a "splendid shining supple creature" (24:239), she comes out to extort "*her* security at any price" (24:244). Maggie "literally caught herself in the act of dodging and ducking, and it told her there vividly, in a single word, what she had all along been most afraid of" (24:239). When we consider how Maggie empathetically cringes at the imagined sound of Charlotte shrieking at the end of the novel, we should remember how Charlotte pitilessly provides "Maggie's own sense . . . of having been thrown over on her back with her neck from the first half broken and her helpless face staring up" (24:242). Maggie's fear is for her own ethical virtue, also, correspondingly, for her own rightful passion. Charlotte's extortion of deception from Maggie implies that Charlotte's deception and adultery will triumph, that Maggie's virtue, because of her need to protect her husband and her father, will be compromised.

Yet Maggie's real hold on the truth of the adulterous situation has only seemed to be compromised. Maggie's "real" virtue — her hold on the truth of the adulterous situation—remains unflaggingly clear to her husband. Ironically, also, Charlotte's handling of surface propriety reaches an incriminatingly baroque excess as she struggles to suppress a truth increasingly volatile: "She had exceeded the limit of discretion in this insistence on her capacity to repay in proportion a service she acknowledged as handsome. 'Why handsome?' Maggie would have been free to ask; since if she had been veracious the service assuredly wouldn't have been huge" (24:279). If Maggie's father had not been suspicious, Charlotte's incriminating excess would have made him so.

Charlotte's fate—to be condemned for eternity to what must seem to her to be an infernal state of existence with a passionless man— has the ring of a Dantesque contrapasso. A woman compromised and thus condemned by her passion must live out her life as an esthete. Perhaps it is within this context that we should understand Maggie's sympathy for Charlotte, as if Maggie is Dante the Pilgrim, her attention, as *she* characterizes, circling and hovering, as she watches her stepmother "doomed" (24:283): "Maggie meanwhile at the window knew the strangest thing to be happening: she had turned suddenly to crying, or was at least on the point of it—the lighted square before her all blurred and dim. The high voice went on; its quaver was doubtless for conscious ears only, but there were verily thirty seconds during which it sounded, for our young woman, like the shriek of a soul in pain" (24:292). Charlotte's unhallowed consecration of her adultery with Amerigo is reminiscent of Francesca's use of the *stilnovisti* platonic love poetry to glorify her adultery with Paolo. Both pairs of lovers might be misinterpreted—in a romantic age—as fully justified.

It would fit, therefore, that in attempting to provide Charlotte with solace, Maggie must avoid the priest: "She feared the very breath of a better wisdom, the jostle of the higher light, of heavenly help itself; and, in addition, however that might be, she drew breath this afternoon, as never yet, in an element heavy to oppression" (24:298). The priest, muses Maggie, would, and might already, in his superior wisdom, have taken away Charlotte's means of solace, her own obfuscated confidence in the redemptive power of surface appearance: "He had possibly prescribed contrition—he had at any rate quickened in her [Charlotte] the beat of that false repose to which our young woman's own act had devoted her at her all so deluded instance" (24:300). Maggie subsequently "saw round about her, through the chinks of the shutters, the hard glare of nature—saw Charlotte somewhere in it virtually at bay and yet denied the last grace of any protecting truth. She saw her off somewhere all unaided, pale in her silence and taking in her fate" (24:303).

Charlotte is hard up against the fatalistic consequences of her naturalism. Maggie determines, for Charlotte's sake, to "shuffle away every link between consequence and cause . . . like some famous poetic line in a dead language, subject to varieties of interpretation" (24:345). Maggie offers Charlotte the *stilnovisti*-like cover that so availed Francesca. Maggie "waited with her intention as Charlotte on the other occasion had waited—allowing, oh allowing, for the difference of the intention! (24:309). Maggie "had come out to her really because she knew her doomed, doomed to a separation that was like a knife in her heart" (24:311). Maggie notes in Charlotte the Francesca-like apprehension that

> pride indeed had the next moment become the mantle caught up for protection and perversity; she flung it round her as a denial of any loss of her freedom. To be doomed was in her situation to have extravagantly incurred a doom, so that to confess to wretchedness was by the same stroke to confess to falsity. She wouldn't confess, she didn't—a thousand times no; she only cast about her, and quite frankly and fiercely, for something else that would give colour to her having burst her bonds. (24:312)

Out of her sympathy for Charlotte, Maggie rejects the Dantesque religious denial of such a need for rationalizing self-deception and falls "in a secret responsive ecstasy, to wondering if there weren't some supreme abjection with which she might be inspired" (24:313). Maggie empathetically perjures herself for Charlotte's sake. Oddly, the transaction is described in the terms of moral rhetoric: "Far down below the level of attention, in she could scarce have said what sacred depths, Maggie's inspiration had come, and it had trebled the next moment into sound. 'Do you mean *I'm* your difficulty?' " (24:315–16). With Maggie's offer of herself as the competitive force for her father's affections, as if Charlotte were really seeking out her husband's, Maggie provides Charlotte with the covering mantle, the pride she requires. And it seems James means the terms of rhetorical inspiration to be taken seriously. The truth that is supposed to be elicited by moral rhetoric is supposed to be the truth of human compassion; and in the instance of Charlotte's doomed soul, the most compassionate truth would have to be a covering lie. In Maggie's choosing the lie of compassion over her own cherished reverence for the truth, "something in her throbbed as it had throbbed the night she stood in the drawing-room and denied that she had suffered. She was ready to lie again if her companion would but give her the opening. Then she should know she had done all" (24:316).

All the use of *three's* in Volume 24[30] suggests Maggie's final resurrection from her cross of deception, but her rebirth is of necessity uneasy because it is a movement back into, not away from, the imperfect world. The balance of truth, trust, genuine emotion, yet continual unease in the concluding scenes between Maggie and Amerigo reveal the problematics of moral rhetoric for imperfect people in an imperfect world. Maggie finally asks Amerigo for both open honesty and an accompanying genuine emotion: " 'Am I to take from you then that you accept and recognise my knowledge?' " Maggie asks of the Prince (24:349). When Amerigo responds by asking if his style has not sufficiently reflected sincerity, Maggie responds, " 'It isn't a question of any beauty . . . it's only a question of the quantity of truth.' " She wishes also to inquire about the necessary accompaniment to an honest transaction, " 'good faith' " (24:350). Even though Maggie "could feel, the thick breath of the definite—which was the intimate, the immediate, the familiar, as she hadn't had them for so long," she fears, because of her husband's desire to wait for a frank discussion until Charlotte and Adam have left Europe, that "they had come too far—too far for where they were; so that the mere act of her quitting him was like the attempt to recover the lost and gone" (24:351).

Maggie consequently asks the Prince to wait in his overtures of passion. Maggie's response to her passion is incremental to her loss or gain of trust in Amerigo, a point with great bearing on the often-quoted final passage of the novel: "He tried, too clearly, to please her—to meet her in her own way; but with the result only that, close to her, her face kept before him, his hands holding her shoulders, his whole act enclosing her, he presently echoed: " 'See?' " I see nothing but *you.*' And the truth of it had with this force after a moment so strangely lighted his eyes that as for pity and dread of them she buried her own in his breast" (24:369). Pearson suggests that "Maggie buries her head in the Prince's breast at the end of the novel in knowledge that she has had to become a predator and he her prey."[31] Yet Maggie's response is to the special truth of her relationship to her husband in the context of the larger ideals of the successful rhetorical transaction. Amerigo's truth is his dependence on Maggie to keep him honest; this provokes her pity for his weakness. Maggie's dread, accordingly, is of the weakening in-fluence of her own passion over which she must constantly be vigilant because the Prince shifts the entire burden for a truthful relationship onto her. Maggie and Amerigo's rhetoric thus becomes a dialogue rid-dled with angst, a tentative truce between two intimate individuals involved in a constant dynamics of suspicion and trust. Thus in *The Golden Bowl*, the easy faith of the Quintilian principle is amended. Yet it is also affirmed. By Maggie's offering the shopkeeper faith, he offers her, in return, his honesty, which allows her to choose consciously a world of imperfection over perfect faith. In *The Golden Bowl*, trust in the virtue of eloquence is an ideal and, through Maggie's agency, a transforming power in the world. In the beginning of a century of ever-increasing cynicism, Henry James wrote his bravest and most complicated testament to the ameliorating force of honest language.

Notes

INTRODUCTION

1. Wayne Booth, *The Company We Keep: An Ethics of Fiction* (Berkeley and Los Angeles: University of California Press, 1988), 90.

2. See Evan Carton, *The Rhetoric of American Romance: Dialectic and Identity in Emerson, Dickinson, Poe, and Hawthorne* (Baltimore: Johns Hopkins University Press, 1985); Fred G. See, *The Desire and the Sign: Nineteenth-Century American Fiction* (Baton Rouge: Louisiana State University Press, 1987); Richard Poirier, *The Renewal of Literature: Emersonian Reflections* (New Haven: Yale University Press, 1987); John P. Miller and William J. Richardson, *The Purloined Poe: Lacan, Derrida, and Psychoanalytic Reading* (Baltimore: Johns Hopkins University Press, 1988); J. Gerald Kennedy, *Poe, Death, and the Life of Writing* (New Haven: Yale University Press, 1987); John Auchard, *Silence in Henry James: The Heritage of Symbolism and Decadence* (University Park: Pennsylvania State University Press, 1986).

3. David W. Smit, *The Language of a Master: Theories of Style and the Late Writing of Henry James* (Carbondale: Southern Illinois University Press, 1988), 19.

4. See, *The Desire and the Sign*, 44, 35, 7, 5.

5. Millicent Bell, "The Obliquity of Signs: *The Scarlet Letter*," *Massachusetts Review* 23 (Spring 1982): 12.

6. Murray Krieger, *Words about Words about Words: Theory, Criticism, and the Literary Text* (Baltimore: Johns Hopkins University Press, 1988), 43.

7. Booth, *The Company We Keep*, 67.

8. These are Booth's words to describe what the New Critics praised (ibid., 58).

9. See Jacques Derrida, "Plato's Pharmacy," in *Dissemination*, trans. Barbara Johnson (Chicago: University of Chicago Press, 1981), 68. Future references to "Plato's Pharmacy" will be noted within the text.

10. See, *The Desire and the Sign*, 19.

11. Nina Baym, *The Shape of Hawthorne's Career* (Ithaca: Cornell University Press, 1976), 139.

12. Barnet Baskerville, "Principal Themes of Nineteenth-Century Critics of Oratory," *Speech Monographs* 19 (1952): 14–16.

13. W.H., "Importance and Obligation of Truth, Philosophically Considered," *New England Magazine* 7 (1834): 302. This essay is signed W.H. and may possibly be the early signature of Oliver Wendell Holmes. A similarly signed essay on a similar theme appeared in *Knickerbocker's*, in September 1836, and Holmes is listed by Mott as an early contributor to both periodicals (Frank Luther Mott, *A History of American Magazines, 1741–1850* [Cambridge, Mass.: Harvard University Press, 1939], 601, 609).

14. Importance and Obligation of Truth," 302.

15. Henry James, *What Maisie Knew*, Vol. 11 in *The Novels and Tales of Henry James*, New York Edition, 24 vols. (New York: Scribner's, 1907–9), 11:137, 151, 145.

16. Despite Aristotle's emphasis on the pragmatics of rhetoric, he sometimes paradoxically sounds the moral note: "For we must not make people believe what is wrong. . . . Things that are true and things that are better are, by their nature, practically always easier to prove and easier to believe in" (Book I, Chap. 1, *The Rhetoric and the Poetics of Aristotle*, trans. W. Rhys Roberts [New York: Modern Library, 1984], 25). Despite Cicero's emphasis on the use of emotion, he also stresses that "no one can be a good speaker who is not a sound thinker" (*Brutus*, trans. G. L. Hendrickson, *Cicero in Twenty-Eight Volumes: Brutus, Orator*, 28 vols. Loeb Classical Library Series [Cambridge, Mass.:, Harvard University Press, 1971], 5:35).

17. Baskerville, "Principal Themes," 15.

18. Cicero, *Orator*, trans. H. M. Hubbell, *Cicero in Twenty-Eight Volumes*, 5: 419.

19. James, Preface, *What Maisie Knew*, 11:xii.

20. Booth suggests that my reading of the ending of *Adventures of Huckleberry Finn* follows my own "ethical program" — see *The Company We Keep*, 470–72. I will respond to this in my chapter on *Adventures of Huckleberry Finn*.

21. Krieger, *Words about Words*, 110.

22. Georges Poulet, "Criticism and the Experience of Interiority," in *The Languages of Criticism and the Sciences of Man: The Structuralist Controversy*, ed. Richard Macksey and Eugenio Donato (Baltimore: Johns Hopkins University Press, 1970), 60.

23. See chapter 2, pp. 8–36, of Smit's *Language of a Master* for a clear discussion of recent reading theory.

24. The literary text and Auchard's analysis are quoted from *Silence in Henry James*, 104–5.

25. I do not mean to slight this reading. Please see ibid., 104–5, for a fuller explanation of this view. Nevertheless, one of the potential antecedents Auchard supposes possible for "her" does not make sense.

26. Herman Melville, *The Confidence-Man: His Masquerade*, Vol. 10 in *The*

Writings of Herman Melville, ed. Harrison Hayford et al., 15 vols. (Evanston and Chicago: Northwestern University Press and the Newberry Library, 1984), 9. Future references to Melville's *The Confidence-Man* are from this edition and will be noted within the text.

27. Watson Branch et al., "Historical Note," ibid., 256.

28. For a good summary of Melville's use of "William Thompson," see Tom Quirk, *Melville's Confidence Man: From Knave to Knight* (Columbia: University of Missouri Press, 1982), Chap. 2, or the Newberry Edition of *The Confidence-Man*, "Historical Note," section 3.

29. Philip Drew, "Appearance and Reality in Melville's *The Confidence-Man*," *ELH* 31 (1964): 441; Lawrence Buell, "The Last Word on 'The Confidence-Man'?" *Illinois Quarterly* 35 (1972): 17, 18.

30. Elizabeth Foster, Introduction, *The Confidence-Man: His Masquerade*, by Herman Melville (New York: Hendricks House, 1954), xlvi.

31. See, for example, Nathalia Wright, *Melville's Use of the Bible* (Durham: Duke University Press, 1949), and Tom Quirk's discussion of the St. Paul allusions in *Melville's Confidence Man*, 61–62, 64–66.

32. See Mary K. Madison's summary of the status of this figure in the critical world in "Hypothetical Friends: The Critics and the Confidence Man," *Melville Society Extracts* 46 (1981): 10–14.

33. I am indebted to Mary K. Madison (ibid.) for this quotation.

34. John Schroeder, "Sources and Symbols for Melville's *Confidence-Man*," *PMLA* 66 (1951): 368, 372.

35. Ibid., 372.

36. Foster, Introduction, xvi.

37. Schroeder, "Sources and Symbols," 379.

38. Buell, "The Last Word on 'The Confidence-Man'?" 21.

39. Branch et al., "Historical Note," 314.

40. Newton Arvin, *Herman Melville*, American Men of Letters Series (New York: Sloane, 1950), 26.

41. Edward Waldo Emerson, Notes, *Society and Solitude: Twelve Chapters*, by Ralph Waldo Emerson, Vol. 7 in *The Complete Works of Ralph Waldo Emerson*, Centenary Edition, ed. Edward Waldo Emerson, 12 vols. (Boston: Houghton Mifflin, 1903–4), 364. Emerson took the Boylston prize for speaking at Harvard.

42. Herman Melville, *White-Jacket or The World in a Man-of-War*, Vol. 5 in *The Writings of Herman Melville*, ed. Harrison Hayford et al., 15 vols. (Evanston and Chicago: Northwestern University Press and the Newberry Library, 1970), 168.

43. Herman Melville, "Notes on 'A Short Patent Sermon," *The Piazza Tales and Other Prose Pieces, 1839–1860*, Vol. 9 in *The Writings of Herman Melville*, ed. Harrison Hayford et al., 15 vols. (Evanston and Chicago: Northwestern University Press and the Newberry Library, 1987), 443–44.

44. Merton Sealts, *Melville's Reading* (Columbia: University of South Carolina Press, 1988), 151, 167.

45. Merton Sealts, "Melville and the Platonic Tradition," in *Pursuing Melville, 1940–1980: Chapters and Essays* (Madison: University of Wisconsin Press, 1982). Interestingly, Sealts notes the use of the *Phaedrus* by Melville in such works as *Moby Dick*, but regarding Plato's influence in *The Confidence-Man*, Sealts mentions that Mark Winsome's allusion to Proclus's translation of Plato in chapter 36 and an earlier reference to Plato in chapter 7 "are the only specific signs of possible Platonic influence on *The Confidence-Man* that I have detected" (327). My suggestion is that the *Phaedrus* was a work immanent within *The Confidence-Man*.

46. Many critics connect Melville's confidence men not only with William Thompson but with other well-known artists of illusion such as P. T. Barnum and the Yankee peddler type.

47. Merton Sealts, "Historical Note," *The Piazza Tales and Other Prose Pieces, 1839–1860*, Vol. 9 in *The Writings of Herman Melville*, ed. Harrison Hayford et al., 15 vols. (Evanston and Chicago: Northwestern University Press and the Newberry Library, 1987), 476–514.

48. Sealts, *Melville's Reading*, 207.

49. "American Orators: Rufus Choate," *Putnam's New Monthly Magazine* 5 (1855): 347. Future references to this essay will be made within the text.

50. Sealts, *Melville's Reading*, 207.

51. Tom Quirk finds the allusions to Hamlet unproductive to analysis of the Cosmopolitan (*Melville's Confidence Man*, 82–83).

52. "Of Fitness in Oratory," *Putnam's New Monthly Magazine* 3 (1854): 417. Future references to this essay will be noted in the text.

53. Plato, *Phaedrus*, trans. W. C. Helmbold and W. G. Rabinowitz (New York: Macmillan, 1956), 32. Future references to the *Phaedrus* will be noted in the text.

54. Richard Weaver, *The Ethics of Rhetoric* (South Bend, Ind.: Regnery/Gateway, 1953), 3–26.

55. Foster, Introduction, li.

56. Although the barber's sign "No Trust" at the beginning of the novel is also written, it is met with no resistance, but Melville may be suggesting that it is easier for a written inscription to represent a lack than a positive virtue.

57. Branch, "The Genesis, Composition, and Structure of *The Confidence-Man*," *Nineteenth-Century Fiction* 27 (1973): 424–48.

58. Noted by Quirk, along with other references to the Confidence Man's other various avatars.

59. Plato defines these virtues as the spiritual good in the *Gorgias*, trans. W. C. Helmbold (New York: Macmillan, 1952), 79–91.

60. Noted in *The Confidence-Man: His Masquerade*, ed. Hershel Parker (New York: Norton, 1971), xi–xiv.

61. Hershel Parker, "The Metaphysics of Indian-hating," *Nineteenth-Century Fiction* 18 (1963): 170, 167.

62. Saint Augustine, *The Confessions of St. Augustine*, trans. F. J. Sheed (New York: Sheed & Ward, 1943), 31–41, quote on 36.

63. Quirk, *Melville's Confidence-Man*, 32.

64. According to John McAleer, "This was the most popular lecture Emerson gave and was always well received" (*Ralph Waldo Emerson: Days of Encounter* [Boston: Little, Brown, 1984], 484).

65. It appeared in *Society and Solitude*.

66. See Merton Sealts, "Melville and Emerson's Rainbow," *ESQ* 26 (1980): 53–78.

67. Ralph Waldo Emerson, "Eloquence," in *Society and Solitude*, 7:98.

68. Ralph Waldo Emerson, "Eloquence," *Letters and Social Aims*, Vol. 8 in *The Complete Works of Ralph Waldo Emerson*, Centenary Edition, ed. Edward Waldo Emerson, 12 vols. (Boston: Houghton Mifflin, 1903–4), 131.

69. Hugh Blair, *Lectures on Rhetoric and Belles Lettres*, ed. Harold F. Harding, 2 vols. (Carbondale: Southern Illinois University Press, 1965), 1:13.

CHAPTER 1. A Full Heart and a Well-Equipped Mind: The Legacy of Rhetorical Idealism in Nineteenth-Century America

1. Baskerville, "Principal Themes," 11.

2. Ibid., 15.

3. James L. Golden and Edward P. J. Corbett, *The Rhetoric of Blair, Campbell, and Whately* (New York: Holt, Rinehart, and Winston, 1968), 6.

4. Plato, *Gorgias*, 79–91.

5. W.H., "Importance and Obligation of Truth," 303–5.

6. Noted also by Michael Davitt Bell, " 'The Double-Tongued Deceiver': Sincerity and Duplicity in the Novels of Charles Brockden Brown," *Early American Literature* 9 (1974): 145.

7. Albert Kitzhaber, "Rhetoric in American Colleges, 1850–1900" (Ph.D. dissertation, University of Washington, 1953), 81.

8. William Charvat, *The Origins of American Critical Thought, 1810–1835* (1936; reprint, New York: A. S. Barnes, 1961), 29–31; Kitzhaber, "Rhetoric in American Colleges," 81.

9. Richard Beale Davis, "James Ogilvie, an Early American Teacher of Rhetoric," *QJS* 28 (1942): 289–97.

10. Ibid., 295, 297.

11. Warren Guthrie, "The Development of Rhetorical Theory in America, 1635–1850," *Speech Monographs* 15 (1948): 70, 68.

12. Ronald F. Reid, "The Boylston Professorship of Rhetoric and Oratory, 1806–1904: A Case Study of Changing Concepts of Rhetoric and Pedagogy," *QJS* 45 (1959): 239.

13. Guthrie, "Development of Rhetorical Theory in America," 68.

14. Richard Whately, *Elements of Rhetoric*, ed. Douglas Ehninger (Carbondale: Southern Illinois University Press, 1963), xxxiii.

15. Quintilian, *On the Teaching of Speaking and Writing: Translations from Books One, Two, and Ten of the Institutio Oratoria*, ed. James J. Murphy (Carbondale: Southern Illinois University Press, 1987), Preface to the *Institutio Oratoria*, p. 6.

16. Blair, *Lectures on Rhetoric and Belles Lettres*, 1:13.

17. Kitzhaber, "Rhetoric in American Colleges," 85.

18. George Campbell, *The Philosophy of Rhetoric* (Boston: J. H. Wilkins, 1835), Book I: 77–78, 101.

19. Reid, "The Boylston Professorship of Rhetoric and Oratory," 243.

20. "Mr. Forrest's Oration," *United States Magazine and Democratic Review* 3 (September 1838): 54. The date of Hawthorne's sketch is noted in C. E. Frazer Clark, *Nathaniel Hawthorne: A Descriptive Bibliography* (Pittsburgh: University of Pittsburgh Press, 1978), 418.

21. "Living Pulpit Orators," *Knickerbocker* 34 (October 1849): 319.

22. "Living Pulpit Orators," *Knickerbocker* 24 (October 1844): 379.

23. "Remarks on the Eloquence of Debate," *New England Magazine* 7 (July 1834): 113.

24. Stephen Chambers and G. P. Mohrmann, "Rhetoric in Some American Periodicals," *Speech Monographs* 37 (1970): 112–13.

25. Dorothy I. Anderson, "Edward T. Channing's Definition of Rhetoric," *Speech Monographs* 14 (1947): 81.

26. Edward T. Channing, "The Orator and His Times," in *Lectures Read to Seniors at Harvard College*, ed. Dorothy I. Anderson and Waldo Braden (Carbondale: Southern Illinois University Press, 1968), 1.

27. In the *Gorgias*, for example, Plato calls the rhetoric during his own time "a form of flattery and a shameless method of addressing the public" and urges an oratory instead that would be "beautiful, a genuine attempt to make the souls of one's fellows as excellent as may be" (77).

28. Channing, *Lectures*, 23.

29. Ibid., 17–18.

30. Dorothy I. Anderson and Waldo Braden, Introduction, ibid., xxix.

31. As told by David G. Hoth, "A Possible Source for Melville's *The Confidence Man*," *Melville Society Extracts* 48 (November 1981): 7–10.

32. Ralph Waldo Emerson, "Eloquence," in *Society and Solitude*, 7:66.

33. Baskerville, "Principal Themes," 20.

34. McAleer, *Ralph Waldo Emerson*, 440–41.

35. Thomas Carlyle, "Stump Orator," *Latter-Day Pamphlets*, Vol. 20 in *The*

Works of Thomas Carlyle, 30 vols. (1896; reprint, New York: AMS Press, 1969), 172, 174.

36. W.H., "Importance and Obligation of Truth," 302.

37. Both appeared in the 1834 November issue of *New England Magazine*, the essay on truth on pages 302–8 and Hawthorne's sketch on pages 352–58, as noted by Clark's *Nathaniel Hawthorne*, p. 413.

38. John P. Hoshor, "American Contributions to Rhetorical Theory and Homiletics," in *A History of Speech Education in America*, ed. Karl R. Wallace et al. (New York: Appleton-Century-Crofts, 1954), 131.

39. As noted by John G. Bayer, "Narrative Techniques and the Oral Tradition in *The Scarlet Letter*," *American Literature* 52 (May, 1980): 252.

40. Channing, *Lectures*, 125.

41. W.H., "Importance and Obligation of Truth," 303.

42. Alan Gribben, *Mark Twain's Library: A Reconstruction*, 2 vols. (Boston: G. K. Hall, 1980), 2:501, 672, 1:55.

43. Henry Ward Beecher, "Eloquence and Oratory," in *Lectures and Orations*, ed. Newell Dwight Hillis (New York: AMS Press, 1970), 128–29.

44. Ibid., 138.

45. Ibid.

46. Henry Ward Beecher, "The Atoning God," in *Plymouth Pulpit Sermons, September, 1873–March, 1874* (New York: Fords, Howard and Hulbert, 1901), 89.

47. John R. Howard, "Review of Mr. Beecher's Personality and Political Influence," in *Patriotic Addresses in America and England, 1850-1885*, by Henry Ward Beecher, ed. John R. Howard (Boston: Pilgrim Press, 1887), 24.

48. A. McE. Wylie, "Mr. Beecher as a Social Force," *Scribner's Monthly* 4 (1872): 751.

49. J. Parton, "Henry Ward Beecher's Church," *Atlantic Monthly* 19 (1867): 43.

50. Lionel Crocker, "The Rhetorical Influence of Henry Ward Beecher," *QJS* 18 (1932): 86.

51. Edward Waldo Emerson, Notes, *Letters and Social Aims*, by Ralph Waldo Emerson, Vol. 8 in *The Complete Works of Ralph Waldo Emerson*, Centenary Edition, ed. Edward Waldo Emerson, 12 vols. (Boston: Houghton Mifflin, 1903–4), 384.

52. In the first epithet, Emerson quotes poetry about the "manly patriot" who "believes the eloquent was aye the true," and in the second epithet he quotes Milton's line "true eloquence I find to be none but the serious and hearty love of truth" ("Eloquence," *Letters and Social Aims*, 8:109–10).

53. Ibid., 130–31.

54. E. L. Godkin, "Rhetorical Training," *Nation* 20 (1875): 146, 171.

55. J. T. Peck, "Rhetoric — Its Philosophy and Principles," *Universalist Quarterly Review* 20 (1863): 255.

56. T. Hunt, "Rhetorical Science," *Presbyterian Quarterly* 3 (1874): 662–63.

57. "Article VI," *National Quarterly Review* 6 (1863): 303–4.

58. Hunt, "Rhetorical Science," 664.

59. See, for example, Mark Seltzer's chapter on *The Golden Bowl* in *Henry James and the Art of Power* (Ithaca: Cornell University Press, 1984), or Carren Kaston's chapters on *The Wings of the Dove* and *The Golden Bowl* in *Imagination and Desire in the Novels of Henry James* (New Brunswick: Rutgers University Press, 1984).

60. Campbell, *Philosophy of Rhetoric*, Book I:48.

61. As quoted by Lloyd F. Bitzer in "A Re-evaluation of Campbell's Doctrine of Evidence," *QJS* 46 (1960): 137.

62. Samuel P. Newman, *Practical System of Rhetoric* (Portland: Wm. Hyde, 1827), 43.

63. Campbell, *Philosophy of Rhetoric*, Book I:77.

64. Lewis E. Gates, Introduction, in *Selections from the Prose Writings of John Henry Cardinal Newman* (New York: Henry Holt, 1895), xxi–xxii.

65. Composition became a concern after Harvard's entrance exams in the 1880s focused attention on the poor writing skills of entering college freshmen, according to Kitzhaber, "Rhetoric in American Colleges," 51–79.

66. Lewis E. Gates, "Newman as a Prose Writer," in *Three Studies in Literature* (New York: Macmillan, 1899), 79.

67. Henry Ward Beecher, "Fact and Fancy," in *Plymouth Pulpit Sermons*, 167.

68. Henry Ward Beecher, "The Departed Christ," ibid., 466–67.

69. Peck, "Rhetoric," 260.

CHAPTER 2. Eloquence a Virtue?
The Evils of Credulity and Imposture in *Wieland*

1. Donald A. Ringe, *Charles Brockden Brown* (New York: Twayne, 1966), 42.

2. A notable exception is William Manley's reading of *Wieland*, "The Importance of Point of View in Brockden Brown's *Wieland*," *American Literature* 35 (1963): 311–21. Manley insists that Clara and Theodore veer dangerously into a world of subjective terror, never fully relying on the sane and logical commonsense world.

3. Alan Axelrod, *Charles Brockden Brown: An American Tale* (Austin: University of Texas Press, 1983), 87.

4. See, for example, Bell, " 'Double-Tongued Deceiver,' " 145.

5. Charles Brockden Brown, *Wieland or The Transformation*, ed. Sydney J. Krause and S. W. Reid (Kent, Ohio: Kent State University Press, 1977), 3. Future references to this edition will be noted in the text.

6. Blair, *Lectures on Rhetoric and Belles Lettres*, 2:308. Future references will be noted in the text.

7. Terence Martin, *The Instructed Vision* (Bloomington: Indiana University Press, 1961), 79, 153.

8. Charvat, *Origins of American Critical Thought*, esp. chap. 3 on Scottish sources.

9. Mark Seltzer, "Saying Makes It So: Language and Event in Brown's *Wieland*," *Early American Literature* 13 (1978): 81–91; Bell, " 'Double-Tongued Deceiver,' " 147.

10. Harold F. Harding, "Editor's Introduction," *Lectures on Rhetoric and Belles Lettres*, by Hugh Blair, 2 vols. (Carbondale: Southern Illinois University Press, 1965), 1:xxv.

11. Reid, "The Boylston Professorship of Rhetoric and Oratory," 245.

12. Charvat, *Origins of American Critical Thought*, 30–31.

13. Davis, "James Ogilvie."

14. Michael T. Gilmore, "Calvanism and Gothicism: The Example of Brown's Wieland," *Studies in the Novel* 9 (1977): 107–18.

15. For a good example of this, see Donna Przybylowicz's discussion of James's male artists in *Desire and Repression: The Dialectic of Self and Other in the Late Works of Henry James* (University, Ala.: University of Alabama Press, 1986), pp. 1–38.

16. Davis, "James Ogilvie," 295.

17. Kitzhaber, "Rhetoric in American Colleges," 84.

18. Martin, *Instructed Vision*, 98.

19. Hugh Henry Brackenridge, "Author's Address to the Reader," in *Modern Chivalry, or the Adventures of Captain Farrago and Teague O'Regan* (Philadelphia: Carey and Hart, 1846), xiii–xvi.

20. Ringe, *Charles Brockden Brown*, 32.

21. Axelrod, *Charles Brockden Brown*, 92.

22. Ibid., 94, 85.

23. Ringe, *Charles Brockden Brown*, 47–48.

24. Axelrod, *Charles Brockden Brown*, 96.

CHAPTER 3. "I Take the Shame Upon Myself": Ethical Veracity in *The Scarlet Letter*

1. Baym, *Shape of Hawthorne's Career*, 139, 147.

2. Louise K. Barnett, "Speech and Society in *The Scarlet Letter*," *ESQ* 29 (1983): 19, 17.

3. See, *Desire and the Sign*, 6, 15, 26, 35.

4. Bell, "Obliquity of Signs," 12.

5. Carton, *Rhetoric of American Romance*, 3.

6. Bell, "Obliquity of Signs," 12.

7. Carton, *Rhetoric of American Romance*, 202–3.

8. Essentially, this is Michael Ragussis's point in "Family Discourse and Fiction in *The Scarlet Letter*," *ELH* 49 (1982): 863–88. But for Ragussis, fiction is mercy because it deflects the scandalous truth that we are all both criminal and victim. Ragussis inverts See's notion of scandal. For See, scandal is the breakdown of determinate language. For Ragussis, scandal would be the eruption of determinate language that would identify the criminal in all of us. Bell also sees narrative indeterminacy as a form of mercy.

9. Seltzer, *Henry James and the Art of Power*. See in particular the introduction.

10. Baym, *Shape of Hawthorne's Career*, 134.

11. Lester H. Hunt, "*The Scarlet Letter*: Hawthorne's Theory of Moral Sentiment," *Philosophy and Literature* 8 (1984): 75–87, quote on 78.

12. Nathaniel Hawthorne, *The Scarlet Letter*, in *Nathaniel Hawthorne: Novels*, ed. Millicent Bell (New York: Library of America, from the Ohio State University Centenary Edition of *The Works of Nathaniel Hawthorne*, 1983), 115–345. All future references to the novel will be noted within the chapter from this source.

13. Murray Krieger, *The Play and Place of Criticism* (Baltimore: Johns Hopkins University Press, 1967), 105, 126–27.

14. Mott, *History of American Magazines*, 679.

15. Clark, *Nathaniel Hawthorne*, 418.

16. "Mr. Forrest's Oration," 51. All future references to this article will be made within the text.

17. Bayer, "Narrative Techniques and the Oral Tradition," 251.

18. Newman's rhetoric textbook was a conventional grammar textbook that did not participate in much of the popular idealizing of rhetoric as truth that could be found in the popular periodicals of the time.

19. Bayer, "Narrative Techniques and the Oral Tradition," 257.

20. Blair, *Lectures on Rhetoric and Belles Lettres*, 2:308.

21. Kennedy, *Poe, Death, and the Life of Writing*.

22. Ibid., 2, 3, 40, 45, 47.

23. Nina Baym, for example, suggests this on page 130 of *The Shape of Hawthorne's Career*.

24. Krieger, *Play and the Place of Criticism*, 127.

25. Hester stands three hours on the platform of the pillory at a time when Pearl is three or four months old. Pearl's age is next mentioned when she is three. The ship is to take Hester, Pearl, and Dimmesdale to Europe three days from Election Sermon day.

26. "How I had entered there I scarce can say, / So full was I of slumber at the point / At which I first abandoned the true way. / But when I

reached the rising of a hill, / Whereunder came that valley to an end / Which on my heart had laid its deadly chill" (Dante, ll.10–15, Canto I, *The Inferno*, in *The Divine Comedy*, trans. Jefferson Butler Fletcher [New York: Columbia University Press, 1931], 3).

27. The Nurse speaks similarly in *Medea* about the way Medea replaces her love for her children with her own passion: "Such a look she will flash on her servants / If any comes near with a message, / Like a lioness guarding her cubs" (ll.186–88 in *The Medea, Euripedes: Four Greek Tragedies*, 4 vols. [Chicago: University of Chicago Press, 1955], 1:65, in *The Complete Greek Tragedies*, ed. David Greene and Richard Lattimore).

28. Przybylowicz, *Desire and Repression*, 4, 50.

29. See, for example, John Carlos Rowe, "The Internal Conflict of Romantic Narrative: Hegel's *Phenomenology* and Hawthorne's *The Scarlet Letter*," *MLN* 95 (1980): 1216.

30. Louise K. Barnett, for example, decides that Pearl's "language consistently fails as social communication" in "Speech and Society in *The Scarlet Letter*," 23.

31. James, Preface, *What Maisie Knew*, viii, ix, x, xiii–xiv.

32. Ibid., viii.

33. John Bayer ("Narrative Techniques and the Oral Tradition") has discussed only the possible role of Hugh Blair's rhetoric in Hawthorne's use of rhetorical strategy in the Preface.

34. Anderson, "Edward T. Channing's Definition of Rhetoric," 81.

35. Emerson's popular lecture "Eloquence" was first delivered in Boston in 1847, when Hawthorne would have been living in Salem and working as surveyor in the Salem Custom House.

36. Arlin Turner, *Nathaniel Hawthorne: A Biography* (New York: Oxford University Press, 1980), 105.

37. Marion L. Kesselring, *Hawthorne's Reading, 1828–1850: A Transcription and Identification of Titles Recorded in the Charge-Books of the Salem Atheneum* (New York: New York Public Library, 1949), 58.

38. "Principles of Elocution," *North American Review* 29 (July 1829): 38–39.

39. "Edward Everett's Addresses," *New England Magazine* 9 (December 1835): 464. All information about Hawthorne's contributions to the periodicals mentioned here comes from C. E. Frazer Clark's *Nathaniel Hawthorne*. The present reference to Hawthorne's entry in the December 1835 *New England Magazine* appears on 415.

40. Lewis Gaylord Clark, "Editors' Tables," *Knickerbocker* 11 (June 1838): 562.

41. "Living Pulpit Orators," *Knickerbocker* 34 (August 1849): 105.

42. "Living Pulpit Orators," *Knickerbocker* 34 (October 1849): 319.

43. "Living Pulpit Orators," *Knickerbocker* 24 (October 1844): 379; "Remarks on the Eloquence of Debate," 113.

44. "Living Pulpit Orators," *Knickerbocker* 24 (October 1844): 381.

45. Clark, *Nathaniel Hawthorne*, 20.

46. George Bancroft, "William Ellery Channing," *Democratic Review* 12 (May 1843): 527. This essay included two separate portraitures of Channing, the first written by George Bancroft and the second an anonymous but apparently well-known source. The quotation is from the second source.

47. Ibid.

48. "Living Pulpit Orators," *Knickerbocker* 34 (October 1849): 310.

49. Baskerville, "Principal Themes," 14–15.

50. Plato, *Gorgias*, 79.

51. "Living Pulpit Orators," *Knickerbocker* 34 (August 1849): 105.

52. Michel Small, "Hawthorne's *The Scarlet Letter:* Arthur Dimmesdale's Manipulation of Language," *American Imago* 37 (Spring 1980): 116, 118, 115, 121.

53. Ibid., 113.

54. " 'If I take not indeed thy words amiss,' / Answered that shade of the Magnanimous, / 'Attainted is thy soul with cowardice, / which oft the spirit of a man so palls / That he is turned away from honorable deed, / Like beasts that shy at shadows when dusk falls' " (Dante, Canto II, ll.43–48, *The Inferno*).

55. Channing, "The Orator and His Times," in *Lectures*, 23.

56. Clark, *Nathaniel Hawthorne*, 413.

57. "Mr. Gardiner's Address to the Phi Beta Kappa Society, on American Education in Classical Learning and Eloquence," *New England Magazine* 7 (December 1834): 417.

58. Small, "Hawthorne's *The Scarlet Letter*," 119.

CHAPTER 4. No More in This World:
An Instance of Moral Rhetoric in *Adventures of Huckleberry Finn*

1. Samuel Clemens, *Adventures of Huckleberry Finn*, ed. Walter Blair and Victor Fischer (Berkeley and Los Angeles: University of California Press, 1985), xxv. Future references are to this edition and will be noted within the text.

2. Henry Nash Smith, *Mark Twain: The Development of A Writer* (Cambridge, Mass.: Harvard University Press, 1962), 118.

3. Kenneth R. Andrews, *Nook Farm: Mark Twain's Hartford Circle* (Cambridge, Mass.: Harvard University Press, 1950), 71.

4. Forrest G. Robinson, *In Bad Faith: The Dynamics of Deception in Mark Twain's America* (Cambridge, Mass.: Harvard University Press, 1986), 71.

5. Lee Mitchell, " 'Nobody but Our Gang Warn't Around': The Authority of Language in *Huckleberry Finn*," in *New Essays on Huckleberry Finn*, ed. Louis J. Budd (Cambridge: Cambridge University Press, 1985), 89–90.

6. J. Hillis Miller, "Three Problems of Fictional Form: First-Person in *David Copperfield* and *Huckleberry Finn, Experiences in the Novel: Selected Papers from the English Institute*, ed. Roy Harvey Pearce (New York: Columbia University Press, 1968), 25, 22, 28.

7. David Sewell has addressed Mark Twain's training in rhetoric from another angle—his knowledge of grammar and the subsequent varieties of dialect in *Adventures of Huckleberry Finn* (*Mark Twain's Languages: Discourse, Dialect, and Linguistic Variety* [Berkeley and Los Angeles: University of California Press, 1987]). Although this reading is on a similar topic, its focus is very different, and it bears no direct relation to my reading of Twain's grounding in rhetoric.

8. Henry Ward Beecher, "The Science of Right Living," in *Plymouth Pulpit Sermons, September, 1873–March, 1874* (New York: Fords, Howard and Hulbert, 1901), 333.

9. Beecher, "Atoning God," 95.

10. John Henry Newman, *Apologia Pro Vita Sua*, ed. A. Dwight Culler (Boston: Houghton Mifflin, 1956), 11.

11. Vincent Ferrer Blehl, "Early Criticism of the *Apologia*," in *Newman's "Apologia": A Classic Reconstructed*, ed. V. F. Blehl and F. X. Connolly (New York: Harcourt, Brace, & World, 1964), 48–49.

12. Parton, "Henry Ward Beecher's Church," 48.

13. Ibid., 43, 41.

14. Mark Twain, "Christian Science," in *Mark Twain: Selected Writings of an American Skeptic*, ed. Victor Doyno (Buffalo, N.Y.: Prometheus Books, 1983), 381.

15. Hunt, "Rhetorical Science," 664.

16. Peck, "Rhetoric," 260.

17. Beecher, "Man's Two Natures," in *Plymouth Pulpit Sermons*, 140.

18. Beecher, "Departed Christ," 461.

19. Robinson, *In Bad Faith*, 239. Stephen Mailloux also makes this point in his essay "Reading *Huckleberry Finn*: The Rhetoric of Performed Ideology," in *New Essays on Huckleberry Finn*, ed. Louis J. Budd (Cambridge: Cambridge University Press, 1985).

20. Beecher, "Shall We Compromise?" in *Patriotic Addresses in America and England, 1850–1885*, ed. John R. Howard (Boston: Pilgrim Press, 1887), 174.

21. Robinson, *In Bad Faith*, 111.

22. Gribben, *Mark Twain's Library*, 1:55.

23. Andrews, *Nook Farm*, 5.

24. This quotation is provided in Howard G. Baetzhold, *Mark Twain and John Bull: The British Connection* (Bloomington: Indiana University Press, 1970), 267.

25. Andrews, *Nook Farm*, 75.

26. Beecher, "Modes and Duties of Emancipation," 322.

27. Beecher, "The Moral Teaching of Suffering," in *Plymouth Pulpit Sermons*, 231, 215–17.

28. Beecher, "Atoning God," 90, 92.

29. Beecher, "The Debt of Strength," in *Plymouth Pulpit Sermons*, 537.

30. Henry Ward Beecher, "The Wastes and Burdens of Society," in *Lectures and Orations*, ed. Newell Dwight Hillis (New York: AMS Press, 1970), 66–67.

31. Robinson, *In Bad Faith*, 161.

32. Kennedy, *Poe, Death, and the Life of Writing*, 16–17.

33. Robinson, *In Bad Faith*, 175.

34. Mitchell, " 'Nobody but Our Gang Warn't Around,' " 101.

35. George C. Carrington, *The Dramatic Unity of Huckleberry Finn* (Columbus: Ohio State University Press, 1976), 5.

36. Robinson, *In Bad Faith*, 192.

37. Ibid., 195.

38. Booth, *The Company We Keep*, 466–67.

39. James Kastely, "The Ethics of Self-Interest: Narrative Logic in *Huckleberry Finn*," *Nineteenth-Century Fiction* 40 (March 1986): 421–22.

40. Booth, *The Company We Keep*, 470.

41. Ibid., 471, 473.

42. Wayne Booth, *The Rhetoric of Fiction* (Chicago: University of Chicago Press, 1961), 386.

43. Robinson, *In Bad Faith*, 181, 198.

44. Mailloux, "Reading *Huckleberry Finn*," 108.

45. Beecher, "Fact and Fancy," 169.

46. Leo Marx, "Mr. Eliot, Mr. Trilling, and *Huckleberry Finn*," *American Scholar* 22 (Autumn 1953): 429.

47. Smith, *Mark Twain*, 4.

48. Kastely, "Ethics of Self-Interest," 433.

49. Beecher, "Wastes and Burdens of Society," 78, 79.

50. Ibid., 79, 76.

51. Beecher, "Fact and Fancy," 167.

52. David Sewell notes that Mark Twain invests Mary Jane Wilks with the moral authority of correct grammar (*Mark Twain's Languages*, 89).

CHAPTER 5. James's *The Bostonians:*
Love and Discourse in the American Marketplace

1. The most recent topical reading is that of John Carlos Rowe, in *The Theoretical Dimensions of Henry James* (Madison: University of Wisconsin Press, 1984), 85–118. *The Bostonians*, according to Rowe, satirizes transcendentalism and addresses the issue of female powerlessness.

2. Henry James, *The Bostonians* (New York: Random House, 1956), 3. Further references to *The Bostonians* will be noted in the text.

3. Beecher, "Eloquence and Oratory," 149.

4. See Mary Margaret Robb's account of the popularity of nineteenth-century oratory, "The Elocutionary Movement and Its Chief Figures," in *A History of Speech Education in America*, ed. Karl R. Wallace (New York: Appleton-Century-Crofts, 1954), 178–79.

5. C. E. Grinnell, "A Few Orators and Their Eloquence at the Bar and Elsewhere," *American Law Review* 16 (1882): 154–55.

6. Information on MacKaye is from Claude L. Shaver, "Steele MacKaye and the Delsartian Tradition," in *History of Speech Education in America*, ed. Wallace, 207–9.

7. Edyth Renshaw, "Five Private Schools of Speech," in *History of Speech Education in America*, ed. Wallace, 302.

8. Henry James, *Autobiography*, ed. Frederick W. Dupee (Princeton: Princeton University Press, 1983), 440–41.

9. William James, "The Stream of Thought," in *The Writings of William James*, ed. John J. McDermott (Chicago: University of Chicago Press, 1977), 50.

10. James, *Autobiography*, 427–28.

11. See Paul E. Ried, "Francis J. Child: The Fourth Boylston Professor of Rhetoric and Oratory," *QJS* 55 (1969): 268–75.

12. Channing, *Lectures*, 18.

13. Ried, "Francis J. Child," 270.

14. Irving Howe, Introduction, *The Bostonians*, xviii.

15. Godkin, "Rhetorical Training," 146.

16. Plato says, for example, that "a man must study, not how to seem good, but to be so, both in public and private life" (*Gorgias*, p. 106).

17. Henry James, *The American Scene*, ed. W. H. Auden (New York: Charles Scribner's Sons, 1946), 298.

18. Socrates claims in the *Gorgias*, for example, that he never carries on his "habitual discussions with a view to gratification, but with my eyes fixed on the highest good" (100).

19. See ibid., 18.

20. Socrates observes, for example, that "the man who partakes of this madness and loves beauty is called a lover," who then can begin "to grow wings" (Plato, *Phaedrus*, 33).

21. Richard E. Young, Alton L. Becker, and Kenneth L. Pike, *Rhetoric, Discovery, and Change* (New York: Harcourt Brace Jovanovich, 1970), 273–90. For the discussion of Rogers's "bridge" see esp. p. 280.

22. Plato, "Apology," in *The Dialogues of Plato*, Vol. 1, trans. B. Jowett (Oxford: Clarendon Press, 1953), 347.

23. "Article VI," 308.

24. Elizabeth Allen, *A Woman's Place in the Novels of Henry James* (New York: St. Martin's Press, 1984), 12, 32, 92.

25. Renshaw, "Five Private Schools of Speech," 310.

26. Donald H. Hayworth, "Review of Whately's *Elements of Rhetoric*," *QJS* 14 (1928): 594.

27. Whately, *Elements of Rhetoric*, 368.

28. Renshaw, "Five Private Schools of Speech," 310.

29. Robb, "Elocutionary Movement," 189.

30. "Article VI," 302.

31. Ibid., 301–2.

32. Peck, "Rhetoric," 255.

33. Beecher, "Eloquence and Oratory," 132.

34. "Article VI," 304.

35. Beecher, "Eloquence and Oratory," 137.

36. Hunt, "Rhetorical Science," 668–69.

37. Ibid., 672, 673.

38. Howe, Introduction, xxi.

39. Theodore C. Miller, "Muddled Politics of Henry James's *The Bostonians*," *Georgia Review* 26 (1972): 336–46. See also Susan Wolstenholme, "Possession and Personality: Spiritualism in *The Bostonians*," *American Literature* 49 (1977–78): 580–91; and David Howard, "The Bostonians," in *The Air of Reality: New Essays on Henry James*, ed. John Goode (London: Methuen, 1972), 76–77.

40. Beecher, "Fact and Fancy," 167.

41. Campbell, *Philosophy of Rhetoric*, 42.

42. Plato, *Phaedrus*, 37.

43. Franz Theremin, *Eloquence: A Virtue; or Outlines of a Systematic Rhetoric*, trans. William G. T. Shedd (Andover: W. F. Draper and Brother, 1854), 15, 16, 20–22.

44. Plato, *Phaedrus*, 33.

45. Beecher, "Moral Teaching of Suffering," 227.

46. Theremin, *Eloquence*, 96.

47. Aristotle, *The Rhetoric of Aristotle*, trans. Lane Cooper (New York: Appleton-Century-Crofts, 1960), 154.

48. Beecher, "Fact and Fancy," 178.

49. Paul Armstrong, *The Phenomenology of Henry James* (Chapel Hill: University of North Carolina Press, 1983), 19.

50. Judith Fetterley, *The Resisting Reader: A Feminist Approach to American Fiction* (Bloomington: Indiana University Press, 1978), 138.

51. Kaston, *Imagination and Desire*, 6.

52. Fetterley, *Resisting Reader*, 126, 128.

53. Rowe, *Theoretical Dimensions*, 95.

54. I am indebted to Alfred Habegger for this connection between Beecher and the James family. See his "The Lessons of the Father: Henry James Sr. on Sexual Difference," *Henry James Review* 8 (Fall 1986): 1–36.

55. Ibid., 21.

56. Rowe, *Theoretical Dimensions*, 95.

CHAPTER 6. The Light That Cannot Fail: The Ideal of Truth in *The Wings of the Dove*

1. Theodore Dreiser, *Sister Carrie*, ed. Donald Pizer (New York: Norton, 1970), 56–57.

2. Ibid., 150–51.

3. Henry James, *The Wings of the Dove*, Vols. 19 and 20 in *The Novels and Tales of Henry James*, New York Edition, 24 vols. (New York: Scribner's, 1907–9), 19:61. Future references to this novel will be noted in the text.

4. See, for example, Allen, *A Woman's Place*, 150; John Goode, "The Pervasive Mystery of Style: *The Wings of the Dove*," in *The Air of Reality: New Essays on Henry James*, ed. John Goode (London: Methuen, 1972), 250.

5. Allen, *A Woman's Place*, 150.

6. John Carlos Rowe, *Henry Adams and Henry James* (Ithaca: Cornell University Press, 1976), 183, 76.

7. Ruth Bernard Yeazell, *Language and Knowledge in the Late Novels of Henry James* (Chicago: University of Chicago Press, 1976), 71.

8. David Potter, Foreword, *The Philosophy of Rhetoric*, by George Campbell, ed. Lloyd F. Bitzer (Carbondale: Southern Illinois University Press, 1963), xiv.

9. Campbell, *Philosophy of Rhetoric*, 51.

10. Goode, "Pervasive Mystery of Style," 293.

11. Allen, *A Woman's Place*, 149.

12. Plato, *Gorgias*, 33–34: "I call a good and honorable man or woman happy, and one who is unjust and evil wretched."

13. Campbell, *Philosophy of Rhetoric*, 51, 54, 48.

14. James, Preface, *Wings of the Dove*, 19:xxii.

15. Goode, "Pervasive Mystery of Style," 261.

16. Ibid., 275.

17. Armstrong, *Phenomenology of Henry James*, for example, the introductory chapter on *What Maisie Knew*.

18. Contrary to Laurence Holland's statement that "Kate alters her scheme so as to do justice not only to the need for receiving Maud and acquiring money but to the genuine pity and affection she feels for her friend" (*The Expense of Vision: Essays on the Craft of Henry James* [Princeton: Princeton University Press, 1964], 292), I think that Kate is primarily focusing at this time

on her own emotional needs. She virtually threatens to drop Milly if Milly does not back off her investigation of Kate and Densher's relationship.

19. Campbell, *Philosophy of Rhetoric*, 60.

20. Gertrude Buck, *The Metaphor—A Study in the Psychology of Rhetoric*, Contributions to Rhetorical Theory, no. 5, ed. Fred Newton Scott (Ann Arbor: Inland Press, 1899), 24, 27, 30.

21. Ibid., 15–18.

22. Ibid., 33–34.

23. Ibid., 40.

24. Allen, *A Woman's Place*, 146–75.

25. Henry Ward Beecher, "The Naturalness of Faith," in *Plymouth Pulpit Sermons, September, 1873–March, 1874* (New York: Fords, Howard and Hulbert, 1901), 485, 492–93.

26. Beecher, "Fact and Fancy," 169.

27. Auchard, *Silence in Henry James*, 10.

28. Campbell, *Philosophy of Rhetoric*, 98.

29. Beecher, "Atoning God," 95–96.

30. Oscar Cargill, *The Novels of Henry James* (New York: Macmillan, 1961), 366.

31. William James, "Pragmatism's Conception of Truth," in *The Writings of William James*, ed. John J. McDermott (Chicago: University of Chicago Press, 1977), 432. Future references to the essays of William James will be from this text.

32. Nicola Bradbury, *Henry James: The Later Novels* (Oxford: Clarendon University Press, 1979), 121.

33. Frederick Crews observes that when Kate challenges Densher, "Your word of honour that you're not in love with her memory," she tests him to see if he will abandon his position of faith and play by her own secular rules (*The Tragedy of Manners* [New Haven: Yale University Press, 1957], 79).

34. William James, "The Moral Philosopher and the Moral Life," in *Writings*, ed. McDermott, 628–29.

35. The latest rendering of this criticism is found in Donna Przybylowicz's *Desire and Repression*, although *The Wings of the Dove* is not explicitly discussed.

36. James, "Stream of Thought," 73, 60.

37. Paul B. Armstrong, "How Maisie Knows: The Phenomenology of James's Moral Vision," *Texas Studies in Literature and Language* 20 (1978): 535.

CHAPTER 7. Maggie's Unfortunate Virtue: Rhetorical Responsibility in *The Golden Bowl*

1. Henry James, *The Golden Bowl*, Vols. 23 and 24 in *The Novels and Tales of Henry James*, New York Edition, 24 vols. (New York: Scribners, 1907–9), 23:31. Future references to this edition will be noted in the text.

2. Bradbury, *Henry James*, 128.

3. Allen, *A Woman's Place*, 186.

4. Anne Throne Margolis, *Henry James and the Problem of Audience: An International Act* (Ann Arbor: UMI Research Press, 1985), esp. 110–12, 118–20, 129–30, 139–40, 166–67, 169.

5. Reid, "The Boylston Professorship of Rhetoric and Pedagogy," 245.

6. Kaston, *Imagination and Desire*, 173.

7. Gabriel Pearson, "The Novel to End All Novels: *The Golden Bowl*," in *The Air of Reality: New Essays on Henry James*, ed. John Goode (London: Methuen, 1972), 348.

8. Kaston, *Imagination and Desire*, 173.

9. Beecher, "Atoning God," 95.

10. See, for example, Allen, *A Woman's Place*, 204.

11. Pearson, "The Novel to End All Novels," 316.

12. Margolis, *Henry James and the Problem of Audience*, 176. Elizabeth Owen also takes a firm stand on the subject of Charlotte's immediate and consistent predatory guile: "In the pages in which Charlotte is introduced, all James's stress is on her preparedness, calculation and deliberate use of her opportunities. There is no softening excuse of blindness or lack of intention" ("The 'Given Appearance' of Charlotte Verver," *Essays in Criticism* 13 [1963]: 364–74).

13. Joseph A. Boone, "Modernist Maneuverings in the Marriage Plot: Breaking Ideologies of Gender and Genre in James's *The Golden Bowl*," *PMLA* 101 (1986): 382, 381.

14. Allen, *A Woman's Place*, 185.

15. Kaston, *Imagination and Desire*, 163.

16. See, for example, ibid., 154, where the shopkeeper is likened to James's self-portrait in *The Portrait of a Lady* Preface.

17. Kaston, *Imagination and Desire*, 159.

18. Brown, *Wieland*, 84.

19. Rowe, *Henry Adams and Henry James*, 216, 213.

20. John Auchard, *Silence in Henry James*, 139, 144.

21. Armstrong, *Phenomenology of Henry James*, esp. 37–68.

22. L. A. Westervelt, "The Individual and the Form: Maggie Verver's Tactics in *The Golden Bowl*," *Renascence* 36 (1984): 150–51.

23. Auchard, *Silence in Henry James*, 120.

24. Armstrong, *The Phenomenology of Henry James*, 169.

25. Ibid., 174.

26. Kaston, *Imagination and Desire*, 156, 170.

27. Auchard, *Silence in Henry James*, 135.

28. "Article VI," 301–2.

29. Beecher, "Eloquence and Oratory," 137.

30. See, for example, pp. 321 and 323: "three days before they start"; "three minutes from her post."

31. Pearson, "The Novel to End All Novels," 351.

Bibliography

Allen, Elizabeth. *A Woman's Place in the Novels of Henry James.* New York: St. Martin's Press, 1984.

"American Orators: Rufus Choate." *Putnam's New Monthly Magazine* 5 (1855): 347–59.

Anderson, Dorothy I. "Edward T. Channing's Definition of Rhetoric." *Speech Monographs* 14 (1947): 81–92.

Anderson, Dorothy I., and Waldo Braden. Introduction. In *Lectures Read to Seniors at Harvard College,* by Edward T. Channing, edited by Dorothy Anderson and Waldo Braden, ix–lii. Carbondale: Southern Illinois University Press, 1968.

Andrews, Kenneth R. *Nook Farm: Mark Twain's Hartford Circle.* Cambridge, Mass.: Harvard University Press, 1950.

Aristotle. *The Rhetoric and Poetics of Aristotle.* Translated by W. Rhys Roberts. New York: Modern Library, 1984.

———. *The Rhetoric of Aristotle.* Translated by Lane Cooper. New York: Appleton-Century-Crofts, 1960.

Armstrong, Paul B. "How Maisie Knows: The Phenomenology of James's Moral Vision." *Texas Studies in Literature and Language* 20 (1978): 517–37.

———. *The Phenomenology of Henry James.* Chapel Hill: University of North Carolina Press, 1983.

"Article VI." *National Quarterly Review* 6 (1863): 299–317.

Arvin, Newton. *Herman Melville.* American Men of Letters Series. New York: Sloane, 1950.

Auchard, John. *Silence in Henry James: The Heritage of Symbolism and Decadence.* University Park: Pennsylvania State University Press, 1986.

Axelrod, Alan. *Charles Brockden Brown: An American Tale.* Austin: University of Texas Press, 1983.

Baetzhold, Howard G. *Mark Twain and John Bull: The British Connection.* Bloomington: Indiana University Press, 1970.

Bancroft, George. "William Ellery Channing." *Democratic Review* 12 (May 1843): 524–28.

Barnett, Louise K. "Speech and Society in *The Scarlet Letter*." *ESQ* 29 (1983): 16–24.

Baskerville, Barnet. "Principal Themes of Nineteenth-Century Critics of Oratory." *Speech Monographs* 19 (1952): 11–26.

Bayer, John G. "Narrative Techniques and the Oral Tradition in *The Scarlet Letter*." *American Literature* 52 (May 1980): 250–63.

Baym, Nina. *The Shape of Hawthorne's Career*. Ithaca: Cornell University Press, 1976.

Beecher, Henry Ward. "The Atoning God." In *Plymouth Pulpit Sermons, September, 1873–March, 1874*, 85–102. New York: Fords, Howard and Hulbert, 1901.

———. "The Debt of Strength." In *Plymouth Pulpit Sermons, September, 1873–March, 1874*, 531–49. New York: Fords, Howard and Hulbert, 1901.

———. "The Departed Christ." In *Plymouth Pulpit Sermons, September 1873–March, 1874*, 455–78. New York: Fords, Howard and Hulbert, 1901.

———. "Eloquence and Oratory." In *Lectures and Orations*. Edited by Newell Dwight Hillis, 128–56. New York: AMS Press, 1970.

———. "Fact and Fancy." In *Plymouth Pulpit Sermons, September, 1873–March, 1874*, 167–89. New York: Fords, Howard and Hulbert, 1901.

———. "Man's Two Natures." In *Plymouth Pulpit Sermons, September, 1873–March, 1874*, 127–46. New York: Fords, Howard and Hulbert, 1901.

———. "Modes and Duties of Emancipation." In *Patriotic Addresses in America and England, 1850–1885*, edited by John R. Howard, 322–41. Boston: Pilgrim Press, 1887.

———. "The Moral Teaching of Suffering." In *Plymouth Pulpit Sermons, September, 1873–March, 1874*, 215–34. New York: Fords, Howard and Hulbert, 1901.

———. "The Naturalness of Faith." In *Plymouth Pulpit Sermons, September, 1873–March, 1874*, 481–504. New York: Fords, Howard and Hulbert, 1901.

———. "The Science of Right Living." In *Plymouth Pulpit Sermons, September, 1873–March, 1874*, 327–49. New York: Fords, Howard and Hulbert, 1901.

———. "Shall We Compromise?" In *Patriotic Addresses in America and England, 1850–1885*, edited by John R. Howard, 167–77. Boston: Pilgrim Press, 1887.

———. "The Wastes and Burdens of Society." In *Lectures and Orations*, edited by Newell Dwight Hillis, 43–93. New York: AMS Press, 1970.

Bell, Michael Davitt. " 'The Double-Tongued Deceiver': Sincerity and Duplicity in the Novels of Charles Brockden Brown." *Early American Literature* 9 (1974): 143–63.

Bell, Millicent. "The Obliquity of Signs: *The Scarlet Letter*." *Massachusetts Review* 23 (Spring 1982): 9–26.

Bitzer, Lloyd, F. "A Re-evaluation of Campbell's Doctrine of Evidence." *QJS* 46 (1960): 134–40.

Blair, Hugh. *Lectures on Rhetoric and Belles Lettres*. Edited by Harold F. Harding. 2 vols. Carbondale: Southern Illinois University Press, 1965.

Blehl, Vincent Ferrer. "Early Criticism of the *Apologia*." *Newman's 'Apologia': A Classic Reconstructed*, edited by V. F. Blehl and F. X. Connolly, 47–63. New York: Harcourt, Brace & World, 1964.

Boone, Joseph A. "Modernist Maneuverings in the Marriage Plot: Breaking Ideologies of Gender and Genre in James's *The Golden Bowl*." *PMLA* 101 (1986): 374–88.

Booth, Wayne. *The Company We Keep: An Ethics of Fiction*. Berkeley and Los Angeles: University of California Press, 1988.

————. *The Rhetoric of Fiction*. Chicago: University of Chicago Press, 1961.

Brackenridge, Hugh Henry. "Author's Address to the Reader." In *Modern Chivalry, or the Adventures of Captain Farrago and Teague O'Regan*, xiii-xvi. Philadelphia: Carey and Hart, 1846.

Bradbury, Nicola. *Henry James: The Later Novels*. Oxford: Clarendon Press, 1979.

Branch, Watson. "The Genesis, Composition, and Structure of *The Confidence-Man*." *Nineteenth-Century Fiction* 27 (1973): 424–48.

Branch, Watson, et al. "Historical Note." In *The Confidence-Man: His Masquerade*, by Herman Melville, Vol. 10 in *The Writings of Herman Melville*, edited by Harrison Hayford et al., 255–357. Evanston and Chicago: Northwestern University Press and the Newberry Library, 1984.

Brown, Charles Brockden. *Wieland or The Transformation*. Edited by Sydney J. Krause and S. W. Reid. Kent, Ohio: Kent State University Press, 1977.

Buck, Gertrude. *The Metaphor—A Study in the Psychology of Rhetoric*. Contributions to Rhetorical Theory, no. 5, edited by Fred Newton Scott. Ann Arbor: Inland Press, 1899.

Buell, Lawrence. "The Last Word on 'The Confidence-Man'?" *Illinois Quarterly* 35 (1972): 15–29.

Campbell, George. *The Philosophy of Rhetoric*. Boston: J. H. Wilkins, 1835.

Cargill, Oscar. *The Novels of Henry James*. New York: Macmillan, 1961.

Carlyle, Thomas. "Stump Orator." *Latter-Day Pamphlets*. In *The Works of Thomas Carlyle*, 20:172–213. 30 vols. London: Chapman and Hall, 1896. Reprint. New York: AMS Press, 1969.

Carrington, George C. *The Dramatic Unity of Huckleberry Finn*. Columbus: Ohio State University Press, 1976.

Carton, Evan. *The Rhetoric of American Romance: Dialectic and Identity in Emerson, Dickinson, Poe, and Hawthorne*. Baltimore: Johns Hopkins University Press, 1985.

Chambers, Stephen, and G. P. Mohrmann. "Rhetoric in Some American Periodicals." *Speech Monographs* 37 (1970): 111–20.

Channing, Edward T. *Lectures Read to Seniors at Harvard College*. Edited by Dorothy I. Anderson and Waldo Braden. Carbondale: Southern Illinois University Press, 1968.

Charvat, William. *The Origins of American Critical Thought, 1810–1835.* 1936. Reprint. New York: A. S. Barnes, 1961.

Cicero. *Brutus.* Translated by G. L. Hendrickson, Loeb Classical Library Series. Cambridge, Mass.: Harvard University Press, 1971. Vol. 5 of *Cicero in Twenty-Eight Volumes: Brutus, Orator.*

———. *Orator.* Translated by H. M. Hubbell, 296–509. Loeb Classical Library Series. Cambridge, Mass.: Harvard University Press, 1971. Vol. 5 of *Cicero in Twenty-Eight Volumes: Brutus, Orator.* 28 vols.

Clark, C. E. Frazer. *Nathaniel Hawthorne: A Descriptive Bibliography.* Pittsburgh: University of Pittsburgh Press, 1978.

Clark, Lewis Gaylord. "Editors' Tables." *Knickerbocker* 11 (June 1838): 562–70.

Clemens, Samuel. *Adventures of Huckleberry Finn.* Edited by Walter Blair and Victor Fischer. Berkeley and Los Angeles: University of California Press, 1985.

Crews, Frederick. *The Tragedy of Manners.* New Haven: Yale University Press, 1957.

Crocker, Lionel. "The Rhetorical Influence of Henry Ward Beecher." *QJS* 18 (1932): 82–87.

Dante. *The Inferno. The Divine Comedy.* Translated by Jefferson Butler Fletcher. New York: Columbia University Press, 1931.

Davis, Richard Beale. "James Ogilvie, an Early American Teacher of Rhetoric." *QJS* 28 (1942): 290–96.

Derrida, Jacques. *Dissemination.* Translated by Barbara Johnson. Chicago: University of Chicago Press, 1981.

Dreiser, Theodore. *Sister Carrie.* Edited by Donald Pizer. New York: Norton, 1970.

Drew, Philip. "Appearance and Reality in Melville's *The Confidence-Man.*" *ELH* 31 (1964): 418–42.

"Edward Everett's Addresses." *New England Magazine* 9 (December 1835): 462–68.

Emerson, Edward Waldo. Notes. *Letters and Social Aims.* By Ralph Waldo Emerson. In *The Complete Works of Ralph Waldo Emerson,* edited by Edward Waldo Emerson, 8:355–441. 12 vols. Centenary Edition. Boston: Houghton Mifflin, 1903–4.

———. Notes. *Society and Solitude: Twelve Chapters.* By Ralph Waldo Emerson. In *The Complete Works of Ralph Waldo Emerson,* edited by Edward Waldo Emerson, 7:339–451. 12 vols. Centenary Edition. Boston: Houghton Mifflin, 1903–4.

Emerson, Ralph Waldo. "Eloquence." *Letters and Social Aims.* In *The Complete Works of Ralph Waldo Emerson,* edited by Edward Waldo Emerson, 8:109–33. 12 vols. Centenary Edition. Boston: Houghton Mifflin, 1903–4.

———. "Eloquence." *Society and Solitude: Twelve Chapters.* In *The Complete Works of Ralph Waldo Emerson,* edited by Edward Waldo Emerson, 7:59–100. 12 vols. Centenary Edition. Boston: Houghton Mifflin, 1903–4.

Euripides. *The Medea*. Translated by Rex Warner. Chicago: University of Chicago Press, 1955. Vol. 1 of *Euripides: Four Greek Tragedies*. 4 vols. *The Complete Greek Tragedies*. Edited by David Greene and Richard Lattimore.

Fetterley, Judith. *The Resisting Reader: A Feminist Approach to American Fiction*. Bloomington: Indiana University Press, 1978.

Foster, Elizabeth. Introduction. In *The Confidence-Man: His Masquerade*, by Herman Melville, xiii–xcv. New York: Hendricks House, 1954.

Gates, Lewis E. Introduction. In *Selections from the Prose Writings of John Henry Cardinal Newman*, ix–lix. New York: Henry Holt, 1895.

———. "Newman as a Prose Writer." In *Three Studies in Literature*. New York: Macmillan, 1899.

Gilmore, Michael T. "Calvinism and Gothicism: The Example of Brown's *Wieland*." *Studies in the Novel* 9 (1977): 107–18.

Godkin, E. L. "Rhetorical Training." *Nation* 20 (1875): 145–46.

Golden, James L., and Edward P. J. Corbett. *The Rhetoric of Blair, Campbell, and Whately*. New York: Holt, Rinehart, and Winston, 1968.

Goode, John. "The Pervasive Mystery of Style: *The Wings of the Dove*." In *The Air of Reality: New Essays on Henry James*, edited by John Goode, 244–300. London: Methuen, 1972.

Gribben, Alan. *Mark Twain's Library: A Reconstruction*. 2 vols. Boston: G. K. Hall, 1980.

Grinnell, C. E. "A Few Orators and Their Eloquence at the Bar and Elsewhere." *American Law Review* 16 (1882): 138–57.

Guthrie, Warren. "The Development of Rhetorical Theory in America, 1635–1850." *Speech Monographs* 15 (1948): 61–71.

Habegger, Alfred. "The Lessons of the Father: Henry James Sr. on Sexual Difference." *Henry James Review* 8 (Fall 1986): 1–36.

Harding, Harold F. "Editor's Introduction." In *Lectures on Rhetoric and Belles Lettres*, by Hugh Blair, vii–xl. 2 vols. Carbondale: Southern Illinois University Press, 1965.

Hawthorne, Nathaniel. *The Scarlet Letter*. In *Nathaniel Hawthorne: Novels*, edited by Millicent Bell, 113–345. New York: Library of America, from the Ohio State University Centenary Edition of *The Works of Nathaniel Hawthorne*, 1983.

Hayworth, Donald H. "Review of Whately's *Elements of Rhetoric*." *QJS* 14 (1928): 594–96.

Holland, Laurence Bedwell. *The Expense of Vision: Essays on the Craft of Henry James*. Princeton: Princeton University Press, 1964.

Hoshor, John P. "American Contributions to Rhetorical Theory and Homiletics." In *A History of Speech Education in America*, edited by Karl R. Wallace et al., 129–52. New York: Appleton-Century-Crofts, 1954.

Hoth, David G. "A Possible Source for Melville's *The Confidence Man*." *Melville Society Extracts* 48 (November 1981): 7–10.

Howard, David. "The Bostonians." In *The Air of Reality: New Essays on Henry James*, edited by John Goode, 60–80. London: Methuen, 1972.

Howard, John R. "Review of Mr. Beecher's Personality and Political Influence." In *Patriotic Addresses in America and England, 1850–1885*, by Henry Ward Beecher, edited by John R. Howard, 11–161. Boston: Pilgrim Press, 1887.

Howe, Irving. Introduction. In *The Bostonians*, by Henry James, v–xxviii. New York: Random House, 1956.

Hunt, Lester H. "*The Scarlet Letter:* Hawthorne's Theory of Moral Sentiment." *Philosophy and Literature* 8 (1984): 75–87.

Hunt, T. "Rhetorical Science." *Presbyterian Quarterly* 3 (1864): 660–78.

James, Henry. *The American Scene*. Edited by W. H. Auden. New York: Charles Scribner's Sons, 1946.

———. *Autobiography*. edited by Frederick W. Dupee. Princeton: Princeton University Press, 1983.

———. *The Bostonians*. New York: Random House, 1956.

———. *The Golden Bowl*. Vols. 23 and 24 in *The Novels and Tales of Henry James*. New York Edition. 24 vols. New York: Scribner's, 1907–9.

———. *What Maisie Knew*. Vol. 11 in *The Novels and Tales of Henry James*. New York Edition. 24 vols. New York: Scribner's, 1907–9.

———. *The Wings of the Dove*. Vols. 19 and 20 in *The Novels and Tales of Henry James*. New York Edition. 24 vols. New York: Scribner's, 1907–9.

James, William. "The Moral Philosopher and the Moral Life." In *The Writings of William James*, edited by John J. McDermott, 610–29. Chicago: University of Chicago Press, 1977.

———. "Pragmatism's Conception of Truth." In *The Writings of William James*, edited by John J. McDermott, 429–43. Chicago: University of Chicago Press, 1977.

———. "The Stream of Thought." In *The Writings of William James*, edited by John J. McDermott, 21–74. Chicago: University of Chicago Press, 1977.

Kastely, James. "The Ethics of Self-Interest: Narrative Logic in *Huckleberry Finn*." *Nineteenth-Century Fiction* 40 (March 1986): 412–37.

Kaston, Carren. *Imagination and Desire in the Novels of Henry James*. New Brunswick: Rutgers University Press, 1984.

Kennedy, J. Gerald. *Poe, Death, and the Life of Writing*. New Haven: Yale University Press, 1987.

Kesselring, Marion L. *Hawthorne's Reading, 1828–1850: A Transcription and Identification of Titles Recorded in the Charge-Books of the Salem Atheneum*. New York: New York Public Library, 1949.

Kitzhaber, Albert. "Rhetoric in American Colleges, 1850–1900." Ph.D. dissertation, University of Washington, 1953.

Krieger, Murray. *The Play and Place of Criticism*. Baltimore: Johns Hopkins University Press, 1967.

————. *Words about Words about Words: Theory, Criticism, and the Literary Text.* Baltimore: Johns Hopkins University Press, 1988.

"Living Pulpit Orators." *Knickerbocker* 24 (October 1844): 379–81.

"Living Pulpit Orators." *Knickerbocker* 34 (August 1849): 95–107.

"Living Pulpit Orators." *Knickerbocker* 34 (October 1849): 308–20.

Madison, Mary K. "Hypothetical Friends: The Critics and the Confidence Man." *Melville Society Extracts* 46 (1981): 10–14.

Mailloux, Stephen. "Reading *Huckleberry Finn:* The Rhetoric of Performed Ideology." In *New Essays on Huckleberry Finn,* edited by Louis J. Budd, 107–33. Cambridge: Cambridge University Press, 1985.

Manley, William. "The Importance of Point of View in Brockden Brown's *Wieland." American Literature* 35 (1963): 311–21.

Margolis, Anne Throne. *Henry James and the Problem of Audience: An International Act.* Ann Arbor: UMI Research Press, 1985.

Martin, Terence. *The Instructed Vision.* Bloomington: Indiana University Press, 1961.

Marx, Leo. "Mr. Eliot, Mr. Trilling, and Huckleberry Finn." *American Scholar* 22 (Autumn 1953): 423–40.

McAleer, John. *Ralph Waldo Emerson: Days of Encounter.* Boston: Little, Brown, 1984.

Melville, Herman. *The Confidence-Man: His Masquerade.* Vol. 10 in *The Writings of Herman Melville,* edited by Harrison Hayford et al. 15 vols. Evanston and Chicago: Northwestern University Press and the Newberry Library, 1984.

————. *The Confidence-Man: His Masquerade,* edited by Hershel Parker. New York: Norton, 1971.

————. "Notes on 'A Short Patent Sermon.'" *The Piazza Tales and Other Prose Pieces, 1839–1860,* 443–44. Vol. 9 in *The Writings of Herman Melville,* edited by Harrison Hayford et al. 15 vols. Evanston and Chicago: Northwestern University Press and the Newberry Library, 1970.

————. *White-Jacket or The World in a Man-of-War.* Vol. 5 in *The Writings of Herman Melville,* edited by Harrison Hayford et al. 15 vols. Evanston and Chicago: Northwestern University Press and the Newberry Library, 1970.

Miller, J. Hillis. "Three Problems of Fictional Form: First-Person in *David Copperfield* and *Huckleberry Finn.*" In *Experiences in the Novel: Selected Papers from the English Institute,* edited by Roy Harvey Pearce, 21–48. New York: Columbia University Press, 1968.

Miller, John P., and William J. Richardson. *The Purloined Poe: Lacan, Derrida, and Psychoanalytic Reading.* Baltimore: Johns Hopkins University Press, 1988.

Miller, Theodore C. "Muddled Politics of Henry James's *The Bostonians.*" *Georgia Review* 26 (1972): 336–46.

Mitchell, Lee. "'Nobody but Our Gang Warn't Around': The Authority of Language in *Huckleberry Finn.*" In *New Essays on Huckleberry Finn,* edited by Louis J. Budd, 83–106. Cambridge: Cambridge University Press, 1985.

Mott, Frank Luther. *A History of American Magazines, 1741–1850*. Cambridge, Mass.: Harvard University Press, 1939.

"Mr. Forrest's Oration." *United States Magazine and Democratic Review* 3 (September 1838): 51–57.

"Mr. Gardiner's Address to the Phi Beta Kappa Society, on American Education in Classical Learning and Eloquence." *New England Magazine* 7 (December 1834): 416–18.

Newman, John Henry. *Apologia Pro Vita Sua*. Edited by A. Dwight Culler. Boston: Houghton Mifflin, 1956.

Newman, Samuel P. *Practical System of Rhetoric*. Portland: Wm. Hyde, 1827.

"Of Fitness in Oratory." *Putnam's New Monthly Magazine* 3 (1854): 417–23.

Owen, Elizabeth. "The 'Given Appearance' of Charlotte Verver." *Essays in Criticism* 13 (1963): 364–74.

Parker, Hershel. "The Metaphysics of Indian-hating." *Nineteenth-Century Fiction* 18 (1963): 165–73.

Parton, J. "Henry Ward Beecher's Church." *Atlantic Monthly* 19 (1867): 38–51.

Pearson, Gabriel. "The Novel to End All Novels: *The Golden Bowl*." In *The Air of Reality: New Essays on Henry James*, edited by John Goode, 301–62. London: Methuen, 1972.

Peck, J. T. "Rhetoric—Its Philosophy and Principles." *Universalist Quarterly Review* 20 (1863): 251–78.

Plato. "The Apology." Translated by B. Jowett. 4th ed. 1871. 4 vols. Vol. 1 of *The Dialogues of Plato*, 341–66. Oxford: Clarendon Press, 1953.

———. *Gorgias*. Translated by W. C. Helmbold. New York: Macmillan, 1952.

———. *Phaedrus*. Translated by W. C. Helmbold and W. G. Rabinowitz. New York: Macmillan, 1956.

Poirier, Richard. *The Renewal of Literature: Emersonian Reflections*. New Haven: Yale University Press, 1987.

Potter, David. Foreword. In *The Philosophy of Rhetoric*, by George Campbell, edited by Lloyd F. Bitzer, ix–xxxvii. Carbondale: Southern Illinois University Press, 1963.

Poulet, Georges. "Criticism and the Experience of Interiority." In *The Languages of Criticism and the Sciences of Man: The Structuralist Controversy*, edited by Richard Macksey and Eugenio Donato, 56–88. Baltimore: Johns Hopkins University Press, 1970.

"Principles of Elocution." *North American Review* 29 (July 1829): 38–67.

Przybylowicz, Donna. *Desire and Repression: The Dialectic of Self and Other in the Late Works of Henry James*. University, Ala.: University of Alabama Press, 1986.

Quintilian. *On the Teaching of Speaking and Writing: Translations from Books One, Two, and Ten of the Institutio Oratoria*. Edited by James J. Murphy. Carbondale: Southern Illinois University Press, 1987.

Quirk, Tom. *Melville's Confidence Man: From Knave to Knight.* Columbia: University of Missouri Press, 1982.

Ragussis, Michael. "Family Discourse and Fiction in *The Scarlet Letter.*" *ELH* 49 (1982): 863–88.

Reid, Ronald F. "The Boylston Professorship of Rhetoric and Oratory, 1806–1904: A Case Study of Changing Concepts of Rhetoric and Pedagogy." *QJS* 45 (1959): 239–57.

"Remarks on the Eloquence of Debate." *New England Magazine* 7 (July 1834): 105–16.

Renshaw, Edyth. "Five Private Schools of Speech." In *A History of Speech Education in America,* edited by Karl R. Wallace, 301–25. New York: Appleton-Century-Crofts, 1954.

Ried, Paul E. "Francis J. Child: The Fourth Boylston Professor of Rhetoric and Oratory." *QJS* 55 (1969): 268–75.

Ringe, Donald A. *Charles Brockden Brown.* New York: Twayne, 1966.

Robb, Mary Margaret. "The Elocutionary Movement and Its Chief Figures." In *A History of Speech Education in America,* edited by Karl R. Wallace, 178–201. New York: Appleton-Century-Crofts, 1954.

Robinson, Forrest G. *In Bad Faith: The Dynamics of Deception in Mark Twain's America.* Cambridge. Mass.: Harvard University Press, 1986.

Rowe, John Carlos. *Henry Adams and Henry James.* Ithaca: Cornell University Press, 1976.

————. "The Internal Conflict of Romantic Narrative: Hegel's *Phenomenology* and Hawthorne's *The Scarlet Letter.*" *MLN* 95 (1980): 1203–31.

————. *The Theoretical Dimensions of Henry James.* Madison: University of Wisconsin Press, 1984.

Saint Augustine. *The Confessions of St. Augustine.* Translated by F. J. Sheed. New York: Sheed & Ward, 1943.

Schroeder, John. "Sources and Symbols for Melville's *Confidence-Man.*" *PMLA* 66 (1951): 363–80.

Sealts, Merton. "Historical Note." In *The Piazza Tales and Other Prose Pieces, 1839–1860,* by Herman Melville. Vol. 9 in *The Writings of Herman Melville,* edited by Harrison Hayford et al., 457–533. 15 vols. Evanston and Chicago: Northwestern University Press and the Newberry Library, 1970.

————. "Melville and Emerson's Rainbow." *ESQ* 26 (1980): 53–78.

————. "Melville and the Platonic Tradition." In *Pursuing Melville, 1940–1980,* 278–336. Madison: University of Wisconsin Press, 1982.

————. *Melville's Reading.* Columbia: University of South Carolina Press, 1988.

See, Fred G. *The Desire and the Sign: Nineteenth-Century American Fiction.* Baton Rouge: Louisiana State University Press, 1987.

Seltzer, Mark. *Henry James and the Art of Power.* Ithaca: Cornell University Press, 1984.

———. "Saying Makes It So: Language and Event in Brown's *Wieland*." *Early American Literature* 13 (1978): 81–91.

Sewell, David. *Mark Twain's Languages: Discourse, Dialect, and Linguistic Variety*. Berkeley and Los Angeles: University of California Press, 1987.

Shaver, Claude L. "Steele MacKaye and the Delsartian Tradition." In *A History of Speech Education in America*, edited by Karl R. Wallace, 202–18. New York: Appleton-Century-Crofts, 1954.

Small, Michel. "Hawthorne's *The Scarlet Letter:* Arthur Dimmesdale's Manipulation of Language." *American Imago* 37 (Spring 1980): 113–23.

Smit, David W. *The Language of a Master: Theories of Style and the Late Writing of Henry James*. Carbondale: Southern Illinois University Press, 1988.

Smith, Henry Nash. *Mark Twain: The Development of a Writer*. Cambridge, Mass.: Harvard University Press, 1962.

Theremin, Franz. *Eloquence: A Virtue; or Outlines of a Systematic Rhetoric*. Translated by William G. T. Shedd. Andover: W. F. Draper and Brother, 1854.

Turner, Arlin. *Nathaniel Hawthorne: A Biography*. New York: Oxford University Press, 1980.

Twain, Mark. "Christian Science." In *Mark Twain: Selected Writings of an American Skeptic*, edited by Victor Doyno, 378–87. Buffalo, N.Y.: Prometheus Books, 1983.

W. H. "Importance and Obligation of Truth, Philosophically Considered." *New England Magazine* 7 (1834): 302–8.

Weaver, Richard. *The Ethics of Rhetoric*. South Bend, Ind. Regnery/Gateway, 1953.

Westervelt, L. A. "The Individual and the Form: Maggie Verver's Tactics in *The Golden Bowl*." *Renascence* 36 (1984): 147–59.

Whately, Richard. *Elements of Rhetoric*. Edited by Douglas Ehninger. Carbondale: Southern Illinois University Press, 1963.

Wolstenholme, Susan. "Possession and Personality: Spiritualism in *The Bostonians*." *American Literature* 49 (1977–78): 580–91.

Wright, Nathalia. *Melville's Use of the Bible*. Durham: Duke University Press, 1949.

Wylie, A. McE. "Mr. Beecher as a Social Force." *Scribner's Monthly* 4 (1872): 751–54.

Yeazell, Ruth Bernard. *Language and Knowledge in the Late Novels of Henry James*. Chicago: University of Chicago Press, 1976.

Young, Richard E., Alton L. Becker, and Kenneth L. Pike. *Rhetoric, Discovery, and Change*. New York: Harcourt Brace Jovanovich, 1970.

Index